4/27/09

# ENDANGERED SPECIES

## PROTECTING BIODIVERSITY

ISSN 1930-3319

# ENDANGERED SPECIES

## PROTECTING BIODIVERSITY

Kim Masters Evans

**INFORMATION PLUS® REFERENCE SERIES**
Formerly Published by Information Plus, Wylie, Texas

GALE
CENGAGE Learning™

Detroit • New York • San Francisco • New Haven, Conn • Waterville, Maine • London

## GALE
### CENGAGE Learning™

**Endangered Species**

**Kim Masters Evans**
**Paula Kepos, Series Editor**

Project Editors: Kathleen J. Edgar, Elizabeth Manar

Rights Acquisition and Management: Scott Bragg, Jacqueline Key, Barb McNeil

Composition: Evi Abou-El-Seoud, Mary Beth Trimper

Manufacturing: Cynde Bishop

Product Management: Carol Nagel

Gale
27500 Drake Rd.
Farmington Hills, MI 48331-3535

ISBN-13: 978-0-7876-5103-9 (set)
ISBN-13: 978-1-4144-0753-1

ISBN-10: 0-7876-5103-6 (set)
ISBN-10: 1-4144-0753-X

ISSN 1930-3319

This title is also available as an e-book.
ISBN-13: 978-1-4144-3819-1 (set)
ISBN-10: 1-4144-3819-2 (set)
Contact your Gale sales representative for ordering information.

Printed in the United States of America
1 2 3 4 5 6 7 12 11 10 09 08

# TABLE OF CONTENTS

**PREFACE** . . . . . . . . . . . . . . . . . . . . . . . . . . . vii

**CHAPTER 1**

Extinction and Endangered Species . . . . . . . . . . . . . . 1

This chapter defines extinction and endangered species and describes some of the repercussions of species loss. Biological diversity, land conservation, and factors contributing to species endangerment are also discussed. Statistics on species loss in the United States and worldwide are presented.

**CHAPTER 2**

The Endangered Species Act. . . . . . . . . . . . . . . . . 23

The idea of conserving nature has a long history, and modern legislation in the United States, notably the Endangered Species Act of 1973, is intended to protect and conserve many forms of life. The policies and protections of the Endangered Species Act are reviewed here, as are controversies that have arisen since its passage.

**CHAPTER 3**

Marine Mammals . . . . . . . . . . . . . . . . . . . . . . . . 39

Marine mammals comprise one of the most popular groups of endangered animals. Whales, seals, sea lions, otters, and manatees face special challenges for recovery. Safeguards for them under the Marine Mammal Protection Act and the Endangered Species Act are discussed.

**CHAPTER 4**

Fish. . . . . . . . . . . . . . . . . . . . . . . . . . . . . . . . 55

Fish species face a variety of threats to their survival in freshwater and marine environments. Such dangers include water pollution, dams and other water obstructions, overfishing, overcrowding, and invasive species. The perils facing these species are described, as are the recovery measures being taken to save them.

**CHAPTER 5**

Clams, Snails, Crustaceans, and Corals . . . . . . . . . . . 71

Clams, snails, crustaceans, and corals are aquatic creatures imperiled for various reasons. Habitat degradation and the spread of invasive species are primary threats to clams, snails, and crustaceans. Global warming is blamed for declining populations of coral species.

**CHAPTER 6**

Amphibians and Reptiles . . . . . . . . . . . . . . . . . . . 81

Large numbers of amphibians and reptiles are endangered. Amphibians have been showing recent sharp declines in population, possibly caused by factors such as habitat destruction, pollution, invasive species, diseases, and human collection, while reptiles are facing some of the same problems.

**CHAPTER 7**

Terrestrial Mammals. . . . . . . . . . . . . . . . . . . . . . 95

Some of the best-known endangered species are terrestrial mammals. Animals such as black-footed ferrets, wolves, bears and pandas, big cats, rhinos, elephants, and primates are facing extinction. This chapter explains the reasons and what is being done about it.

**CHAPTER 8**

Birds . . . . . . . . . . . . . . . . . . . . . . . . . . . . . . . 113

Threats to bird species include habitat loss, pesticides, oil spills, house cats, the pet trade, and invasive species. This chapter examines some threatened bird species, as well as some that are recovering from the threats against them.

**CHAPTER 9**

Insects and Spiders . . . . . . . . . . . . . . . . . . . . . . . 131

There are dozens of threatened or endangered insect and arachnid species in the United States alone. Discussed here are vulnerable butterflies, grasshoppers, dragonflies, beetles, and spiders.

**CHAPTER 10**

Plants. . . . . . . . . . . . . . . . . . . . . . . . . . . . . . . 139

Over half of the species on the Endangered Species List are plants. This chapter covers American plants in danger, the reasons they are endangered, and how and why plant species should be conserved.

**IMPORTANT NAMES AND ADDRESSES**. . . . . . . 161

**RESOURCES**. . . . . . . . . . . . . . . . . . . . . . . . . . 163

**INDEX** . . . . . . . . . . . . . . . . . . . . . . . . . . . . . 165

# PREFACE

*Endangered Species: Protecting Biodiversity* is part of the *Information Plus Reference Series*. The purpose of each volume of the series is to present the latest facts on a topic of pressing concern in modern American life. These topics include today's most controversial and studied social issues: abortion, capital punishment, care for the elderly, crime, health care, the environment, immigration, minorities, social welfare, women, youth, and many more. Even though this series is written especially for high school and undergraduate students, it is an excellent resource for anyone in need of factual information on current affairs.

By presenting the facts, it is the intention of Gale, a part of Cengage Learning, to provide its readers with everything they need to reach an informed opinion on current issues. To that end, there is a particular emphasis in this series on the presentation of scientific studies, surveys, and statistics. These data are generally presented in the form of tables, charts, and other graphics placed within the text of each book. Every graphic is directly referred to and carefully explained in the text. The source of each graphic is presented within the graphic itself. The data used in these graphics are drawn from the most reputable and reliable sources, in particular from the various branches of the U.S. government and from major independent polling organizations. Every effort has been made to secure the most recent information available. Readers should bear in mind that many major studies take years to conduct, and that additional years often pass before the data from these studies are made available to the public. Therefore, in many cases the most recent information available in 2008 is dated from 2005 or 2006. Older statistics are sometimes presented as well, if they are of particular interest and no more-recent information exists.

Even though statistics are a major focus of the *Information Plus Reference Series*, they are by no means its only content. Each book also presents the widely held positions and important ideas that shape how the book's subject is discussed in the United States. These positions are explained in detail and, where possible, in the words of their proponents. Some of the other material to be found in these books includes historical background; descriptions of major events related to the subject; relevant laws and court cases; and examples of how these issues play out in American life. Some books also feature primary documents, or have pro and con debate sections giving the words and opinions of prominent Americans on both sides of a controversial topic. All material is presented in an even-handed and unbiased manner; readers will never be encouraged to accept one view of an issue over another.

## HOW TO USE THIS BOOK

The status of endangered species is an issue of concern both for many Americans and for people around the world. In particular, balancing biodiversity with economics has led to much controversy. This book looks at what has been done to protect endangered species in the United States and around the world, and examines the debate over what future actions are warranted.

*Endangered Species: Protecting Biodiversity* consists of ten chapters and three appendixes. Each chapter is devoted to a particular aspect of endangered species. For a summary of the information covered in each chapter, please see the synopses provided in the Table of Contents at the front of the book. Chapters generally begin with an overview of the basic facts and background information on the chapter's topic, then proceed to examine subtopics of particular interest. For example, Chapter 8: Birds begins by explaining the taxonomy of birds and how they are broadly classified by physical characteristics. It then discusses the bird species that are endangered and threatened in the United States, including woodpeckers, passerines (perching birds or songbirds), Hawaiian honeycreepers, and raptors (e.g., owls and condors). The chapter then highlights the types of threats that that U.S. bird species face: habitat loss and environmental decline, pesticides, oil spills, domestic cats, trade in exotic birds, and invasive species. These threats have drastically reduced the population size of dozens of bird species and have even driven some species into extinction. Next, the success stories of the bald eagle, peregrine falcon, Aleutian Canada goose, and brown pelican are provided. Finally, the chapter discusses foreign species that are endangered and threatened. Readers can find their way through a chapter by looking for the section and subsection headings, which are clearly set off from the text. Or, they can refer to the book's extensive index if they already know what they are looking for.

## Statistical Information

The tables and figures featured throughout *Endangered Species: Protecting Biodiversity* will be of particular use to readers in learning about this issue. The tables and figures represent an extensive collection of the most recent and important statistics on endangered species, as well as related issues—for example, graphics in the book cover the number of endangered species and the reasons for their endangerment; the locations of national parks; the types of invasive plants; and the life cycle of Pacific salmon. The photographs illustrate some of the most threatened species on Earth, including the Asian box turtle, the Texas horned lizard, and the red wolf. Gale, a part of Cengage Learning, believes that making this information available to readers is the most important way to fulfill the goal of this book: to help readers understand the issues and controversies surrounding endangered species and reach their own conclusions.

Each table or figure has a unique identifier appearing above it, for ease of identification and reference. Titles for the tables and figures explain their purpose. At the end of each table or figure, the original source of the data is provided.

To help readers understand these often complicated statistics, all tables and figures are explained in the text. References in the text direct readers to the relevant statistics. Furthermore, the contents of all tables and figures are fully indexed. Please see the opening section of the index at the back of this volume for a description of how to find tables and figures within it.

## Appendixes

Besides the main body text and images, *Endangered Species: Protecting Biodiversity* has three appendixes.

The first is the Important Names and Addresses directory. Here readers will find contact information for a number of government and private organizations that can provide further information on aspects of endangered species. The second appendix is the Resources section, which can also assist readers in conducting their own research. In this section, the author and editors of *Endangered Species: Protecting Biodiversity* describe some of the sources that were most useful during the compilation of this book. The final appendix is the detailed index, which facilitates reader access to specific topics in this book.

## ADVISORY BOARD CONTRIBUTIONS

The staff of Information Plus would like to extend its heartfelt appreciation to the Information Plus Advisory Board. This dedicated group of media professionals provides feedback on the series on an ongoing basis. Their comments allow the editorial staff who work on the project to continually make the series better and more user-friendly. Our top priorities are to produce the highest-quality and most useful books possible, and the Advisory Board's contributions to this process are invaluable.

The members of the Information Plus Advisory Board are:

- Kathleen R. Bonn, Librarian, Newbury Park High School, Newbury Park, California

- Madelyn Garner, Librarian, San Jacinto College–North Campus, Houston, Texas

- Anne Oxenrider, Media Specialist, Dundee High School, Dundee, Michigan

- Charles R. Rodgers, Director of Libraries, Pasco-Hernando Community College, Dade City, Florida

- James N. Zitzelsberger, Library Media Department Chairman, Oshkosh West High School, Oshkosh, Wisconsin

## COMMENTS AND SUGGESTIONS

The editors of the *Information Plus Reference Series* welcome your feedback on *Endangered Species: Protecting Biodiversity*. Please direct all correspondence to:

Editors
*Information Plus Reference Series*
27500 Drake Rd.
Farmington Hills, MI  48331 3535

# CHAPTER 1
# EXTINCTION AND ENDANGERED SPECIES

The earth is richly supplied with different types of living organisms, including animals, plants, fungi, and bacteria. Various living organisms coexist in their environments, forming complex, interrelated communities. Living organisms depend on one another for nutrients, shelter, and other benefits. The extinction of any one species can set off a chain reaction that affects many other species, particularly if the loss occurs near the bottom of the food chain. For example, the extinction of a particular insect or plant might seem inconsequential. However, there may be fish or small animals that depend on that resource for foodstuff. The loss can threaten the survival of these creatures and of the larger predators that prey on them. Extinction can have a ripple effect that spreads throughout nature.

Besides its biological consequences, extinction poses a moral dilemma for humans, the only species capable of saving other species. The presence of humans on the planet has affected all other life forms, particularly plants and animals. Human lifestyles have proven to be incompatible with the survival of some other species. Purposeful efforts have been made to eliminate animals that prey on people, livestock, crops, or pose any threat to human livelihoods. Some wild animals have been decimated by human desire for meat, hides, fur, or other body parts with commercial value. Likewise, demand for land, water, timber, and other natural resources has left many wild plants and animals with little to no suitable habitat. Humans have also affected nature by introducing non-native species to local areas and producing pollutants that have a negative impact on the environment. The combination of these anthropogenic (human-related) effects with natural obstacles that limit survival, such as disease or low birthrates, have proven to be too much for some species to overcome. They have no chance of survival without human help.

As a result, societies have difficult choices to make about the amount of effort and money they are willing to spend to keep imperiled species from becoming extinct. Will people accept limits on their property rights, recreational activities, and means of livelihood to save a plant or animal? Should saving popular species such as whales and dolphins take priority over saving obscure, annoying, or feared species? Is it the responsibility of humans to save every kind of life form from disappearing, or is extinction an inevitable part of nature, in which the strong survive and the weak perish? These are some of the difficult questions that people face as they ponder the fate of other species living on this planet.

## DEFINING AND NAMING LIFE ON EARTH

Living organisms are named and categorized according to a taxonomy, a hierarchical system of order based on the natural relationships among all types of life. For example, Table 1.1 shows the taxonomic chart for blue whales, the largest creatures on Earth. Blue whales are described by eight taxonomic levels ending with "species." A species is a term assigned to a group of organisms that are considered capable of interbreeding with one another. There is another category called subspecies that ranks immediately below species. A subspecies (abbreviated ssp.) is a population of a particular geographical region that is genetically different from other populations of the same species, but can still interbreed with them.

Animals and plants are identified by their common names and by unique scientific names. Some organisms have more than one common name. The animal known as the mountain lion is also called a puma or a cougar. To avoid confusion, scientific bodies have established a system of nomenclature (naming) for animals and plants. This system is based on the example set by Carolus Linnaeus (1707–1778), a Swedish botanist who published classifications for thousands of plants and animals. Linnaeus popularized the use of a binary naming system in

## TABLE 1.1

**Taxonomic chart for blue whales**

| Classification | Blue whale example | Explanation |
|---|---|---|
| Kingdom | Animalia | Whales belong to the kingdom Animalia because whales have many cells, ingest food, and are formed from a "blastula" (from a fertilized egg). |
| Phylum | Chordata | An animal from the phylum Chordata has a spinal cord and gill pouches. |
| Class | Mammalia | Whales and other mammals are warm blooded, have glands to provide milk for their offspring, and have a four-chambered heart. |
| Order | Cetacea | Cetaceans are mammals that live completely in the water. |
| [Suborder] | Mysticeti | Whales that belong to the suborder Mysticeti have baleen plates (big filters in their mouths) rather than teeth. |
| Family | Balaenidae | The family Balaenidae, also called rorqual whales. They have pleats around their throat that allow them to hold lots of water (which contains their food). |
| Genus | *Balaenoptera* | A genus is a group of species that are more closely related to one another than any group in the family. *Balaenoptera* refers to the genus. |
| Species | *Musculus* | A species is a grouping of individuals that interbreed successfully. The blue whale species name is *musculus*. |

SOURCE: "The Chart Below Is a Sample Taxonomic Chart for Blue Whales," in *What Is Taxonomy?* National Oceanic and Atmospheric Administration, Alaska Fisheries Science Center, National Marine Mammal Laboratory, March 3, 2004, http://www.afsc.noaa.gov/nmml/education/taxonomy.php (accessed January 17, 2008)

which the first word names the genus of the organism. The genus, which identifies a group of closely related species, is followed by a specific epithet (a descriptive word or phrase) that differentiates one species from another. Linnaeus used Latin words in his nomenclature because Latin was the preferred language for scientific publications during the eighteenth century.

Since the time of Linnaeus many thousands of additional plants and animals have been discovered or intentionally bred. Modern convention dictates that the scientist who first describes an organism in a scholarly publication chooses the scientific name for that organism. The scientific name must be in Latin or contain words that have been Latinized (rendered to appear Latin). During the 1800s the American researcher Frank Higgins discovered a new species of mussel (clam) in the Mississippi River. He called it Higgins' eye. The scientific name is *Lampsilis higginsii*. In this case the specific epithet reflects the common name of the organism, but it is not required to do; it can be any descriptive term.

Scientific names are either italicized or underlined in print to distinguish them from surrounding text. The genus is capitalized, whereas the specific epithet is not capitalized.

Subspecies are indicated in scientific nomenclature with an additional term. For example, the scientific name of the blue whale is *Balaenoptera musculus*. A subspecies, the pygmy blue whale, is called *Balaenoptera musculus brevicauda*. Genus reassignments are indicated with the "=" sign in a scientific name. When the royal snail was discovered in 1977, it was assigned to the genus *Marstonia*. Ten years later biologists decided the snail was more properly a member of the genus *Pyrgulopsis*. Thus, the scientific name of the royal snail is written as *Pyrgulopsis (=Marstonia) ogmorhaphe*. When the species is not known for an organism of known genus, the scientific name is written with sp. (indicating a single species) or spp. (indicating multiple species) as the specific epithet. The latter format is also used when referring to all species in a genus. For example, *Pyrgulopsis* spp. refers to all species within the genus *Pyrgulopsis*.

The rules governing scientific names for animals are overseen by the International Commission on Zoological Nomenclature, which is headquartered in London, England. The International Code of Botanical Nomenclature for plants is managed by the International Botanical Congress (IBC), a meeting of botanists from around the world that is held every six years. The most recent IBC took place in Vienna, Austria, in 2005.

## BIODIVERSITY

Biodiversity is short for biological diversity. It refers to the richness and variety of living organisms across the planet. Biodiversity is important at levels within the taxonomic table and at the genetic level. For example, all humans are members of one species (*Homo sapiens*), but humans can vary widely in their personal characteristics, such as race, hair color, and eye color. These differences are due to slight variations in genetic material from person to person. Genetic biodiversity results in different individual properties within a species. It also helps ensure that deformities or disorders in genetic material do not become concentrated in a population.

Inbreeding is mating between closely related individuals with extremely similar genetic material. It is almost certain that if one of these individuals has any kind of gene disorder, the other individual will also have it. This disorder might not cause any notable problems in the parents, but it could become concentrated in the offspring and cause serious health problems for them. This explains why there is a certain lower limit to the population of some species, particularly those that are isolated in a specific location. If the population falls too low, the remaining individuals will be so closely related that any inherent gene problems can kill off the resulting offspring and ultimately wipe out the entire species.

## WHAT ARE ENDANGERED SPECIES?

A species is described as extinct when no living members remain. Scientists know from the study of fossils that dinosaurs, mammoths, saber-toothed cats, and countless other animal and plant species that once lived on Earth no longer exist. These species have "died out," or become extinct. Once a species is extinct, there is no way to bring it back.

The U.S. government defines endangered species as those that are at risk of extinction through all or a significant portion of their natural habitats. Threatened species are defined as those likely to become endangered in the future. The management at the federal level of endangered and threatened species is handled by two agencies: the U.S. Fish and Wildlife Service (USFWS) and the National Marine Fisheries Service (NMFS). The USFWS is an agency of the U.S. Department of the Interior and oversees the terrestrial (land-based) and freshwater species. The NMFS is an agency of the National Oceanic and Atmospheric Administration under the U.S. Department of Commerce. The NMFS is responsible for marine (ocean-dwelling) species and those that are anadromous (migrate between the ocean and freshwater).

The USFWS maintains a list of species that are endangered or threatened in the United States and abroad. Both endangered and threatened species are protected by laws intended to save them from extinction. In many cases recovery plans for endangered species have also been developed and implemented. These include measures designed to protect endangered and threatened species and to help their populations grow.

## MASS EXTINCTION

In the billions of years since life began on Earth, species have formed, existed, and then become extinct. Scientists call the natural extinction of a few species per million years a background, or normal, rate. When the extinction rate doubles for many different groups of plants and animals at the same time, this is described as a mass extinction. Mass extinctions have occurred infrequently in Earth's history and, in general, have been attributed to major cataclysmic geological or astronomical events. Five mass extinctions have occurred in the last six hundred million years. These episodes, known as the Big Five, occurred at the end of five geologic periods:

- Ordovician (505 million to 440 million years ago)

- Devonian (410 million to 360 million years ago)

- Permian (286 million to 245 million years ago)

- Triassic (245 million to 208 million years ago)

- Cretaceous (146 million to 65 million years ago)

After each mass extinction the floral (plant) and faunal (animal) composition of the earth changed drastically. The largest mass extinction on record occurred at the end of the Permian, when an estimated 90% to 95% of all species became extinct. The Cretaceous extinction is perhaps the most familiar—it was at the end of the Cretaceous that many species of dinosaurs became extinct. The Cretaceous extinction is hypothesized to have resulted from the collision of an asteroid with the earth.

### The Sixth Mass Extinction?

Scientists estimate that hundreds, or even thousands, of species are being lost around the world each year. This suggests that another mass extinction is taking place in the twenty-first century. However, unlike previous mass extinctions the current extinction does not appear to be associated with a cataclysmic physical event. Rather, the heightened extinction rate has coincided with the success and spread of human beings. Researchers predict that as humans continue to alter natural ecosystems through destruction of natural habitats, pollution, introduction of nonnative species, and global climate change, the extinction rate may eventually approach several hundred species per day. This would be a rate millions of times higher than normal background levels. The United Nations (UN) concludes in *Global Biodiversity Outlook 2* (2006, http://www.cbd.int/doc/gbo2/cbd-gbo2-en.pdf) that without immediate intervention, more species of flora and fauna may disappear than were lost in the mass extinction that wiped out the dinosaurs sixty-five million years ago.

In 1948 an international conference on conservation resulted in the formation of the International Union for the Protection of Nature. In 1956 its name was changed to the International Union for the Conservation of Nature and Natural Resources (IUCN). The IUCN is based in Gland, Switzerland, and is the world's largest conservation organization. According to the IUCN (2008, http://cms.iucn.org/about/union/members/index.cfm), in March 2008, 84 nations and 785 nongovernmental organizations were members.

## U.S. HISTORY—SOME EXTINCTIONS AND SOME CLOSE CALLS

The colonization of the North American by European settlers severely depleted the ranks of some native wild species. The introduction of livestock brought new animal diseases that devastated some native animals. Widespread hunting and trapping led to the demise of other species. During the early 1800s the United States was home to millions, perhaps billions, of passenger pigeons. These migratory birds traveled in enormous flocks and were extremely popular with hunters. By the beginning of the twentieth century the species was virtually exterminated. The last known passenger pigeon died in the Cincinnati Zoo in 1914. The heath hen, a small wild fowl native to the United States and once very abundant, was wiped out

FIGURE 1.1

Bison (or American buffaloes) are the largest terrestrial animals in North America. *Field Mark Publications*

of existence by 1932. Stocks of other animals—beaver, elk, and bison (American buffalo)—were driven to the brink of extinction, but saved by conservation efforts.

### Bison Comeback

The bison is the largest terrestrial animal in North America. It has short, pointed horns and a hump over the front shoulders. The head, neck, and front parts of the body are covered by a thick, dark coat of long, curly hair, and the rear has shorter, lighter hair. Adult males weigh as much as 1,800 to 2,400 pounds (816.5 to 1,088.6 kg); females are smaller. Adult males also have black "beards" about a foot (30.5 cm) long. Bison are social animals and travel in herds. Bison were central to the existence of Native Americans, who used them for food and made clothing from their hides and tools from their bones. The dried dung, called buffalo chips, was used for fuel.

According to the National Park Service, in "Buffalo Hunters" (May 8, 2007, http://www.nps.gov/archive/jeff/buffalo_hunters.html), approximately forty million bison (or buffalo) once roamed the grasslands of North America. (See Figure 1.1.) Historical accounts describe herds stretching as far as the eye could see. Even though Native Americans hunted bison, it was not until European settlers came with firearms that their numbers fell drastically. Many people shot the animals for fun, whereas others sold the hides. Bison numbers were eventually reduced to fewer than one thousand.

Bison first received protection from the U.S. government in 1872, with the establishment of Yellowstone National Park in Wyoming and Montana. However, the welfare of the small herd of bison in the park was largely ignored until 1901, when it was discovered that only twenty-five individuals remained. The herd was restored to one thousand by 1930 with bison imported from the Great Plains. As the Yellowstone herd multiplied, the park service shot animals to keep the population under control. However, this practice was unnecessary because harsh winters caused the herd to dwindle naturally. The park service stopped shooting bison in the 1960s. The National Park Service indicates that in 2007 there were over 150,000 bison on public and private lands across the United States.

Some populations of bison are managed as livestock because they have become a food source for humans. Bison are a source of high-protein, low-fat, low-cholesterol meat. In *National Bison Association Update* (2007, http://www.canadianbison.ca/producer/documents/NBAPresentationforCBANov2007.pdf), the National Bison Association notes that over forty thousand bison were slaughtered for food during 2006.

### HOW MANY SPECIES ARE ENDANGERED?

Since 1960 the IUCN has compiled the *Red List of Threatened Species* (http://cms.iucn.org/), which aims to examine the status of biological species across the globe. The so-called Red List categorizes species based on the level of risk of their extinction in the wild as follows:

- Critically endangered—extremely high risk

- Endangered—very high risk

- Vulnerable—high risk

- Near threatened—likely to qualify for a risk category soon

The IUCN refers to species in all these categories as "threatened" species.

Determining how many species of plants and animals are threatened or endangered is difficult. In fact, only a small fraction of the species in existence have even been identified and named, let alone studied in detail. Various estimates of the total number of species on Earth range from three million to more than one hundred million with most estimates figuring around ten million species worldwide. Of these, the IUCN states in *2007 Red List of Threatened Species* (2007, http://www.iucnredlist.org/)

TABLE 1.2

**Count of endangered and threatened species and U.S. species with recovery plans, February 1, 2008**

| Group | United States | | | Foreign | | | Total listings (US and foreign) | US listings with active recovery plans |
|---|---|---|---|---|---|---|---|---|
| | Endangered | Threatened | Total listings | Endangered | Threatened | Total listings | | |
| Mammals | 69 | 12 | 81 | 256 | 20 | 276 | 357 | 56 |
| Birds | 75 | 14 | 89 | 179 | 6 | 185 | 274 | 84 |
| Reptiles | 13 | 24 | 37 | 66 | 16 | 82 | 119 | 38 |
| Amphibians | 13 | 10 | 23 | 8 | 1 | 9 | 32 | 17 |
| Fishes | 74 | 65 | 139 | 11 | 1 | 12 | 151 | 101 |
| Clams | 62 | 8 | 70 | 2 | 0 | 2 | 72 | 70 |
| Snails | 64 | 11 | 75 | 1 | 0 | 1 | 76 | 69 |
| Insects | 47 | 10 | 57 | 4 | 0 | 4 | 61 | 35 |
| Arachnids | 12 | 0 | 12 | 0 | 0 | 0 | 12 | 6 |
| Crustaceans | 19 | 3 | 22 | 0 | 0 | 0 | 22 | 18 |
| Corals | 0 | 2 | 2 | 0 | 0 | 0 | 2 | 0 |
| **Animal subtotal** | **448** | **159** | **607** | **527** | **44** | **571** | **1178** | **494** |
| Flowering plants | 570 | 143 | 713 | 1 | 0 | 1 | 714 | 628 |
| Conifers and cycads | 2 | 1 | 3 | 0 | 2 | 2 | 5 | 3 |
| Ferns and allies | 24 | 2 | 26 | 0 | 0 | 0 | 26 | 26 |
| Lichens | 2 | 0 | 2 | 0 | 0 | 0 | 2 | 2 |
| **Plant subtotal** | **598** | **146** | **744** | **1** | **2** | **3** | **747** | **659** |
| **Grand total** | **1046** | **305** | **1351** | **528** | **46** | **574** | **1925** | **1153** |

Notes: 34 animal species (17 in the U.S. and 17 foreign) are counted more than once in the above table, primarily because these animals have distinct population segments (each with its own individual listing status). There are a total of 579 distinct active (draft and final) recovery plans. Some recovery plans cover more than one species, and a few species have separate plans covering different parts of their ranges. This count includes only plans generated by the US Fish and Wildlife Service (USFWS) (or jointly by the USFWS and National Marine Fisheries Service), and only listed species that occur in the United States.

SOURCE: "Summary of Listed Species: Listed Populations and Recovery Plans as of 02/01/2008," in *USFWS Threatened and Endangered Species System (TESS)*, U.S. Department of the Interior, U.S. Fish and Wildlife Service, February 1, 2008, http://ecos.fws.gov/tess_public/Boxscore.do (accessed February 1, 2008)

that nearly 1.6 million species have been named and described. Mammals, which are probably the best-studied group—and the one that includes humans—make up 0.3% (5,416) of all known organisms. Insects are a particularly rich biological group—over 950,000 insect species have been identified, with countless more to be described.

According to the IUCN's 2007 Red List, a total of 16,306 species were listed as threatened. More than 41,000 species were examined out of the nearly 1.6 million species that the IUCN considers "described species." Thus, only 2.6% of all known species were evaluated by the IUCN.

The listed species were as follows:

- 1,217 of 9,956 bird species evaluated (12%)
- 1,808 of 5,915 amphibian species evaluated (31%)
- 1,201 of 3,119 fish species evaluated (39%)
- 1,094 of 4,863 mammal species evaluated (22%)
- 978 of 2,212 mollusk species evaluated (44%)
- 623 of 1,255 insect species evaluated (50%)
- 422 of 1,385 reptile species evaluated (30%)
- 460 of 553 crustacean species evaluated (83%)
- 5 of 13 coral species evaluated (38%)
- 42 of 83 other species evaluated (51%)

In addition, the IUCN listed 8,447 plant species as threatened in 2007 out of 12,043 species evaluated. More than 297,000 plant species are known to the IUCN.

According to the IUCN, nearly all described bird, amphibian, and mammal species were evaluated during 2007. The other species have not yet been thoroughly assessed. Further study will likely result in many more species being added to the Red List.

Table 1.2 lists the number of species identified as threatened or endangered under the Endangered Species Act (ESA) as of February 2008. Of the 1,178 animal species listed, 607 are found in the United States. Among these, 448 are endangered and 159 are threatened. Among animals, the greatest numbers of listed species occur among fish, birds, and mammals. Of the 747 plant species listed, 744 are found in the United States. Among these, 598 are endangered and 146 are threatened. Nearly all the endangered plants are flowering plants.

Figure 1.2 shows the number of U.S. species listed per calendar year from 1967 through 2007. The peak year was 1994, when 127 species were listed. In 2007 only two species were added to the list.

Within the United States, endangered and threatened species are not evenly distributed but are clustered in specific geographical areas. Figure 1.3 shows the number of federally listed endangered and threatened species in each state as of February 1, 2008. Regions where the

FIGURE 1.2

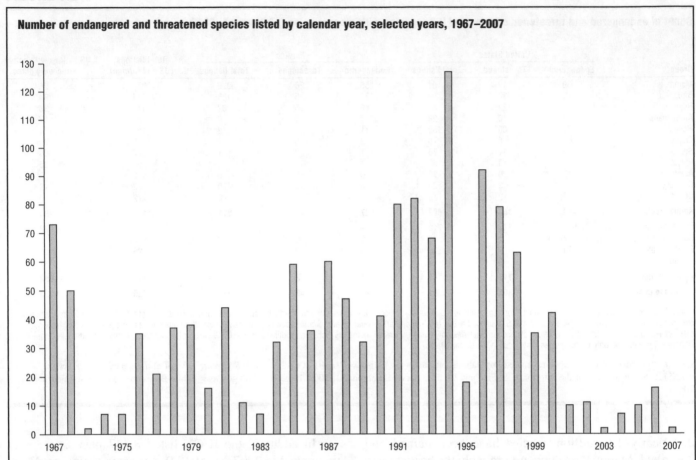

**Number of endangered and threatened species listed by calendar year, selected years, 1967–2007**

SOURCE: Adapted from "Federal Endangered and Threatened Species by Calendar Year," in *USFWS Threatened and Endangered Species System (TESS)*, U.S. Department of the Interior, U.S. Fish and Wildlife Service, February 1, 2008, http://ecos.fws.gov/tess_public/SpeciesCountByYear.do (accessed February 1, 2008)

number of listed species is particularly high include southern Appalachia, Florida, the Southwest, California, and Hawaii. Hawaii harbors more threatened and endangered species than any other state, despite its small size. This is due largely to the fact that a significant proportion of Hawaiian plant and animal life is endemic—that is, they are found nowhere else on Earth. Endemism is dangerous for imperiled species for a variety of reasons. A single calamitous event, such as a hurricane, earthquake, or disease epidemic, could wipe out the entire population at one time. The likelihood of interbreeding and resulting genetic problems is also higher for a species that is so geographically limited

## SPECIES LOSS—CRISIS OR FALSE ALARM?

Environmental issues, which tend to pit conservation against business or economic development, are often hotly debated. With respect to current threats to biodiversity, some critics argue that the scale of loss is not as great as what is imagined. They point to the uncertainty regarding the total number of species and to the geographic distributions of species. Other challengers claim that loss of

habitat and disruption by human activity are not powerful enough to cause the massive extinction being documented. Still other challengers contend that extinction is inevitable and that the earth has experienced, and recovered from, mass extinctions before. They conclude that the current biodiversity loss, while huge, is not disastrous.

In addition, opponents of conservation frequently argue that "green" policies such as the ESA place the needs of wildlife before those of humans. This was the central issue in one of the bitterest battles over an endangered species: the protection of the northern spotted owl habitat. (See Figure 1.4.) In 1990 declining populations resulted in the listing of the northern spotted owl as a threatened species. In 1992 the USFWS set aside 7 million acres (3 million ha) of forestland in the Pacific Northwest—both private and public—as critical habitat for the species. Logging was banned on federal lands within these areas. Loggers protested this ban, arguing that jobs would be lost. By contrast, supporters of the ban claimed that the logging industry in the area was already in decline and that continued logging would preserve existing jobs only for a short time. Eventually, a com-

FIGURE 1.3

**Number of endangered and threatened species, by state or territory, February 1, 2008**

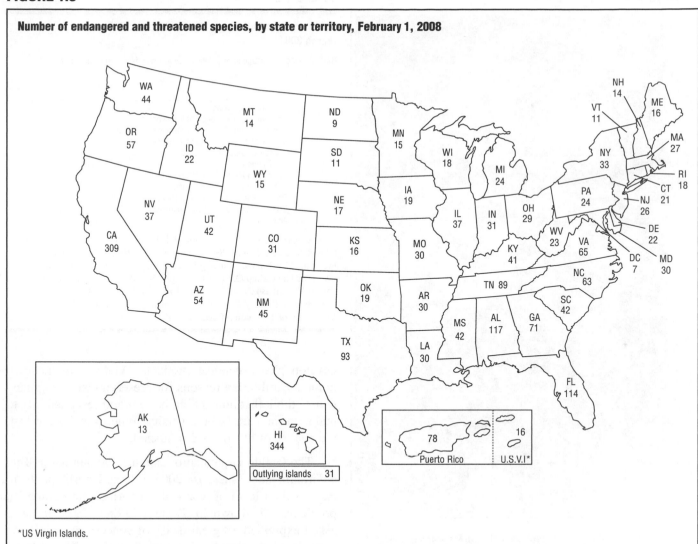

*US Virgin Islands.

SOURCE: "Listed Species Range by State/Territory as of Fri Feb 1 08:19:28 MST 2008," in *USFWS Threatened and Endangered Species System (TESS)*, U.S. Department of the Interior, U.S. Fish and Wildlife Service, February 1, 2008, http://ecos.fws.gov/tess_public/StateListing.do?state=all (accessed February 1, 2008)

promise was reached in which logging was limited to trees under a certain size, leaving the mature growth for owl habitat. By early 1993 almost all old-growth logging on federal lands had been stopped by court action.

In 1994 a group of federal agencies adopted the Northwest Forest Plan (http://www.fs.fed.us/r6/nwfp.htm) for the management of old-growth forests in the Pacific Northwest. The plan has three goals:

- Manage federal forests so that sustainable timber production and biological diversity are achieved

- Coordinate actions by various federal agencies involved in forest management and ensure that they receive input from nonfederal parties

- Provide economic assistance and job retraining for displaced timber workers and other parties adversely affected by reduced timber harvesting

The compromise worked out in the plan did not fully please either side in the controversy. In 2002 organizations representing the timber industry sued the USFWS claiming that northern spotted owl populations had recovered enough to remove the bird from the list of threatened species. The USFWS conducted a status review and concluded in 2004 that the threatened listing should remain in place. The agency noted that the Northwest Forest Plan had successfully minimized habitat loss on federal lands. However, populations of northern spotted owls in Washington, Oregon, and California continued to decline due to a combination of threats, including forest fires, bird and tree diseases, and competition for habitat from barred owls.

## WHY SAVE ENDANGERED SPECIES?

Proponents of conservation believe that saving species from extinction is important for many reasons. Species

**FIGURE 1.4**

The northern spotted owl, which inhabits old-growth forests in the Pacific Northwest, was the subject of a lengthy battle pitting environmentalists against logging interests. *U.S. Fish and Wildlife Service*

**TABLE 1.3**

**Public opinion poll on greatest environmental worries, March 2007**

[Based on the percentage saying they worry a "great deal" about each problem]

|  | % |
|---|---|
| Pollution of drinking water | 58 |
| Pollution of rivers, lakes, and reservoirs | 53 |
| Contamination of soil and water by toxic waste | 52 |
| Maintenance of the nation's supply of fresh water for household needs | 51 |
| Air pollution | 46 |
| Damage to the earth's ozone layer | 43 |
| The loss of tropical rain forests | 43 |
| The "greenhouse effect" or global warming | 41 |
| Extinction of plant and animal species | 39 |
| Acid rain | 25 |

SOURCE: Joseph Carroll, "Environmental Worries, March 11–14, 2007, (Based on the Percentage Saying They Worry a 'Great Deal' about Each Problem)," in *Polluted Drinking Water Is Public's Top Environmental Concern*, The Gallup Organization, April 20, 2007, http://brain.gallup.com/content/default.aspx?ci=27274&pg=1 (accessed January 17, 2008). Copyright © 2008 by The Gallup Organization. Reproduced by permission of The Gallup Organization.

develop pharmaceutical products. Aside from the economic or utilitarian reasons for preserving species, many people think that humankind has a moral responsibility to maintain the earth's biodiversity. When species are lost, the quality of all life is diminished.

The Gallup Organization conducts an annual poll on environmental issues. In 2007 it asked participants to express their level of worry about various environmental problems. As shown in Table 1.3, only 39% of those asked expressed a "great deal" of concern regarding the extinction of plant and animal species. This placed extinction ninth in the listing of environmental problems in terms of amount of worry.

### Are Some Species More Important than Others?

In general, the public places high value on some endangered species and not on others. For example, whales and seals are popular animals for which protection measures receive widespread support. By contrast, there are several species listed under the ESA that are considered pests or predators, because they pose a threat to human livelihoods or safety. Utah prairie dogs are burrowing animals that produce networks of underground tunnels. The resulting holes and dirt mounds can ruin cropland and trip and injure livestock. The protection of Utah prairie dogs and other imperiled rodents is a source of contention for people who believe that the ESA puts animal interests above human interests. The same debate rages over predators such as wolves and mountain lions that may prey on livestock, pets, and even people.

From a scientific standpoint, some species are more valued because they are the last remnants of biological groups that once flourished. Examples of these include

have both aesthetic and recreational value, as the tremendous popularity of zoos, wildlife safaris, recreational hiking, and wildlife watching (bird watching, whale watching, etc.) indicate. Wildlife also has educational and scientific value. In addition, because all species depend on other species for resources, the impact of a single lost species is difficult to predict and could potentially be immense. Scientists have shown that habitats with greater biodiversity are more stable—that is, they are better able to adjust to and recover from disturbances. This is because different species may perform overlapping functions in a biologically diverse ecosystem. Habitats with less diversity are more vulnerable, because a disturbance affecting one species may cause the entire network of interactions to collapse. Furthermore, many species have great economic value to human beings. Plants provide the genetic diversity used to breed new strains of agricultural crops, and many have been used to

the coelacanth, one of the few species (along with lung-fish) that help document the transition from aquatic to terrestrial life in vertebrates, and the tuatara, a highly endangered reptile found only in New Zealand. The extinction of species that have no closely related species left on Earth represent particularly significant losses to the genetic diversity of the planet.

## Biological Indicator Species

The rapid rate of species loss should also concern human beings because many are dying out due to pollution and environmental degradation, problems that affect human health and well-being as well. Species that are particularly useful in reporting on the health of ecosystems are called biological indicator species. Environmental scientists rely on sensitive indicator species just as coal miners once relied on canaries to check air safety in underground tunnels, where dangerous gases frequently became concentrated enough to be poisonous. Miners carried a canary into the mineshaft, knowing that the air was safe to breathe as long as the canary lived. If the bird started to sicken, however, miners evacuated the tunnel. In the same way, the sudden deaths of large numbers of bald eagles and peregrine falcons warned people about the dangers of dichlorodiphenyltrichloroethane, a powerful pesticide in wide use at the time. The disappearance of fish from various rivers, lakes, and seas also alerted people to the presence of dangerous chemicals in the water.

During the final decades of the twentieth century, many scientists became concerned about the sudden disappearance of many amphibians, particularly frogs, all over the world. Most troubling was the fact that many species disappeared from protected parks and wildlife refuges, areas that appeared relatively pristine and undisturbed. Amphibians are believed to be particularly sensitive to environmental disturbances such as pollution because their skins readily absorb substances from the environment. Their decline suggests that all may not be well with the environment.

## HABITAT AND ECOSYSTEM CONSERVATION
### U.S. Land Conservation Efforts

The early North American colonists were impressed by the abundance of natural resources they found and by the vast expanses of land available for settlement. Settlers migrated to the west and south, building towns and developing land for agriculture and industry. New modes of transportation allowed access to areas previously undisturbed by humans. Widespread development and demand for food, water, lumber, and other goods began to stress some natural resources. Massive areas of forest were cleared of trees. Passenger pigeons and heath hens were driven to extinction. Buffalo, elk, and beaver stocks were nearly destroyed.

The Bureau of Land Management (February 21, 1997, http://www.access.gpo.gov/blm/pls96/part1.html) explains that in the United States' first century as a nation, the federal government owned about 80% of the nation's land. The government started surveying and selling its landholdings to states, settlers, and railroad companies in about 1785. During the nineteenth century, awareness began growing in the United States about the scarcity and value of natural resources. In 1892 John Muir (1838–1914) established the Sierra Club, an organization devoted to recreation, education, and conservation. President Theodore Roosevelt (1858–1919) set aside millions of acres of land under federal government control for national refuges, forests, and parks.

By the end of the nineteenth century the government had transferred most of its lands to private ownership. It also allowed private use of remaining federal lands. After several decades of rapid development and unrestricted use, much of the nation's land and natural resources were significantly degraded. Responding to mounting concerns, Congress slowly redefined the federal government's role in land management from temporary to permanent retention and active stewardship.

During the 1960s increasing scientific and public concern about the declining condition of the country's natural resources led Congress to enact a number of laws to conserve both federal and nonfederal lands. These laws regulate activities that affect air, water, soil, plants, and animals. With increasing environmental legislation, the land management framework evolved into a complex collection of agencies, land units, and laws. Different agencies have different priorities, which are reflected in how they manage the resources under their care. The effects of these different missions are particularly evident in places where two agencies hold adjacent lands. For example, the National Park Service (Department of the Interior) oversees Yellowstone National Park, where timber harvesting is prohibited, whereas the U.S. Forest Service (Department of Agriculture) allows large areas to be clear-cut (removing all the trees in a designated area) in the adjacent Targhee National Forest in Idaho.

### The National Park System

In 1849 Congress passed a bill creating the U.S. Department of the Interior (DOI). The DOI was responsible for a wide variety of matters, including constructing water systems, exploring wilderness areas in the West, and managing public lands and public parks. In 1872 Yellowstone National Park was created by an act of Congress and was the first national park established in the world. Over the next four decades more than a dozen national parks were established in the United States, along with twenty-one national monuments. In 1916 a new agency, the National Park Service (NPS), was created under the DOI to manage these federal lands.

According to the NPS (2008, http://www.nps.gov/faqs.htm), in 2008 there were 391 units in the National Park System covering more than 84 million acres (34 million ha). The units include national parks, monuments, preserves, lakeshores, seashores, wild and scenic rivers, trails, historic sites, military parks, battlefields, historical parks, recreation areas, memorials, and parkways. Besides preserving habitats that range from arctic tundra to tropical rain forest, the system protects many imperiled plant and animal species.

The national parks have played a significant role in the return of several species, including red wolves and peregrine falcons. The national parks also contain designated critical habitat for many listed species. However, not all these are publicly disclosed, to protect rare species from collectors, vandals, or curiosity seekers.

## The National Forests

In 1905 the U.S. Forest Service was established as an agency of the U.S. Department of Agriculture. In 2008 the Forest Service (March 7, 2008, http://www.fs.fed.us/aboutus/meetfs.shtml) managed nearly 193 million acres (78 million ha) of public lands in 155 national forests and 20 national grasslands. National Forest lands also include many lakes and ponds. National Forest land is, in general, not conserved to the same degree as NPS lands. For example, much logging occurs within these forests.

Table 1.4 shows the number of threatened and endangered species that occurred in national forests or were potentially affected by National Forest Service management as of 2007. Within the Forest Service, the Threatened, Endangered, and Sensitive Species Program focuses on wildlife conservation. According to the Forest Service (2008, http://www.fs.fed.us/r9/wildlife/tes/faq.shtml), it is directed by the Secretary of Agriculture's Policy on Fish and Wildlife to "manage habitats for all native and desired nonnative plants, fish and wildlife species to maintain viable populations of each species; identify and recover threatened and endangered plant and animal species" and to avoid actions "which may cause species to become threatened or endangered." In addition, the Forest Service has another designation called "sensitive species" for species considered unique, rare, endemic, or meeting other criteria.

Endangered, threatened, and sensitive species on National Forest lands are subjected to biological evaluations to determine the effects on them of management activities. Conservation measures are also incorporated to preserve these species.

## The National Wildlife Refuge System

In 1903 President Theodore Roosevelt established the National Wildlife Refuge System (NWRS) and designated the first refuge at Pelican Island, Florida. The

**TABLE 1.4**

**Numbers of threatened and endangered species under the management of the National Forest Service, 2007**

| Taxonomic group | T&E species |
|---|---|
| 1. Plants | 170 |
| 2. Amphibians | 9 |
| 3. Arachnids | 1 |
| 4. Birds | 30 |
| 5. Clams/Molluscs | 50 |
| 6. Crustaceans | 8 |
| 7. Fishes | 89 |
| 8. Insects | 11 |
| 9. Mammals | 39 |
| 10. Reptiles | 11 |
| 11. Other invertebrate | 7 |
| **Total** | **425** |

Note: T&E=threatened and endangered.

SOURCE: Adapted from "Table 5. Numbers of Threatened and Endangered Species, and Designated Sensitive Species, by Taxonomic Group, That Occur on National Forest System Lands or Are Potentially Affected by NFS Management," in *Opportunities for Threatened, Endangered and Sensitive Species Conservation, 2008*, U.S. Department of Agriculture, U.S. Forest Service, February 21, 2007, http://www.fs.fed.us/biology/resources/pubs/tes/tes_opps_fy08_21feb07.pdf (accessed January 22, 2008)

refuge was home to a population of brown pelicans, which were being slaughtered for their popular feathers. Over the next century hundreds of additional refuges were designated throughout the country.

The NWRS is the only network of federal lands and waters managed principally for the protection of fish and wildlife. In 2007 the NWRS (2007, http://www.fws.gov/refuges/refugeLocatorMaps/index.html) included 548 refuges and thousands of small wetlands around the country. Approximately one-third of the total refuge acreage was wetland habitat, reflecting the importance of wetlands for wildlife survival.

Fifty-nine of the refuges were established specifically for endangered species. (See Table 1.5.) Protected species include a variety of plants and animals. Many other listed animal species use refuge lands on a temporary basis for breeding or migratory rest stops. Virtually every species of bird in North America has been recorded in the refuge system.

## Wilderness Preservation System Areas

In 1964 Congress passed the Wilderness Act. Its purpose was to designate certain areas of undeveloped federal land as the National Wilderness Preservation System. The act noted that these areas were to be "where the earth and its community of life are untrammeled by man, where man himself is a visitor who does not remain."

According to Wilderness.net (June 12, 2007, http://www.wilderness.net/index.cfm?fuse=NWPS&sec=fast

TABLE 1.5

**National Wildlife Refuges established for endangered species**

| State | Unit name | Species of concern | Unit acreage |
|---|---|---|---|
| Alabama | Sauta Cave NWR | Indiana bat, gray bat | 264 |
| | Fern Cave NWR | Indiana bat, gray bat | 199 |
| | Key Cave NWR | Alabama cavefish, gray bat | 1,060 |
| | Watercress Darter NWR | Watercress darter | 7 |
| Arkansas | Logan Cave NWR | Cave crayfish, gray bat, Indiana bat, Ozark cavefish | 124 |
| Arizona | Buenos Aires NWR | Masked bobwhite quail | 116,585 |
| | Leslie Canyon | Gila topminnow, yaqui chub, peregrine falcon | 2,765 |
| | San Bernardino NWR | Gila topminnow, yaqui chub, yaqui catfish, beautiful shiner, huachuca water umbel | 2,369 |
| California | Antioch Dunes NWR | Lange's metalmark butterfly, Antioch Dunes evening-primrose, Contra Costa wallflower | 55 |
| | Bitter Creek NWR | California condor | 14,054 |
| | Blue Ridge NWR | California condor | 897 |
| | Castle Rock NWR | Aleutian Canada goose | 14 |
| | Coachella Valley NWR | Coachello valley fringe-toed lizard | 3,592 |
| | Don Edwards San Francisco Bay NWR | California clapper rail, California least tern, salt marsh harvest mouse | 21,524 |
| | Ellicott Slough NWR | Santa Cruz long-toed salamander | 139 |
| | Hopper Mountain NWR | California condor | 2,471 |
| | Sacramento River NWR | Valley elderberry longhorn beetle, bald eagle, least bell's vireo | 7,884 |
| | San Diego NWR | San Diego fairy shrimp, San Diego mesa mint, otay mesa mint, California orcutt grass, San Diego button-celery | 1,840 |
| | San Joaquin River NWR | Aleutian Canada goose | 1,638 |
| | Seal Beach NWR | Light-footed clapper rail, California least tern | 911 |
| | Sweetwater Marsh NWR | Light-footed clapper rail | 316 |
| | Tijuana Slough NWR | Light-footed clapper rail | 1,023 |
| Florida | Archie Carr NWR | Loggerhead sea turtle, green sea turtle | 29 |
| | Crocodile Lake NWR | American crocodile | 6,686 |
| | Crystal River NWR | West Indian manatee | 80 |
| | Florida Panther NWR | Florida panther | 23,379 |
| | Hobe Sound NWR | Loggerhead sea turtle, green sea turtle | 980 |
| | Lake Wales Ridge NWR | Florida scrub jay, snakeroot, scrub blazing star, Carter's mustard, papery whitlow-wort, Florida bonamia, scrub lupine, highlands scrub hypericum, Garett's mint, scrub mint, pygmy gringe-tree, wireweed, Florida ziziphus, scrub plum, eastern indigo snake, bluetail mole skink, sand skink | 659 |
| | National Key Deer Refuge | Key deer | 8,542 |
| | St. Johns NWR | Dusky seaside sparrow | 6,255 |
| Hawaii | Hakalau Forest NWR | Akepa, akiapolaau, 'O'u, Hawaiian hawk, Hawaiian creeper | 32,730 |
| | Hanalei NWR | Hawaiian stilt, Hawaiian coot, Hawaiian moorhen, Hawaiian duck | 917 |
| | Huleia NWR | Hawaiian stilt, Hawaiian coot, Hawaiian moorhen, Hawaiian duck | 241 |
| | James C. Campbell NWR | Hawaiian stilt, Hawaiian coot, Hawaiian moorhen, Hawaiian duck | 164 |
| | Kakahaia NWR | Hawaiian stilt, Hawaiian coot | 45 |
| | Kealia Pond NWR | Hawaiian stilt, Hawaiian coot | 691 |
| | Pearl Harbor NWR | Hawaiian stilt | 61 |
| Iowa | Driftless area NWR | Iowa Pleistocene snail | 521 |
| Massachusetts | Massasoit NWR | Plymouth red-bellied turtle | 184 |
| Michigan | Kirtland's warbler WMA | Kirtland's warbler | 6,535 |
| Mississippi | Mississippi Sandhill crane NWR/TD> | Mississippi sandhill crane | 19,713 |
| Missouri | Ozark cavefish NWR | Ozark cavefish | 42 |
| | Pilot Knob NWR | Indiana bat | 90 |
| Nebraska | Karl E. Mundt NWR | Bald eagle | 19 |
| Nevada | Ash Meadows NWR | Devil's hole pupfish, warm springs pupfish, ash meadows amargosa pupfish, ash meadows speckled dace, ash meadows naucorid, ash meadows blazing star, amargosa niterwort, ash meadows milk-vetch, ash meadows sunray, spring-loving centaury, ash meadows gumplant, ash meadows invesia | 13,268 |
| | Moapa Valley NWR | Moapa dace | 32 |
| Oklahoma | Ozark Plateau NWR | Ozark big-eared bat, gray bat | 2,208 |
| Oregon | Bear Valley NWR | Bald eagle | 4,200 |
| | Julia Butler Hansen Refuge for Columbian white-tail deer | Columbian white-tailed deer | 2,750 |
| | Nestucca Bay NWR | Aleutian Canada goose | 457 |

Facts), in 2007, 703 of these so-called wilderness areas had been designated across the country covering more than 107.4 million acres (43.5 million ha). (See Figure 1.5.) The lands are owned or administered by the USFWS, the Forest Service, the NPS, or the Bureau of Land Management. Alaska, California, and other western states are home to most of the wilderness areas.

Unlike national parks, which are intended for use by large numbers of visitors, wilderness areas are intended to be pristine, with limited access and no amenities.

### The Debate over Use of Federally Protected Lands

Since federal conservation lands were first set aside, a national debate has raged over how they should be

**TABLE 1.5**

**National Wildlife Refuges established for endangered species** [CONTINUED]

| State | Unit name | Species of concern | Unit acreage |
|---|---|---|---|
| South Dakota | Karl E. Mundt NWR | Bald eagle | 1,044 |
| Texas | Attwater prairie chicken NWR | Attwater's greater prairie chicken | 8,007 |
| | Balcones Canyonlands NWR | Black-capped vireo, golden-cheeked warbler | 14,144 |
| Virgin Islands | Green Cay NWR | St. Croix ground lizard | 14 |
| | Sandy Point NWR | Leatherback sea turtle | 327 |
| Virginia | James River NWR | Bald eagle | 4,147 |
| | Mason Neck NWR | Bald eagle | 2,276 |
| Washington | Julia Butler Hansen Refuge for Columbian white-tail deer | Columbian white-tailed deer | 2,777 |
| Wyoming | Mortenson Lake NWR | Wyoming toad | 1,776 |

Note: NWR = National Wildlife Refuge. WMA = Wildlife Management Area.

SOURCE: "National Wildlife Refuges Established for Endangered Species," in *America's National Wildlife Refuge System*, U.S. Department of the Interior, U.S. Fish and Wildlife Service, 2008, http://www.fws.gov/refuges/habitats/endSpRefuges.html (accessed January 18, 2008)

used. Many of these lands contain natural resources of great value in commercial markets, including timber, oil, gas, and minerals. Political and business interests that wish to harvest these resources are pitted against environmentalists, who want to preserve the lands in as pristine condition as possible. During the 1990s such a battle raged over the issue of logging in old-growth forests of the Pacific Northwest—the same forests that provided habitat for endangered northern spotted owls. A similar controversy has been brewing for decades over the drilling of oil and gas in the Arctic National Wildlife Refuge.

**OIL DRILLING IN THE ARCTIC NATIONAL WILDLIFE REFUGE?** The Arctic National Wildlife Refuge (ANWR) is located in northern Alaska. (See Figure 1.6.) Covering 19 million acres (8 million ha), it is the largest National Wildlife Refuge in the United States. ANWR was established in 1980 by passage of the Alaska National Interest Lands Conservation Act. In Section 1002 of the act, Congress deferred a decision on the future management of 1.5 million acres (607,000 ha) of ANWR, because of conflicting interests between potential oil and gas resources thought to be located there and the area's importance as a wildlife habitat. This disputed area of coastal plain came to be known as the 1002 area. (See Figure 1.7.)

There has been interest in tapping the oil deposits in northern Alaska since the mid-1900s. The area was first explored for oil and gas resources in the 1940s and 1950s. It was also in the 1950s, however, that people became aware of the ecological value of these lands, and a compromise was reached in which the northeastern part of the state was set aside as a wildlife range (later refuge), while drilling began (and continues) in the northwestern part of the state. Production of oil and gas in the refuge area— the 5% of Alaska's North Slope not already open to drilling—was also prohibited at that time unless specifically authorized by Congress.

In 1987 the DOI submitted a report to Congress on the resources of the 1002 area. At that time only a few oil

accumulations had been found near ANWR. Over the next decade, much larger oil fields were discovered as shown by the shaded areas in Figure 1.7. In 1998 the U.S. Geological Survey (USGS) performed a petroleum assessment of the 1002 area and the adjacent state waters. In *Arctic National Wildlife Refuge, 1002 Area, Petroleum Assessment, 1998, Including Economic Analysis* (April 2001, http://pubs.usgs.gov/fs/fs-0028-01/fs-0028-01.pdf), an updated assessment, the USGS finds that there is a 95% probability of 5.7 billion barrels of oil being recoverable from the assessed area, with most of the oil coming from the undeformed part of the 1002 area. The undeformed area has a geologic structure composed of rock layers that are mostly horizontal. This makes for more successful drilling than in the deformed area, where rock layers are folded and faulted.

The protected status of ANWR has been challenged by large oil companies and their political supporters. When Republicans took control of Congress in 1995, they passed legislation to allow for drilling in ANWR, but President Bill Clinton (1946–) vetoed the bill. The succeeding administration under President George W. Bush (1946–) has been much more supportive of drilling in the refuge.

Environmentalists argue that USFWS studies suggest that oil drilling in the refuge will harm many arctic species by taking over habitat, damaging habitats through pollution, interfering with species activities directly, or increasing opportunities for invasive species. ANWR harbors the greatest number of plant and animal species of any park or refuge in the arctic, including a multitude of unique species such as caribou, musk oxen, polar bears, arctic foxes, and snow geese. Because of the harsh climate, arctic habitats are generally characterized by short food chains and extreme vulnerability to habitat disturbance. Furthermore, the majority of arctic species already live "on the edge." Consequently, the decline of even a single species is likely to have dramatic effects on the entire community.

FIGURE 1.5

**National Wilderness Preservation System areas**

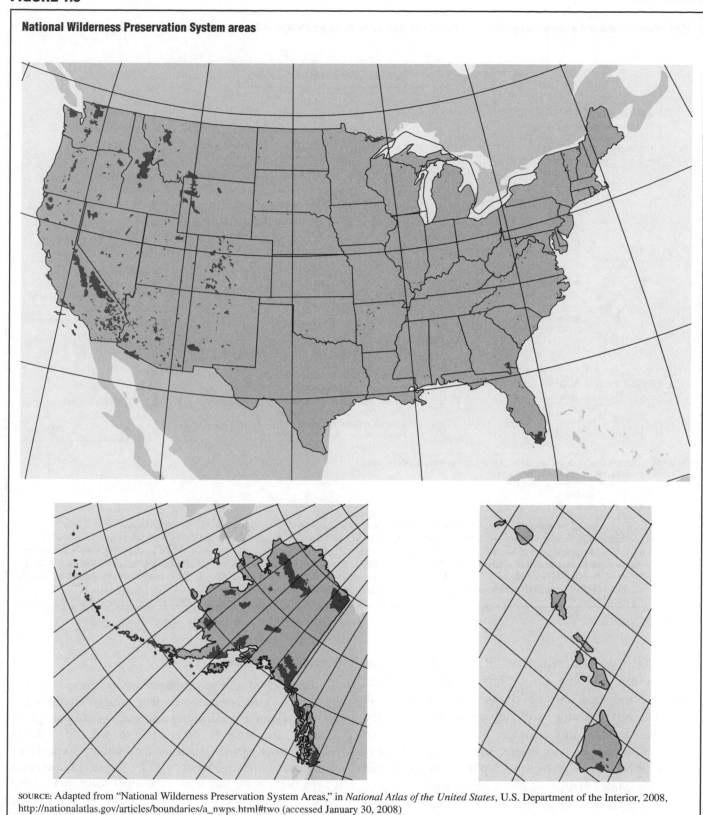

SOURCE: Adapted from "National Wilderness Preservation System Areas," in *National Atlas of the United States*, U.S. Department of the Interior, 2008, http://nationalatlas.gov/articles/boundaries/a_nwps.html#two (accessed January 30, 2008)

Some environmentalists consider the 1002 area to be one of the most ecologically diverse and valuable parts of the refuge. Among the species that would be affected if drilling is permitted are polar bears, whose preferred sites for building dens are in the 1002 area, and caribou, which use this area for calving (giving birth to young). (See Figure 1.8 and Figure 1.9).

**FIGURE 1.6**

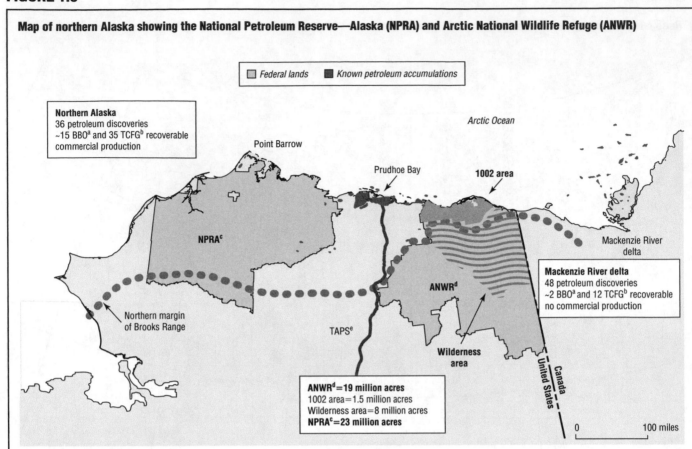

Map of northern Alaska showing the National Petroleum Reserve—Alaska (NPRA) and Arctic National Wildlife Refuge (ANWR)

[Legend] ☐ Federal lands  ■ Known petroleum accumulations

**Northern Alaska**
36 petroleum discoveries
~15 BBO[a] and 35 TCFG[b] recoverable
commercial production

Point Barrow

Arctic Ocean

Prudhoe Bay

1002 area

NPRA[c]

Mackenzie River delta

**Mackenzie River delta**
48 petroleum discoveries
~2 BBO[a] and 12 TCFG[b] recoverable
no commercial production

ANWR[d]

Northern margin of Brooks Range

TAPS[e]

Wilderness area

Canada
United States

**ANWR[d]=19 million acres**
1002 area=1.5 million acres
Wilderness area=8 million acres
**NPRA[c]=23 million acres**

0          100 miles

[a]BBO=billion barrels of oil (includes cumulative production plus recoverable resources).
[b]TCFG=trillion cubic feet of gas recoverable resources.
[c]NPRA=National Petroleum Reserve—Alaska.
[d]ANWR=Arctic National Wildlife Refuge.
[e]TAPS=Trans-Alaska Pipeline System.

SOURCE: "Figure 1. Map of Northern Alaska and Nearby Parts of Canada Showing Locations of the Arctic National Wildlife Refuge (ANWR), the 1002 Area, and the National Petroleum Reserve—Alaska (NPRA). Locations of Known Petroleum Accumulations and the Trans-Alaska Pipeline System (TAPS) Are Shown, As Well As Summaries of Known Petroleum Volumes in Northern Alaska and the Mackenzie River Delta of Canada. BBO, Billion Barrels of Oil (Includes Cumulative Production Plus Recoverable Resources); TCFG, Trillion Cubic Feet of Gas Recoverable Resources," in *Arctic National Wildlife Refuge, 1002 Area, Petroleum Assessment, 1998, Including Economic Analysis,* U.S. Department of the Interior, U.S. Geological Survey, April 2001, http://pubs.usgs.gov/fs/fs-0028-01/fs-0028-01.pdf (accessed January 30, 2008)

In 2001 the U.S. House of Representatives again passed a bill allowing for drilling within the refuge. However, the U.S. Senate rejected this proposal in 2002. The terrorist attacks of September 11, 2001, and heightened tensions in the Middle East have encouraged some politicians to emphasize the national security aspects of oil development in ANWR. They argue that the United States cannot be truly secure until it reduces its dependence on foreign oil. The Bush administration has continued to press for oil drilling in ANWR. During 2005 ANWR drilling measures were added to bills related to energy, the fiscal year 2006 budget, and defense appropriations. Various versions of these bills were approved by either the House or the Senate at one time or another; however, the drilling measures were ultimately dropped from the final bills.

**Private Lands Conservation**

Federal and state governments are not the only entities involved in land conservation. Increasingly, environment-minded private organizations and citizens are purchasing land with the intent of preserving it for wildlife. National environmental groups such as the Nature Conservancy participate in these endeavors. The Nature Conservancy (2008, http://www.nature.org/aboutus/) states that it helps protect more than 117 million acres (47 million ha) worldwide. Other major groups engaged in private land conservation include the Conservation Fund, the Trust for Public Land, the Land Trust Alliance, the Society for the Protection of New Hampshire Forests, and the Rocky Mountain Elk Foundation.

Every five years the Land Trust Alliance conducts a census on lands held for private conservation; the most

**FIGURE 1.7**

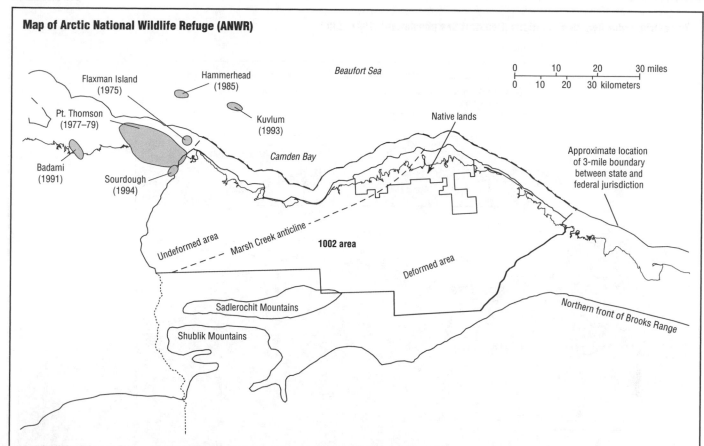

**Map of Arctic National Wildlife Refuge (ANWR)**

SOURCE: E.D. Attanasi, "Figure 1. Map Showing the Entire Study Area That Included the Federal Part of the 1002 Area of the Arctic National Wildlife Refuge, Native Lands within the 1002 Area, and Lands Underlying Adjacent Alaska State Waters and the Undeformed and Deformed Areas of the 1002 Area. Also Shown Are Oil Accumulations Discovered Near the Entire Study Area during the Past Three Decades," in *Economics of 1998 U.S. Geological Survey's 1002 Area Regional Assessment: An Economic Update*, U.S. Department of the Interior, U.S. Geological Survey, 2005, http://pubs.usgs.gov/of/2005/1359/OF2005-1359.pdf (accessed January 30, 2008)

recent census was completed in 2005. The alliance (November 30, 2006, http://www.lta.org/census/) states that in 2005 approximately 37 million acres (15 million ha) of land were held in local, regional, or national land trusts. Land trusts either purchase land outright or develop private, voluntary agreements called conservation easements or restrictions that limit future development of the land.

## INTERNATIONAL EFFORTS AT CONSERVATION

The UN Environment Programme (UNEP) was established to address diverse environmental issues on an international level. Many of its conventions have been extremely valuable in protecting global biodiversity and natural resources. The UNEP has also helped regulate pollution and the use of toxic chemicals.

### Convention on International Trade in Endangered Species of Wild Fauna and Flora

The Convention on International Trade in Endangered Species of Wild Fauna and Flora (CITES) is an international agreement administered under the UNEP

that regulates international trade in wildlife. CITES is perhaps the single most important international agreement relating to endangered species and has contributed critically to the protection of many threatened species. The international wildlife trade is estimated to involve hundreds of millions of specimens annually.

CITES was first drafted in 1963 at a meeting of the IUCN and went into effect in 1975. Protected plant and animals are listed in three separate CITES appendices, depending on the degree of endangerment. Appendix I includes species that are in immediate danger of extinction. CITES generally prohibits international trade of these species. Appendix II lists species that are likely to become in danger of extinction without strict protection from international trade. Permits may be obtained for the trade of Appendix II species only if trade will not harm the survival prospects of the species in the wild. Appendix III lists species whose trade is regulated in one or more nations. Any member nation can list a species in Appendix III to request international cooperation to prevent unsustainable levels of international trade. Nations agree to abide by CITES rules voluntarily. In 2008 there were more than 170 nations participating in the agreement.

FIGURE 1.8

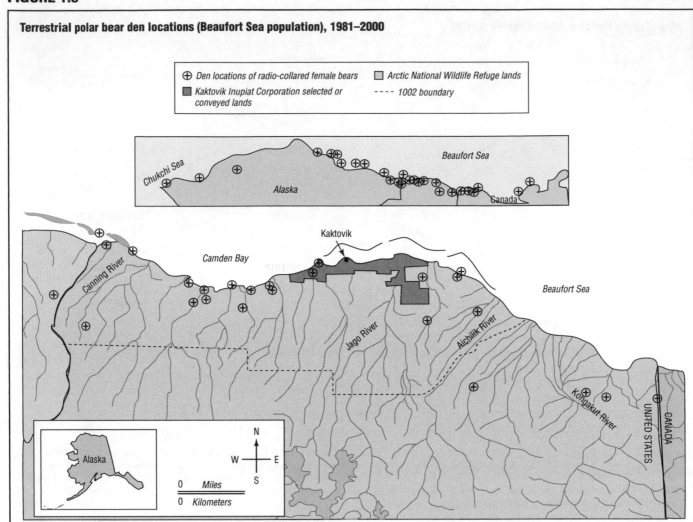

**Terrestrial polar bear den locations (Beaufort Sea population), 1981–2000**

⊕ Den locations of radio-collared female bears

▪ Kaktovik Inupiat Corporation selected or conveyed lands

☐ Arctic National Wildlife Refuge lands

---- 1002 boundary

SOURCE: "Terrestrial Polar Bear Den Locations (Beaufort Sea Population) 1981–2000," in *Potential Impacts of Proposed Oil and Gas Development on the Arctic Refuge's Coastal Plain: Historical Overview and Issues of Concern*, U.S. Fish and Wildlife Service, January 17, 2001, http://library.fws.gov/Pubs7/ arctic_oilandgas_impact.pdf (accessed February 6, 2008)

## Convention on Biological Diversity

The Convention on Biological Diversity was set up to conserve biodiversity and to promote the sustainable use of biodiversity. The convention supports national efforts in the documentation and monitoring of biodiversity, the establishment of refuges and other protected areas, and the restoration of degraded ecosystems. It also supports goals related to the maintenance of traditional knowledge of sustainable resource use, the prevention of invasive species introductions, and the control of invasive species that are already present. Finally, it funds education programs promoting public awareness of the value of natural resources.

## Convention on the Conservation of Migratory Species of Wild Animals

The Convention on the Conservation of Migratory Species of Wild Animals (also known as the CMS or the Bonn Convention) recognizes that certain migratory spe-

cies cross national boundaries and require protection throughout their range. The convention (December 28, 2007, http://www.cms.int/about/intro.htm) aims to "conserve terrestrial, marine and avian migratory species throughout their range." It was originally signed in Bonn, Germany, in 1979 and went into force in November 1983. According to the CMS (March 1, 2008, http://www.cms.int/ about/part_lst.htm), as of March 2008, 108 nations in Africa, Central and South America, Asia, Europe, and Oceania were involved in the agreement. The United States and several other nations are not official parties to the agreement but nonetheless abide by its rules.

The CMS provides two levels of protection to migratory species. Appendix I species are endangered and strictly protected. Appendix II species are less severely threatened but would nonetheless benefit from international cooperative agreements. Appendix II agreements have been drawn up for groups such as European bats,

**FIGURE 1.9**

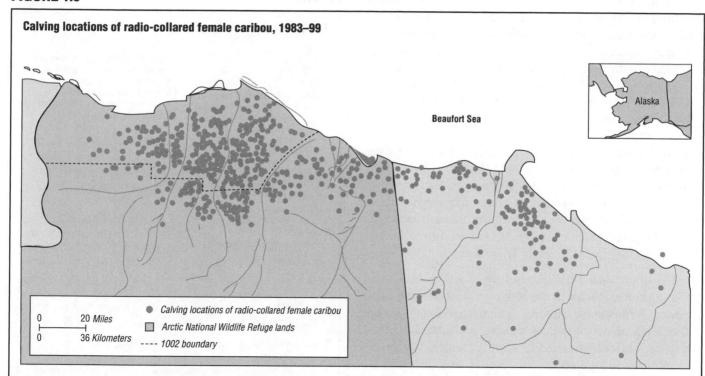

**Calving locations of radio-collared female caribou, 1983–99**

SOURCE: "Calving Locations of Radio-Collared Female Caribou during 1983–1999," in *Potential Impacts of Proposed Oil and Gas Development on the Arctic Refuge's Coastal Plain: Historical Overview and Issues of Concern*, U.S. Fish and Wildlife Service, January 17, 2001, http://library.fws.gov/Pubs7/arctic_oilandgas_impact.pdf (accessed February 6, 2008)

Mediterranean and Black Sea cetaceans (whales and related species), Baltic and North Sea cetaceans, Wadden Sea seals, African-Eurasian migratory water birds, and marine turtles. In 2004 the Agreement on the Conservation of Albatrosses and Petrels came into effect. Because these seabirds are highly migratory, their conservation requires broad international agreements besides efforts by individual nations.

## World Commission on Protected Areas

The IUCN's World Commission on Protected Areas (WCPA) is the leading international body dedicated to the selection, establishment, and management of national parks and protected areas. It helps establish natural areas around the world for the protection of plant and animal species and maintains a database of protected areas. Protected areas often consist of a core zone, in which wildlife cannot legally be disturbed by human beings, and a buffer zone, a transitional space that acts as shield for the core zone. On the periphery are areas for managed human living. According to the WCPA (2004, http://www.unep-wcmc.org/protected _areas/categories/index.html), a protected area is defined as "an area of land and/or sea especially dedicated to the protection and maintenance of biological diversity, and of natural and associated cultural resources, and managed through legal or other effective means."

Conservation biology theory advocates that protected areas should be as large as possible to increase biological diversity and to buffer refuges from outside pressures. The world's largest protected areas are Greenland National Park (Greenland), Ar-Rub'al-khali Wildlife Management Area (Saudi Arabia), Great Barrier Reef Marine Park (Australia), Qiang Tang Nature Reserve (China), Cape Churchill Wildlife Management Area (Canada), and the Northern Wildlife Management Zone (Saudi Arabia).

## FACTORS THAT CONTRIBUTE TO SPECIES ENDANGERMENT

Experts believe that the increasing loss and decline of species cannot be attributed to natural processes, but results instead from the destructive effect of human activities. People hunt and collect wildlife. They destroy natural habitats by clearing trees and filling swamps for development. Aquatic habitats are altered or destroyed by the building of dams. Humans also poison habitats with polluting chemicals and industrial waste. Indeed, human activity may be causing changes in climate patterns on a global scale.

### Habitat Destruction

Habitat destruction is probably the single most important factor leading to the endangerment of species. It plays a role in the decline of nearly all listed species and has had an impact on nearly every type of habitat and ecosystem.

Many types of human activity result in habitat destruction. Agriculture is a leading cause, with nearly half of the total land area in the United States used for farming. Besides causing the direct replacement of natural habitat with fields, agricultural activity also results in soil erosion, pollution from pesticides and fertilizers, and runoff into aquatic habitats. Agriculture has compromised forest, prairie, and wetland habitats in particular. Brian Czech, Paul R. Krausman, and Patrick K. Devers note in "Economic Associations among Causes of Species Endangerment in the United States" (*Bioscience*, vol. 50, no. 7, July 2000) that the role of agriculture in the endangerment of species is greatest in the Southeast and California. However, agriculture affects threatened and endangered species throughout the country, contributing to endangerment in thirty-five states.

Urban expansion has also destroyed wild habitat areas and is a primary factor in the endangerment of many plant species. As with agriculture, urbanization leads to the direct replacement of natural habitat. It also results in the depletion of local resources, such as water, which are important to many species. According to Czech, Krausman, and Devers, urbanization contributes to the endangerment of species in thirty-one states. The greatest impact is in California, Florida, and Texas, the three states that are urbanizing the most rapidly. In contrast, only two species are endangered by urbanization in Utah, Nevada, and Idaho. The researchers argue that this is because a large proportion of land in these states is public land and therefore not available for private development.

Logging, particularly the practice of clear-cutting, destroys important habitat for many species. Clear-cutting or extensive logging can also lead to significant erosion, harming both soils and aquatic habitats, which become blocked with soil.

Many other forms of human activity result in habitat destruction and degradation. Grazing by domestic livestock has a direct impact on many plant species, as well as on animal species that compete with livestock. Mining destroys vegetation and soil and degrades habitat through pollution. Dams destroy aquatic habitats in rivers and streams. Finally, human recreational activity, particularly the use of off-road vehicles, results in the destruction of natural habitat. Czech, Krausman, and Devers report that recreational activity has a particularly detrimental effect on species in California, Hawaii, Florida, as well as on species in the Mojave Desert, which includes portions of Arizona, California, Nevada, and Utah.

## Habitat Fragmentation

Human land-use patterns often result in the fragmentation of natural habitat areas that are available to species. Studies show that habitat fragmentation is occurring in most habitat types. Habitat fragmentation can have sig-

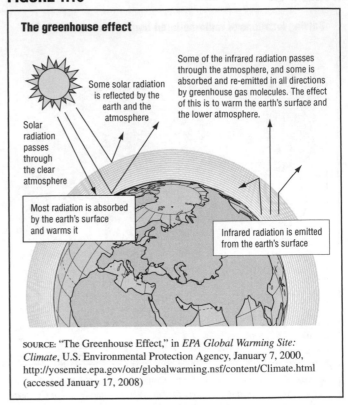

**FIGURE 1.10**

**The greenhouse effect**

Some solar radiation is reflected by the earth and the atmosphere

Solar radiation passes through the clear atmosphere

Some of the infrared radiation passes through the atmosphere, and some is absorbed and re-emitted in all directions by greenhouse gas molecules. The effect of this is to warm the earth's surface and the lower atmosphere.

Most radiation is absorbed by the earth's surface and warms it

Infrared radiation is emitted from the earth's surface

SOURCE: "The Greenhouse Effect," in *EPA Global Warming Site: Climate*, U.S. Environmental Protection Agency, January 7, 2000, http://yosemite.epa.gov/oar/globalwarming.nsf/content/Climate.html (accessed January 17, 2008)

nificant effects on species. Small populations can become isolated, so that dispersal from one habitat patch to another is impossible. Smaller populations are also more likely to become extinct. Finally, because there are more "edges" when habitats are fragmented, there can be increased exposure to predators and increased vulnerability to disturbances associated with human activity.

## Global Warming

Global warming is a phenomenon associated with the enhanced greenhouse effect. Gases such as carbon dioxide and methane in the atmosphere absorb and maintain heat in the same way that glass traps heat in a greenhouse. This natural greenhouse effect keeps Earth warm and habitable for life. (See Figure 1.10.)

An enhanced greenhouse effect refers to the possible increase in the temperature of Earth's surface due to the release of excessive amounts of greenhouse gases from the burning of fossil fuels. Figure 1.11 shows that the global average of carbon dioxide in the atmosphere has increased dramatically since the early 1980s. A global temperature increase has also been compellingly documented and has already had important effects on ecosystems worldwide. (See Figure 1.12.)

Chris D. Thomas et al. suggest in "Extinction Risk from Climate Change" (*Nature*, vol. 427, January 8, 2004), a study of habitats comprising 20% of the earth's surface, that 15% to 37% of the world's species may be extinct by 2050 if recent warming trends continue.

## FIGURE 1.11

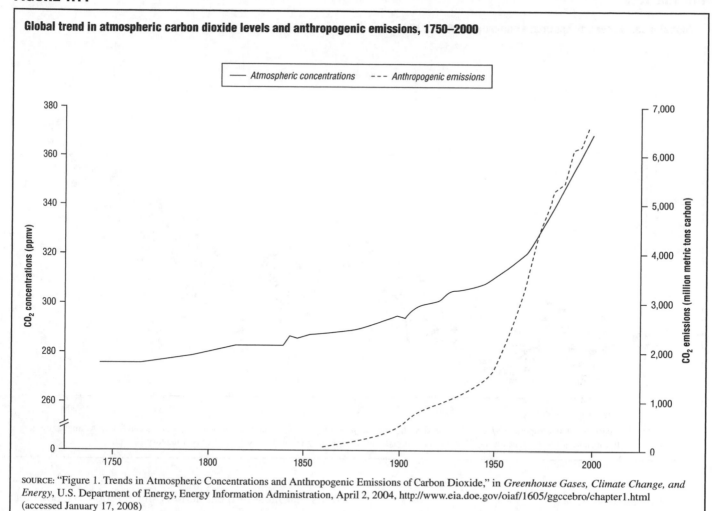

**Global trend in atmospheric carbon dioxide levels and anthropogenic emissions, 1750–2000**

— Atmospheric concentrations    --- Anthropogenic emissions

SOURCE: "Figure 1. Trends in Atmospheric Concentrations and Anthropogenic Emissions of Carbon Dioxide," in *Greenhouse Gases, Climate Change, and Energy*, U.S. Department of Energy, Energy Information Administration, April 2, 2004, http://www.eia.doe.gov/oiaf/1605/ggccebro/chapter1.html (accessed January 17, 2008)

Continued warming of the earth would alter habitats drastically, with serious consequences for many species. In places such as Siberia and the northernmost regions of Canada, habitats such as the tundra (permanently frozen land supporting only low-growing plant life such as mosses and lichens) and the taiga (expanses of evergreen forests located immediately south of the tundra) are shrinking. Deserts are expanding. Forests and grasslands are beginning to shift toward more appropriate climate regimes. Animal and plant species that cannot shift their ranges quickly enough, or have no habitat to shift into, are dying out. Some plants and animals that are found in precise, narrow bands of temperature and humidity, such as monarch butterflies or edelweiss, are likely to find their habitats wiped out entirely. Global warming is already endangering some of the most diverse ecosystems on Earth, such as coral reefs and tropical cloud forests. The impact on endangered species, which are already in a fragile state, may be particularly great.

### Pollution

Pollution is caused by the release of industrial and chemical wastes into the land, air, and water. It can damage habitats and kill or sicken animals and plants. Pollution comes from a wide variety of sources, including industrial operations, mining, automobiles, and agricultural products such as pesticides and fertilizers. Even animals that are not directly exposed to pollution can be affected, if other species they rely on die out. According to Czech, Krausman, and Devers, pollution currently affects many species in the Southeast, particularly aquatic species such as fish or mussels.

### Hunting and Trade

Humans have hunted many animal species to extinction, and hunting continues to be a major threat to some species. In the United States, gray wolves were nearly wiped out because they were considered a threat to livestock. The Caribbean monk seal was exterminated because it was viewed as a competitor for fish. Other animals are hunted for the value of their hides, tusks, or horns, including elephants and rhinoceroses. Many exotic species, such as parrots and other tropical birds, are taken from their natural habitats for the pet trade.

FIGURE 1.12

**Global mean surface temperature anomalies, 1880–2007**

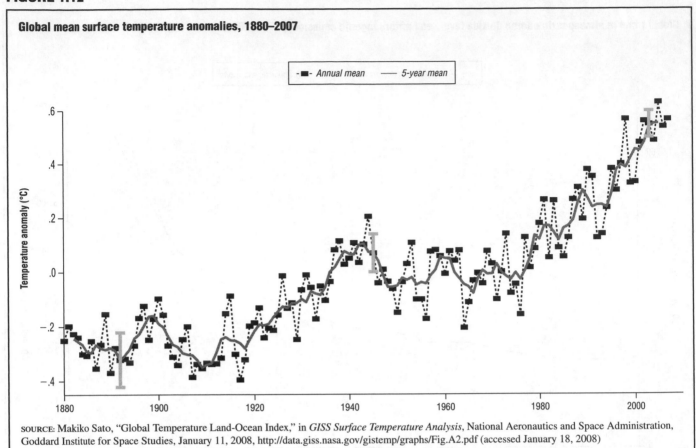

SOURCE: Makiko Sato, "Global Temperature Land-Ocean Index," in *GISS Surface Temperature Analysis*, National Aeronautics and Space Administration, Goddard Institute for Space Studies, January 11, 2008, http://data.giss.nasa.gov/gistemp/graphs/Fig.A2.pdf (accessed January 18, 2008)

## Invasive Species

Invasive species are those that have been introduced from their native habitat into a new, nonnative habitat and cause environmental harm. Most introductions of invasive species are accidental, resulting from "stowaways" on ships and planes. Invasive species harm native life forms by competing with them for food and other resources, or by preying on them or parasitizing them. In "Environmental and Economic Costs of Nonindigenous Species in the United States" (*BioScience*, vol. 50, no. 1, January 2000), David Pimentel et al. indicate that approximately fifty thousand species are believed to have been introduced into the United States alone. Even though there are sometimes beneficial effects from introducing nonnative species, most of the effects are harmful.

The introduction of invasive species can lead to genetic swamping. This is a condition that arises when large numbers of one species breed with a much smaller population of another related species. The genetic material of the invasive species becomes overwhelming, causing the resulting generations to lose many of the characteristics that made the smaller population a unique species in the first place.

Many species in peril are endangered partly or entirely because of invasive species. In fact, the IUCN finds that most bird extinctions since 1800 have been due to invasive species such as rats and snakes. In 2003 the IUCN (http://www.iucn.org/themes/ssc/redlist_archive/redlist2003/English/newsreleaseEn.htm) reported in a press release that the unique flora and fauna of islands such as the Galapagos Islands, Hawaii, the Seychelles, the Falkland Islands, and the British Virgin Islands have been devastated by invasive species. Human commensals (species that are used by and associated with humans) can be among the most destructive introduced species. For example, in Hawaii grazing by feral pigs, goats, cattle, and sheep is responsible for the endangerment of many plants and birds.

The introduction of invasive species by humans has also taken a toll on mammalian wildlife. Australia is overrun with domestic cats whose ancestors were brought by settlers to the island continent two hundred years ago. Stray domestic cats have driven indigenous species such as bandicoots, bettongs, numbats, wallabies, and dozens of other bird and mammal species, most of which are found nowhere else on Earth, toward extinction.

Recognizing the threat posed by invasive species, President Clinton signed Executive Order 13112 on Invasive Species in 1999. This order required federal agencies to make every possible effort to control the spread of invasive species and resulted in the formation of the Invasive Species Council, which drafted the first National Invasive Species Management Plan in 2001. The plan emphasizes prevention of the introduction of alien species, early detection of invasions, rapid response to them, and coordination of national and international efforts in management and control of these species.

In "Update on the Environmental and Economic Costs Associated with Alien-Invasive Species in the United States" (*Ecological Economics*, vol. 52, no. 3, February 15, 2005), David Pimentel, Rodolfo Zuniga, and Doug Morrison report that invasive species cause environmental damages and losses that cost the country nearly $120 billion per year. Invasive species are blamed, in part, for imperiling approximately 42% of the species on the list of threatened and endangered species in the United States.

# CHAPTER 2
# THE ENDANGERED SPECIES ACT

The Endangered Species Act (ESA) of 1973 is generally considered one of the most far-reaching laws ever enacted by any nation for the preservation of wildlife. The passage of the ESA resulted from alarm at the decline of many species worldwide, as well as from recognition of the importance of preserving species diversity. The purpose of the ESA is to identify species that are either endangered (at risk of extinction throughout all or a significant portion of their range) or threatened (likely to become endangered in the future). Except for recognized insect pests, all animals and plants are eligible for listing under the ESA. Listed species are protected without regard to either commercial or sport value.

The ESA is also one of the most controversial and contentious laws ever passed. It affects the rights of private landowners and how they manage their property if endangered species are found there. It also allows private individuals and groups to sue federal agencies for alleged failures in carrying out the law. The result has been a flood of litigation since the 1990s by conservation organizations. They believe that full and effective implementation of the ESA will help ensure the survival of imperiled species. However, critics charge that the ESA has saved virtually no species, puts too many restrictions on land and water development projects, and is too expensive for the results that it achieves.

## HISTORY OF SPECIES PROTECTION

Conservation has a long history. One of the oldest examples dates to 242 B.C., when the Indian emperor Asoka (300–238? B.C.) created nature reserves in Asia. Marco Polo (c. 1254–c. 1324) reported that the Asian ruler Kublai Khan (1215–1294) helped conserve bird and mammal species valued for hunting by banning hunting during their reproductive periods. He also helped increase their numbers by planting food and providing protected cover areas. In South America, during the reign of the Incas, many species of seabirds were protected.

By the mid-nineteenth century many governments had developed an interest in wildlife conservation and an awareness of the need to protect natural habitats. In 1861 painters of the Barbizon school established the first French nature reserve, which covered over 3,400 acres (1,376 ha) of forest at Fontainebleau near Paris. Three years later the U.S. government set aside the Yosemite Valley in California as a national reserve. This became Yosemite National Park in 1890. Wyoming's Yellowstone National Park was created in 1872 and became the first U.S. national park.

Organizations and laws dedicated to the protection of species soon followed. In 1895 the first international meeting for the protection of birds was held in Paris and resulted in new laws protecting species in several countries. The first international conference for the protection of nature was held in 1913. The International Whaling Commission was established in 1946, and two years later the International Union for the Protection of Nature was founded. In 1956 its name was changed to the International Union for Conservation of Nature and Natural Resources (IUCN).

In 1961 the World Wildlife Fund (WWF), a private conservation organization, was founded. The Chinese giant panda was selected as the WWF symbol, not only because of the animal's great popularity but also to reaffirm the international character of nature conservation and to emphasize the independence of wildlife conservation from political differences. The Convention on International Trade in Endangered Species of Wild Fauna and Flora (CITES), an international treaty established to regulate commerce in wildlife, was first ratified in 1975 in an attempt to block both the import and export of endangered species and to regulate international trade in threatened species.

**TABLE 2.1**

## First list of endangered species, 1967

In accordance with section 1(c) of the Endangered Species Preservation Act of October 15, 1966 (80 Stat. 926; 16 U.S.C. 668aa(c) I [the Secretary of the Interior] find after consulting the states, interested organizations, and individual scientists, that the following listed native fish and wildlife are threatened with extinction.

**Mammals**

- Indiana bat—*Myotis sodalis*
- Delmarva Peninsula fox squirrel—*Sciurus niger cinereus*
- Timber wolf—*Canis lupus lycaon*
- Red wolf—*Canis niger*
- San Joaquin kit fox—*Vulpes macrotis mutica*
- Grizzly bear—*Ursus horribilis*
- Black-footed ferret—*Mustela nigripes*
- Florida panther—*Felis concolor coryi*
- Caribbean monk seal—*Monachus tropicalis*
- Guadalupe fur seal—*Arctocephalus philippi townsendi*
- Florida manatee or Florida sea cow—*Trichechus manatus latirostris*
- Key deer—*Odocoileus virginianus clavium*
- Sonoran pronghorn—*Antilocapra americana sonoriensis*

**Birds**

- Hawaiian dark-rumped petrel—*Pterodroma phaeopygia sandwichensis*
- Hawaiian goose (nene)—*Branta sandvicensis*
- Aleutian Canada goose—*Branta canadensis leucopareia*
- Tule white-fronted goose—*Anser albifrons gambelli*
- Laysan duck—*Anas laysanensis*
- Hawaiian duck (or koloa)—*Anas wyvilliana*
- Mexican duck—*Anas diazi*
- California condor—*Gymnogyps californianus*
- Florida Everglade kite (Florida Snail Kite)—*Rostrhamus sociabilis plumbeus*
- Hawaiian hawk (or ii)—*Buteo solitarius*
- Southern bald eagle—*Haliaeetus t. leucocephalus*
- Attwater's greater prairie chicken—*Tympanuchus cupido attwateri*
- Masked bobwhite—*Colinus virginianus ridgwayi*
- Whooping crane—*Grus americana*
- Yuma clapper rail—*Rallus longirostris yumanensis*
- Hawaiian common gallinule—*Gallinula chloropus sandvicensis*
- Eskimo curlew—*Numenius borealis*
- Puerto Rican parrot—*Amazona vittata*
- American ivory-billed woodpecker—*Campephilus p. principalis*
- Hawaiian crow (or alala)—*Corvus hawaiiensis*
- Small Kauai thrush (puaiohi)—*Phaeornis palmeri*
- Nihoa millerbird—*Acrocephalus kingi*
- Kauai oo (or oo aa)—*Moho braccatus*
- Crested honeycreeper (or akohekohe)—*Palmeria dolei*
- Akiapolaau—*Hemignathus wilsoni*
- Kauai akialoa—*Hemignathus procerus*
- Kauai nukupuu—*Hemignathus lucidus hanapepe*

- Laysan finchbill (Laysan Finch)—*Psittirostra c. cantans*
- Nihoa finchbill (Nihoa Finch)—*Psittirostra cantans ultima*
- Ou—*Psittirostra psittacea*
- Palila—*Psittirostra bailleui*
- Maui parrotbill—*Pseudonestor xanthophyrys*
- Bachman's warbler—*Vermivora bachmanii*
- Kirtland's warbler—*Dendroica kirtlandii*
- Dusky seaside sparrow—*Ammospiza nigrescens*
- Cape Sable sparrow—*Ammospiza mirabilis*

**Reptiles and Amphibians**

- American alligator—*Alligator mississippiensis*
- Blunt-nosed leopard lizard—*Crotaphytus wislizenii silus*
- San Francisco garter snake—*Thamnophis sirtalis tetrataenia*
- Santa Cruz long-toed salamander—*Ambystoma macrodactylum croceum*
- Texas blind salamander—*Typhlomolge rathbuni*
- Black toad, Inyo County toad—*Bufo exsul*

**Fishes**

- Shortnose sturgeon—*Acipenser brevirostrum*
- Longjaw Cisco—*Coregonus alpenae*
- Paiute cutthroat trout—*Salmo clarki seleniris*
- Greenback cutthroat trout—*Salmo clarki stomias*
- Montana Westslope cutthroat trout—*Salmo clarki*
- Gila trout—*Salmo gilae*
- Arizona (*Apache*) trout—*Salmo sp.*
- Desert dace—*Eremichthys acros*
- Humpback chub—*Gila cypha*
- Little Colorado spinedace—*Lepidomeda vittata*
- Moapa dace—*Moapa coriacea*
- Colorado River squawfish—*Ptychocheilus lucius*
- Cui-ui—*Chasmistes cujus*
- Devils Hole pupfish—*Cyprinodon diabolis*
- Commanche Springs pupfish—*Cyprinodon elegans*
- Owens River pupfish—*Cyprinodon radiosus*
- Pahrump killifish—*Empetrichthys latos*
- Big Bend gambusia—*Gambusia gaigei*
- Clear Creek gambusia—*Gambusia heterochir*
- Gila topminnow—*Poeciliopsis occidentalis*
- Maryland darter—*Etheostoma sellare*
- Blue pike—*Stizostedion vitreum glaucum*

SOURCE: Stewart L. Udall, "Native Fish and Wildlife Endangered Species," in *Federal Register*, vol. 32, no. 48, March 11, 1967

---

In the United States, Congress passed the Endangered Species Preservation Act in 1966, and the first species were listed in 1967. (See Table 2.1.) This established a process for listing species as endangered and provided some measure of protection. The Endangered Species Conservation Act of 1969 provided protection to species facing worldwide extinction, prohibiting their import and sale within the United States.

## THE ENDANGERED SPECIES ACT OF 1973—A LANDMARK PROTECTION

Passed by Congress in 1973, the ESA was substantially amended in 1978, 1982, and 1987. The ESA is administered by the U.S. Department of the Interior (DOI) through the U.S. Fish and Wildlife Service (USFWS). The U.S. Department of Commerce, through the National Marine Fisheries Service (NMFS), is responsible for most marine (ocean-based) species and those

that are anadromous (migrate between freshwaters and marine waters). The Biological Resources Division of the U.S. Geological Survey conducts research on species for which the USFWS has management authority.

It should be noted that the original ESA defined the word *species* to include species, subspecies, or "smaller taxa." Taxa is the plural of taxon, which is a grouping on the taxonomic table. In 1978 the ESA was amended to define a smaller taxon for vertebrates (animals with a backbone) as a distinct population segment (DPS). A DPS is a distinct population of vertebrates capable of interbreeding with each other that live in a specific geographical area. A DPS is usually described using geographical terms, such as northern or southern, or by a given latitude or longitude. In 1991 the NMFS developed a policy defining the DPS for Pacific salmon populations. Salmon are anadromous, and most salmon migrate in groups at particular times of the year. Each of these groups is called a stock. The NMFS developed a new term, the evolutionarily significant unit (ESU), to refer to a distinct stock of Pacific salmon.

In summary, the word *species* as used in the ESA can mean a species, a subspecies, a DPS (vertebrates only), or an ESU (Pacific salmon only).

## LISTING UNDER THE ESA

According to the USFWS, in "Listing a Species as Threatened or Endangered" (September 2007, http://www.fws.gov/endangered/factsheets/listing.pdf), the ESA stipulates that there are five criteria that must be evaluated before a decision is made to list a species:

- The present or threatened destruction, modification, or curtailment of the species' habitat or range

- Overutilization for commercial, recreational, scientific, or educational purposes

- Disease or predation

- The inadequacy of existing regulatory mechanisms

- Other natural or manmade factors affecting the species' survival

The primary status codes assigned to listed species are E for endangered and T for threatened. However, there are many other status codes for specific types of listings. (See Table 2.2.) Details of these listing actions are provided in the following sections.

In February 2008 there were 1,046 U.S. species (448 animals and 598 plants) and 528 foreign species (527 animals and 1 plant) listed as endangered, and 305 U.S. species (159 animals and 146 plants) and 46 foreign species (44 animals and 2 plants) listed as threatened under the ESA. (See Table 1.2 in Chapter 1.)

### The Listing Process

The process by which a species becomes listed under the ESA is a legal process with specifically defined steps. Successful listing results in regulations that are legally enforceable within all U.S. jurisdictions. At various stages of the listing process, the USFWS or the NMFS publishes its actions in the *Federal Register* (http://www.gpoaccess.gov/fr/index.html), an official document published daily by the National Archives and Records Administration in Washington, D.C. The *Federal Register* details specific legal actions of the federal government, such as rules, proposed rules, notices from federal agencies, executive orders, and miscellaneous presidential documents.

There are three ways for the listing process to be initiated:

- Submittal of a petition to the USFWS or the NMFS

- Initiative of the USFWS or the NMFS

- Emergency designation by the USFWS or the NMFS

**TABLE 2.2**

**Endangered Species Act status codes**

| | |
|---|---|
| E | Endangered |
| T | Threatened |
| EmE | Emergency listing, endangered |
| EmT | Emergency listing, threatened |
| EXPE, XE | Experimental population, essential |
| EXPN, XN | Experimental population, non-essential |
| SAE, E(S/A) | Similarity of appearance to an endangered taxon |
| SAT, T(S/A) | Similarity of appearance to a threatened taxon |
| PE | Proposed endangered |
| PT | Proposed threatened |
| PEXPE, PXE | Proposed experimental population, essential |
| PEXPN, PXN | Proposed experimental population, non-essential |
| PSAE, PE(S/A) | Proposed similarity of appearance to an endangered taxon |
| PSAT, PT(S/A) | Proposed similarity of appearance to a threatened taxon |
| C | Candidate taxon, ready for proposal |
| D3A | Delisted taxon, evidently extinct |
| D3B | Delisted taxon, invalid name in current scientific opinion |
| D3C | Delisted taxon, recovered |
| DA | Delisted taxon, amendment of the act |
| DM | Delisted taxon, recovered, being monitored first five years |
| DO | Delisted taxon, original commercial data erroneous |
| DP | Delisted taxon, discovered previously unknown additional populations and/or habitat |
| DR | Delisted taxon, taxonomic revision (improved understanding) |
| AD | Proposed delisting |
| AE | Proposed reclassification to endangered |
| AT | Proposed reclassification to threatened |

SOURCE: "Endangered Species Act Status Codes," in *USFWS Threatened and Endangered Species System (TESS)*, U.S. Department of the Interior, U.S. Fish and Wildlife Service, Undated, http://ecos.fws.gov/tess_public/html/db-status.html (accessed February 1, 2008)

Figure 2.1 diagrams the most common listing process under the ESA, one that begins with a petition submittal.

**PETITION SUBMITTAL.** The process for listing a new species as endangered or threatened begins with a formal petition from a person, organization, or government agency. This petition is submitted to the USFWS for terrestrial and freshwater species or to the NMFS for marine and anadromous species. All petitions must be backed by published scientific data supporting the need for listing. Within ninety days, the USFWS or the NMFS determines whether there is "substantial information" to suggest that a species requires listing under the ESA.

**STATUS REVIEW.** A status review is triggered when a petition is found to suggest that listing may be necessary or on the initiative of the USFWS or the NMFS. The purpose of a status review is to determine whether a listing is warranted and what that listing should be.

In *Endangered Species Petition Management Guidance* (July 1996, http://www.fws.gov/southwest/es/arizona/Documents/ESAGuidance/Petn%20Guidance.pdf), the USFWS defines a status review as "the act of reviewing all the available information on a species to determine if it should be provided protection under the ESA. A status review should also use the knowledge of experts; the greater the extent to which Service biologists can

## FIGURE 2.1

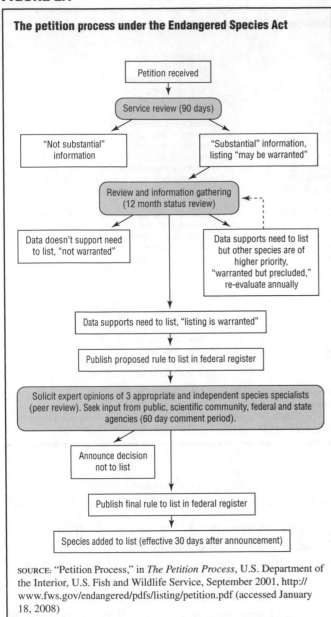

**The petition process under the Endangered Species Act**

Petition received

↓

Service review (90 days)

↓

"Not substantial" information

"Substantial" information, listing "may be warranted"

↓

Review and information gathering (12 month status review)

↓

Data doesn't support need to list, "not warranted"

Data supports need to list but other species are of higher priority, "warranted but precluded," re-evaluate annually

↓

Data supports need to list, "listing is warranted"

↓

Publish proposed rule to list in federal register

↓

Solicit expert opinions of 3 appropriate and independent species specialists (peer review). Seek input from public, scientific community, federal and state agencies (60 day comment period).

↓

Announce decision not to list

↓

Publish final rule to list in federal register

↓

Species added to list (effective 30 days after announcement)

SOURCE: "Petition Process," in *The Petition Process*, U.S. Department of the Interior, U.S. Fish and Wildlife Service, September 2001, http://www.fws.gov/endangered/pdfs/listing/petition.pdf (accessed January 18, 2008)

## TABLE 2.3

**Listing priority numbers for candidate species**

| Threat | | | |
|---|---|---|---|
| Magnitude | Immediacy | Taxonomy | Priority |
| High | Imminent | Monotypic genus | 1 |
| | | Species | 2 |
| | | Subspecies/population | 3 |
| | Non-imminent | Monotypic genus | 4 |
| | | Species | 5 |
| | | Subspecies/population | 6 |
| Moderate to low | Imminent | Monotypic genus | 7 |
| | | Species | 8 |
| | | Subspecies/population | 9 |
| | Non-imminent | Monotypic genus | 10 |
| | | Species | 11 |
| | | Subspecies/population | 12 |

SOURCE: John J. Fay and W.L. Thomas, "Table 1. Priorities for Listing or Reclassification from Threatened to Endangered," in *Federal Register*, vol. 48, no. 184, September 21, 1983, http://www.fws.gov/endangered/pdfs/1983_LPN_Policy_FR_pub.pdf (accessed February 11, 2008)

petitioned action or why there are not enough data to make an appropriate determination.

**LISTING IS WARRANTED BUT PRECLUDED—CANDIDATE SPECIES.** In some cases it may be decided that a species should be proposed for listing, but development of the listing regulation is precluded by other listing activities with higher priorities. In other words, the USFWS or the NMFS acknowledges that a species deserves protection under the ESA, but the USFWS or the NMFS has other priorities that it believes must come first. The species is designated as a "candidate species."

Candidate species are assigned a listing priority number ranging from 1 to 12, with lower numbers (1 to 3) indicating greater priority compared to other candidates. (See Table 2.3.) Priority is determined based on three considerations:

- The magnitude of the threats facing the species
- The immediacy of the threats facing the species
- The taxonomic uniqueness of the species

The NMFS has a different definition for candidate species. It calls them "species of concern" and does not propose them for listing on the basis that available information is inadequate to justify doing so.

Candidate species are reevaluated annually to confirm that listing continues to be appropriate. These reevaluations continue until the species is proposed for listing or until its status improves sufficiently to remove it from consideration for listing. The USFWS or the NMFS works with state wildlife agencies and other groups to help preserve and improve the status of candidate species, hoping that populations may recover enough that species will not require listing.

build an external consensus using the expertise of various parties (e.g., Federal, State, Tribal, University, Heritage programs), the better." Comments and information are also requested from the general public through publication of a notice in the *Federal Register*.

The status review must be completed within twelve months. There are three possible determinations from the status review:

- Listing is not warranted
- Listing is warranted but precluded
- Listing is warranted

**LISTING IS NOT WARRANTED.** A finding that listing is not warranted must be accompanied by information explaining why the data presented do not support the

FIGURE 2.2

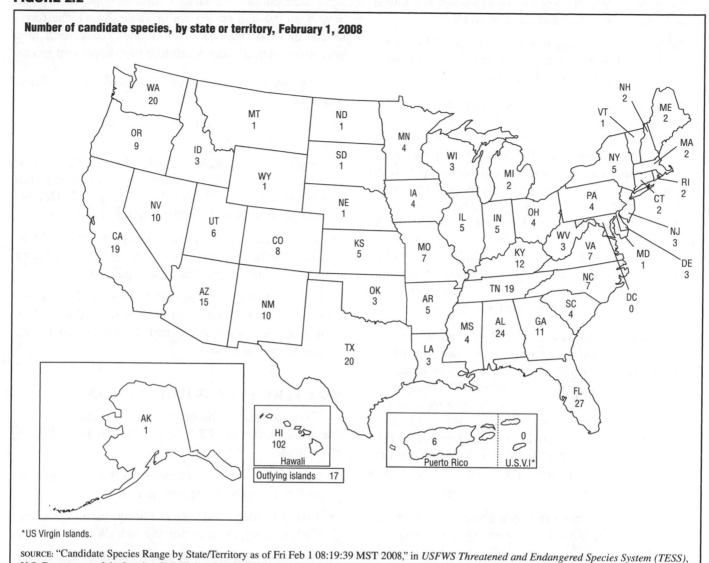

**Number of candidate species, by state or territory, February 1, 2008**

*US Virgin Islands.

SOURCE: "Candidate Species Range by State/Territory as of Fri Feb 1 08:19:39 MST 2008," in *USFWS Threatened and Endangered Species System (TESS)*, U.S. Department of the Interior, U.S. Fish and Wildlife Service, February 1, 2008, http://ecos.fws.gov/tess_public/StateListing.do?state=all&status=candidate (accessed February 1, 2008)

The USFWS (April 17, 2008, http://ecos.fws.gov/tess_public/SpeciesReport.do?listingType=C) states that in February 2008 there were 282 candidate species designated under the ESA, and distributed as shown in Figure 2.2. Note that some species are found in more than one state. Hawaii had the most candidate species of any state (102), followed by Florida (27) and Alabama (24).

**LISTING IS WARRANTED.** A determination that listing is warranted means that a species is officially proposed for listing through the publication of this action in the *Federal Register*. At this point, the USFWS or the NMFS asks at least three independent biological experts to verify that the petitioned species requires listing under either threatened or endangered status. After that, input from the public, from other federal and state agencies, and from the scientific community is welcomed. This period of public comment typically lasts sixty days, but may be extended in some cases. Within forty-five days of pro-

posal issuance, interested parties can request public hearings be held on the issues involved with listing. Such hearings are also held in cases where public interest is high in the listing outcome.

According to the USFWS (http://ecos.fws.gov/tess_public/SpeciesReport.do?listingType=P), in February 2008 there were nine species proposed for listing under the ESA: polar bears, a DPS of gray wolves, an ESU of coho salmon, and six tropical birds.

**FINAL DECISION.** After a listing has been proposed, the USFWS or the NMFS must take one of three possible actions:

- Withdraw the proposal—the biological information is found not to support listing the species.

- Extend the proposal period—there is substantial disagreement within the scientific community regarding the listing. Only one six-month extension is allowed, and then a final decision must be made.

- Publish a final listing rule in the *Federal Register*—the listing becomes effective thirty days after publication, unless otherwise indicated.

Section 4(c)(2)(A) of the ESA requires a review of the condition and situation of a listed species at least every five years to decide whether it still requires government protection. However, USFWS records indicate that these so-called five-year reviews are seldom performed on time. In fact, they are frequently late by several years or even decades. For example, the eastern cougar was listed under the ESA as endangered in 1973, and its recovery plan was issued in 1982. The first five-year review for the species was begun in 2007. The USFWS (2008, http://www.fws.gov/northeast/ECougar) notes that "limited resources and higher priorities" are to blame for this long delay in conducting the five-year review.

**EMERGENCY LISTING.** The ESA authorizes the USFWS or the NMFS to issue temporary emergency listings for species when evidence indicates an immediate and significant risk to the well-being of a species (e.g., following a natural disaster). Two designations are possible: endangered emergency listing (EmE) and threatened emergency listing (EmT). The listing must be published in the *Federal Register* and is effective for only 240 days. During this time the normal status review procedure continues.

Petitioners also have the right under the ESA to ask the USFWS or the NMFS for an emergency listing for a species. In July 2005 a coalition of groups petitioned the USFWS for an EmE listing for the *rufus* subspecies of the red knot, an imperiled shorebird found in New Jersey. The petitioners argued that the species faced imminent threats and required immediate protection under the ESA. The USFWS denied the petition claiming that recent population data showed the bird's condition was improving and steps were already being taken to protect the bird's status. In 2006 the red knot was designated a candidate species under the ESA.

The USFWS (http://ecos.fws.gov/tess_public/pub/adHocSpeciesCountForm.jsp) indicates that as of February 2008 there were no emergency listings in effect for endangered or threatened species listed under the ESA.

**DELISTING.** Delisting occurs when a species is removed from the candidate list, proposed list, or final list of endangered and threatened species. Delisting takes place for a variety of reasons, as indicated by the D codes in Table 2.2. In general, delisting occurs when the USFWS or the NMFS finds that a species has recovered or become extinct, or on various procedural grounds, including discovery of additional habitats or populations.

Listed entities (species or distinct populations) that have been delisted are shown in Table 2.4. Of the forty-seven delisted entities, twenty-one recovered, nine became extinct, and the remainder had procedural issues.

The twelve recovered entities found in the United States are:

- Marine mammal—gray whale (eastern north Pacific Ocean population)
- Terrestrial mammals—grizzly bear (Yellowstone National Park DPS), Columbian white-tailed deer (Douglas County, Oregon DPS), gray wolf (Minnesota population and western Great Lakes DPS)
- Birds—bald eagle, American peregrine falcon, Arctic peregrine falcon, Aleutian Canada goose, and brown pelican (Florida and Alabama populations)
- Plants—Robbins' cinquefoil (native to New Hampshire), Eggert's sunflower (native to Alabama, Tennessee, and Kentucky), and Hoover's woolly-star (native to California).

## RECOVERY ACTIONS UNDER THE ESA

Once a species becomes listed as endangered or threatened under the ESA, it is afforded the following protections:

- Import, export, and interstate or foreign sales are prohibited without a special permit.
- Taking is illegal—taking is killing, harming, harassing, pursuing, or removing the species from the wild.
- Federal agencies must conduct their activities in such a way as to conserve the species.
- Federal agencies that manage lands and/or waters must consult with the USFWS or the NMFS regarding conserving listed species in those habitats. Any activities funded or authorized by these federal agencies or carried out on lands or waters managed by them cannot jeopardize the survival of the listed species.

Civil and criminal penalties can be levied for violations of these provisions. However, exemptions are granted for native peoples of Alaska that rely on certain endangered or threatened animals for food or other products needed for subsistence. In addition, section 4(d) of the ESA allows the USFWS to grant other exemptions from the taking rule for threatened species. For example, the Chiricahua leopard frog in Arizona and New Mexico falls under a 4(d) rule that exempts livestock owners from the take prohibition if the frogs are accidentally killed due to livestock activities. A 4(d) rule is commonly referred to as a "special rule" under the ESA.

**TABLE 2.4**

## Delisted U.S. and foreign species, February 1, 2008

| Date species first listed | Date delisted | Species name | Reason delisted |
|---|---|---|---|
| 05/18/1984 | 06/19/2006 | Agave, Arizona (*Agave arizonica*) | Original data in error-not a listable entity |
| 12/06/1979 | 10/01/2003 | Barberry, Truckee (*Berberis* (=*Mahonia*) *sonnei*) | Original data in error-taxonomic revision |
| 03/29/2007 | 03/29/2007 | Bear, grizzly Yellowstone DPS (*Ursus arctos horribilis*) | Recovered |
| 02/17/1984 | 02/06/1996 | Bidens, cuneate (*Bidens cuneata*) | Original data in error-taxonomic revision |
| 08/27/1984 | 02/23/2004 | Broadbill, Guam (*Myiagra freycineti*) | Extinct |
| 04/28/1976 | 08/31/1984 | Butterfly, Bahama swallowtail (*Heraclides andraemon bonhotei*) | Original data in error-act amendment |
| 11/28/1979 | 06/24/1999 | Cactus, Lloyd's hedgehog (*Echinocereus lloydii*) | Original data in error-taxonomic revision |
| 12/07/1979 | 09/22/1993 | Cactus, spineless hedgehog (*Echinocereus triglochidiatus var. inermis*) | Original data in error-not a listable entity |
| 09/17/1980 | 08/27/2002 | Cinquefoil, Robbins' (*Potentilla robbinsiana*) | Recovered |
| 03/11/1967 | 09/02/1983 | Cisco, longjaw (*Coregonus alpenae*) | Extinct |
| 07/24/2003 | 07/24/2003 | Deer, Columbian white-tailed Douglas County DPS (*Odocoileus virginiainus leucurus*) | Recovered |
| 06/02/1970 | 09/12/1985 | Dove, Palau ground (*Gallicolumba canifrons*) | Recovered |
| 03/11/1967 | 07/25/1978 | Duck, Mexican U.S.A. only (*Anas diazi*) | Original data in error - taxonomic revision |
| 03/11/1967 | 07/09/2007 | Eagle, bald lower 48 states (*Haliaeetus leucocephalus*) | Recovered |
| 06/02/1970 | 08/25/1999 | Falcon, American peregrine (*Falco peregrinus anatum*) | Recovered |
| 06/02/1970 | 10/05/1994 | Falcon, Arctic peregrine (*Falco peregrinus tundrius*) | Recovered |
| 06/02/1970 | 09/12/1985 | Flycatcher, Palau fantail (*Rhipidura lepida*) | Recovered |
| 04/30/1980 | 12/04/1987 | Gambusia, Amistad (*Gambusia amistadensis*) | Extinct |
| 04/29/1986 | 06/18/1993 | Globeberry, Tumamoc (*Tumamoca macdougalii*) | Original data in error-new information discovered |
| 03/11/1967 | 03/20/2001 | Goose, Aleutian Canada (*Branta canadensis leucopareia*) | Recovered |
| 10/11/1979 | 11/27/1989 | Hedgehog cactus, purple-spined (*Echinocereus engelmannii var. purpureus*) | Original data in error-taxonomic revision |
| 12/30/1974 | 03/09/1995 | Kangaroo, eastern gray (*Macropus giganteus*) | Recovered |
| 12/30/1974 | 03/09/1995 | Kangaroo, red (*Macropus rufus*) | Recovered |
| 12/30/1974 | 03/09/1995 | Kangaroo, western gray (*Macropus fuliginosus*) | Recovered |
| 12/08/1977 | 02/23/2004 | Mallard, Mariana (*Anas oustaleti*) | Extinct |
| 05/27/1978 | 09/14/1989 | Milk-vetch, Rydberg (*Astragalus perianus*) | Original data in error-new information discovered |
| 06/02/1970 | 09/21/2004 | Monarch, Tinian (old world flycatcher) (*Monarcha takatsukasae*) | Recovered |
| 06/02/1970 | 09/12/1985 | Owl, Palau (*Pyrroglaux podargina*) | Recovered |
| 06/14/1976 | 01/09/1984 | Pearlymussel, Sampson's (*Epioblasma sampsoni*) | Extinct |
| 06/02/1970 | 02/04/1985 | Pelican, brown U.S. Atlantic coast, FL, AL (*Pelecanus occidentalis*) | Recovered |
| 07/13/1982 | 09/22/1993 | Pennyroyal, Mckittrick (*Hedeoma apiculatum*) | Original data in error-new information discovered |
| 03/11/1967 | 09/02/1983 | Pike, blue (*Stizostedion vitreum glaucum*) | Extinct |
| 10/13/1970 | 01/15/1982 | Pupfish, Tecopa (*Cyprinodon nevadensis calidae*) | Extinct |
| 03/10/1997 | 04/14/2006 | Pygmy-owl, cactus ferruginous AZ pop. (*Glaucidium brasilianum cactonm*) | Original data in error-not a listable entity |
| 09/26/1986 | 02/28/2000 | Shrew, Dismal Swamp southeastern (*Sorex longirostris fisheri*) | Original data in error-new information discovered |
| 06/04/1973 | 10/12/1983 | Sparrow, Santa Barbara song (*Melospiza melodia graminea*) | Extinct |
| 03/11/1967 | 12/12/1990 | Sparrow, dusky seaside (*Ammodramus maritimus nigrescens*) | Extinct |
| 12/14/1992 | 08/06/2007 | Springsnail, Idaho (*Pyrgulopsis idahoensis*) | Original data in error-taxonomic revision |
| 05/22/1997 | 08/18/2005 | Sunflower, Eggert's (*Helianthus eggertii*) | Recovered |
| 12/18/1977 | 11/22/1983 | Treefrog, pine barrens FL pop. (*Hyla andersonii*) | Original data in error-new information discovered |
| 09/13/1996 | 04/26/2000 | Trout, coastal cutthroat Umpqua R. (*Oncorhynchus clarki clarki*) | Original data in error-taxonomic revision |
| 06/14/1976 | 02/29/1984 | Turtle, Indian flap-shelled (*Lissemys punctata punctatia*) | Original data in error-erroneous data |
| 06/16/1994 | 06/16/1994 | Whale, gray except where listed (*Eschrichtius robustus*) | Recovered |
| 03/28/2008 | 02/27/2008 | Wolf, gray Northern Rocky Mountain Gray Wolf Distinct Population Segment (*Canis lupus*) | Recovered |
| 04/10/1978 | 02/08/2007 | Wolf, gray MN (*Canis lupus*) | Recovered |
| 03/27/2006 | 02/08/2007 | Wolf, gray Western Great Lakes DPS (*Canis lupus*) | Recovered |
| 07/19/1990 | 10/07/2003 | Woolly-star, Hoover's (*Eriastrum hooveri*) | Recovered |

SOURCE: "Delisted Species," in *USFWS Threatened and Endangered Species System (TESS)*, U.S. Department of the Interior, U.S. Fish and Wildlife Service, February 1, 2008, http://ecos.fws.gov/tess_public/DelistingReport.do (accessed February 1, 2008)

Endangered species have different needs and require different conservation measures. Some fish are endangered because of a history of overfishing. Halting or reducing fishing is sufficient for population recovery. In most cases, however, more active forms of intervention are necessary. The single most important conservation measure for many threatened and endangered species is habitat conservation or restoration. For some species, captive breeding followed by reintroduction into the wild may help increase numbers. In all cases, knowledge of the natural history of endangered species is essential to acquiring a better understanding of species' needs, as well as to the development of measures that will aid in conservation.

## Critical Habitat

Under the ESA, the USFWS or the NMFS must decide whether critical habitat should be designated for a listed species. Critical habitat is specific geographical areas of land, water, and/or air space that contain features essential for the conservation of a listed species and that may require special management and protection. For example, these could be areas used for breeding, resting, and feeding. If the agency decides that critical habitat should be designated, a proposal notice is published in the *Federal Register* for public comment. If it is decided that critical habitat is needed, then the final boundaries are published in the *Federal Register*.

TABLE 2.5

**Number of U.S. endangered and threatened species with critical habitat specified, February 1, 2008**

| | |
|---|---:|
| Mammals | 25 |
| Birds | 23 |
| Reptiles | 16 |
| Amphibians | 9 |
| Fish | 61 |
| Clams | 25 |
| Snails | 3 |
| Insects | 16 |
| Arachnids | 6 |
| Crustaceans | 9 |
| Flowering plants | 303 |
| Ferns and allies | 12 |
| **Total** | **508** |

SOURCE: Adapted from "Listed Species with Critical Habitat," in *USFWS Threatened and Endangered Species System (TESS)*, U.S. Department of the Interior, U.S. Fish and Wildlife Service, February 1, 2008, http://ecos.fws.gov/tess_public/CriticalHabitat.do?listings=0&nmfs=1 (accessed February 1, 2008)

The role of critical habitat is often misunderstood by the public. Critical habitat designation does not set up a refuge or sanctuary for a species in which no development can take place. It can provide additional protection for a specific geographical area that might not occur without the designation. For example, if the USFWS determines that an area not currently occupied by a species is needed for species recovery and designates that area as critical habitat, any federal actions involving that area have to avoid adverse modifications. Critical habitat designation has no regulatory impact on private landowners unless they wish to take actions on their land that involve federal funding or permits.

The original ESA did not provide a time limit for the setting of critical habitat. In 1978 the law was amended to require that critical habitat be designated at the same time a species is listed. However, the designation is only required "when prudent." For example, the USFWS or the NMFS can refuse to designate critical habitat for a species if doing so would publicize the specific locations of organisms known to be targets for illegal hunting or collection. Historically, both agencies have broadly used the "when prudent" clause to justify not setting critical habitat for many listed species. This has been a contentious issue between the government and conservation groups.

As of February 2008, critical habitat had been designated for 508 species. (See Table 2.5.) This represents approximately 38% of all U.S. species listed under the ESA. (See Table 1.2 in Chapter 1.) Plants make up more than half of the listed species for which critical habitat has been designated.

**Experimental Populations**

For some species, primarily mammals, birds, fish, and aquatic invertebrates, recovery efforts include the introduction of individuals into new areas. Typically, this is accomplished by moving a small group of imperiled animals from an established area to one or more other locations within their historical range of distribution.

Experimental populations of a species are not subject to the same rigorous protections under the ESA as other members of the species. Experimental populations can be considered threatened, even if the rest of the species is listed as endangered. In addition, the USFWS can designate an experimental population as essential or nonessential. A nonessential designation indicates that the survival of this population is not believed essential to the survival of the species as a whole. A nonessential experimental population is treated under the law as if it is proposed for listing, not already listed. This results in less protection under the ESA.

As of February 2008, there were fifty-seven experimental populations listed under the ESA for forty separate species. (See Table 2.6.) Clams and snails make up more than half the animals represented. Notable experimental populations for mammals include the grizzly bear and the gray wolf. Both have been reintroduced into portions of western states.

**Recovery Plans**

The ESA requires that a recovery plan be developed and implemented for every listed species unless "such a plan will not promote the conservation of the species." The USFWS and the NMFS are directed to give priority to those species that are most likely to benefit from having a plan in place. The recovery potential of species is ranked from 1 to 18 by the USFWS. (See Table 2.7.) Low rankings indicate a greater likelihood that the species can be recovered. Priority is based on the degree of threat, the potential for recovery, and taxonomy (genetic distinctiveness). In addition, rankings can be appended with the letter "c" when species recovery is in conflict with economic activities. Species with a "c" designation have higher priority than other species within the same numerical ranking. The NMFS uses a different rating system that ranges from 1 (highest recovery potential) to 12 (lowest recovery potential). (See Table 2.8.)

Each recovery plan must include the following three elements:

- Site-specific management actions to achieve the plan's goals

- Objective and measurable criteria for determining when a species is recovered

- Estimates of the amount of time and money that will be required to achieve recovery

Recovery plans include precisely defined milestones for recovery achievement. For example, recovery may be

## TABLE 2.6

**Experimental populations, February 2008**

| Inverted common name | Scientific name | Species group | Where listed |
|---|---|---|---|
| Bean, Cumberland (pearlymussel) | *Villosa trabalis* | Clams | AL-The free-flowing reach of the Tennessee River from the base of Wilson Dam downstream to the backwaters of Pickwick Reservoir [about 12 RM (19 km)] and the lower 5 RM [8 km] of all tributaries to this reach in Colbert and Lauderdale Counties |
| Bean, Cumberland (pearlymussel) | *Villosa trabalis* | Clams | TN-Specified portions of the French Broad and Holston Rivers |
| Bear, grizzly | *Ursus arctos horribilis* | Mammals | Experimental non-essential (portions of ID and MT) |
| Blossom, tubercled (pearlymussel) | *Epioblasma torulosa torulosa* | Clams | See locations for Bean, Cumberland (pearlymussel) |
| Blossom, turgid (pearlymussel) | *Epioblasma turgidula* | Clams | See locations for Bean, Cumberland (pearlymussel) |
| Blossom, yellow (pearlymussel) | *Epioblasma florentina florentina* | Clams | See locations for Bean, Cumberland (pearlymussel) |
| Catspaw (=purple cat's paw pearlymussel) | *Epioblasma obliquata obliquata* | Clams | See locations for Bean, Cumberland (pearlymussel) |
| Chub, slender | *Erimystax cahni* | Fishes | TN-Specified portions of the French Broad and Holston Rivers |
| Chub, spotfin | *Erimonax monachus* | Fishes | Tellico River, between the backwaters of the Tellico Reservoir and the Tellico Ranger Station, in Monroe County, Tennessee |
| Chub, spotfin | *Erimonax monachus* | Fishes | Shoal Creek |
| Chub, spotfin | *Erimonax monachus* | Fishes | TN-Specified portions of the French Broad and Holston Rivers |
| Clubshell | *Pleurobema clava* | Clams | See locations for Bean, Cumberland (pearlymussel) |
| Combshell, Cumberlandian | *Epioblasma brevidens* | Clams | See locations for Bean, Cumberland (pearlymussel) |
| Combshell, Cumberlandian | *Epioblasma brevidens* | Clams | TN-Specified portions of the French Broad and Holston Rivers |
| Condor, California | *Gymnogyps californianus* | Birds | Specific portions of Arizona, Nevada, and Utah |
| Crane, whooping | *Grus americana* | Birds | CO, ID, FL, NM, UT, and the western half of Wyoming |
| Crane, whooping | *Grus americana* | Birds | AL, AR, GA, IL, IN, IA, KY, LA, MI, MN, MS, MO, NC, OH, SC, TN, VA, WI, WV |
| Darter, boulder | *Etheostoma wapiti* | Fishes | Shoal Creek |
| Darter, duskytail | *Etheostoma percnurum* | Fishes | Tellico River, between the backwaters of the Tellico Reservoir and the Tellico Ranger Station, in Monroe County, Tennessee |
| Darter, duskytail | *Etheostoma percnurum* | Fishes | TN-Specified portions of the French Broad and Holston Rivers |
| Fanshell | *Cyprogenia stegaria* | Clams | TN-Specified portions of the French Broad and Holston Rivers |
| Ferret, black-footed | *Mustela nigripes* | Mammals | Specific portions of AZ, CO, MT, SD, UT, and WY |
| Lampmussel, Alabama | *Lampsilis virescens* | Clams | See locations for Bean, Cumberland (pearlymussel) |
| Madtom, pygmy | *Noturus stanauli* | Fishes | TN-Specified portions of the French Broad and Holston Rivers |
| Madtom, smoky | *Noturus baileyi* | Fishes | Tellico River, between the backwaters of the Tellico Reservoir and the Tellico Ranger Station, in Monroe County, Tennessee |
| Madtom, yellowfin | *Noturus flavipinnis* | Fishes | North Fork Holston River, VA, TN; S. Fork Holston River, upstream to Ft. Patrick Henry Dam, TN; Holston River, downstream to John Sevier Detention Lake Dam, TN; and all tributaries thereto |
| Madtom, yellowfin | *Noturus flavipinnis* | Fishes | Tellico River between the backwaters of the Tellico Reservoir and the Tellico Ranger Station, in Monroe County, Tennessee |
| Madtom, yellowfin | *Noturus flavipinnis* | Fishes | TN-Specified portions of the French Broad and Holston Rivers |
| Mapleleaf, winged | *Quadrula fragosa* | Clams | See locations for Bean, Cumberland (pearlymussel) |
| Monkeyface, Appalachian (pearlymussel) | *Quadrula sparsa* | Clams | TN-Specified portions of the French Broad and Holston Rivers |
| Monkeyface, Cumberland (pearlymussel) | *Quadrula intermedia* | Clams | See locations for Bean, Cumberland (pearlymussel) |
| Monkeyface, Cumberland (pearlymussel) | *Quadrula intermedia* | Clams | TN-Specified portions of the French Broad and Holston Rivers |
| Mussel, oyster | *Epioblasma capsaeformis* | Clams | See locations for Bean, Cumberland (pearlymussel) |
| Otter, Southern Sea | *Enhydra lutris nereis* | Mammals | All areas subject to U.S. jurisdiction south of Pt. Conception, CA |
| Pearlymussel, birdwing | *Conradilla caelata* | Clams | See locations for Bean, Cumberland (pearlymussel) |
| Pearlymussel, birdwing | *Conradilla caelata* | Clams | TN-Specified portions of the French Broad and Holston Rivers |
| Pearlymussel, cracking | *Hemistena lata* | Clams | See locations for Bean, Cumberland (pearlymussel) |
| Pearlymussel, cracking | *Hemistena lata* | Clams | TN-Specified portions of the French Broad and Holston Rivers |
| Pearlymussel, dromedary | *Dromus dromas* | Clams | See locations for Bean, Cumberland (pearlymussel) |
| Pearlymussel, dromedary | *Dromus dromas* | Clams | TN-Specified portions of the French Broad and Holston Rivers |

**TABLE 2.6**

**Experimental populations, February 2008** [CONTINUED]

| Inverted common name | Scientific name | Species group | Where listed |
|---|---|---|---|
| Pigtoe, finerayed | *Fusconaia cuneolus* | Clams | See locations for Bean, Cumberland (pearlymussel) |
| Pigtoe, finerayed | *Fusconaia cuneolus* | Clams | TN-Specified portions of the French Broad and Holston Rivers |
| Pigtoe, rough | *Pleurobema plenum* | Clams | TN-Specified portions of the French Broad and Holston Rivers |
| Pigtoe, shiny | *Fusconaia cor* | Clams | See locations for Bean, Cumberland (pearlymussel) |
| Pigtoe, shiny | *Fusconaia cor* | Clams | TN-Specified portions of the French Broad and Holston Rivers |
| Pikeminnow (=squawfish), Colorado | *Ptychocheilus lucius* | Fishes | Salt and Verde River drainages, AZ |
| Pimpleback, orangefoot (pearlymussel) | *Plethobasus cooperianus* | Clams | TN-Specified portions of the French Broad and Holston Rivers |
| Rail, Guam | *Rallus owstoni* | Birds | Rota |
| Ring pink (mussel) | *Obovaria retusa* | Clams | TN-Specified portions of the French Broad and Holston Rivers |
| Riversnail, Anthony's | *Athearnia anthonyi* | Snails | See locations for Bean, Cumberland (pearlymussel) |
| Riversnail, Anthony's | *Athearnia anthonyi* | Snails | TN-Specified portions of the French Broad and Holston Rivers |
| Squirrel, Delmarva Peninsula fox | *Sciurus niger cinereus* | Mammals | DE-Assawoman Wildlife Area in Sussex Co. |
| Wartyback, white (pearlymussel) | *Plethobasus cicatricosus* | Clams | TN-Specified portions of the French Broad and Holston Rivers |
| Wolf, gray | *Canis lupus* | Mammals | WY and portions of ID and MT |
| Wolf, gray | *Canis lupus* | Mammals | Portions of AZ, NM, and TX |
| Wolf, red | *Canis rufus* | Mammals | Portions of NC and TN |
| Woundfin | *Plagopterus argentissimus* | Fishes | Gila River drainage, AZ, NM |

SOURCE: Adapted from "Experimental Populations," in *USFWS Threatened and Endangered Species System (TESS)*, U.S. Department of the Interior, U.S. Fish and Wildlife Service, February 7, 2008, http://ecos.fws.gov/tess_public/SpeciesReport.do?dsource=experimental (accessed February 7, 2008)

considered accomplished when a certain number of individuals is reached and specifically named threats are eliminated.

Notices regarding proposed new or revised recovery plans must be placed in the *Federal Register* so that public comment can be obtained and considered before a plan is finalized.

### Incidental Take Permits and Habitat Conservation Plans

When the original ESA was passed, it included exceptions that allowed taking of listed species only for scientific research or other conservation activities authorized by the act. In 1982 Congress added a provision in section 10 of the ESA that allows "incidental take" of listed species of wildlife by nonfederal entities. Incidental take is defined as take that is incidental to, but not the purpose of, an otherwise lawful activity. Incidental taking cannot appreciably reduce the likelihood of the survival and recovery of listed species in the wild. The incidental take provision was added to allow private landowners some freedom to develop their land even if it provides habitat to listed species.

To obtain an incidental take permit, an applicant has to prepare a Habitat Conservation Plan (HCP). An HCP describes the impacts likely to result from the taking of the species and the measures the applicant will take to minimize and mitigate the impacts. HCPs are generally partnerships drawn up by people at the local level who are working with officials from the USFWS or the NMFS. The plans frequently represent compromises between developers and environmentalists.

Included in the agreement is a "no surprise" provision that assures landowners and developers that the overall cost of species protection measures will be limited to what has been agreed to under the HCP. In return, landowners make a long-term commitment to conservation as negotiated in the HCP. Many HCPs include the preservation of significant areas of habitat for endangered species.

Even though the HCP program was implemented in 1982, it was hardly ever used before 1992, with only fourteen permits issued in that time period. The USFWS (April 17, 2008, http://ecos.fws.gov/conserv_plans/servlet/gov.doi.hcp.servlets.PlanReport) states that in April 2008 there were 544 HCPs in place covering dozens of species. Information about HCPs is provided by the Conservation Plans and Agreements Database (http://ecos.fws.gov/conserv_plans/public.jsp). The database includes the locations covered by the plans as well as information on the applicants and the listed and unlisted species involved.

### Enhancement of Survival Permits

Another type of permit issued under the ESA is the enhancement of survival permit. This permit authorizes future incidental take by nonfederal landowners in exchange for management of listed species on their property. Permit applicants must agree to participate in a Candidate Conservation Agreement with Assurances or a Safe Harbor Agreement. These agreements provide assurances to landowners that no additional future regulatory restrictions will be imposed.

TABLE 2.7

**U.S. Fish and Wildlife Service recovery potential priority ranking system**

| Degree of threat | Recovery potential | Taxonomy | Priority | Conflict |
|---|---|---|---|---|
| High | High | Monotypic genus | 1 | 1C |
| | | | | 1 |
| | High | Species | 2 | 2C |
| | | | | 2 |
| | High | Subspecies | 3 | 3C |
| | | | | 3 |
| | Low | Monotypic genus | 4 | 4C |
| | | | | 4 |
| | Low | Species | 5 | 5C |
| | | | | 5 |
| | Low | Subspecies | 6 | 6C |
| | | | | 6 |
| Moderate | High | Monotypic genus | 7 | 7C |
| | | | | 7 |
| | High | Species | 8 | 8C |
| | | | | 8 |
| | High | Subspecies | 9 | 9C |
| | | | | 9 |
| | Low | Monotypic genus | 10 | 10C |
| | | | | 10 |
| | Low | Species | 11 | 11C |
| | | | | 11 |
| | Low | Subspecies | 12 | 12C |
| | | | | 12 |
| Low | High | Monotypic genus | 13 | 13C |
| | | | | 13 |
| | High | Species | 14 | 14C |
| | | | | 14 |
| | High | Subspecies | 15 | 15C |
| | | | | 15 |
| | Low | Monotypic genus | 16 | 16C |
| | | | | 16 |
| | Low | Species | 17 | 17C |
| | | | | 17 |
| | Low | Subspecies | 18 | 18C |
| | | | | 18 |

SOURCE: John J. Fay and W.L. Thomas, "Table 3. Recovery Priority," in *Federal Register*, vol. 48, no. 184, September 21, 1983, and *Federal Register*, vol. 48, no. 221, November 15, 1983 (correction), http://www.fws.gov/Endangered/pdfs/FR/48fr43098-43105.pdf (accessed February 23, 2008)

TABLE 2.8

**U.S. Fish and Wildlife Service recovery potential priority ranking system**

| Magnitude of threat | Recovery potential | Conflict | Priority |
|---|---|---|---|
| High | High | Conflict | 1 |
| | | No conflict | 2 |
| | Low to moderate | Conflict | 3 |
| | | No conflict | 4 |
| Moderate | High | Conflict | 5 |
| | | No conflict | 6 |
| | Low to moderate | Conflict | 7 |
| | | No conflict | 8 |
| Low | High | Conflict | 9 |
| | | No conflict | 10 |
| | Low to moderate | Conflict | 11 |
| | | No Conflict | 12 |

SOURCE: "Table 3. Species Recovery Priority," in *Federal Register*, vol. 55, no. 116, June 15, 1990, http://www.nmfs.noaa.gov/pr/pdfs/fr/fr55-24296.pdf (accessed February 29, 2008)

rior, described the ESA as "a powerful law designed for confrontation." Many confrontations over the law have taken place in the courts. The ESA includes provisions for civil lawsuits against government agencies alleged to be in violation of the ESA. Citizens can also sue if they believe the USFWS has failed to perform actions required under the ESA or to compel the USFWS to apply ESA prohibitions regarding taking. Only two lawsuits were filed against the agency regarding the ESA between 1974 and 1991. Over the next decade more than three dozen suits were filed.

In *Endangered Species Act: Successes and Challengesin Agency Collaboration and the Use of Scientific Information in the Decision Making Process* (May 19, 2005, http://www.gao.gov/new.items/d05732t.pdf), the U.S. Government Accountability Office notes that the USFWS has become "overburdened by litigation." Many of the lawsuits have been filed by conservationist and animal groups regarding the listing process and designation of critical habitat. In 1992 a coalition of groups sued the DOI charging that the listing process was proceeding too slowly. At that time more than five hundred species were awaiting listing. The suit was settled out of court later that year when the USFWS agreed to specific time limits for listings of the species at issue.

Designation of critical habitat has also been a contentious issue. In 1997 the Natural Resources Defense Council sued the DOI over the long-standing policy of the USFWS to avoid designating critical habitat under the "when prudent" clause. At that time the agency had set critical habitat for only approximately 10% of all listed species. The USFWS lost the lawsuit, as well as many subsequent suits in the same vein. In 2000 the agency put a one-year hold on all work related to listing new species so that court-ordered critical habitat work could be tackled.

In 2006 the Mokelumne River Programmatic Safe Harbor Agreement was created for landowners along California's Mokelumne River, which provides habitat for several listed species, particularly the endangered valley elderberry longhorn beetle. It was the state's first regional agreement available to multiple landowners. Participants agree to restore, enhance, and manage native riparian (riverbank) vegetation on their property for the benefit of the beetle. In exchange, the landowners are granted exemption from penalty if they accidentally kill the beetles during their restoration/enhancement activities or during normal farming and ranching activities.

## ESA LITIGATION

In a 2004 speech to the American Farm Bureau Federation, Gale Norton (January 11, 2004, http://www.doi.gov/news/040111hawaii), the secretary of the inte-

In 2004 the USFWS lost a case that focused on the agency's decision to ignore petitions submitted for species that are candidate species. The lawsuit specifically dealt with the Gunnison sage grouse, a large ground-dwelling bird found only in parts of Colorado and Utah. In January 2000 a coalition of conservationist groups submitted a petition to the USFWS on behalf of the species. The USFWS responded that no action was needed on its part, because it planned to designate the species as a candidate species. This decision was in keeping with the agency's *Endangered Species Petition Management Guidance*. In September 2000 the petitioning groups sued the agency claiming that the guidance violated the intent of the ESA. In 2004 the U.S. District Court for the District of Columbia ruled against the USFWS and ordered the agency to respond to petitions that had been submitted for more than two hundred candidate species.

Since the 1990s the USFWS has repeatedly complained that many of its decisions and activities are driven by court orders, rather than by scientific priorities. Conservation and animal groups have taken advantage of ESA provisions that allow citizen involvement in petition submittals and lawsuits. Critics claim that the groups flood the USFWS with petitions so that lawsuits can be brought when the agency is unable to respond in a timely manner. Environmentalists counter that the lawsuits are necessary, because the USFWS fails to do the job assigned to the agency under the ESA to protect imperiled species.

## ESA SPENDING

Various federal agencies spend money in support of the ESA. The primary spending agencies are the USFWS and the NMFS. For accounting purposes, the federal government operates on a fiscal year (FY) that begins in October and runs through the end of September. Thus, FY 2009 covers the time period of October 1, 2008, through September 30, 2009. Each year by the first Monday in February the president of the United States must present a proposed budget to the U.S. House of Representatives. This is the amount of money that the president estimates will be required to operate the federal government during the next fiscal year.

### USFWS Budget

In February 2008 the president proposed a $1.3 billion budget for the USFWS for FY 2009. (See Figure 2.3.) This was a reduction from nearly $1.4 billion requested the previous year. An additional $947 million was available in FY 2009 under permanent appropriations. (This is money allocated to the agency on a continuing basis, not requested each year.) According to the USFWS, most of the permanent appropriations for FY

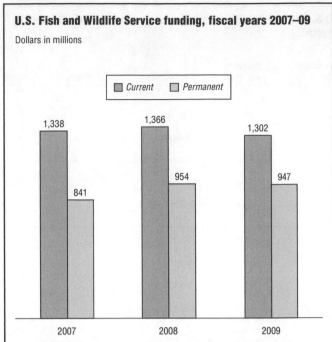

**FIGURE 2.3**

**U.S. Fish and Wildlife Service funding, fiscal years 2007–09**

Dollars in millions

SOURCE: "FWS Funding," in *The Department of the Interior Fiscal Year 2009 Interior Budget in Brief*, U.S. Department of the Interior, February 2008, http://www.doi.gov/budget/2009/09Hilites/BH055.pdf (accessed February 7, 2008)

2009 will be turned over to the states for restoration and conservation of fish and wildlife resources.

In *The Department of the Interior Fiscal Year 2009 Interior Budget in Brief* (February 2008, http://www.doi.gov/budget/2009/09Hilites/BH055.pdf), the DOI notes that $146.8 million was requested for endangered species programs. Most of the money is allocated to recovery programs (47%), followed by consultations with other agencies and groups (35%), listing activities (12%), and candidate species conservation (6%). (See Figure 2.4.)

### NMFS Budget

The NMFS handles ESA management of marine mammals, such as whales and seals, and anadromous fish. According to the National Oceanic and Atmospheric Administration, in *Budget Estimates, Fiscal Year 2009: Congressional Submission* (2008, http://www.corporateservices.noaa.gov/~nbo/FY09_Rollout_Materials/NOAA_FY09_Final_CJ.pdf), the FY 2009 budget request for the NMFS was $782 million. This was down from $829 million allocated the previous fiscal year. Even though the agency does not specifically break down ESA activities within its budget summary, the agency reports that it requested $167.2 million for its Protected Species Research and Management program in FY 2009, including the following major components:

## FIGURE 2.4

**Budget breakdown for endangered species activities by the U.S. Fish and Wildlife Service, fiscal year 2009**

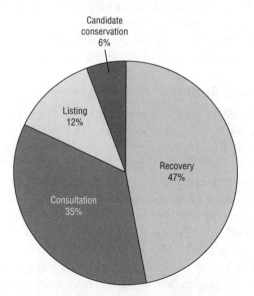

Candidate conservation 6%

Listing 12%

Consultation 35%

Recovery 47%

SOURCE: Adapted from "Highlights of Budget Changes, by Appropriation Activity/Subactivity," in *The Department of the Interior Fiscal Year 2009 Interior Budget in Brief*, U.S. Department of the Interior, February 2008, http://www.doi.gov/budget/2009/09Hilites/BH055.pdf (accessed February 7, 2008)

## TABLE 2.9

**Twenty-seven species accounting for 75% of spending under the Endangered Species Act, fiscal year 2006**

| Ranking | Species | Expenditure |
|---|---|---|
| 1 | Chinook salmon | $188,999,257 |
| 2 | Steelhead | $130,606,467 |
| 3 | Pallid sturgeon | $38,892,982 |
| 4 | Coho salmon | $35,141,511 |
| 5 | Steller sea-lion | $30,504,422 |
| 6 | Bull trout (lower 48 states) | $23,863,886 |
| 7 | Sockeye salmon | $22,485,620 |
| 8 | Southwestern willow flycatcher | $14,668,834 |
| 9 | Red-cockaded woodpecker | $13,875,377 |
| 10 | Gopher tortoise | $13,348,459 |
| 11 | Bald eagle | $12,309,254 |
| 12 | Chum salmon | $11,713,091 |
| 13 | Desert tortoise | $10,890,015 |
| 14 | Razorback sucker | $10,540,595 |
| 15 | West Indian manatee | $9,737,769 |
| 16 | Rio Grande silvery minnow | $9,701,954 |
| 17 | Colorado pikeminnow (=squawfish) | $9,670,160 |
| 18 | Right whale | $9,349,875 |
| 19 | White sturgeon (ID and MT) | $9,113,933 |
| 20 | Gray wolf | $8,309,256 |
| 21 | Piping plover | $8,295,377 |
| 22 | Grizzly bear | $7,457,850 |
| 23 | Humpback chub | $7,410,806 |
| 24 | Leatherback sea turtle | $6,824,249 |
| 25 | Whooping crane | $6,796,708 |
| 26 | Loggerhead sea turtle | $6,791,863 |
| 27 | Least tern | $6,577,825 |

SOURCE: Adapted from "Table 2. Species Ranked in Descending Order of Total FY 2006 Reported Expenditures, Not Including Land Acquisition Costs," in *Federal and State Endangered and Threatened Species Expenditures: Fiscal Year 2006*, U.S. Department of the Interior, U.S. Fish and Wildlife Service, draft, 2008

- Pacific salmon ESA recovery and research ($62.9 million)

- Marine mammal conservation and recovery ($41.3 million)

- Recovery and habitat needs of Atlantic salmon ($10 million)

## ESA Expenditures

The ESA requires the USFWS (http://www.fws.gov/endangered/expenditures/expenditurereports.html) to file an annual report detailing certain expenditures made for the conservation of threatened and endangered species under the act. As of April 2008, reports for FYs 2005 and 2006 were undergoing review and comment. However, the USFWS released data tables from the reports with the understanding that, even though the data are not expected to change, they are considered draft data until the reports are finalized later in the year. In *Federal and State Endangered and Threatened Species Expenditures: Fiscal Year 2006* (draft, 2008), the USFWS indicates that nearly $885 million was spent by federal agencies that year to protect 1,111 specific entities (species, subspecies, DPS, or ESUs) under the ESA.

**ESA EXPENDITURES BY SPECIES.** Table 2.9 shows the twenty-seven species with the highest reported expenditures under the ESA in FY 2006. Together, these species accounted for nearly $664 million in spending, 75% of the total spent that year. The list is dominated by fish species. Nearly $189 million was spent on the Chinook salmon, followed by $130 million for the steelhead. Both species are anadromous and found in the waters of the Pacific Northwest. Coho salmon, sockeye salmon, and chum salmon are also anadromous, whereas the other fish on the list are freshwater species. There are three marine (ocean-based) mammals on the list: the Steller sea lion, the West Indian manatee, and the right whale. Other species among the top twenty-seven include birds, reptiles, and one terrestrial mammal: the gray wolf.

How best to use the funds allocated to endangered species has been a contentious issue for years. Three-fourths of the money allocated to individual species in FY 2006 was spent on only twenty-seven species. They represent approximately 2.5% of all listed species for that year.

The number of species being added to the federal threatened and endangered species list is likely to continue to grow. Even though vertebrate species dominated the list during the first years of the act, plants and invertebrate animals now make up a much greater proportion of listed species. (See Table 1.2 in Chapter 1.) These species are politically more difficult to defend than either mammals or birds, which are more inherently appealing to most Americans because of the "warm and fuzzy" factor. These circumstances raise questions about the continued feasibility of a species-by-species preservation strategy, and the USFWS struggles under intense legal and political pressures to decide which species to protect first.

## THE ECOSYSTEM APPROACH

During the 1990s there was a growing concern that traditional methods of species protection, which take a species-by-species approach, were ineffective. Many alternatives were proposed. One of the most popular was a method variously called the habitat, ecosystem, or community approach. In "What Is an Ecosystem?" (April 15, 2008, http://www.fws.gov/midwest/EcosystemConservation/ecosystem.html), the USFWS defines an ecosystem as a "a geographic area and all its living components (e.g., people, plants, animals, and microorganisms), their physical surroundings (e.g., soil, water, and air), and the natural cycles that sustain them." Central to the new approach is a focus on conservation of large intact areas of habitat. It is hoped that by focusing on entire habitats, rather than on individual species recovery, many species will be protected before they reach critically low population sizes.

Ecosystem conservation considers entire communities of species as well as their interactions with the physical environment and aims to develop integrated plans involving wildlife, physical resources, and sustainable use. Such an approach sometimes requires compromise between environmentalists and developers. This is the case for several HCPs developed by the USFWS in recent years. In Southern California developers and environmentalists had long battled over hundreds of thousands of biologically rich acres lying between Los Angeles and Mexico that were home to uncounted species of plants and animals. Developers wanted to build there, whereas federal regulators wanted to protect the habitat for wildlife. Haggling over small parcels of land had already cost significant time and money and caused frustration on both sides. A compromise resolution permitted developers to develop some large parcels of land while setting aside other large, intact regions as conservation areas. A similar agreement between developers and environmentalists was reached in the Texas Hill Country in 1996 and is effective for thirty years from that date. The Balcones Canyonlands Conservation Plan set aside 111,428 acres (45,093 ha) for ecosystem enhancement while allowing uncontested development of many thousands of acres of land in the central Texas corridor.

## OPPOSITION TO THE ESA

Opponents of the ESA believe the law violates private property rights and stifles economic growth by curbing development. They charge that environmental protection often results in the loss of jobs and business profits. There are also accusations that poor scientific data are used to make decisions about which species should be listed as endangered or threatened. Finally, opponents contend that the ESA has a poor success rate, because it has resulted in the recovery of only a handful of species during its more than three-decade history.

### Property Rights and Economic Issues

In 1996 Congressman Richard W. Pombo (1961–; R-CA) coauthored (with Joseph Farah) *This Land Is Our Land: How to End the War on Private Property*, in which he asserted that the ESA and other federal laws infringe on private property rights. After taking office in 1993, the conservative congressman sponsored several bills calling for sweeping reforms of the ESA. The most recent legislation (H.R. 3824) was introduced in 2005 and had ninety-five cosponsors. The bill called for the elimination of critical habitat designation, authorized government payments for landowners prevented from carrying out planned developments, and granted greater decision-making powers to the secretary of the interior regarding the scientific data involved in ESA decisions. The bill was passed by the House, but failed to pass the U.S. Senate. Pombo was defeated in his November 2006 reelection bid. His loss was attributed, in part, to the concerted efforts of conservation groups who funded an aggressive advertising campaign against him.

### Does the ESA Rely on Sound Science?

Section 4 of the ESA describes how the secretary of the interior is to determine which species are endangered or threatened. Subsection 4(b)(1)(A) states that the determination shall be made "solely on the basis of the best scientific and commercial data available." These words are at the center of a fierce debate about the scientific validity of ESA decisions. Critics of the law complain that the term *best available* is not well defined and allows the USFWS too much latitude to declare species endangered or threatened based on incomplete data. Pambo and other ESA critics in Congress have championed what they call a "sound science" approach to species protection.

Eugene H. Buck, M. Lynne Corn, and Pamela Baldwin of the Congressional Research Service discuss in *The Endangered Species Act and "Sound Science"* (January 8, 2007, http://www.fas.org/sgp/crs/misc/RL32992.pdf) the "sound science" debate at length. They note that some ESA decisions have raised congressional concern about the interpretation of scientific data. The following are two examples:

- In 2001 the USFWS and the NMFS issued "biological opinions" regarding the imperiled salmon and sucker species in the Klamath River in California. The agencies recommended restricting irrigation water use to protect the fishes' habitat—a controversial decision widely protested by local farmers dependent on river water to grow crops. The National Research Council, an agency of the National Academy of Sciences, reviewed the USFWS and NMRS decisions and recommendations and determined they were not based on sound scientific data.

- In 2002 an investigation by the Government Accountability Office revealed problems with fur collection and sampling conducted as part of the habitat survey for the Canada lynx. The lynx was listed as threatened under the ESA in 2000. Investigators found that some government researchers had submitted fur samples that were not collected from naturally occurring wild populations of the animals. This raised speculation that the USFWS had inflated the known range of Canada lynx based on faulty data.

Regarding congressional action on this subject, Buck, Corn, and Baldwin state:

> Proponents of "sound science" legislation believe that ESA amendments are necessary to rein in the perceived extremism of the ESA that allowed federal agencies to use "shoddy science" (e.g., to prevent Klamath Basin farmers from receiving the irrigation water they needed). Furthermore, supporters believe amendments are needed to help those who have to deal with an "unreasonable" ESA. They claim that private property rights would be helped by these proposals because a species would have to actually be endangered to be listed and that it would be nearly impossible to use falsified data, which they charged was being done by government agencies.

Critics of the "sound science" movement protest that obtaining comprehensive biological data on an imperiled species is unfeasible. Due to their very scarcity, these species are difficult to locate and count with complete reliability. Buck, Corn, and Baldwin point out that court rulings have interpreted the statutory language in the ESA to mean that federal agencies must use the best scientific data available, not the best scientific data possible. ESA supporters believe legislative efforts to incorporate "sound science" requirements in the law are veiled attempts to weaken the law in favor of the economic interests of landowners and developers. They note that the word *solely* in "solely on the basis of the best scientific and commercial data available" was added to the ESA in the 1982 amendments to the law to ensure that nonscientific concerns, such as economic and social factors, did not influence listing decisions.

### Recovery Rate Controversy

One of the most frequent criticisms leveled against the ESA is that it has achieved recovery for few species

since its passage in 1973. As shown in Table 2.4 and discussed earlier, only twelve U.S. entities (species or distinct populations) have been delisted due to recovery under the ESA as of February 2008. All the recovered mammal entities are not entire species, but subpopulations of the wider population (e.g., the grizzly bear in Yellowstone National Park).

In 2005 Pombo wrote a report for the Center for the Defense of Free Enterprise calling for reforms in the ESA. In "The ESA at 30: Time for Congress to Update & Strengthen the Law" (http://www.cdfe.org/esa_reform1.htm), Pombo argues that the law has failed to achieve its stated goal of saving imperiled species. He notes that "none of the species listed by the FWS to have been 'recovered' in the United States may reasonably be claimed to have recovered as a result of the ESA. The fact is that the few recovery success stories are not even attributable to regulatory protections under the ESA, but unrelated factors such as bans on DDT and other organochlorides."

In "Don't List the Polar Bear under the Endangered Species Act" (January 25, 2008, http://www.heritage.org/Research/EnergyandEnvironment/wm1781.cfm), Ben Lieberman of the Heritage Foundation, a conservative organization and vocal critic of the ESA, argues that "while being highly successful in violating private property rights and hampering economic activities—especially for farmers, ranchers, and loggers in the rural West and elsewhere—the statute has done little to protect species. In its decades-long existence, only a very small percentage of the listed species have actually recovered or even shown any increase in their numbers."

## IS THE ESA ENOUGH?

In May 2005 a group of ten prominent scientists sent a letter (http://www.saveesa.org/letter.pdf) to the U.S. Senate in which they urged strengthening of the ESA. The letter was spearheaded by Professors Edward O. Wilson (1929–) of Harvard University and Paul R. Ehrlich (1932–) of Stanford University. It warns that Earth is facing an "extinction crisis" and that large numbers of species could be lost over the next few decades. The scientists note the importance of the ESA in U.S. efforts to preserve biological diversity and conclude, "Viewing our looming extinction crisis as a crisis for humans as well as wildlife, the importance of the Endangered Species Act takes on even greater significance. In the face of this crisis, we must strengthen the Act and broaden its protections, not weaken them."

In January 2006 over fifty-seven hundred U.S. scientists signed the letter "A Letter from Biologists to the United States Senate" (http://www.ucsusa.org/scientific_integrity/restoring/biologists-letter-on.html) regarding concerns of the scientific community about proposed changes to the ESA. The letter highlights the historical successes of the ESA as encouraging signs that progress is being made against the loss of imperiled species. It argues that the ESA does not need a substantial overhaul, but a greater emphasis on implementation and use of objective scientific information in decision making. The scientists state that "for species conservation to continue, it is imperative both that the scientific principles embodied in the Act are maintained, and that the Act is strengthened, fully implemented, and adequately funded."

# CHAPTER 3
# MARINE MAMMALS

Marine mammals live in and around the ocean. They are warm blooded, breathe air, have hair at some point in their life, give birth to live young (as opposed to laying eggs), and nourish their young by secreting milk. Dolphins, whales, seals, sea lions, walruses, polar bears, manatees, and dugongs (manatee relatives) fall into this category.

Historically, marine mammals have garnered a high level of public support and legal protection. During the 1960s the television show *Flipper* entertained American audiences with stories about a highly intelligent and loveable dolphin that befriended and helped a family. Tourist attractions such as Marineland in Florida and SeaWorld in California began featuring acrobatic dolphins and whales in popular shows. The growing environmental movement seized on the public interest in marine mammals and lobbied for measures to protect animals that many people believed to be extremely smart and sociable.

At the time, purse-seine fishing was widely practiced by commercial tuna fishers in the eastern tropical Pacific Ocean. This fishing method involved the use of enormous nets, often hundreds of miles long that were circled around schools of tuna. Many dolphins were inadvertently captured because they tend to mingle with fleets of tuna in this part of the ocean. Nontargeted animals captured during commercial fishing activities are called bycatch. Dolphin bycatch became a major public issue. Hauling in the enormous tuna-filled nets was a long process. As a result, the air-breathing dolphins were trapped for long periods underwater and often drowned. Public outcry over these killings and general concern for the welfare of marine mammals led Congress to pass the Marine Mammal Protection Act of 1972.

## THE MARINE MAMMAL PROTECTION ACT

The Marine Mammal Protection Act (MMPA) was passed in 1972 and was substantially amended in 1994.

The original act noted that "certain species and population stocks of marine mammals are, or may be, in danger of extinction or depletion as a result of man's activities." However, it was acknowledged that "inadequate" information was available concerning the population dynamics of the animals being protected.

The MMPA prohibits the taking (hunting, killing, capturing, and harassing) of marine mammals. The act also bars the importation of most marine mammals or their products. Exceptions are occasionally granted for scientific research, public display in aquariums, traditional subsistence hunting by Alaskan Natives, and some incidental capture during commercial fishing operations. The goal of the MMPA is to maintain marine populations at or above "optimum sustainable" levels.

Whales, dolphins, seals, and sea lions were put under the jurisdiction of the National Marine Fisheries Service (NMFS), an agency of the National Oceanic and Atmospheric Administration in the U.S. Department of Commerce. Polar bears, walruses, sea otters, manatees, and dugongs were placed under the jurisdiction of the U.S. Fish and Wildlife Service (USFWS), an agency of the U.S. Department of the Interior.

The MMPA requires the NMFS and the USFWS to conduct periodic surveys to estimate populations and to predict population trends for marine mammals in three regions of U.S. waters: the Pacific Ocean coast (excluding Alaska), the Atlantic Ocean coast (including the Gulf of Mexico), and the Alaskan coast. The survey results are published by the NMFS in an annual *Stock Assessment Report* (http://www.nmfs.noaa.gov/pr/sars/).

The MMPA was passed a year before the Endangered Species Act (ESA). The MMPA was driven largely by public affection for marine mammals, rather than by specific knowledge about impending species extinction. According to Eugene H. Buck of the Congressional

**TABLE 3.1**

Endangered and threatened aquatic mammals, February 1, 2008

**U.S. Species**

| Status | Type | Common name | Scientific name | Note |
|---|---|---|---|---|
| E | Whale | Blue whale | *Balaenoptera musculus* | Baleen plate |
| E | Whale | Bowhead whale | *Balaena mysticetus* | Baleen plate |
| E | Whale | Finback whale | *Balaenoptera physalus* | Baleen plate |
| E | Whale | Humpback whale | *Megaptera novaeangliae* | Baleen plate |
| E | Whale | Killer whale | *Orcinus orca* | Toothed |
| E | Whale | Right whale (northern & southern) | *Balaena glacialis incl. australis* | Baleen plate |
| E | Whale | Sei whale | *Balaenoptera borealis* | Baleen plate |
| E | Whale | Sperm whale | *Physeter catodon=macrocephalus* | Toothed |
| E, T | Sea-lion | Steller sea-lion | *Eumetopias jubatus* | Eared |
| E | Seal | Caribbean monk seal | *Monachus tropicalis* | Earless, presumed extinct |
| T | Seal | Guadalupe fur seal | *Arctocephalus townsendi* | Eared |
| E | Seal | Hawaiian monk seal | *Monachus schauinslandi* | Earless |
| T | Otter | Northern sea otter | *Enhydra lutris kenyoni* | Southwest Alaska stock |
| T, XN | Otter | Southern sea otter | *Enhydra lutris nereis* | California stock |
| E | Manatee | West Indian manatee | *Trichechus manatus* | Florida stock |

**Foreign species**

| Status | Type | Common name | Scientific name | Region |
|---|---|---|---|---|
| E | Whale | Gray whale | *Eschrichtius robustus* | Western North Pacific Ocean |
| E | Dolphin | Chinese River dolphin | *Lipotes vexillifer* | China |
| E | Dolphin | Indus River dolphin | *Platanista minor* | Pakistan |
| E | Porpoise | Cochito (or vaquita) | *Phocoena sinus* | Mexico (Gulf of California) |
| E | Seal | Mediterranean monk seal | *Monachus monachus* | Mediterranean, Northwest African Coast and Black Sea |
| E | Seal | Saimaa seal | *Phoca hispida saimensis* | Finland |
| E | Otter | Cameroon clawless otter | *Aonyx congicus=congica microdon* | Nigeria |
| E | Otter | Giant otter | *Pteronura brasiliensis* | South America |
| E | Otter | Long-tailed otter | *Lontra=Lutra longicaudis* | South America |
| E | Otter | Marine otter | *Lontra=Lutra felina* | Peru south to Straits of Magellan |
| E | Otter | Southern river otter | *Lontra=Lutra provocax* | Argentina, Chile |
| E | Manatee | Amazonian manatee | *Trichechus inunguis* | South America |
| T | Manatee | West African manatee | *Trichechus senegalensis* | West coast of Africa |
| E | Dugong | Dugong | *Dugong dugon* | Palau (Western Pacific Ocean) |

Status codes: E = Endangered; T = Threatened; XN = Experimental Population, Non-Essential.

SOURCE: Adapted from "Listed U.S. Species by Taxonomic Group: Vertebrate Animals" and "Foreign Species," in *USFWS Threatened and Endangered Species System (TESS)*, U.S. Department of the Interior, U.S. Fish and Wildlife Service, February 1, 2008, http://ecos.fws.gov/tess_public/SpeciesReport.do?kingdom=V&listingType=L&mapstatus=1 (accessed February 1, 2008).

Research Service, in *Fishery, Aquaculture, and Marine Mammal Legislation in the 109th Congress* (August 3, 2006, http://digital.library.unt.edu/govdocs/crs/permalink/meta-crs-10140:1), "some critics assert that the MMPA is scientifically irrational because it identifies one group of organisms for special protection unrelated to their abundance or ecological role." However, the MMPA is credited with promoting research about marine mammals and drawing attention to issues associated with bycatch mortality.

## THE ENDANGERED SPECIES ACT

There were only three marine mammal species on the first list of native endangered species issued in 1967. (See Table 2.1 in Chapter 2.) Over the following decades additional marine mammals were added as information became available on their population status. As of February 2008, there were fifteen species of marine mammals listed as endangered or threatened in the United States. (See Table 3.1.) Another fourteen foreign species were also listed.

**TABLE 3.2**

The ten listed marine mammal entities with the highest expenditures under the Endangered Species Act, fiscal year 2006

| Ranking | Species | Expenditure |
|---|---|---|
| 1 | Steller sea-lion (western) | $24,791,913 |
| 2 | West Indian manatee | $9,737,769 |
| 3 | Right whale | $9,349,875 |
| 4 | Steller sea-lion (eastern) | $5,712,509 |
| 5 | Bowhead whale | $4,020,096 |
| 6 | Humpback whale | $3,920,313 |
| 7 | Hawaiian monk seal | $2,839,166 |
| 8 | Southern sea otter | $1,042,860 |
| 9 | Northern sea otter | $772,700 |
| 10 | Sperm whale | $707,417 |

SOURCE: Adapted from "Table 2. Species Ranked in Descending Order of Total FY 2006 Reported Expenditures, Not Including Land Acquisition Costs," in *Federal and State Endangered and Threatened Species Expenditures: Fiscal Year 2006*, U.S. Department of the Interior, U.S. Fish and Wildlife Service, draft, 2008

During fiscal year 2006 nearly $62.8 million was spent by federal and state agencies on the ten marine mammal species with the highest spending that year. (See Table 3.2.)

FIGURE 3.1

A humpback whale, seen off the coast of Massachusetts. *AP/Wide World Photos*

As of February 2008, ESA-listed endangered and threatened marine mammals fell into five main categories: whales, dolphins and porpoises, seals and sea lions, sea otters, and manatees and dugongs. In May 2008 the polar bear was listed under the ESA as threatened. In addition, the USFWS was conducting a status review to determine if polar bears should be proposed for listing under the ESA as a threatened species.

## WHALES

Whales are cetaceans, marine mammals that live in the water all the time and have torpedo-shaped nearly hairless bodies. (See Figure 3.1.) There are approximately seventy known whale species. The so-called great whales are the largest animals on Earth. In general, the great whale species range in size from 30 to 100 feet (9.1 to 30.5 m) in length. There are thirteen whale species normally considered to be great whales. The blue whale is the largest of these species.

Whales are found throughout the world's oceans; however, many species are concentrated in cold northern waters. Even though they are warm blooded and do not have fur, whales can survive in cold waters because they have a thick layer of dense fat and tissue known as blubber lying just beneath the skin. This blubber layer can be up to a foot (30.5 cm) thick in larger species.

Most whales have teeth. A handful of species filter their food through strong flexible plates called baleen. (See Figure 3.2.) Baleen is informally known as "whalebone." It is composed of a substance similar to human fingernails. Baleen whales strain large amounts of water to obtain their food, mostly zooplankton and tiny fish and crustaceans. Nearly all the great whales are baleen whales.

Many marine mammals can vocalize (make sound). Whales, in particular, use sound to communicate with each other and for navigational purposes. Some whale vocalizations are audible to human ears. These sounds are known as "whalesong."

FIGURE 3.2

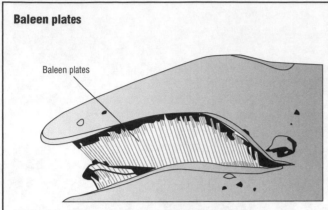

**Baleen plates**

Baleen plates

SOURCE: "How Were Baleen Whales Named?" in *Marine Mammal Education Web: Baleen Whales*, National Oceanic and Atmospheric Administration, Alaska Fisheries Science Center, National Marine Mammal Laboratory, March 3, 2004, http://www.afsc.noaa.gov/nmml/education/cetaceans/baleen1.php (accessed January 23, 2008)

Whales are believed to be highly intelligent. Scientists use a measure called the encephalization quotient (EQ) to compare the relative intelligence of different species. EQ is a number based on the ratio of brain mass to body mass. For example, the average human brain is much larger than needed just to operate an organism the size of a human. This extra capacity indicates higher intelligence. Likewise, the brains of cetaceans, such as whales, are larger than expected, indicating that they are probably very intelligent animals.

## Imperiled Whale Populations

As of February 2008, eight whale species had been listed for protection under the ESA in U.S. waters: blue whales, bowhead whales, finback whales, humpback whales, killer whales, northern right whales, sei whales, and sperm whales. (See Table 3.1.) In addition, the ESA covers southern right whales in the southern hemisphere and gray whales, a species that inhabits the northwest Pacific Ocean. All of these whales are considered great whales. All but the sperm and killer whales have baleen plates.

In the annual *Stock Assessment Report*, the NMFS provides population estimates for endangered whale species in U.S. waters. Surveys of all species are not conducted every year. As of February 2008, draft reports were available for the Pacific coast (2006), the Atlantic and Gulf coasts (2006), and the Alaskan coast (2006).

The northern right whale is also known as the North Atlantic right whale because it is primarily found along the eastern coast of the United States. Even though a few sightings have been confirmed in the North Pacific Ocean, there is no official estimate of that population. The NMFS considers both populations to be of the same species. However, this opinion is disputed by some scientists.

The northern right whale is the most endangered of the great whales. It was once the "right" whale to hunt because it swims slowly, prefers shallow coastal waters, and floats when it dies. The species was nearly driven to extinction by whaling, which was banned in 1937 when the population had been reduced to an estimated one hundred. Despite decades of protection, the northern right whale population has not recovered, and some scientists believe the animal is in grave danger of becoming extinct within only a few decades.

## Threats to Whales

Whale populations are imperiled due to a long history of hunting by humans. As early as the eighth century, humans hunted whales for meat and baleen. Whales were relatively easy for fishermen to catch because the animals spend a great deal of time at the surface of the water and provide a large target for harpoons. Advances in shipbuilding and the invention of the steam engine allowed fishermen greater access to whale populations, even those in Arctic areas that had previously been out of reach. By the nineteenth century, large numbers of whales were being killed for blubber and baleen. Blubber was rendered to extract whale oil, which was used to light lamps. Baleen was valued for making fans, corsets, and other consumer goods.

On December 2, 1946, the representatives of fourteen nations signed the International Convention for the Regulation of Whaling (http://www.iwcoffice.org/_documents/commission/convention.pdf), which formed the International Whaling Commission (IWC). The signatory nations were Argentina, Australia, Brazil, Canada, Chile, Denmark, France, the Netherlands, New Zealand, Peru, South Africa, the United Kingdom, the United States, and the Union of Soviet Socialist Republics. The IWC was formed as a means to regulate the industry and limit the number and type of whales that could be killed. The MMPA of 1972 banned commercial whaling in U.S. waters. The IWC (February 11, 2008, http://www.iwcoffice.org/commission/members.htm) states that in February 2008 it had seventy-nine member nations.

Centuries of whaling severely depleted whale populations. Low birth rates and high mortality rates due to a variety of factors have prevented many species from recovering. Like other marine animals, whales are endangered by water pollution and loss or degradation of habitat. However, the biggest threats to the northern right whale and other whale species are believed to be entanglement in fishing gear and ship strikes. Table 3.3 lists the number of reports of whale entanglements and ship strikes for 2001 through 2005 along the northern Gulf of Mexico coast, the U.S. East Coast, and the adjacent Canadian coasts. More than 400 reports are recorded, including 151 cases of entanglement and 48 ship strikes.

TABLE 3.3

**Summary of reported incidents involving whales along the northern Gulf of Mexico Coast, U.S. East Coast, and adjacent Canadian Maritimes, 2001–05**

| Species | Western North Atlantic right whale | Northwest Atlantic humpback whale[b] | Western North Atlantic fin whale | Nova Scotian sei whale | Western North Atlantic blue whale | Canadian East Coast minke whale | Western North Atlantic Brydes whale | Unidentified fin/sei whale | Unidentified balaenopterid[d] | Unidentified whale spp. | Totals |
|---|---|---|---|---|---|---|---|---|---|---|---|
| Total reports[a] | 51 | 162 | 47 | 6 | 1 | 86 | 1 | 9 | 15 | 39 | 417 |
| Total entanglement reports[a] | 25 | 79[c] | 8 | 0 | 1 | 30 | 1 | 1 | 1 | 5 | 151 |
| Total ship strike reports | 15 | 16[c] | 12 | 3 | 0 | 1 | 0 | 0 | 0 | 1 | 48 |
| Confirmed entanglement events | 24 | 70[c] | 8 | 0 | 1 | 25 | 1 | 1 | 1 | 2 | 133 |
| Confirmed ship strike events | 14 | 12[c] | 10 | 3 | 0 | 2 | 0 | 0 | 0 | 1 | 42 |
| Total confirmed mortalities | 22 | 91 | 40 | 6 | 0 | 78 | 1 | 8 | 14 | 32 | 292 |
| Confirmed entanglement mortalities | 3 | 8 | 3 | 0 | 0 | 11 | 1 | 0 | 0 | 0 | 26 |
| Confirmed ship strike mortalities | 8 | 7 | 8 | 2 | 0 | 2 | 0 | 0 | 0 | 0 | 27 |
| Confirmed entanglement serious injuries | 4 | 6 | 1 | 0 | 0 | 0 | 0 | 0 | 0 | 0 | 11 |
| Confirmed ship strike serious injuries | 1 | 0 | 0 | 0 | 0 | 0 | 0 | 0 | 0 | 0 | 1 |

[a]Excludes resightings of previously entangled individuals unless a new entanglement was documented.
[b]Includes all humpback reports, whether confirmed as members of the Gulf of Maine feeding stock or not.
[c]One humpback report included as both a confirmed entanglement and confirmed ship strike event.
[d]Described as having throat grooves (rorqual pleats).

SOURCE: Adapted from Misty Nelson et al., "Table 1. Summary of All Reported Baleen and Unidentified Whale Events along the Northern Gulf of Mexico Coast, U.S. East Coast and Adjacent Canadian Maritimes, 2001–2005," in *Mortality and Serious Injury Determinations for Baleen Whale Stocks along the United States Eastern Seaboard and Adjacent Canadian Maritimes, 2001–2005*, U.S. Department of Commerce, National Oceanic and Atmospheric Administration, Northeast Fisheries Science Center, 2007, http://www.nefsc.noaa.gov/nefsc/publications/crd/crd0705/t1.html (accessed January 23, 2008)

A total of 292 whales were confirmed killed by these events.

ENTANGLEMENT IN FISHING GEAR. The NMFS explains in "What Kinds of Fishing Gear Most Often Entangle Right Whales?" (*Right Whale News*, November 2005) that entanglement of whales in fishing gear is a major problem. According to studies conducted in 2003 by the New England Aquarium, 71.9% of all known northern right whales have been entangled at least once in fishing gear. In 2005 researchers from Duke University investigated thirty-one cases of right whale entanglements and tried to identify the type of fishing gear involved in each case. They found that nearly a third of the whales had become entangled in lobster pot gear, mostly buoy lines. It was concluded that any type of fishing line that rises vertically in the water column poses a "significant entanglement risk" to northern right whales.

The article "Max Sues MA Lobsterman over Entanglement" (*Commercial Fisheries News*, April 2007) reports that in February 2007 Max Strahan, an environmental activist concerned about whale entanglement, filed a lawsuit under the ESA against a Maine lobsterman whose gear had been found wrapped around a humpback whale during the summer of 2006. The whale was freed unharmed by a team from the Provincetown Center for Coastal Studies, a private whale organization based in Massachusetts. The entangled gear was turned over to the NMFS, which identified the owner. No charges were filed, however, because the gear was deemed to be of a legal type and had been legally set. The commercial fishing industry fears that the suit could unleash a wave of litigation against individual fishermen and force new restrictions on fishing gear. As of April 2008, the suit had not been brought to trial.

SHIP STRIKES. In "NOAA Fisheries: North Atlantic Right Whales and Ship Strikes off the U.S. East Coast" (2004, http://nefsc.noaa.gov/press_release/2004/advisory 04.02.pdf), the National Oceanic and Atmospheric Administration reports that between 1975 and 2002 there were 292 ship strikes on large whales off the U.S. East Coast. Between 2001 and 2005 the NMFS documented forty-eight ship strikes on large whales. (See Table 3.3.) Strikes on northern right whales are particularly troublesome because so few of the animals remain in existence. The NMFS states in "Ship Strike Reduction" (March 11, 2008, http://www.nero.noaa.gov/shipstrike/) that "collision with vessels is the leading human-caused source of mortality for the endangered North Atlantic right whale."

Figure 3.3 shows the locations of ship strikes on northern right whales that occurred between 1990 and 2000 along the North American coastline. Most strikes in U.S. waters occurred along the Massachusetts coast near Cape Cod and along the Georgia and northern Florida coastline. These areas are near or within critical habitats designated by the NMFS for the whales. The southern critical habitat is the only known calving area of the northern right whale and is used from mid-November to mid-April. During calving season the NMFS performs aerial surveys and alerts ships about whales in their vicinity. In addition, federal law requires that ships

**FIGURE 3.3**

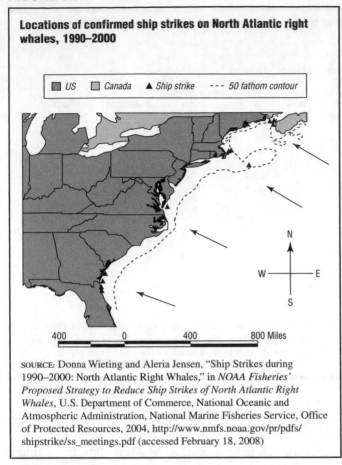

**Locations of confirmed ship strikes on North Atlantic right whales, 1990–2000**

☐ US ☐ Canada ▲ Ship strike --- 50 fathom contour

400    0    400    800 Miles

SOURCE: Donna Wieting and Aleria Jensen, "Ship Strikes during 1990–2000: North Atlantic Right Whales," in *NOAA Fisheries' Proposed Strategy to Reduce Ship Strikes of North Atlantic Right Whales*, U.S. Department of Commerce, National Oceanic and Atmospheric Administration, National Marine Fisheries Service, Office of Protected Resources, 2004, http://www.nmfs.noaa.gov/pr/pdfs/ shipstrike/ss_meetings.pdf (accessed February 18, 2008)

remain five hundred yards from right whales. Any sightings of dead, injured, or entangled whales must be reported to authorities.

In 2004 the NMFS announced plans to propose rules requiring routing changes and speed limits for large vessels traveling in U.S. coastal waters frequented by northern right whales. The agency was still developing the rules in May 2005 when several environmental and animal rights groups petitioned the NMFS requesting that a temporary emergency regulation be imposed until the permanent rules could be issued. In September 2005 the NMFS formally denied the petition. Two months later, three of the petitioners—the Defenders of Wildlife, the Humane Society of the United States, and the Ocean Conservancy—filed a lawsuit against the NMFS accusing the agency of "failing to protect" northern right whales as required by law.

In 2006 the NMFS published "Proposed Rule to Implement Speed Restrictions to Reduce the Threat of Ship Collisions with North Atlantic Right Whales" (*Federal Register*, vol. 71, no. 122, June 26, 2006). As of April 2008, a final decision on the proposal had not been issued. Reports such as the article "White House Blocks Ship Speed Limits Meant to Protect Whales" (Environment News Service, July 16, 2007) and the University of

New Hampshire press release "Right Whales in the Wrong Place—No Bones about It!" (October 22, 2007, http://www.ceps.unh.edu/news/news_releases08/whales .html) claim the administration of George W. Bush (1946–) has stalled implementation of the speed limits due to opposition from foreign shipping companies.

In July 2007 the NMFS and the U.S. Coast Guard modified shipping lanes off the coast of Boston to reduce the threat of ship collisions with whales in the area. The NMFS reports in the press release "Shift of the Boston Traffic Separation Scheme" (July 1, 2007, http://www .nmfs.noaa.gov/pr/shipstrike/) that the realignment is expected to reduce the risk of ship strikes to right whales by 58% and reduce the risk to other large whale species by 81%.

**Whale Recovery Plans**

Table 3.4 lists information about population trends, recovery priority numbers, critical habitat designation, and recovery plan status for the eight whale species listed as endangered under the ESA in U.S. waters. As of February 2008, critical habitat had been designated only for the northern right whale and killer whale. Draft or final recovery plans had been developed for all species except the bowhead whale. Populations of bowhead, humpback, and killer whales were believed to be increasing, but information was inadequate to determine population trends for the other species.

Table 3.4 also shows the recovery priority numbers assigned by the NMFS to each endangered whale species. Priority numbers can range from a value of 1 (highest priority) to 12 (lowest priority). The northern right whale has a priority level of 1, indicating strong concern about its abundance and chances for survival as a species.

In *Recovery Plan for the North Atlantic Right Whale* (August 2004, http://www.nmfs.noaa.gov/pr/pdfs/recovery/ whale_right_northatlantic.pdf), the NMFS lists five goals for recovering the species. In order of importance, the goals are:

• Significantly reduce sources of human-caused death, injury, and disturbance

• Develop recovery criteria based on demographic criteria

• Identify, characterize, protect, and monitor important habitats

• Monitor the status and trends of abundance and distribution of the whale population

• Coordinate federal, state, local, international, and private efforts to implement the recovery plan

TABLE 3.4

**Endangered and threatened whale species, 2008**

| Species//DPS[a] | Date listed or reclassified | Endangered species act status | Population trend | Recovery priority number[b] | Status of recovery plan | Critical habitat |
|---|---|---|---|---|---|---|
| Blue whale | 6/2/1970 | Endangered | Unknown | 7 | Final 07/98 | None |
| Bowhead whale | 6/2/1970 | Endangered | Increasing | 9 | None | None |
| Fin whale | 6/2/1970 | Endangered | Unknown | 7 | Draft completed 06/06 | None |
| Humpback whale | 6/2/1970 | Endangered | Increasing | 3 | Final 11/91 | None |
| Northern right whale | 6/2/1970 | Endangered | Unknown | 1 | Final 05/05 (Atlantic); under development (Pacific) | Final |
| Sei whale | 6/2/1970 | Endangered | Unknown | 3 | Draft completed 07/98 - under revision | None |
| Sperm whale | 6/2/1970 | Endangered | Unknown | 7 | Draft completed 06/06 | None |
| Killer whale (DPS[a]) | 11/18/2005 | Endangered | Increasing | 3 | Final 01/08 | Final |

[a]DPS = distinct population segment.
[b]Recovery priority numbers are designated according to guidelines published by the National Marine Fisheries Service on June 15, 1990. Priorities are designated from 1 (high) to 12 (low) based on the following factors: degree of threat, recovery potential, and conflict with development projects or other economic activity.

SOURCE: Adapted from "Table 1. ESA-Listed Species under NMFS Jurisdiction Including Listing Status, Trends, Priority Numbers, and Recovery Plan Status," in *Biennial Report to Congress on the Recovery Program for Threatened and Endangered Species, October 1, 2004–September 30, 2006*, U.S. Department of Commerce, National Oceanic and Atmospheric Administration, National Marine Fisheries Service, 2007, http://www.nmfs.noaa.gov/pr/pdfs/laws/esabiennial2006.pdf (accessed January 23, 2008), and "Marine Mammals," in *Marine Mammal Species under the Endangered Species Act (ESA)*, U.S. Department of Commerce, National Oceanic and Atmospheric Administration, National Marine Fisheries Service, 2008, http://www.nmfs.noaa.gov/pr/species/esa/mammals.htm (accessed February 1, 2008)

## DOLPHINS AND PORPOISES

Dolphins and porpoises are toothed cetaceans. They are similar in shape; however, dolphins are generally larger than porpoises and prefer shallower, warmer waters. Dolphins tend to have long bottlenoses and cone-shaped teeth, as opposed to the flatter noses and teeth found in porpoises. Porpoises are members of the Phocoenidae family, which includes only six existing species. Dolphins are members of the Delphinidae family, a large family containing at least thirty known species. Most dolphin and porpoise populations around the world are hardy and not in danger of extinction. However, there are several species that are in trouble due to limited geographical distribution.

There are no U.S. species of dolphin or porpoises listed under the ESA. There are, however, three foreign species listed as endangered: the Chinese River dolphin, the Indus River dolphin, and the cochito. (See Table 3.1.) The Chinese River and Indus River dolphins live in freshwater rivers in China and Pakistan, respectively. Their numbers are considered to be extremely small. In both cases extensive river damming, water drawdown due to human consumption, fishing, and pollution are blamed for the declines.

The cochito (or vaquita) is a kind of porpoise found only in the Gulf of California, a narrow body of water that separates the western Mexican mainland from the Baja California peninsula. This stretch of water is known in the United States as the Sea of Cortez and contains a great diversity of sea life. Cochitos are among the rarest of all marine mammals. According to the NMFS, the cochito species has been nearly eliminated because so many of the animals have become entangled in fishing lines and drowned.

### Protection of Prevalent Dolphins

Even though they are not considered endangered or threatened, dolphins receive special consideration under U.S. law because of public concern about them. Dolphins are believed to be highly intelligent. They have a high EQ, perhaps the highest of any animal, besides humans. In addition, many people have been exposed to dolphins through marine entertainment parks, movies, television shows, and even personal encounters and sightings at tourist beaches. As a result, there is widespread public fondness for the animals.

Dolphins are protected by the MMPA and by laws designed to limit their capture during tuna fishing. In 1990 large U.S. tuna canning companies announced they would no longer purchase tuna caught in a manner that endangered dolphins. The companies began labeling their products "Dolphin Safe" if their practices met specific standards established by the U.S. government. The International Dolphin Conservation Program Act, passed in 1992, reduced the number of legally permitted dolphin deaths. This act also made the United States a dolphin-safe zone in 1994, when it became illegal to sell, buy, or ship tuna products obtained using methods that kill dolphins.

### SEALS AND SEA LIONS

Seals, sea lions, and walruses are considered pinnipeds. This designation comes from the Latin word *pinnipedia*, which means "feather or fin foot." Pinnipeds have finlike flippers. Even though they spend most of their time in the ocean, pinnipeds come on shore to rest, breed, give birth, and nurse their young. Areas preferred for breeding, birthing, and nursing are called rookeries. Pinnipeds not yet of reproductive age congregate at shore areas known as haul-outs.

Seals and sea lions were hunted extensively during the 1800s and early 1900s for their blubber, fur, and meat. They continue to be imperiled by human encroachment of haul-out beaches, entanglement in marine debris and fishing nets, incidental catches, disease, and lack of food due to competition from humans for prey species.

## Imperiled Seal and Sea Lion Populations

As of February 2008, there were six species of seals and sea lions listed under the ESA. (See Table 3.1.) The U.S. species are Caribbean monk seal, Guadalupe fur seal (also found in Mexico), Hawaiian monk seal, and Steller sea lion. The Caribbean monk seal has not been sighted since 1952 and is presumed by the NMFS to be extinct. The foreign species listed under the ESA are Mediterranean monk seal and Saimaa seal.

GUADALUPE FUR SEALS. The Guadalupe fur seal breeds along the eastern coast of Isla de Guadalupe, Mexico. The island is approximately 400 miles (644 km) west of Baja California. The Seal Conservation Society (SCS; January 6, 2006, http://www.pinnipeds .org/species/guadfur.htm) notes that even though populations once included as many as twenty thousand to one hundred thousand individuals, decline and endangerment resulted from extensive fur hunting in the 1700s and 1800s. The species was believed extinct in the early twentieth century, but a small population was discovered in 1954. NMFS scientists believe the population is now on the increase.

HAWAIIAN MONK SEALS. Hawaiian monk seals are the only pinnipeds found on Hawaii and are endemic to those islands—that is, they occur nowhere else on Earth. Hunting was the primary cause of population decline. Hawaiian monk seals are also extremely sensitive to human activity and disturbance and now breed exclusively on the remote northwestern Hawaiian islands, which are not inhabited by humans. Most females give birth to a single pup every two years, a reproductive rate lower than other pinniped species.

In *Recovery Plan for the Hawaiian Monk Seal* (August 2007, http://www.nmfs.noaa.gov/pr/pdfs/recovery/hawaii anmonkseal.pdf), the NMFS indicates that in 2007 the population was estimated at around twelve hundred individuals. Significant threats to the seals include starvation due to food limitations, entanglement in marine debris, and predation of young seals by sharks. The recovery plan warns "the Hawaiian monk seal is headed to extinction if urgent action is not taken." Scientists intend to implement a captive care program for juvenile females to ensure that more of them survive into adulthood. Otherwise, they fear there will not be sufficient females in the overall population to guarantee the species' survival.

STELLER SEA LIONS. Steller sea lions are large animals, with males reaching a length of about 11 feet (3.54 m) and weight of 2,500 pounds (1,133 kg). Females are significantly smaller. Steller sea lions are found in Pacific waters from Japan to central California, but most populations breed near Alaska and the Aleutian Islands. The breeding season is from May through July. The species was named after Georg Wilhelm Steller (1709–1746), a German naturalist who studied the animals when he accompanied the Danish explorer Vitus Jonassen Bering (1681–1741) on an expedition to Alaska in 1741.

The Steller sea lion population is divided into two stocks. (See Figure 3.4.) The eastern stock inhabits the area east of 144 degrees West longitude (near Cape Suckling, Alaska), and extends down the west coast of Canada and the U.S. mainland. The western stock is found west of 144 degrees West longitude and extends across the Aleutian Islands to Russia and Japan.

According to the NMFS, in *Recovery Plan for Steller Sea Lion: Eastern and Western Distinct Population Segments* (March 2008, http://www.nmfs.noaa.gov/pr/pdfs/ recovery/stellersealion.pdf), the western stock numbered between 220,000 and 265,000 individuals in the mid-1970s. The population declined by 72% between 1976 and 1990. In April 1990 the Steller sea lion was listed under the ESA as threatened. Over the following decade the western stock continued to decline, dropping to 18,325 individuals. This stock was declared endangered in 1997. Between 2000 and 2004 the western population increased by 12% to 20,533 individuals. The eastern stock has been increasing at a rate of approximately 3% per year since the 1970s. This stock remains classified as threatened. Figure 3.5 and Figure 3.6 show population trends for the western and eastern stocks, respectively.

Steller sea lion populations have declined for a variety of reasons including bycatch, illegal and legal hunting, predation, and disease. In addition, scientists believe the animal has experienced reduced productivity due to the indirect effects of climate change and competition from humans for prey species (food fish).

The North Pacific Universities Marine Mammal Consortium reports in "Leapin' Lipids! In Search of the Ultimate Steller Diet" (June 14, 2005, http://www.mar inemammal.org/2005/composition.php) that population declines may be explained by the fact that Steller sea lions have switched from eating fatty fish to fish with low fat content. In particular, their diet now consists primarily of pollock, rather than of herring. The low fat content of the new diet prevents Steller sea lions from building up enough blubber to survive and reproduce in their cold aquatic habitat.

The NMFS has been conducting surveys of Steller sea lion populations since 1985. These surveys are pri-

**FIGURE 3.4**

**Range and rookeries of Steller sea lions**

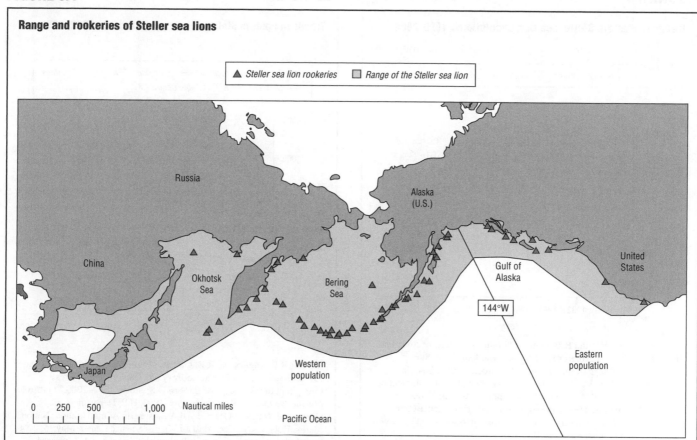

SOURCE: "Steller Sea Lion Range and Rookeries," in *Steller Sea Lions in Alaska: Complexity of the Problem*, National Oceanic and Atmospheric Administration, National Marine Fisheries Service, Alaska Fisheries Science Center, Undated, http://www.afsc.noaa.gov/stellers/range.htm (accessed January 24, 2008)

marily aerial. The most popular rookeries and haul-outs are photographed from the air, and the animals are counted from examination of detailed photographs. During the summer of 2005 the first Alaska-wide aerial pup count was conducted. Researchers found that pup populations had declined dramatically since the 1980s. However, the numbers appeared to level off during the early 2000s.

In fiscal year 2006 species-specific expenditures under the ESA for Steller sea lions totaled $30.5 million, accounting for nearly 50% of expenditures on all marine mammals. (See Table 3.2.) The Steller sea lion ranked fifth in spending among all species covered by the ESA. (See Table 2.9 in Chapter 2.)

**MEDITERRANEAN MONK SEALS.** Mediterranean monk seals inhabit remote areas around the Mediterranean Sea and northwestern African coast. Most are found off the coasts of Mauritania/Western Sahara, Greece, and Turkey. According to the SCS (January 6, 2006, http://www.pinnipeds.org/species/medmonk.htm), there are less than four hundred of the seals believed to be in existence. Mediterranean monk seals are extremely sensitive to disturbance. As humans have encroached on beaches

and coastal areas, the seals have retreated to isolated caves.

In 1997 there was a massive die-off in a colony of the seals near Mauritania. The exact cause is not known; however, a virus or red tide (a reddish discoloration of coastal surface waters due to concentrations of certain toxin-producing algae) is generally blamed. This was a severe blow to the seal population. The animals are also purposely killed by fishermen, who consider them a nuisance and competition for limited fish stocks. Scientists fear that Mediterranean monk seals could become extinct with a few decades.

**SAIMAA SEALS.** Saimaa seals are found only in the cold waters of the Saimaa Lake system in eastern Finland. Their numbers were decimated by hunting over the centuries to the point of extinction. However, protection measures and fishing restrictions allowed some measure of recovery. The SCS (January 6, 2006, http://www.pinnipeds.org/species/ringed.htm) estimates that there are approximately 220 to 250 Saimaa seals remaining, making them one of the most endangered species in the world. Even though the number of seals has been slowly increasing, they are still imperiled by entanglement in fishing nets when they leave protected areas of the lake.

**FIGURE 3.5**

**FIGURE 3.6**

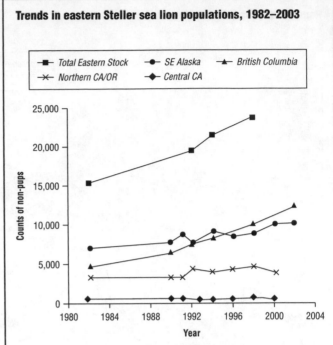

**Trends in western Steller sea lion populations, 1990–2004**

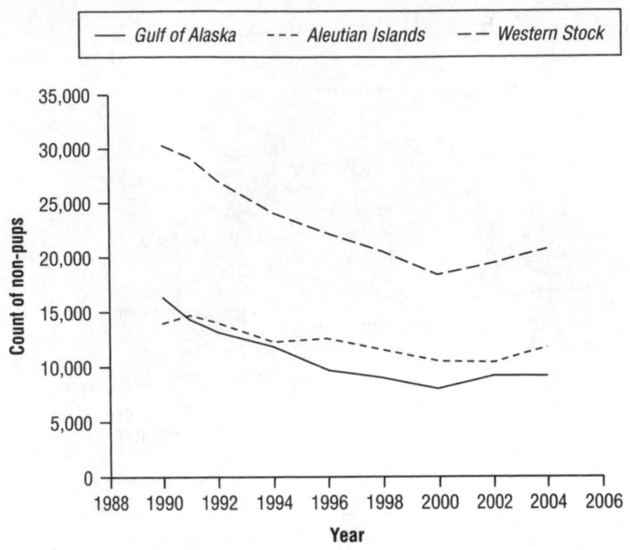

Gulf of Alaska — Aleutian Islands - - - Western Stock - -

SOURCE: R.P. Angliss and R.B. Outlaw, "Figure 2. Counts of Adult and Juvenile Steller Sea Lions at Rookery and Haulout Trend Sites throughout the Range of the Western U.S. Stock, 1990–2004," in *Alaska Marine Mammal Stock Assessments, 2006*, U.S. Department of Commerce, National Oceanic and Atmospheric Administration, National Marine Fisheries Service, Alaska Fisheries Science Center, May 15, 2006, http://www.nmfs.noaa.gov/pr/pdfs/sars/ak2006_slst-w .pdf (accessed February 21, 2008)

**Trends in eastern Steller sea lion populations, 1982–2003**

SOURCE: R.P. Angliss and R.B. Outlaw, "Figure 4. Counts of Adult and Juvenile Steller Sea Lions at Rookery and Haulout Trend Sites throughout the Range of the Eastern U.S. Stock, 1982–2003," in *Alaska Marine Mammal Stock Assessments, 2006*, U.S. Department of Commerce, National Oceanic and Atmospheric Administration, National Marine Fisheries Service, Alaska Fisheries Science Center, May 15, 2006, http://www.nmfs.noaa.gov/pr/pdfs/sars/ak2006_slste.pdf (accessed February 21, 2008)

## Recovery Plans for Seals and Sea Lions

Table 3.5 lists information about population trends, recovery priority numbers, critical habitat designation, and recovery plan status for the Caribbean monk seal, Hawaiian monk seal, and Steller sea lion (eastern and western distinct population segments [DPSs]). Critical habitat and a recovery plan have not been developed for Caribbean monk seals, because they are believed to be extinct. Critical habitat has been designated and recovery plans developed for the Hawaiian monk seal and both Steller sea lion DPSs.

Table 3.5 also shows the recovery priority numbers assigned by the NMFS to each endangered seal and sea lion species. Priority numbers can range from a value of 1 (highest priority) to 12 (lowest priority). The Hawaiian monk seal has a priority level of 1, indicating strong concern about its abundance and chances for survival as a species.

## SEA OTTERS

Sea otters are the smallest marine mammals in North America. They are furry creatures that grow to be about 4 feet (1.2 m) in length and weigh up to 65 pounds (30 kg). Otters are related to weasels and mink and are members of the Mustelidae family. Sea otters are almost entirely aquatic and inhabit relatively shallow waters along the

rocky coasts of the North Pacific Ocean. They eat a wide variety of marine invertebrate. Sea otters are the only animals, besides primates, known to use tools. They use rocks and other objects to smash open the hard shells of clams and crabs to get the meat inside.

Even though they inhabit cold waters, sea otters do not have a blubber layer to keep them warm. Instead, they have extremely dense fur coats and high metabolism rates. Their fur coats are waterproof, but only if kept clean. This makes sea otters susceptible to water contaminants, such as oil.

## Imperiled Otter Populations

At one time sea otters were populous along the entire U.S. West Coast from Southern California to Alaska. Their thick and lustrous fur made them a target of intensive hunting for many centuries. By the dawn of the twentieth century sea otters were on the brink of extinction. In 1911 they became protected under the International Fur Seal Treaty, and their numbers began to increase.

Figure 3.7 shows the distribution of sea otters in 1995. Biologists recognize two distinct populations. The northern sea otter extends from Russia across the Aleu-

TABLE 3.5

**Endangered and threatened seal and sea lion species, 2008**

| Species/DPS[a] | Date listed or reclassified | Endangered species act status | Population trend | Recovery priority number[b] | Status of recovery plan | Critical habitat |
|---|---|---|---|---|---|---|
| Caribbean monk seal | 1979 | Endangered | Presumed extinct | 12 | None | None |
| Guadalupe fur seal | 1985 | Threatened | Increasing | 10 | None | None |
| Hawaiian monk seal | 1976 | Endangered | Mixed | 1 | Final 03/83; revision 08/07 | Final |
| Steller sea lion (DPSs)[a] | | | | | | |
|    Eastern | 1990 | Threatened | Increasing | 10 | Final 12/92; draft revision 05/07 | Draft revision |
|    Western | 1997 | Endangered | Declining | 7 | Final 12/92; draft revision 05/07 | Draft revision |

[a]DPS = distinct population segment.

[b]Recovery priority numbers are designated according to guidelines published by the National Marine Fisheries Service on June 15, 1990. Priorities are designated from 1 (high) to 12 (low) based on the following factors: degree of threat, recovery potential, and conflict with development projects or other economic activity.

SOURCE: Adapted from "Table 1. ESA-Listed Species under NMFS Jurisdiction Including Listing Status, Trends, Priority Numbers, and Recovery Plan Status," in *Biennial Report to Congress on the Recovery Program for Threatened and Endangered Species, October 1, 2004–September 30, 2006,* U.S. Department of Commerce, National Oceanic and Atmospheric Administration, National Marine Fisheries Service, 2007, http://www.nmfs.noaa.gov/pr/pdfs/laws/ esabiennial2006.pdf (accessed January 23, 2008), and "Marine Mammals," in *Marine Mammal Species Under the Endangered Species Act (ESA),* U.S. Department of Commerce, National Oceanic and Atmospheric Administration, National Marine Fisheries Service, 2008, http://www.nmfs.noaa.gov/pr/species/ esa/mammals.htm (accessed February 4, 2008)

---

tian Islands and the coast of Alaska south to the state of Washington. The southern sea otter is found only off the California coast.

Beginning in the 1960s the USFWS began translocating (moving) limited numbers of sea otters from established locations to new locations within their traditional range of distribution. Attempted translocations to Oregon failed; however, translocated colonies were established at four locations: southeastern Alaska, Washington, and San Nicolas Island, California, in the United States, and Vancouver, British Columbia, in Canada. (See Figure 3.7.)

**SOUTHERN SEA OTTERS.** Southern (or California) sea otters were designated a threatened species in 1977. At that time the animals inhabited a small stretch of coastline in central California. Scientists feared that this isolated population was in grave danger of being wiped out by a single catastrophe, such as an oil spill. In 1987 the USFWS decided to establish an "experimental population" of sea otters at another location. Over the next few years 140 sea otters were moved, a few at a time, to San Nicolas Island. It was hoped that these translocated animals would thrive and develop an independent growing colony. However, the venture achieved only limited success. Many of the otters swam back to their original habitat; others died, apparently from the stress of moving. During the early 1990s the transport effort was abandoned.

In October 2005 the USFWS proposed officially ending the translocation program and removing the designation of "experimental population" for the thirty or so sea otters remaining at San Nicolas Island. These animals would be considered threatened under the ESA, just like their fellow southern sea otters. As of April 2008, a final decision had not been reached on this proposal.

**FIGURE 3.7**

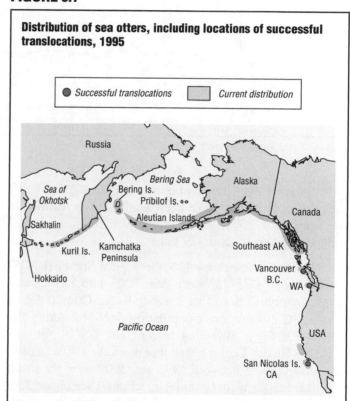

**Distribution of sea otters, including locations of successful translocations, 1995**

SOURCE: James L. Bodkin, Ronald J. Jameson, and James A. Estes, "Fig. 1b. Current Distribution of Sea Otters Including Locations of Successful Translocations," in "Alaska," *Our Living Resources: A Report to the Nation on the Distribution, Abundance, and Health of U.S. Plants, Animals, and Ecosystems,* U.S. Department of the Interior, U.S. Geological Survey, National Biological Service, 1995, http://biology .usgs.gov/status_trends/reptspubs.html (accessed January 30, 2008)

Figure 3.8 shows annual survey results for southern sea otter populations from 1983 through 2007. These surveys were conducted during the springtime and count

**FIGURE 3.8**

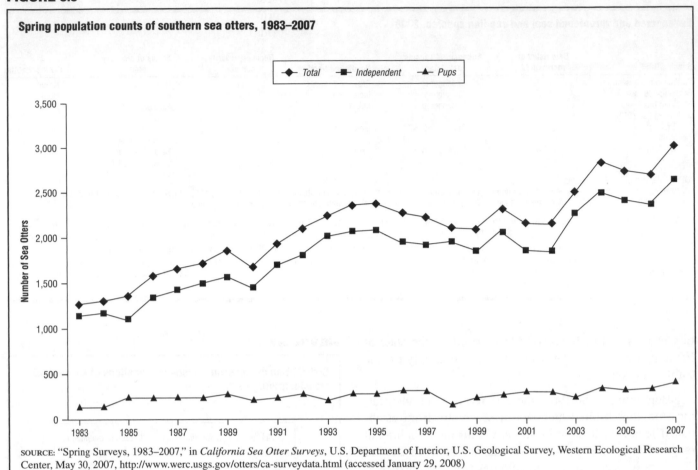

**Spring population counts of southern sea otters, 1983–2007**

Legend: ◆ Total ■ Independent ▲ Pups

Y-axis: Number of Sea Otters

SOURCE: "Spring Surveys, 1983–2007," in *California Sea Otter Surveys*, U.S. Department of Interior, U.S. Geological Survey, Western Ecological Research Center, May 30, 2007, http://www.werc.usgs.gov/otters/ca-surveydata.html (accessed January 29, 2008)

both independent otters and pups. As indicated in Figure 3.8, the populations have been gradually increasing. In the spring of 2007, 3,026 otters were counted (2,637 independent otters and 389 pups).

Nancy Thomas of the U.S. Geological Survey (USGS) reports in *Sea Otter Mortality* (May 2005, http://www.nwhc .usgs.gov/publications/fact_sheets/pdfs/SeaOtter2005.pdf) that the California otter population declined during the late 1990s for a surprising reason. The USGS National Wildlife Health Center found that more than 40% of otter deaths occurring between 1992 and 2002 were the result of parasitic, fungal, or bacterial infections. (See Figure 3.9.) Toxicological analyses indicated that the immune systems of the animals had been damaged by water pollutants, particularly butyltins and organochlorine compounds, such as polychlorinated biphenyls. Butyltins are tin compounds widely used as wood preservatives and as a component of ship paints.

In *Final Revised Recovery Plan for the Southern Sea Otter* (2003, http://ecos.fws.gov/docs/recovery_plans/2003/ 030403.pdf), the USFWS notes that the primary recovery objective is the management of human activities (e.g., oil spills) that can damage or destroy habitat. The USFWS

**FIGURE 3.9**

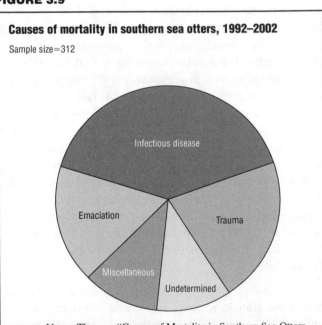

**Causes of mortality in southern sea otters, 1992–2002**

Sample size=312

Infectious disease
Trauma
Emaciation
Miscellaneous
Undetermined

SOURCE: Nancy Thomas, "Causes of Mortality in Southern Sea Otters 1992–2002," in *Sea Otter Mortality*, U.S. Department of the Interior, U.S. Geological Survey, National Wildlife Health Center, May 2005, http://www.nwhc.usgs.gov/publications/fact_sheets/pdfs/SeaOtter2005 .pdf (accessed February 21, 2008)

indicates that southern sea otters can be considered for delisting under the ESA when the average population level over a three-year period exceeds 3,090 animals. As shown in Figure 3.8, population trends through 2007 were encouraging. Absent of any catastrophic events, the southern sea otter could achieve delisting within the next decade.

SOUTHWEST ALASKA DPS. Translocations of northern sea otters to southeast Alaska, British Columbia, and Washington established thriving colonies in those areas. Likewise, populations in south central Alaska are believed to be stable or increasing. However, the stock of sea otters in southwest Alaska has experienced severe decline. In August 2005 the USFWS listed the southwest Alaska DPS of the northern sea otter as threatened under the ESA.

The southwest Alaska DPS extends from the tip of the Aleutian Islands to a point roughly halfway up the coast of Alaska. In the press release "U.S. Fish and Wildlife Service Lists Northern Sea Otters in Southwest Alaska as 'Threatened' under Endangered Species Act" (August 9, 2005, http://alaska.fws.gov/media/seaotter 2004/finalpressrelease.pdf), the USFWS indicates that populations in this area have decreased dramatically since the mid-1980s, when between fifty-five thousand and seventy-four thousand sea otters inhabited southwest Alaska. According to the USFWS, in the fact sheet "Alaska Sea Otters: The Southwest Decline Continues" (February 2004, http://alaska.fws.gov/media/seaotter 2004/factsheet.pdf), surveys conducted in 2003 in the Aleutian Islands found that sea otter counts were down by 63% from 2000. Scientists are not sure of the reasons for the decline; however, there is suspicion that orca whales are preying on the otters.

## Foreign Species of Sea Otters

As of February 2008, five foreign otter species were listed as endangered under the ESA. (See Table 3.1.) They populate areas of Africa and South America. All species are imperiled by illegal hunting for meat and fur. Loss of habitat and water pollution are also threats to their survival. The southern river otter of South America is in dire danger of extinction. The International Union for Conservation of Nature and Natural Resources explains that the species is found in only a handful of isolated areas, all of which are threatened by massive deforestation and expanding fishing operations.

## MANATEES AND DUGONGS

Manatees are large stout mammals that inhabit freshwaters and coastal waterways. They are from the Sirenian order, along with dugongs. There are only five Sirenian species, and all are endangered or extinct. Scientists believe Steller's sea cow, the only species of cold water manatee, was hunted to extinction during the 1700s.

The West Indian manatee, also known as the Florida manatee, primarily swims in the rivers, bays, and estuaries of Florida and surrounding states. As February 2008, this species is listed as endangered under the ESA. (See Table 3.1.)

Manatees are often called "sea cows" and can reach weights of up to 2,000 pounds (907 kg). They swim just below the surface of the water and feed on vegetation. West Indian manatees migrate north in the summer, though generally no farther than the North Carolina coast. In 1995 a manatee nicknamed Chessie made headlines by swimming all the way to Chesapeake Bay. Eventually, biologists, concerned about his health in cooler waters, had him airlifted back to Florida. During the winter many manatees huddle around warm-water discharges from power plants and other industrial facilities. Even though this can keep them warm, scientists worry that overcrowding in small areas makes the animals more susceptible to sickness.

## Imperiled Manatee Populations

Each year during cold weather biologists conduct surveys to determine the number of Florida manatees remaining in the wild. The numbers are estimates based on surveys conducted at known wintering habitats. Elsa Haubold of the Florida Fish and Wildlife Research Institute states in "Manatee Synoptic Surveys" (2008, http://research.myfwc.com/features/view_article.asp?id=15246) that the most recent survey was performed in January to February 2007 and found 2,812 manatees living along the Florida coast. This number is down from 3,113 manatees reported in 2006, but up from 1,267 reported in 1991. Many manatees have scars on their backs from motorboat propellers—these allow individual manatees to be recognized.

## Threats to Manatees

Manatees are imperiled for a variety of reasons. Even though they can live for fifty or sixty years, their birth rate is low. Mature females bear a single offspring only every three to five years. Many baby manatees die in the womb or soon after birth for unknown reasons. These are called perinatal fatalities. Disease, natural pathogens, and cold water temperatures are also deadly. However, motorboat strikes are the major documented cause of manatee mortalities. Manatees are large and swim slowly at the surface of the water. They often cannot move away from boats quickly enough to avoid being hit. Environmentalists have tried to protect manatees from boat collisions, and have successfully had several Florida waterways declared boat-free zones. There are also areas where boaters are required to lower their speeds.

During 1995 and 1996 a pneumonia-like virus killed more than one hundred manatees in southern Florida. John

**FIGURE 3.10**

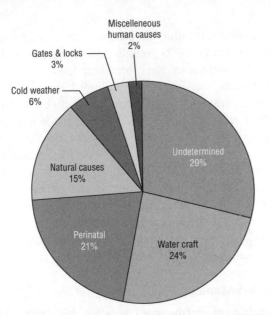

**Causes of mortality in Florida manatees, April 1974–November 2007**

- Miscelleneous human causes 2%
- Gates & locks 3%
- Cold weather 6%
- Natural causes 15%
- Perinatal 21%
- Water craft 24%
- Undetermined 29%

SOURCE: Adapted from "Summary Report by County, Month, Year, and Probable Cause of Death," in *Manatee Mortality Database*, Florida Fish and Wildlife Conservation Commission, Fish and Wildlife Research Institute, 2008, http://research.myfwc.com/manatees/search_summary_results.asp?c=&txt_description1=Watercraft&txt_description2=Gate%2FLock&txt_description3=Human%2C+Other&txt_description4=Perinatal&txt_description5=Cold+stress&txt_description6=Natural&txt_description7=Undetermined&d=&m=&mn1=January%3C&mn2=February%3C&mn3=March%3C&mn4=April%3C&mn5=May%3C&mn6=June%3C&mn7=July%3C&mn8=August%3C&mn9=September%3C&mn10=October%3C&mn11=November%3C&mn12=December%3C&y=&bln_standardOutput=1&btn_submit=Search (accessed January 30, 2008)

H. Paul et al. indicate in "A Filterable Lytic Agent Obtained from a Red Tide Bloom That Caused Lysis of *Karenia brevis* (*Gymnodinum breve*) Cultures" (*Aquatic Microbial Ecology*, vol. 27, no. 1, 2002) that the disease was caused by a red tide that occurred when toxin-producing aquatic organisms called *dinoflagellates* bloomed in large quantities. The Florida Fish and Wildlife Research Institute reported in 2008 that human-related activity—watercraft (24%), gates and locks (3%), and other types of activities (2%)—accounted for 29% of all manatee deaths between April 1974 and November 2007. (See Figure 3.10.) The cause of death could not be determined in 29% of the cases. Non-human causes—perinatal (21%), natural causes (15%), and cold weather (6%)—were blamed for 42% of the deaths.

A lawsuit by the Save the Manatee Club and other environmental and conservation organizations in 2000 successfully required the state to implement new low-speed zones for boats and establish safe-haven areas for manatees. The rules were immediately challenged by individual boaters and boating organizations; however, the restrictions were upheld by Florida courts in 2002.

**Foreign Manatee and Dugong Species**

There are two surviving foreign species of manatees found in western Africa and in and around the Amazon River in South America. Both species are designated under the ESA as endangered and are in grave danger of extinction due to illegal hunting, deforestation, habitat destruction, and water pollution. The only remaining dugongs live in the coastal waters of the Indian Ocean and the Pacific Ocean. Their populations are also considered imperiled. Dugongs around the tiny island of Palau in the western Pacific Ocean are considered endangered under the ESA.

**POLAR BEARS**

Polar bears are the largest of the bear species. They are believed to have evolved from grizzly bears hundreds of thousands of years ago. Polar bears have stocky bodies and weigh up to 700 pounds (320 kg) when fully grown. Their fur includes water-repellent guard hairs and a dense undercoat and is white to pale yellow in color. They have large paddle-like paws that help make them excellent swimmers.

Polar bears are considered a marine mammal, because sea ice is their primary habitat. They are found throughout the arctic and near-arctic regions of the northern hemisphere. There are two stocks in and around Alaska: the Beaufort Sea stock and the Chukchi/Bering Sea stock. (See Figure 3.11.) The bears prefer coastal sea ice and other areas in which water conditions are conducive to providing prey. Seals are their primary food source, particularly ringed seals.

In 2005 the USFWS was petitioned by the Center for Biological Diversity (later joined by the Natural Resources Defense Council and Greenpeace) to list the polar bear as threatened throughout its range. Due to a heavy workload, the agency failed to issue a ninety-day finding to the petition. The organizations sued in the U.S. District Court. In February 2006 the agency issued its ninety-day finding, noting that there was sufficient scientific information to warrant the listing. In January 2007 the polar bear was officially proposed for listing as a threatened species.

In March 2008 the original petitioners filed a lawsuit in the U.S. District Court against the USFWS for failing to make a listing decision in a timely manner. The court ruled in favor of the plaintiffs, forcing the USFWS to make a decision by May 15, 2008. On that date the agency officially published "Endangered and Threatened Wildlife and Plants; Special Rule for the Polar Bear" (*Federal Register*, vol. 73, no. 95), which listed the polar bear as threatened. The USFWS also issued a "special

FIGURE 3.11

**Distribution of polar bears in Alaska, 2004**

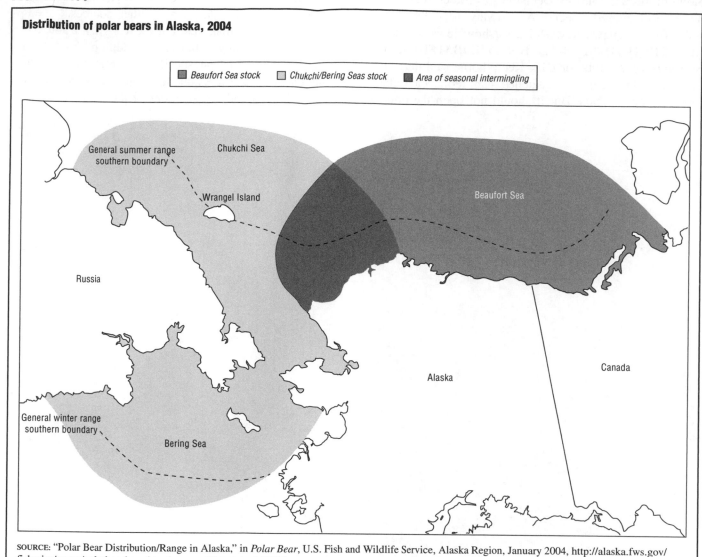

| | | |
|---|---|---|
| ■ Beaufort Sea stock | □ Chukchi/Bering Seas stock | ■ Area of seasonal intermingling |

SOURCE: "Polar Bear Distribution/Range in Alaska," in *Polar Bear*, U.S. Fish and Wildlife Service, Alaska Region, January 2004, http://alaska.fws.gov/fisheries/mmm/polarbear/map.htm (accessed February 4, 2008)

rule" under section 4(d) of the ESA adopting the existing conservation regulatory requirements for polar bears under the MMPA and the Convention on International Trade in Endangered Species of Wild Fauna and Flora. In other words, activities already authorized in these regulations would take precedence over the general prohibitions under U.S. law that apply to threatened species. Such activities include "take," import and export, and shipment in interstate or foreign commerce for commercial purposes.

The polar bear's situation is unique among other endangered and threatened species in the United States, because the principal and most significant threat to its survival is believed to be climate change. The USFWS notes in "Endangered and Threatened Wildlife and Plants; 12-Month Petition Finding and Proposed Rule to List the Polar Bear (Ursus maritimus) as Threatened throughout Its Range" (*Federal Register*, vol. 72, no. 5,

January 9, 2007) that melting and thinning sea ice have already stressed polar bear populations. Computer models indicate these conditions are expected to worsen in the future as temperatures continue to warm. Polar bears have evolved to move on ice. They have special "suckers" on their paws to help them walk on the ice. They are poorly suited to walking on ground and expend a great deal of energy when they are forced to do so, because of a lack of sea ice. In addition, warmer temperatures are degrading the snowy birthing dens of ringed seals, the major prey of the polar bears, and endangering seal pup survival. Thus, both populations face problems due to the warming of their icy ecosystems.

Environmentalists hoped the listing status granted to polar bears would facilitate legal restrictions on oil and gas exploration in Alaska and on U.S. emissions of carbon dioxide (a suspected cause of global warming). However, according to the USFWS press release "Secretary

Kempthorne Announces Decision to Protect Polar Bears under Endangered Species Act" (May 14, 2008, http://www.fws.gov/news/NewsReleases/showNews.cfm?newsId=ECB61DD1-0D74-1D7B-4A67E9B51FB1626B), Secretary of the Interior Dirk Kempthorne said that "listing the polar bear as threatened can reduce avoidable losses of polar bears. But it should not open the door to use of the ESA to regulate greenhouse gas emissions from automobiles, power plants, and other sources." Kempthorne vowed "to make certain the ESA isn't abused to make global warming policies." In addition, the 4(d) rule issued for the polar bear specifically noted that the incidental take of the species due to oil and gas exploration is already allowed under regulations of the MMPA.

# CHAPTER 4
# FISH

Fish are cold-blooded vertebrates with fins. They occur in nearly all permanent water environments, from deep oceans to remote alpine lakes and desert springs. Marine fish inhabit the salty waters of oceans and seas, whereas freshwater fish inhabit inland rivers, lakes, and ponds. Some fish species migrate between fresh and marine waters. These include species called anadromous fish that are born in freshwater, migrate to the ocean to spend their adulthood, and then return to freshwater to spawn.

Fish are the most diverse vertebrate group on the planet and include thousands of different species. The largest known fish are the whale sharks, which can grow to be more than 50 feet (15.2 m) long and weigh several tons. At the other end of the spectrum is *Paedocypris progenetica*, a tiny fish discovered in Sumatra, Indonesia, that is less than one-third of an inch (0.8 cm) in length.

FishBase (http://filaman.ifm-geomar.de/home.htm) is a comprehensive online database of scientific information about fish. It was developed by the WorldFish Center of Malaysia in collaboration with the United Nations Food and Agriculture Organization and is supported by many government and research institutions. As of April 2008, FishBase (http://filaman.ifm-geomar.de/search.php) contained information on 30,200 fish species around the world. Scientists report that only a small fraction of these species have been assessed for their conservation status.

As of February 2008, the U.S. Fish and Wildlife Service (USFWS) listed a total of 139 endangered and threatened fish species in the United States. (See Table 1.2 in Chapter 1.) In *Federal and State Endangered and Threatened Species Expenditures: Fiscal Year 2006* (draft, 2008), the USFWS indicates that more than $500 million was spent under the Endangered Species Act (ESA) during fiscal year (FY) 2006 on imperiled fish.

## GENERAL THREATS TO FISH

Fish species have become endangered and threatened in the United States for a variety of reasons, both natural and anthropogenic (caused by humans). Most fish are not imperiled by a single threat to their survival, but by multiple threats that combine to produce daunting challenges to recovery. Some scientists believe that natural threats, such as disease, have been aggravated by human actions that stress fish populations. Dams and other structures used for power generation, flood control, irrigation, and navigation have dramatically changed water flow patterns in many rivers. These impediments disrupt migration patterns and affect water temperature and quality. Likewise, the dredging of river and stream beds to produce channels and the filling of wetlands and swamps have changed water habitats.

### The Problem with Dams

Dams affect rivers, the lands abutting them, the water bodies they join, and aquatic wildlife throughout the United States. Water flow is reduced or stopped altogether downstream of dams, altering aquatic habitats and drying wetlands. Arthur C. Benke and Colbert E. Cushing, the editors of *Rivers of North America* (2005), note that it is difficult to find any river in the United States that has not been dammed or channeled. According to Benke and Cushing, "All human alterations of rivers, regardless of whether they provide services such as power or drinking water supply, result in degradation."

The U.S. Army Corps of Engineers maintains the National Inventory of Dams (NID; http://crunch.tec.army .mil/nidpublic/webpages/nid.cfm). As of April 2008, the inventory included approximately seventy-nine thousand dams throughout the country. To be included in this inventory, dams have be at least 6 feet (21.8 m) tall or hold back a minimum of fifteen acre-feet (nearly five million gallons [19 million L]) of water. Dams are built

## FIGURE 4.1

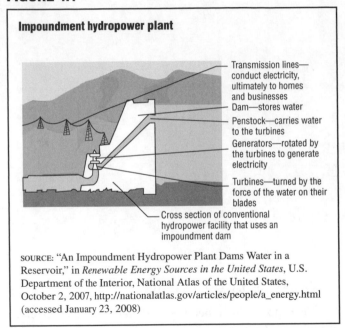

**Impoundment hydropower plant**

Transmission lines—conduct electricity, ultimately to homes and businesses

Dam—stores water

Penstock—carries water to the turbines

Generators—rotated by the turbines to generate electricity

Turbines—turned by the force of the water on their blades

Cross section of conventional hydropower facility that uses an impoundment dam

SOURCE: "An Impoundment Hydropower Plant Dams Water in a Reservoir," in *Renewable Energy Sources in the United States*, U.S. Department of the Interior, National Atlas of the United States, October 2, 2007, http://nationalatlas.gov/articles/people/a_energy.html (accessed January 23, 2008)

for a variety of purposes. The most frequent purposes listed in the NID are recreation, fire protection, stock or small farm pond creation, flood control, and storm water management.

Even though only a small percentage of dams listed with the NID produce hydroelectric power, these dams tend to be the largest in size and affect large watersheds. Figure 4.1 shows the components of a typical impoundment dam producing hydroelectric power. These structures provide many challenges to aquatic species, besides impeding water flow and migration paths. Turbines operate like massive underwater fans. Passage through running turbine blades can result in the death of many small aquatic creatures unable to escape their path. Some modern hydroelectric dams include stairlike structures called fish ladders that provide migrating fish a watery path to climb up and over the dams.

SNAIL DARTERS. The snail darter, a small fish species related to perch, was at the center of a dam-building controversy during the 1970s. The USFWS listed the snail darter as endangered in 1975. At the time it was believed to exist only in the Little Tennessee River, and this area was designated as critical habitat for the species. That same year, the Tellico Dam was near completion on the Little Tennessee River, and the filling of the Tellico Reservoir would have destroyed the entire habitat of the snail darter. A lawsuit was filed to prevent this from happening. The case went all the way to the U.S. Supreme Court, which ruled in 1978 that under the ESA species protection must take priority over economic and developmental concerns. One month after this court decision, Congress amended the ESA to allow for exemptions under certain circumstances.

In late 1979 the Tellico Dam received an exemption and the Tellico Reservoir was filled. The snail darter is now extinct in that habitat. However, snail darter populations were later discovered in other river systems. In addition, the species has been introduced into several other habitats. Because of an increase in numbers, the snail darter was reclassified as threatened in 1984.

### Entrainment and Impingement

Entrainment occurs when fish are pulled or diverted away from their natural habitat by mechanical equipment or other nonnatural structures in water bodies. A prime example is a freshwater intake structure in a river or lake. Small fish, in particular, are susceptible to being sucked into pipes through which water is being pumped out of a water body. Even if the pipe end is screened, the force of the suction can impinge (crush) fish against the screen, causing serious harm. In a more general sense entrainment refers to diversions that occur when fish accidentally feed through artificial water structures, such as gates, locks, or dams, and cannot return to their original location.

### Excessive Sediment

Many river and stream banks and adjacent lands have been stripped of vegetation by timber harvesting, crop growing, and excessive grazing of livestock. This eliminates habitat for insects and other tiny creatures that serve as foodstuff for fish. It also aggravates erosion problems and allows large amounts of dirt to enter into water bodies. Once in the water, this dirt is known as silt or sediment. Most of these particles settle to the bottom. However, sediment is easily stirred up by the movement of fish and other aquatic creatures, many of which spawn or lay eggs at the bed of their habitat. The dirt that remains in suspension in the water is said to make water turbid. The measure of the dirtiness (lack of clarity) of a water body is called its turbidity.

Freshwater aquatic creatures are sensitive to turbidity levels and choose their habitats based in part on their sediment preferences. Some fish prefer waters with large amounts of sediment. It provides cover that prevents predator fish from seeing them. Other species prefer clean waters with low turbidity levels. Excessive sediment may clog their gills or smother their eggs. (See Figure 4.2.)

Forestry and agricultural practices can drastically affect the sediment levels in a water system through the deforestation of banks and nearby lands. Excessive grazing of livestock along riverbanks can strip vegetation and permit large amounts of dirt to enter the water. Likewise, timber harvesting and crop production can expose loosened dirt to wind and rain that carry it into water bodies. Dams and diversion structures trap sediments behind

**FIGURE 4.2**

**Effects of siltation on aquatic life**

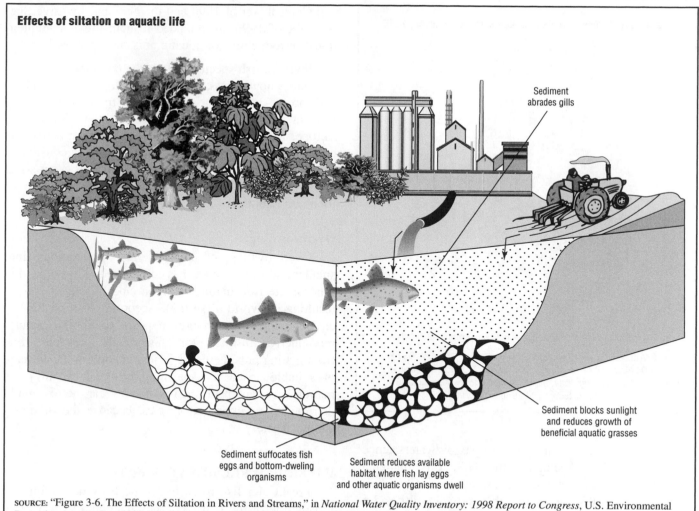

SOURCE: "Figure 3-6. The Effects of Siltation in Rivers and Streams," in *National Water Quality Inventory: 1998 Report to Congress*, U.S. Environmental Protection Agency, June 2000, http://www.epa.gov/305b/98report/chap3.pdf (accessed January 23, 2008)

them, interrupting the natural downstream flow of sediments that takes place in moving waters.

## Chemical and Biological Pollutants

Water pollution poses a considerable threat to many aquatic species. Industrial pollution introduces metal and organic chemicals to water bodies. In agricultural areas there is runoff of manure, fertilizers, and pesticides. U.S. pesticide use in the 1960s centered around chlorine-containing organic compounds, such as dichlorodiphenyltrichloroethane (DDT) and chlordane. Scientists eventually learned that these chemicals are extremely persistent in the environment and have damaging effects on wildlife, particularly fish and bird species. DDT was banned in the United States in 1972, and chlordane in 1983; however, nearly four decades later both pesticides continue to show up in water, sediment, and fish samples.

In general, aquatic creatures are not killed outright by water contamination. A major exception is an oil spill, which can kill many creatures through direct contact. The more widespread and common threat is overall degrada-

tion of water quality and habitats due to pollutants. Exposure to contaminants can weaken the immune systems of aquatic animals and make them more susceptible to disease and to other health and reproductive problems.

Bioaccumulative contaminants are those that accumulate in the tissues of aquatic organisms at much higher concentrations than are found in the water body itself. This biomagnification effect occurs with mercury (a metal), the pesticides DDT and chlordane, and dioxins. Dioxins are a category of several hundred chlorinated organic compounds. Polychlorinated biphenyls (PCBs) are dioxins that were widely used to cool and lubricate electrical equipment before a 1977 ban on their manufacture. Bioaccumulative contaminants are a particular concern for fishes at the higher end of the aquatic food chain, such as salmon and large freshwater species.

**TOXIC POLLUTANT ADVISORIES.** The states issue advisories to protect residents from the adverse health risk of eating fish contaminated with certain pollutants. In the fact sheet *2005/2006 National Listing of Fish*

FIGURE 4.3

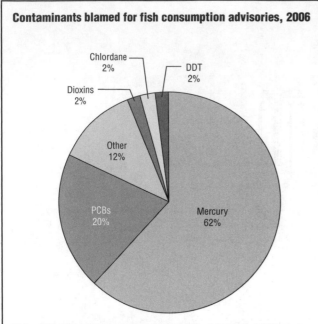

**Contaminants blamed for fish consumption advisories, 2006**

Note: DDT=Dichlorodiphenyltrichloroethane; PCB=Polychlorinated Biphenyls.

SOURCE: Adapted from "Bioaccumulative Pollutants," in *EPA Fact Sheet: 2005/2006 National Listing of Fish Advisories*, U.S. Environmental Protection Agency, July 2007, http://www.epa.gov/waterscience/fish/advisories/2006/tech.pdf (accessed February 15, 2008)

*Advisories* (July 2007, http://www.epa.gov/waterscience/fish/advisories/2006/tech.pdf), the U.S. Environmental Protection Agency states that 3,852 advisories had been issued during 2006. Nearly two-thirds (62%) of the advisories were issued due to mercury contamination. (See Figure 4.3.) PCBs accounted for another 20% of the advisories. Dioxins, chlordane, and DDT each accounted for 2% of the total. All of these chemicals are bioaccumulative. Other contaminants, primarily pesticides and heavy metals, comprised the remaining 12% of the total.

Even though the purpose of fish advisories is to protect human health, the underlying data illustrate that toxic pollutants pose a worrisome threat to the nation's fish species.

**Unwelcome Guests: Aquatic Invasive Species**

Invasive species can be domestic or foreign. Some aquatic invasive species have been introduced purposely to U.S. water bodies, for example, to improve sport and recreational fishing. Others have been introduced unintentionally. The primary source of these aquatic invasive species has traditionally been ship ballast water, which is generally picked up in one location and released in another. Invasive species are also established through transfer from recreational boating vessels, dumping of live bait, release of aquarium species, and accidental escapes from research facilities and aquaculture pens.

The Nonindigenous Aquatic Nuisance Prevention and Control Act of 1990 and the National Invasive Species Act of 1996 are intended to help prevent unintentional introductions of aquatic nuisance species.

Invasive fish species include the common carp, bluegill, largemouth bass, smallmouth bass, shad, walleye, and brook trout. The common carp was purposely brought to the United States during the 1800s from Europe. It thrived so well that it soon spread across the country. In the twenty-first century the fish is considered a pest. Like many large nonnative fish, it preys on small imperiled fish and competes against native species for food and habitat.

**Overcrowding**

Overcrowding of stressed fish populations into smaller and smaller areas has contributed to hybridization (uncharacteristic mating between closely related species resulting in hybrid offspring). According to the USFWS, environmental degradation appears to inhibit natural reproductive instincts that historically prevented fish from mating outside their species. In addition, a shortage of suitable space for spawning has resulted in more mating between species. Cross-mating can be extremely detrimental to imperiled species, because the offspring can be sterile.

**IMPERILED FRESHWATER FISH**

Freshwater fish listed under the ESA fall within the jurisdiction of the USFWS. They include a wide variety of species and are found all over the country. Stephen J. Walsh, Noel M. Burkhead, and James D. Williams estimate in "Southeastern Freshwater Fishes" (Edward T. Laroe et al., eds., *Our Living Resources: A Report to the Nation on the Distribution, Abundance, and Health of U.S. Plants, Animals, and Ecosystems*, 1995) that the United States contains approximately eight hundred native freshwater species. Even though most of these species are found in the eastern part of the country, the highest percentages of imperiled fish species are in the western states. According to Walsh, Burkhead, and Williams, this is because aquatic ecosystems in the western United States, particularly in the Southwest, have high rates of endemism (i.e., species found there are particular to that location).

As of February 2008, there were 107 freshwater fish species listed as endangered (66 species) or threatened (41 species) under the ESA. (See Table 4.1.) Most of the species have recovery plans in place. In general, imperiled freshwater fish are small in size and associated with flowing (lotic) waters, such as rivers and streams, rather than still (lentic) waters, such as lakes and ponds. Nearly half of the listed freshwater fish fall into four species groups: darters, chubs, daces, and shiners.

**TABLE 4.1**

**Endangered and threatened freshwater fish species, February 2008**

| Common name | Scientific name | Listing status[a] | Recovery plan date | Recovery plan stage[b] |
|---|---|---|---|---|
| Alabama cavefish | *Speoplatyrhinus poulsoni* | E | 10/25/1990 | RF(2) |
| Alabama sturgeon | *Scaphirhynchus suttkusi* | E | None | — |
| Amber darter | *Percina antesella* | E | 6/20/1986 | F |
| Apache trout | *Oncorhynchus apache* | T | 7/27/2007 | RD(2) |
| Arkansas River shiner | *Notropis girardi* | T | None | — |
| Ash Meadows Amargosa pupfish | *Cyprinodon nevadensis mionectes* | E | 9/28/1990 | F |
| Ash Meadows speckled dace | *Rhinichthys osculus nevadensis* | E | 9/28/1990 | F |
| Bayou darter | *Etheostoma rubrum* | T | 7/10/1990 | RF(1) |
| Beautiful shiner | *Cyprinella formosa* | T | 3/29/1995 | F |
| Big Bend gambusia | *Gambusia gaigei* | E | 9/19/1984 | F |
| Big Spring spinedace | *Lepidomeda mollispinis pratensis* | T | 1/20/1994 | F |
| Blackside dace | *Phoxinus cumberlandensis* | T | 8/17/1988 | F |
| Blue shiner | *Cyprinella caerulea* | T | 8/30/1995 | F |
| Bluemask (=jewel) darter | *Etheostoma sp.* | E | 7/25/1997 | F |
| Bonytail chub | *Gila elegans* | E | 9/9/2002 | RF(2) |
| Borax Lake chub | *Gila boraxobius* | E | 2/4/1987 | F |
| Boulder darter | *Etheostoma wapiti* | E;XN | 7/27/1989 | F |
| Bull trout | *Salvelinus confluentus* | T | Various | D |
| Cahaba shiner | *Notropis cahabae* | E | 4/23/1992 | F |
| Cape Fear shiner | *Notropis mekistocholas* | E | 10/7/1988 | F |
| Cherokee darter | *Etheostoma scotti* | T | 11/17/2000 | F |
| Chihuahua chub | *Gila nigrescens* | T | 4/14/1986 | F |
| Clear Creek gambusia | *Gambusia heterochir* | E | 1/14/1982 | F |
| Clover Valley speckled dace | *Rhinichthys osculus oligoporus* | E | 5/12/1998 | F |
| Colorado pikeminnow (=squawfish) | *Ptychocheilus lucius* | E;XN | 8/28/2002 | RF(2) |
| Comanche Springs pupfish | *Cyprinodon elegans* | E | 9/2/1981 | F |
| Conasauga logperch | *Percina jenkinsi* | E | 6/20/1986 | F |
| Cui-ui | *Chasmistes cujus* | E | 5/15/1992 | RF(2) |
| Delta smelt | *Hypomesus transpacificus* | T | 11/26/1996 | F |
| Desert dace | *Eremichthys acros* | T | 5/27/1997 | F |
| Desert pupfish | *Cyprinodon macularius* | E | 12/8/1993 | F |
| Devils Hole pupfish | *Cyprinodon diabolis* | E | 9/28/1990 | F |
| Devils River minnow | *Dionda diaboli* | T | 9/13/2005 | F |
| Duskytail darter | *Etheostoma percnurum* | E;XN | 3/30/1994 | F |
| Etowah darter | *Etheostoma etowahae* | E | 11/17/2000 | F |
| Foskett speckled dace | *Rhinichthys osculus ssp.* | T | 4/27/1998 | F |
| Fountain darter | *Etheostoma fonticola* | E | 2/14/1996 | RF(1) |
| Gila chub | *Gila intermedia* | E | None | — |
| Gila topminnow (incl. Yaqui) | *Poeciliopsis occidentalis* | E | 3/5/1999 | RD(1) |
| Gila trout | *Oncorhynchus gilae* | T | 9/10/2003 | RF(3) |
| Goldline darter | *Percina aurolineata* | T | 11/17/2000 | F |
| Greenback cutthroat trout | *Oncorhynchus clarki stomias* | T | 3/1/1998 | RF(2) |
| Hiko White River springfish | *Crenichthys baileyi grandis* | E | 5/26/1998 | F |
| Humpback chub | *Gila cypha* | E | 9/19/1990 | RF(2) |
| Hutton tui chub | *Gila bicolor ssp.* | T | 4/27/1998 | F |
| Independence Valley speckled dace | *Rhinichthys osculus lethoporus* | E | 5/12/1998 | F |
| June sucker | *Chasmistes liorus* | E | 6/25/1999 | F |
| Kendall Warm Springs dace | *Rhinichthys osculus thermalis* | E | 7/12/1982 | F |
| Lahontan cutthroat trout | *Oncorhynchus clarki henshawi* | T | 1/30/1995 | F |
| Leon Springs pupfish | *Cyprinodon bovinus* | E | 8/14/1985 | F |
| Leopard darter | *Percina pantherina* | T | 5/3/1993 | RD(1) |
| Little Colorado spinedace | *Lepidomeda vittata* | T | 1/9/1998 | F |
| Little Kern golden trout | *Oncorhynchus aguabonita whitei* | T | Exempt | — |
| Loach minnow | *Tiaroga cobitis* | T | 9/30/1991 | F |
| Lost River sucker | *Deltistes luxatus* | E | 3/17/1993 | F |
| Maryland darter | *Etheostoma sellare* | E | 2/2/1982 | F |
| Moapa dace | *Moapa coriacea* | E | 5/16/1996 | RF(1) |
| Modoc sucker | *Catostomus microps* | E | Exempt | — |
| Mohave tui chub | *Gila bicolor mohavensis* | E | 9/12/1984 | F |
| Neosho madtom | *Noturus placidus* | T | 9/30/1991 | F |
| Niangua darter | *Etheostoma nianguae* | T | 7/17/1989 | F |
| Okaloosa darter | *Etheostoma okaloosae* | E | 4/7/1997 | RF(1) |
| Oregon chub | *Oregonichthys crameri* | E | 9/3/1998 | F |
| Owens pupfish | *Cyprinodon radiosus* | E | 9/30/1998 | F |
| Owens tui chub | *Gila bicolor snyderi* | E | 9/30/1998 | F |
| Ozark cavefish | *Amblyopsis rosae* | T | 12/17/1986 | F |
| Pahranagat roundtail chub | *Gila robusta jordani* | E | 5/26/1998 | F |
| Pahrump poolfish | *Empetrichthys latos* | E | 3/17/1980 | F |
| Paiute cutthroat trout | *Oncorhynchus clarki seleniris* | T | 9/10/2004 | RF(1) |
| Palezone shiner | *Notropis albizonatus* | E | 7/7/1997 | F |
| Pallid sturgeon | *Scaphirhynchus albus* | E | 11/7/1993 | F |
| Pecos bluntnose shiner | *Notropis simus pecosensis* | T | 9/30/1992 | F |

| Common name | Scientific name | Listing status[a] | Recovery plan date | Recovery plan stage[b] |
|---|---|---|---|---|
| Pecos gambusia | *Gambusia nobilis* | E | 5/9/1985 | F |
| Pygmy madtom | *Noturus stanauli* | E;XN | 9/27/1994 | F |
| Pygmy sculpin | *Cottus paulus (=pygmaeus)* | T | 8/6/1991 | F |
| Railroad Valley springfish | *Crenichthys nevadae* | T | 3/15/1997 | F |
| Razorback sucker | *Xyrauchen texanus* | E | 8/28/2002 | RF(1) |
| Relict darter | *Etheostoma chienense* | E | 7/31/1994 | D |
| Rio Grande silvery minnow | *Hybognathus amarus* | E | 1/18/2007 | F |
| Roanoke logperch | *Percina rex* | E | 3/20/1992 | F |
| San Marcos gambusia | *Gambusia georgei* | E | 2/14/1996 | RF(1) |
| Santa Ana sucker | *Catostomus santaanae* | T | None | — |
| Scioto madtom | *Noturus trautmani* | E | Exempt | — |
| Shortnose sucker | *Chasmistes brevirostris* | E | 3/17/1993 | F |
| Slackwater darter | *Etheostoma boschungi* | T | 3/8/1984 | F |
| Slender chub | *Erimystax cahni* | T;XN | 7/29/1983 | F |
| Smoky madtom | *Noturus baileyi* | E;XN | 8/9/1985 | F |
| Snail darter | *Percina tanasi* | T | 5/5/1983 | F |
| Sonora chub | *Gila ditaenia* | T | 9/30/1992 | F |
| Spikedace | *Meda fulgida* | T | 9/30/1991 | F |
| Spotfin chub | *Erimonax monachus* | T;XN | 11/21/1983 | F |
| Tidewater goby | *Eucyclogobius newberryi* | E | 12/7/2005 | F |
| Topeka shiner | *Notropis topeka (=tristis)* | E | None | — |
| Unarmored threespine stickleback | *Gasterosteus aculeatus williamsoni* | E | 12/26/1985 | RF(1) |
| Vermilion darter | *Etheostoma chermocki* | E | 8/6/2007 | D |
| Virgin River chub | *Gila seminuda (=robusta)* | E | 4/19/1995 | RF(2) |
| Waccamaw silverside | *Menidia extensa* | T | 8/11/1993 | F |
| Warm Springs pupfish | *Cyprinodon nevadensis pectoralis* | E | 9/28/1990 | F |
| Warner sucker | *Catostomus warnerensis* | T | 4/27/1998 | F |
| Watercress darter | *Etheostoma nuchale* | E | 3/29/1993 | RF(2) |
| White River spinedace | *Lepidomeda albivallis* | E | 3/28/1994 | F |
| White River springfish | *Crenichthys baileyi baileyi* | E | 5/26/1998 | F |
| White sturgeon | *Acipenser transmontanus* | E | 9/30/1999 | F |
| Woundfin | *Plagopterus argentissimus* | E;XN | 4/19/1995 | RF(2) |
| Yaqui catfish | *Ictalurus pricei* | T | 3/29/1995 | F |
| Yaqui chub | *Gila purpurea* | E | 3/29/1995 | F |
| Yellowfin madtom | *Noturus flavipinnis* | T;XN | 6/23/1983 | F |

[a]E = Endangered; T = Threatened; XN = Experimental Population, Non-Essential.
[b]F = Final; D = Draft; RF = Final RevisioN.

SOURCE: Adapted from "Listed FWS/Joint FWS and NMFS Species and Populations with Recovery Plans (Sorted by Listed Entity)" and "Listed U.S. Species by Taxonomic Group," in *USFWS Threatened and Endangered Species System (TESS)*, U.S. Department of the Interior, U.S. Fish and Wildlife Service, February 4, 2008, http://ecos.fws.gov/tess_public/SpeciesRecovery.do?sort=1 and http://ecos.fws.gov/tess_public/SpeciesReport.do?kingdom=V&listing Type=L (accessed February 4, 2008)

Table 4.2 shows the ten freshwater species with the highest expenditures under the ESA during FY 2006. Nearly $62.8 million was spent on only two of the fish: pallid sturgeon ($38.9 million) and bull trout ($23.9 million).

## Pallid Sturgeon

The pallid sturgeon is a unique and rare freshwater fish that is sometimes called the "swimming dinosaur." It is descended from fishes that were common more than fifty million years ago. The pallid sturgeon has a long flat snout and a slender body that ends with a pronounced tail fin. (See Figure 4.4.) Adults range in size from 3 to 5 feet (1 to 1.5 m) and typically weigh 25 to 50 pounds (11.3 to 22.7 kg). The fish is a bottom-feeder and prefers large rivers of relatively warm free-flowing water with high turbidity (high mud content).

Historically, the pallid sturgeon was found throughout the Mississippi and Missouri river systems from Montana and North Dakota south to the Gulf of Mexico.

**TABLE 4.2**

**Freshwater fish species with the highest expenditures under the Endangered Species Act, fiscal year 2006**

| Ranking | Species | Expenditure |
|---|---|---|
| 1 | Pallid sturgeon | $38,892,982 |
| 2 | Bull trout (lower 48 states) | $23,863,886 |
| 3 | Razorback sucker | $10,540,595 |
| 4 | Rio Grande silvery minnow | $9,701,954 |
| 5 | Colorado pikeminnow (=squawfish) | $9,670,160 |
| 6 | White sturgeon (ID and MT) | $9,113,933 |
| 7 | Humpback chub | $7,410,806 |
| 8 | Bonytail chub | $5,733,982 |
| 9 | Lost River sucker | $3,958,514 |
| 10 | Shortnose sucker | $3,755,014 |

SOURCE: Adapted from "Table 2. Species Ranked in Descending Order of Total FY 2006 Reported Expenditures, Not Including Land Acquisition Costs," in *Federal and State Endangered and Threatened Species Expenditures: Fiscal Year 2006*, U.S. Department of the Interior, U.S. Fish and Wildlife Service, draft, 2008

In the early 1900s specimens as large as 85 pounds (38.5 kg) and 6 feet (1.8 m) long were reported. Over the next

**FIGURE 4.4**

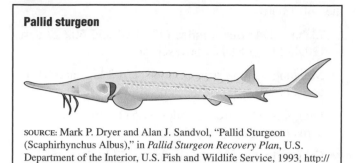

**Pallid sturgeon**

SOURCE: Mark P. Dryer and Alan J. Sandvol, "Pallid Sturgeon (Scaphirhynchus Albus)," in *Pallid Sturgeon Recovery Plan*, U.S. Department of the Interior, U.S. Fish and Wildlife Service, 1993, http://ecos.fws.gov/docs/recovery_plans/1993/931107.pdf (accessed January 30, 2008)

**FIGURE 4.5**

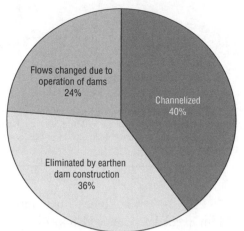

**Consequences of Missouri River alterations on pallid sturgeon habitat**

Flows changed due to operation of dams 24%

Channelized 40%

Eliminated by earthen dam construction 36%

SOURCE: Adapted from Mark P. Dryer and Alan J. Sandvol, "Habitat Loss," in *Pallid Sturgeon Recovery Plan*, U.S. Department of the Interior, U.S. Fish and Wildlife Service, 1993, http://ecos.fws.gov/docs/recovery_plans/1993/931107.pdf (accessed February 21, 2008)

century the fish virtually disappeared. In 1990 it was listed as endangered under the ESA. Three years later the USFWS published *Pallid Sturgeon Recovery Plan* (1993, http://ecos.fws.gov/docs/recovery_plans/1993/931107.pdf). The agency blames human destruction and modification of habitat as the primary cause for the pallid sturgeon's decline.

Figure 4.5 shows the consequences of human alteration on the main stem of the Missouri River, one of the last known habitats of the fish. Forty percent of the river has been channelized (reconfigured to flow in a restricted path). Another 36% has been removed from contention due to the construction of earthen dams during the early decades of the 1900s. The last 24% of river habitat has experienced changes in water flows due to dam operations. The middle portion of the Mississippi River has also been extensively channelized and diked to prevent flooding and improve barge navigation.

Pallid sturgeons are believed to be extremely sensitive to changes in the velocity and volume of river flows. They are nearly blind and forage along muddy river bottoms feeding on tiny fish and other creatures that prefer turbid waters. Dams and channelization have reduced the erosion of riverbank soil into the Missouri and Mississippi rivers. This has given other fish species with better eyesight an advantage over the pallid sturgeon at finding small prey. In addition, mating between the pallid sturgeon and the shovelnose sturgeon in the lower Mississippi River has produced a population of hybrid sturgeon that is thriving compared to their imperiled parents.

All of these factors combine to provide a bleak outlook for the future of the pallid sturgeon. The USFWS recovery plan notes that "it is unlikely that successfully reproducing populations of pallid sturgeon can be recovered without restoring the habitat elements (morphology, hydrology, temperature regime, cover, and sediment/organic matter transport) of the Missouri and Mississippi Rivers necessary for the species continued survival."

In the press release "U.S. Fish and Wildlife Service Stocks Endangered Pallid Sturgeons in Missouri River"

(September 2, 2005, http://mountain-prairie.fws.gov/PRESSREL/05-62.htm), the USFWS reports that since 1994 over one hundred thousand pallid sturgeons have been bred in captivity and placed in river waters in Montana, North Dakota, Nebraska, Iowa, Kansas, Missouri, and Louisiana. The fish are spawned and reared at the agency's Gavins Point National Fish Hatchery near Yankton, South Dakota. This is the only hatchery in the nation engaged in breeding the pallid sturgeon. During 2004 the facility underwent a major construction program that included the addition of new specially designed tanks for the endangered fish. Despite the success of the breeding operation, the USFWS notes that "this stocking effort alone will not recover the species." Habitat improvement is the only step that biologists believe will save the pallid sturgeon from extinction.

The USFWS examines in *5-Year Review: Summary and Evaluation* (June 13, 2007, http://ecos.fws.gov/docs/five_year_review/doc1059.pdf) the scientific and commercial data that have become available since the species was listed as endangered in 1990. The agency concludes that the pallid sturgeon should remain listed as endangered with a recovery priority number of 2c. The USFWS ranks recovery priority on a scale from 1 to 18 with lower numbers indicating higher priority. The "c" designation means that recovery of this species is in conflict with economic activities in its region.

**Bull Trout**

Bull trout are relatively large fish that live in streams, lakes, and rivers. They can grow to weigh more than 20

## FIGURE 4.6

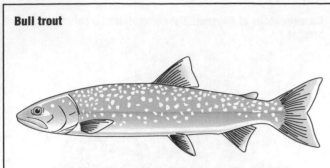

**Bull trout**

pounds (9.1 kg); however, those that inhabit small streams seldom exceed 4 pounds (1.8 kg) in weight. Bull trout are members of the char subgroup of the salmon family (Salmonidae). (See Figure 4.6.) Their backs are dark in color (green to brown) with small light-colored spots (crimson to yellow), and their undersides are pale. The fish prefer cold and clean inland waters in the Northwest.

Historically, bull trout were found throughout much of the northwestern United States and as far north as Alaska. Large populations have disappeared from major rivers, leaving mostly isolated pockets of smaller-sized fish in headwater streams. A variety of factors have contributed to the decline of the bull trout. The species is extremely sensitive to changes in water temperature and purity. Its survival is threatened by water pollution, degraded habitat, and dams and other diversion structures. In addition, the introduction of a nonnative game fish called brook trout has been devastating. The two species are able to mate, but produce mostly sterile offspring—a genetic dead-end for the imperiled bull trout.

The legal history of the bull trout is extensive. In 1992 three environmental groups petitioned the USFWS to list the fish as an endangered species under the ESA. In 1993 the agency concluded that listing for the species was warranted, but low in priority. This set off a long series of court battles that culminated in 1999 when all bull trout in the coterminous United States (the lower forty-eight states) were listed as threatened under the ESA. In 2001 two of the original petitioners (Alliance for the Wild Rockies and Friends of the Wild Swan) filed a lawsuit against the USFWS for failing to designate critical habitat for the bull trout. A settlement was reached in 2002. According to the press release "U.S. Fish and Wildlife Service Designates Critical Habitat for Bull Trout" (September 23, 2005, http://www.fws.gov/news/NewsReleases/showNews.cfm?newsId=F0E6823C-65BF-03E7-21348B612A1081D7), in September 2005

the USFWS designated the following critical habitat for the bull trout:

- Idaho—294 stream miles (473 km) and 50,627 acres (20,488 ha) of lakes or reservoirs

- Montana—1,058 stream miles (1,703 km) and 31,916 acres (12,916 ha) of lakes or reservoirs

- Oregon—939 stream miles (1,511 km) and 27,322 acres (11,057 ha) of lakes or reservoirs

- Oregon/Idaho—17 stream miles (27 km)

- Washington—1,519 stream miles (2,445 km), 33,353 acres (13,497 ha) of lakes or reservoirs, and 985 miles (1,585 km) of marine shoreline

**RECOVERY PLANS FOR FRESHWATER FISH.** As of February 2008, there were recovery plans for more than one hundred populations of listed freshwater fish populations. (See Table 4.1.) Most of the plans have been finalized. Details of the plans can be found in "Listed FWS/Joint FWS and NMFS Species and Populations with Recovery Plans" (2008, http://ecos.fws.gov/tess_public/TESSWebpageRecovery?sort=1).

## IMPERILED MARINE AND ANADROMOUS FISH

Marine and anadromous fish primarily inhabit salty waters. As of February 2008, there were ten such species listed under the ESA. (See Table 4.3.) They are under the jurisdiction of the National Marine Fisheries Service (NMFS). All of the species migrate between freshwater and the sea at various times. The smalltooth sawfish and shortnose sturgeon prefer coastal marine and estuarine waters—that is, areas where saltwater and freshwater meet. Their current distribution is in the eastern United States. The gulf sturgeon migrates between river and coastal seawaters in the Southeast. The North American green sturgeon is anadromous. It inhabits Pacific Coast waters. Five other imperiled anadromous species are found in the Pacific northwest:

- Chinook Salmon

- Chum Salmon

- Coho Salmon

- Sockeye Salmon

- Steelhead

In addition, there is an endangered species of Atlantic salmon that inhabits the Gulf of Maine.

Approximately $399.2 million was spent under the ESA on marine and anadromous fish in FY 2006. Expenditures are broken down by species in Table 4.4. Note that the North American green sturgeon was not listed under the ESA until 2007.

TABLE 4.3

**Endangered and threatened anadromous fish species, February 2008**

| Common name | Scientific name | Listing status* | Recovery plan date | Recovery plan stage |
|---|---|---|---|---|
| Atlantic salmon | Salmo salar | E | 4/7/2006 | Final |
| Chinook salmon | Oncorhynchus (=salmo) tshawytscha | E;T | None | — |
| Chum salmon | Oncorhynchus (=salmo) keta | T | None | — |
| Coho salmon | Oncorhynchus (=salmo) kisutch | E;T | None | — |
| Gulf sturgeon | Acipenser oxyrinchus desotoi | T | 9/22/1995 | Final |
| North American green sturgeon | Acipenser medirostris | T | None | — |
| Shortnose sturgeon | Acipenser brevirostrum | E | None | — |
| Sockeye salmon | Oncorhynchus (=salmo) nerka | E;T | None | — |
| Smalltooth sawfish | Pristis pectinata | E | None | — |
| Steelhead | Oncorhynchus (=salmo) mykiss | E;T | None | — |

*E = Endangered; T = Threatened.

SOURCE: Adapted from "Listed FWS/Joint FWS and NMFS Species and Populations with Recovery Plans (Sorted by Listed Entity)" and "Listed U.S. Species by Taxonomic Group," in *USFWS Threatened and Endangered Species System (TESS)*, U.S. Department of the Interior, U.S. Fish and Wildlife Service, February 4, 2008, http://ecos.fws.gov/tess_public/SpeciesRecovery.do?sort=1 and http://ecos.fws.gov/tess_public/SpeciesReport.do?kingdom=V&listingType=L (accessed February 4, 2008)

## Pacific Salmonids

Pacific salmonids are found in waters of the northwestern United States and belong to the genus *Oncorhynchus*. There are five species of Pacific salmon: chinook, chum, coho, pink, and sockeye. All but the pink salmon are listed under the ESA as endangered and/or threatened and accounted for over $264 million in spending under the ESA in FY 2006. (See Table 4.4.)

Chinook salmon are the largest of the Pacific salmonids, averaging about 25 pounds (11.3 kg) in adulthood. (See Figure 4.7.) They spend two to seven years in the ocean and travel up to 2,500 miles (4,025 km) from their home streams. Coho, sockeye, and chum salmon adults average approximately 10 to 12 pounds (4.5 to 5.4 kg).

**PERILS OF MIGRATION.** Pacific salmon pose unique protection challenges because they are anadromous. Salmon eggs (or roe) are laid in the bottom gravel of cold freshwater streams, where they incubate for five to ten weeks. Each egg ranges in size from 0.25 to 0.5 inches (0.6 to 1.3 cm) in size, depending on species. The eggs hatch to release baby fish (or alevin) that are called fry as they mature. Once a fry reaches about 3 inches (7.6 cm) in length, it is called a fingerling. This typically takes less than a year.

At some point during their first two years the young salmon (now called smolts) migrate downstream to the ocean. There they spend several months or years of their adulthood. When they reach sexual maturity, males and females journey back to the streams where they were born to mate and deposit eggs. This is called spawning. Pacific salmon make the roundtrip only once. They expend all their energy swimming back upstream and die soon after the eggs are laid and fertilized. Their upstream habitats can be hundreds and even thousands of miles away from their ocean habitats. It is a long and dangerous journey both ways.

**TABLE 4.4**

**Marine and anadromous fish species with the highest expenditures under the Endangered Species Act, fiscal year 2006**

| Ranking | Species | Expenditure |
|---|---|---|
| 1 | Chinook salmon | $188,999,257 |
| 2 | Steelhead | $130,606,467 |
| 3 | Coho salmon | $35,141,511 |
| 4 | Sockeye salmon | $22,485,620 |
| 5 | Chum salmon | $11,713,091 |
| 6 | Atlantic salmon | $6,177,575 |
| 7 | Shortnose sturgeon | $2,067,906 |
| 8 | Gulf sturgeon | $1,385,841 |
| 9 | Smalltooth sawfish | $638,744 |

SOURCE: Adapted from "Table 2. Species Ranked in Descending Order of Total FY 2006 Reported Expenditures, Not Including Land Acquisition Costs," in *Federal and State Endangered and Threatened Species Expenditures: Fiscal Year 2006*, U.S. Department of the Interior, U.S. Fish and Wildlife Service, draft, 2008

Predator fish and birds eat salmon fry, fingerlings, and smolts as they make their way to the ocean. Bears, birds, marine mammals, and humans prey on the adult fish as they migrate upstream. Waterfalls, rapids, dams, and other water diversions pose tremendous obstacles to Pacific salmon as they try to travel across long distances.

**STOCKS.** Salmon heading to the same general location travel upstream in groups called stocks (or runs). Stocks migrate at different times of the year, depending on geographical and genetic factors. Figure 4.8 illustrates the life cycle of a stock that migrates upstream from late summer through early fall. During its lifetime a Pacific salmon is exposed to three different water environments: freshwater streams and rivers, estuaries (areas where freshwater and saltwater meet), and the ocean.

**DECLINING POPULATIONS.** Daniel L. Bottom et al. estimate in *Salmon at River's End: The Role of the Estuary in the Decline and Recovery of Columbia River*

FIGURE 4.7

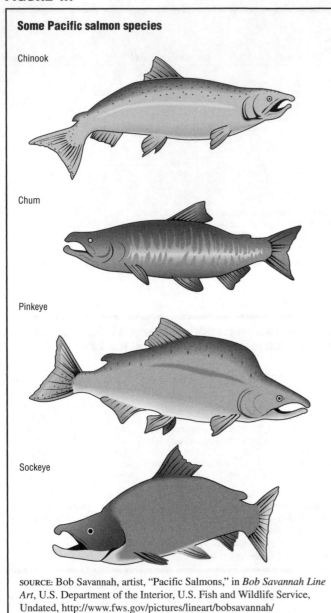

**Some Pacific salmon species**

Chinook

Chum

Pinkeye

Sockeye

SOURCE: Bob Savannah, artist, "Pacific Salmons," in *Bob Savannah Line Art*, U.S. Department of the Interior, U.S. Fish and Wildlife Service, Undated, http://www.fws.gov/pictures/lineart/bobsavannah/ pacificsalmons.html (accessed January 30, 2008)

*Salmon* (August 2005, http://www.nwfsc.noaa.gov/assets/ 25/6294_09302005_153156_SARETM68Final.pdf) that between eleven million and sixteen million salmon per year migrated upstream in waters of the northwestern United States before the arrival of European settlers. Extensive fishing and canning operations quickly decimated the salmon population. As early as 1893 federal officials warned that the future of salmon fisheries had a "disastrous outlook." During the 1890s hatcheries began operating and stocking rivers and streams with "farm-raised" salmon. Over the next century salmon populations were further stressed as natural river flows were dramatically altered with dams, navigational structures, and irrigation systems. Figure 4.9 shows the distribution of salmon hatcheries and dams in the Columbia River basin of the Pacific Northwest. As of 2003 there were twenty-three major dams on mainstream rivers in the basin, more than three hundred smaller dams on tributaries, and over eighty hatcheries.

Endangered and threatened salmon are identified by their water of origin and, in most cases, by their upstream migration season. In 1990 the winter-run stock of Chinook salmon from the Sacramento River was designated as threatened under the ESA, the first Pacific salmon to be listed. It was reclassified to endangered four years later. During the 1990s and early 2000s the NMFS identified thirty-five Evolutionarily Significant Units (ESUs) of Pacific salmonids. As of February 2008, seventeen of them were listed as endangered or threatened. (See Table 4.5.) Two ESUs are "species of concern," meaning that the agency has some concerns regarding threats to these species, but lacks sufficient information indicating the need to list them under the ESA.

According to the press release "'Fishery Failure' Declared for West Coast Salmon Fishery" (http://www .nmfs.noaa.gov/mediacenter/docs/disaster_declaration_2008 _FINAL.pdf), the National Oceanic and Atmospheric Administration announced on May 1, 2008, the closing or severely limiting of recreational and commercial salmon fishing along the West Coast due to "a commercial fishery failure." NOAA explained that in previous years hundreds of thousands of Chinook salmon returned to the Sacramento River to spawn, but that in 2008 only sixty thousand salmon were estimated to return to the river. Jim Balsiger of the NMFS said, "This is far below what is needed to sustain the population and we have decided to shut down the commercial ocean salmon fishery for all of California and most of Oregon to aid their recovery. It's a tough decision, but the condition of the salmon fishery forces us to close most of it to ensure healthy runs of this valuable fish in the future."

**THREATS TO SURVIVAL.** Biologists blame four main threats (sometimes called the "four H's") for the imperiled state of Pacific salmonids:

- Habitat degradation—channelization, dredging, water withdrawals for irrigation, wetland losses, and diking have changed river, stream, and estuary environments.

- Harvesting levels—overfishing for more than a century has decimated salmon populations.

- Hydropower—impassable dams have rendered some historical habitat unreachable by salmon. Most modern dams have fish ladders, stepping-stone waterfalls that allow salmon a path up and over the dams. However, all dams affect water temperature, flow, and quality.

- Hatcheries—biologists fear that hatchery releases overburden estuaries with too many competing fish at the same time.

**FIGURE 4.8**

**Life cycle of Pacific salmon**

Ecological context

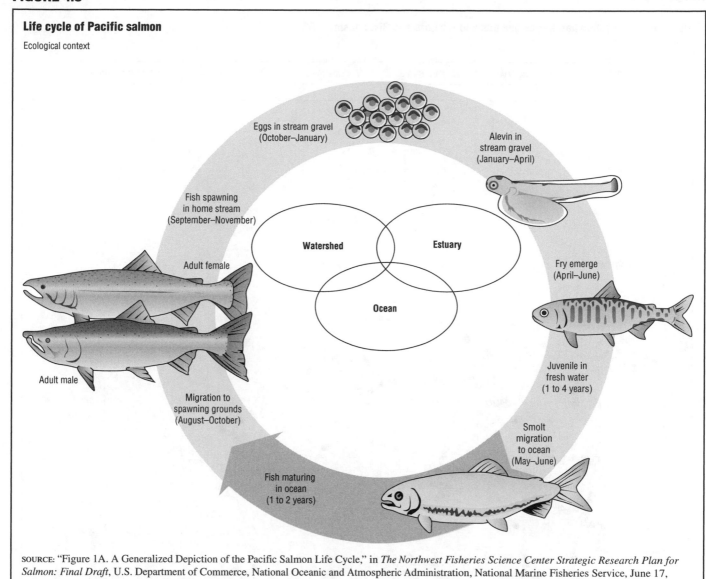

SOURCE: "Figure 1A. A Generalized Depiction of the Pacific Salmon Life Cycle," in *The Northwest Fisheries Science Center Strategic Research Plan for Salmon: Final Draft*, U.S. Department of Commerce, National Oceanic and Atmospheric Administration, National Marine Fisheries Service, June 17, 2004, http://www.nwfsc.noaa.gov/publications/researchplans/salmon_research_plan6.17.04%20.pdf (accessed January 30, 2008)

Besides these threats, scientists believe climate change and the presence of nonnative aquatic species are detrimental to salmon populations.

Scientists are increasingly learning of the importance of estuaries to juvenile salmon in the Pacific Northwest. Juvenile salmon pass through estuaries on their downstream trip to the ocean. Before excessive damming of the Columbia River system, spring and summer floods (called freshets) spread juvenile salmon throughout the estuaries into various marshes and natural channels. From there the salmon would make their way to the sea. Flow regulation has dramatically changed the river flows in this area and limited the amount of estuary habitat available to the salmon. Before damming, river flows were highly variable on a seasonal basis, reflecting the natural effects of melting snows and heavy spring rains. Damming the river dampened these seasonal changes and virtually eliminated freshets from occurring. This result has been beneficial for residents and farmers living along the river, but detrimental to the habitat of the Pacific salmon.

**THE KLAMATH BASIN CONTROVERSY.** The Klamath Basin in southern Oregon and northern California is the site of a heated battle pitting farmers against a coalition of fishermen and environmentalists who wish to protect three listed species: coho salmon, shortnose sucker fish, and Lost River sucker fish. Opponents are battling over water, which is needed for irrigation purposes by farmers in the area.

The Klamath River once supported the third-largest salmon run in the country. However, in recent years, water diversion has caused river water levels to be too low to maintain healthy stream conditions and temperatures.

**FIGURE 4.9**

**Distribution of salmon hatcheries and dams in the Columbia River basin, 2003**

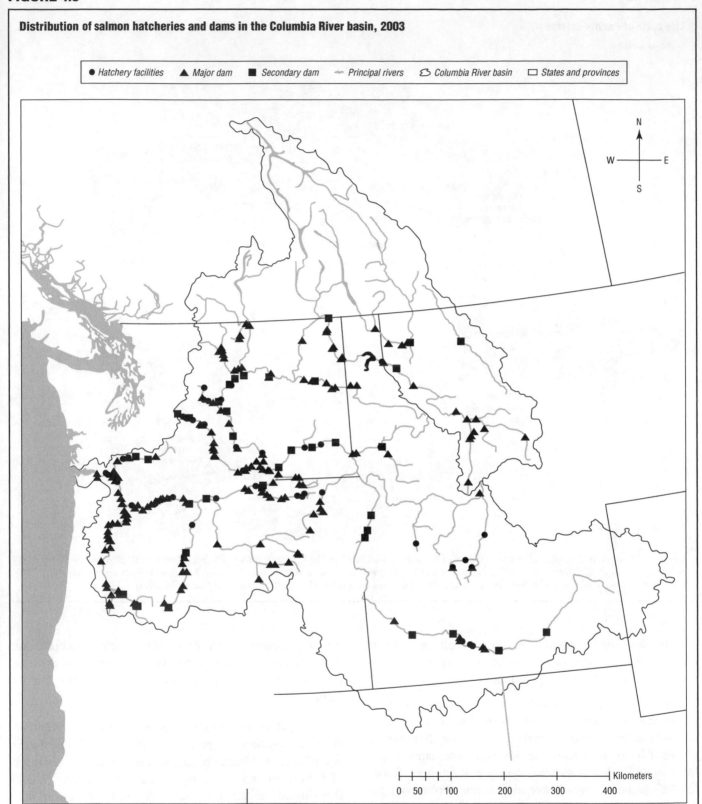

SOURCE: D.L. Bottom et al., "Figure 6. Present Distribution of Salmon Hatcheries and Mainstem and Secondary Dams (StreamNet 2003) along Rivers and Streams of the Columbia River Basin," in *Salmon at River's End: The Role of the Estuary in the Decline and Recovery of Columbia River Salmon*, U.S. Department of Commerce, National Oceanic and Atmospheric Administration, National Marine Fisheries Service, Northwest Fisheries Science Center, 2005, http://www.nwfsc.noaa.gov/assets/25/6294_09302005_153156_SARETM68Final.pdf (accessed February 21, 2008)

**TABLE 4.5**

**Listing status of West Coast salmon populations, February 2008**

| | | Species* | Current Endangered Species Act (ESA) listing status | ESA listing actions under review |
|---|---|---|---|---|
| Sockeye salmon | 1 | Snake River | Endangered | |
| (*Oncorhynchus nerka*) | 2 | Ozette Lake | Threatened | |
| | 3 | Baker River | Not warranted | |
| | 4 | Okanogan River | Not warranted | |
| | 5 | Lake Wenatchee | Not warranted | |
| | 6 | Quinalt Lake | Not warranted | |
| | 7 | Lake Pleasant | Not warranted | |
| Chinook salmon | 8 | Sacramento River Winter-run | Endangered | |
| (*O. tshawytscha*) | 9 | Upper Columbia River Spring-run | Endangered | |
| | 10 | Snake River Spring/Summer-run | Threatened | |
| | 11 | Snake River Fall-run | Threatened | |
| | 12 | Puget Sound | Threatened | |
| | 13 | Lower Columbia River | Threatened | |
| | 14 | Upper Willamette River | Threatened | |
| | 15 | Central Valley Spring-run | Threatened | |
| | 16 | California Coastal | Threatened | |
| | 17 | Central Valley Fall and late Fall-run | Species of concern | |
| | 18 | Upper Klamath-Trinity Rivers | Not warranted | |
| | 19 | Oregon Coast | Not warranted | |
| | 20 | Washington Coast | Not warranted | |
| | 21 | Middle Columbia River Spring-run | Not warranted | |
| | 22 | Upper Columbia River Summer/Fall-run | Not warranted | |
| | 23 | Southern Oregon and Northern California Coast | Not warranted | |
| | 24 | Deschutes River Summer/Fall-run | Not warranted | |
| Coho salmon | 25 | Central California Coast | Endangered | |
| (*O. kisutch*) | 26 | Southern Oregon/Northern California | Threatened | |
| | 27 | Lower Columbia River | Threatened | Critical habitat |
| | 28 | Oregon Coast | Threatened | |
| | 29 | Southwest Washington | Undetermined | |
| | 30 | Puget Sound/Strait of Georgia | Species of concern | |
| Chum salmon | 31 | Olympic Peninsula | Not warranted | |
| (*O. keta*) | 32 | Hood Canal Summer-run | Threatened | |
| | 33 | Columbia River | Threatened | |
| | 34 | Puget Sound/Strait of Georgia | Not warranted | |
| | 35 | Pacific Coast | Not warranted | |

*The ESA defines a "species" to include any distinct population segment of any species of vertebrate fish or wildlife. For Pacific salmon, the National Oceanic and Atmospheric Administration (NOAA) considers an evolutionarily significant unit (ESU), a "species" under the ESA.

SOURCE: Adapted from "Endangered Species Act Status of West Coast Salmon & Steelhead," in *ESA Salmon Listings*, U.S. Department of Commerce, National Oceanic and Atmospheric Administration, National Marine Fisheries Service, February 4, 2008, http://www.nwr.noaa.gov/ESA-Salmon-Listings/upload/snapshot0208.pdf (accessed February 15, 2008).

Over seven thousand fishing jobs have been lost due to salmon declines. Water diversion practices also violate agreements with Native American tribes to avoid harming healthy salmon runs. Over the years many of the wetlands in the Klamath Basin have been drained for agricultural purposes; however, there are still scattered wetlands and lakes throughout the area. This habitat supports the short-nose sucker and the Lost River sucker, which were listed as endangered in their entire ranges in California and Oregon in 1988.

A lawsuit regarding the distribution of Klamath Basin waters was brought against the U.S. Bureau of Reclamation (BOR) by the Pacific Coast Federation of Fishermen's Associations, the Klamath Forest Alliance, the Institute for Fisheries Resources, the Oregon Natural Resources Council, and other groups. The plaintiffs argued that the BOR had met farmers' demands for water but left Klamath River flows much lower than required for survival of the coho salmon, the shortnose suckerfish,

and the Lost River suckerfish. Furthermore, the BOR was charged with violating the ESA by not consulting with the NMFS regarding endangered species conservation. Farmers were also accused of wasting water.

In April 2001 the BOR was found by a federal district court to have knowingly violated the ESA when it allowed delivery of irrigation water required to maintain habitat of the three listed species. As a result of the court decision, federal agencies cut water to irrigation canals to preserve water levels in the Upper Klamath Lake for the two species of suckerfish and to increase water flow in the Klamath River for coho salmon. In April 2002 a lawsuit was filed on behalf of the farmers to remove all three species from the Endangered Species List. Water flow was an issue again in 2002. After a federal judge decided not to force the BOR to provide water for the listed species in 2002, there was a massive fish kill involving approximately thirty-three thousand salmon.

Between 2000 and 2002 the BOR developed many operating plans for water flows in the Klamath Basin; however, these plans were continually challenged in court. In 2002 the agency issued a ten-year plan designed to achieve full protection for the river's salmon by 2012. A long court battle over the plan culminated in March 2006 when a federal judge ruled that the plan had to be implemented immediately. The judge noted that salmon water requirements must outweigh the needs of farmers for irrigation water. Because a wet winter had produced large flows in the Klamath River, no immediate effects of the ruling on irrigation supply were anticipated.

Meanwhile, a separate legal battle has waged over efforts by PacifiCorp—an Oregon-based utility company—to renew federal licenses for a series of dams it owns on the Klamath River. In 2006 federal regulators ruled that PacifiCorp must install costly fish ladders across its dams to help imperiled salmon populations in the river. The decision was upheld in 2007 following legal challenges by the utility company. An Environmental Impact Statement released in November 2007 by the Federal Energy Regulatory Commission (a federal agency that oversees power companies) noted that removing the dams would be less expensive for PacifiCorp than building the fish ladders.

In January 2008 a two-year collaborative effort between dozens of stakeholders—federal, state, and local government agencies; irrigation districts; property owners; Native American tribes; and private conservation organizations—resulted in a proposed Klamath Basin Restoration Agreement (KBRA; http://www.edsheets.com/Klamathdocs.html). The KBRA seeks to restore thriving fish populations in the river and satisfy local needs for irrigation water and power generation. It calls on PacifiCorp to remove four of its dams from the Klamath River. As of April 2008, PacifiCorp was not a party to the KBRA and had not decided on the dam removal proposal.

## Steelhead

Steelhead are members of the *Oncorhynchus* genus and have the scientific name *Oncorhynchus mykiss*. Freshwater steelhead are called rainbow trout. Anadromous steelhead are also trout, but they are associated with salmon due to similarities in habitat and behavior. Steelhead are found in the Pacific Northwest and are anadromous like salmon with two major differences: steelhead migrate individually, rather than in groups, and can spawn many times, not just once.

As of February 2008, the NMFS had identified fifteen distinct population segments (DPSs) of steelhead. (See Table 4.6.) Eleven of these DPSs are listed under the ESA as endangered or threatened. In addition,

**TABLE 4.6**

**Listing status of West Coast steelhead populations, February 2008**

| Species* | | Current Endangered Species Act (ESA) listing status | ESA listing actions under review |
|---|---|---|---|
| Steelhead (O. mykiss) | Southern California | Endangered | |
| | Upper Columbia River | Endangered | |
| | Central California Coast | Threatened | |
| | South Central California Coast | Threatened | |
| | Snake River Basin | Threatened | |
| | Lower Columbia River | Threatened | |
| | California Central Valley | Threatened | |
| | Upper Willamette River | Threatened | |
| | Middle Columbia River | Threatened | |
| | Northern California | Threatened | |
| | Oregon Coast | Species of concern | |
| | Southwest Washington | Not warranted | |
| | Olympic Peninsula | Not warranted | |
| | Puget Sound | Threatened | Critical habitat Protective regulations |
| | Klamath Mountains Province | Not warranted | |

*The ESA defines a "species" to include any distinct population segment of any species of vertebrate fish or wildlife. For Pacific steelhead, the National Oceanic and Atmospheric Administration (NOAA) has delineated distinct population segments for consideration as "species" under the ESA.

SOURCE: Adapted from "Endangered Species Act Status of West Coast Salmon & Steelhead," in *ESA Salmon Listings*, U.S. Department of Commerce, National Oceanic and Atmospheric Administration, National Marine Fisheries Service, February 4, 2008, http://www.nwr.noaa.gov/ESA-Salmon-Listings/upload/snapshot0208.pdf (accessed February 15, 2008)

there is one DPS classified as a "species of concern." The USFWS indicates that $130.6 million was spent on steelhead under the ESA during FY 2006. (See Table 4.4.)

Steelhead face the same threats as Pacific salmon: habitat loss and alteration, overharvesting, dams and other water obstacles, and competition with hatchery fish.

### Recovery Plans for Marine and Anadromous Fish

The NMFS has published several recovery plans, including *Gulf Sturgeon Recovery/Management Plan* (September 1995, http://www.nmfs.noaa.gov/pr/pdfs/recovery/sturgeon_gulf.pdf) and *Final Recovery Plan for the Gulf of Maine Distinct Population Segment of Atlantic Salmon* (November 2005, http://www.nmfs.noaa.gov/pr/pdfs/recovery/salmon_atlantic.pdf). Copies of the other recovery plans are available at the NMFS Web site: http://www.nmfs.noaa.gov/pr/recovery/plans.htm.

### Imperiled Fish around the World

The International Union for Conservation of Nature and Natural Resources (IUCN) listed 1,201 species of fish as threatened in *2007 Red List of Threatened Species* (2007, http://www.iucnredlist.org/), less than half

TABLE 4.7

**Foreign endangered and threatened fish species, February 2008**

| Common name | Scientific name | Listing status* | Foreign range | U.S. and/or foreign listed |
|---|---|---|---|---|
| Ala balik (trout) | Salmo platycephalus | E | Turkey | Foreign |
| Asian bonytongue | Scleropages formosus | E | Thailand, Indonesia, Malaysia | Foreign |
| Ayumodoki (loach) | Hymenophysa curta | E | Japan | Foreign |
| Beautiful shiner | Cyprinella formosa | T | Mexico | US/foreign |
| Beluga sturgeon | Huso huso | T | Black Sea, Caspian Sea, Adriatic Sea and Sea of Azov | Foreign |
| Catfish | Pangasius sanitwongsei | E | Thailand | Foreign |
| Chihuahua chub | Gila nigrescens | T | Mexico | US/foreign |
| Cicek (minnow) | Acanthorutilus handlirschi | E | Turkey | Foreign |
| Desert pupfish | Cyprinodon macularius | E | Mexico | US/foreign |
| Devils River minnow | Dionda diaboli | T | Mexico | US/foreign |
| Gila chub | Gila intermedia | E | Mexico | US/foreign |
| Ikan temoleh (minnow) | Probarbus jullieni | E | Thailand, Cambodia, Vietnam, Malaysia, Laos | Foreign |
| Loach minnow | Tiaroga cobitis | T | Mexico | US/foreign |
| Mexican blindcat (catfish) | Prietella phreatophila | E | Mexico | Foreign |
| Miyako tango (=Toyko bitterling) | Tanakia tanago | E | Japan | Foreign |
| Nekogigi (catfish) | Coreobagrus ichikawai | E | Japan | Foreign |
| North American green sturgeon | Acipenser medirostris | T | Canada | US/foreign |
| Razorback sucker | Xyrauchen texanus | E | Mexico | US/foreign |
| Rio Grande silvery minnow | Hybognathus amarus | E | Mexico | US/foreign |
| Sonora chub | Gila ditaenia | T | Mexico | US/foreign |
| Spikedace | Meda fulgida | T | Mexico | US/foreign |
| Thailand giant catfish | Pangasianodon gigas | E | Thailand | Foreign |
| Totoaba (seatrout or weakfish) | Cynoscion macdonaldi | E | Mexico | Foreign |
| White sturgeon | Acipenser transmontanus | E | Canada | US/foreign |
| Yaqui catfish | Ictalurus pricei | T | Mexico | US/foreign |
| Yaqui chub | Gila purpurea | E | Mexico | US/foreign |

*E=Endangered; T=Threatened.

SOURCE: Adapted from "Listed FWS/Joint FWS and NMFS Species and Populations with Recovery Plans (Sorted by Listed Entity)" and "Listed U.S. Species by Taxonomic Group," in *USFWS Threatened and Endangered Species System (TESS)*, U.S. Department of the Interior, U.S. Fish and Wildlife Service, February 5, 2008, http://ecos.fws.gov/tess_public/SpeciesRecovery.do?sort=1 and http://ecos.fws.gov/tess_public/SpeciesReport.do?kingdom=V&listing Type=L (accessed February 5, 2008)

of the 3,119 species evaluated. However, the IUCN notes that there are approximately thirty thousand known fish species. It is expected that many more fish species will be listed in the future as more evaluations are completed.

As of February 2008, the USFWS listed twenty-six foreign species of fish as endangered or threatened (See Table 4.7.) Fourteen of the species are found both in the United States and in other countries. The remaining twelve species are foreign only.

# CHAPTER 5
# CLAMS, SNAILS, CRUSTACEANS, AND CORALS

## CLAMS, SNAILS, AND CRUSTACEANS

Clams, snails, and crustaceans are small aquatic creatures. They are invertebrates, meaning they lack an internal skeleton made of bone or cartilage. Clams and snails are in the phylum Mollusca. Mollusks have soft bodies usually enclosed in a thin hard shell made of calcium. The U.S. Fish and Wildlife Service (USFWS) uses the generic term *clam* to refer to clams and mussels, but there are physical and reproductive differences between the two creatures. In general, mussels are larger than clams and have an oblong lopsided shell, as opposed to the round symmetrical shell of the clam.

Crustaceans are a large class of creatures with a hard exoskeleton (external skeleton), appendages, and antennae. This class includes lobsters, shrimps, and crabs.

As of February 2008, there were 170 species of clams (including mussels), snails, and crustaceans listed under the Endangered Species Act (ESA) as endangered or threatened. (See Table 1.2 in Chapter 1.) The most imperiled are snails (75 U.S. species and 1 foreign species). As of February 2008, there were seventy U.S. species of snails and two foreign species listed under the ESA. (See Table 5.1 for a list of the U.S. species.) Listed crustaceans include twenty-two U.S. species. (See Table 5.2.) Table 5.3 shows the ten clam, snail, and crustacean entities with the highest expenditures under the ESA during fiscal year (FY) 2006.

## FRESHWATER MUSSELS IN THE UNITED STATES

The vast majority of imperiled clams and mussels in the United States are freshwater species that inhabit inland rivers, primarily in the Southeast.

Mussels are bivalved (two-shelled) creatures encased in hard hinged shells made of calcium. The freshwater species can grow to be up to six inches (15 cm) in length. The United States, with nearly three hundred species, has the greatest diversity of freshwater mussels in the world. According to the U.S. Geological Survey (USGS), in "Conservation of Southeastern Mussels" (December 26, 2007, http://cars.er.usgs.gov/Southeastern_Aquatic_Fauna/Freshwater_Mussels/freshwater_mussels.html), approximately 90% of these creatures live in southeastern states. Most of them are found burrowed into the sand and gravel beds of rivers and streams making up the Mississippi River system. Mussels have a foot-like appendage that acts like an anchor to hold them in place. They can use this appendage to move themselves slowly over small distances. Mussels tend to congregate in large groups called colonies.

Mussels are filter-feeders. They have a siphoning system that sucks in food and oxygen from the water. Their gills can filter impurities out of the water. Thus, mussels are tiny natural water purifiers.

Most mussel species have a unique way of spreading their offspring. A female mussel can produce several thousand eggs in a year. After the eggs are fertilized, they develop into larva and are released. The larva latch onto the fins or gills of passing fish and they stay there until they have grown into baby clams. At that point they turn loose of the fish and drop to the river bottom. The larvae are called glochidia. It is believed that glochidia are harmless to the fish on which they hitchhike. This parasitic relationship allows mussels to spread and distribute beyond their usual range.

### Mussel Declines

The decline of freshwater mussels began in the 1800s. Many of the creatures have an interior shell surface with a pearl-like sheen. These pearlymussels were in great demand as a source of buttons for clothing until the invention of plastic. Collectors also killed many mussels by prying them open looking for pearls. Until the 1990s mussel shells were ground up and used in the oyster pearl industry. Another cause for decline has been habitat disturbance, especially water pollution and the modification of aquatic habitats by dams. The invasive zebra mussel has also harmed native freshwater mussel species, such as

**TABLE 5.1**

**Endangered and threatened clam species, February 2008**

| Common name | Scientific name | Listing status[a] | Recovery plan date | Recovery plan stage[b] |
|---|---|---|---|---|
| Alabama (=inflated) heelsplitter | *Potamilus inflatus* | T | 4/13/1993 | F |
| Alabama lampmussel | *Lampsilis virescens* | E;XN | 7/2/1985 | F |
| Alabama moccasinshell | *Medionidus acutissimus* | T | 11/17/2000 | F |
| Appalachian elktoe | *Alasmidonta raveneliana* | E | 8/26/1996 | F |
| Appalachian monkeyface (pearlymussel) | *Quadrula sparsa* | E;XN | 7/9/1984 | F |
| Arkansas fatmucket | *Lampsilis powelli* | T | 2/10/1992 | F |
| Birdwing pearlymussel | *Conradilla caelata* | E;XN | 7/9/1984 | F |
| Black clubshell | *Pleurobema curtum* | E | 11/14/1989 | F |
| Carolina heelsplitter | *Lasmigona decorata* | E | 1/17/1997 | F |
| Catspaw (=purple cat's paw pearlymussel) | *Epioblasma obliquata obliquata* | E;XN | 3/10/1992 | F |
| Chipola slabshell | *Elliptio chipolaensis* | T | 9/30/2003 | F |
| Clubshell | *Pleurobema clava* | E;XN | 9/21/1994 | F |
| Coosa moccasinshell | *Medionidus parvulus* | E | 11/17/2000 | F |
| Cracking pearlymussel | *Hemistena lata* | E;XN | 7/11/1991 | F |
| Cumberland bean (pearlymussel) | *Villosa trabalis* | E;XN | 8/22/1984 | F |
| Cumberland elktoe | *Alasmidonta atropurpurea* | E | 5/24/2004 | F |
| Cumberland monkeyface (pearlymussel) | *Quadrula intermedia* | E;XN | 7/9/1984 | F |
| Cumberland pigtoe | *Pleurobema gibberum* | E | 8/13/1992 | F |
| Cumberlandian combshell | *Epioblasma brevidens* | E;XN | 5/24/2004 | F |
| Curtis pearlymussel | *Epioblasma florentina curtisii* | E | 2/4/1986 | F |
| Dark pigtoe | *Pleurobema furvum* | E | 11/17/2000 | F |
| Dromedary pearlymussel | *Dromus dromas* | E;XN | 7/9/1984 | F |
| Dwarf wedgemussel | *Alasmidonta heterodon* | E | 2/8/1993 | F |
| Fanshell | *Cyprogenia stegaria* | E;XN | 7/9/1991 | F |
| Fat pocketbook | *Potamilus capax* | E | 11/14/1989 | RF(1) |
| Fat three-ridge (mussel) | *Amblema neislerii* | E | 9/30/2003 | F |
| Finelined pocketbook | *Lampsilis altilis* | T | 11/17/2000 | F |
| Finerayed pigtoe | *Fusconaia cuneolus* | E;XN | 9/19/1984 | F |
| Flat pigtoe | *Pleurobema marshalli* | E | 11/14/1989 | F |
| Green blossom (pearlymussel) | *Epioblasma torulosa gubernaculum* | E | 7/9/1984 | F |
| Gulf moccasinshell | *Medionidus penicillatus* | E | 9/30/2003 | F |
| Heavy pigtoe | *Pleurobema taitianum* | E | 11/14/1989 | F |
| Higgins eye (pearlymussel) | *Lampsilis higginsii* | E | 7/14/2004 | RF(1) |
| James spinymussel | *Pleurobema collina* | E | 9/24/1990 | F |
| Littlewing pearlymussel | *Pegias fabula* | E | 9/22/1989 | F |
| Louisiana pearlshell | *Margaritifera hembeli* | T | 12/3/1990 | F |
| Northern riffleshell | *Epioblasma torulosa rangiana* | E | 9/21/1994 | F |
| Ochlockonee moccasinshell | *Medionidus simpsonianus* | E | 9/30/2003 | F |
| Orangefoot pimpleback (pearlymussel) | *Plethobasus cooperianus* | E;XN | 9/30/1984 | F |
| Orangenacre mucket | *Lampsilis perovalis* | T | 11/17/2000 | F |
| Ouachita rock pocketbook | *Arkansia wheeleri* | E | 6/2/2004 | F |
| Oval pigtoe | *Pleurobema pyriforme* | E | 9/30/2003 | F |
| Ovate clubshell | *Pleurobema perovatum* | E | 11/17/2000 | F |
| Oyster mussel | *Epioblasma capsaeformis* | E;XN | 5/24/2004 | F |
| Pale lilliput (pearlymussel) | *Toxolasma cylindrellus* | E | 8/22/1984 | F |
| Pink mucket (pearlymussel) | *Lampsilis abrupta* | E | 1/24/1985 | F |
| Purple bankclimber (mussel) | *Elliptoideus sloatianus* | T | 9/30/2003 | F |
| Purple bean | *Villosa perpurpurea* | E | 5/24/2004 | F |
| Ring pink (mussel) | *Obovaria retusa* | E;XN | 3/25/1991 | F |
| Rough pigtoe | *Pleurobema plenum* | E;XN | 8/6/1984 | F |
| Rough rabbitsfoot | *Quadrula cylindrica strigillata* | E | 5/24/2004 | F |
| Scaleshell mussel | *Leptodea leptodon* | E | 8/6/2004 | D |
| Shiny pigtoe | *Fusconaia cor* | E;XN | 7/9/1984 | F |
| Shinyrayed pocketbook | *Lampsilis subangulata* | E | 9/30/2003 | F |
| Southern acornshell | *Epioblasma othcaloogensis* | E | 11/17/2000 | F |
| Southern clubshell | *Pleurobema decisum* | E | 11/17/2000 | F |
| Southern combshell | *Epioblasma penita* | E | 11/14/1989 | F |
| Southern pigtoe | *Pleurobema georgianum* | E | 11/17/2000 | F |
| Speckled pocketbook | *Lampsilis streckeri* | E | 1/2/1992 | F |
| Stirrupshell | *Quadrula stapes* | E | 11/14/1989 | F |
| Tan riffleshell | *Epioblasma florentina walkeri (=E. walkeri)* | E | 10/22/1984 | F |

the Higgins' eye pearlymussel, by competing with them for food and other resources.

## Higgins' Eye Pearlymussel

Higgins' eye is a species of freshwater pearlymussel native to the United States. These mussels are found in the waters of Iowa, Illinois, Minnesota, Missouri, Nebraska, and Wisconsin. The species was named after its discoverer, Frank Higgins, who found some of the mussels in the Mississippi River near Muscatine, Iowa, during the mid-1800s. Over the next few decades Muscatine developed a thriving pearl-button industry that lasted into the 1940s. Higgins' eye was also harvested for the commercial pearl industry.

## TABLE 5.1

### Endangered and threatened clam species, February 2008 [CONTINUED]

| Common name | Scientific name | Listing status[a] | Recovery plan date | Recovery plan stage[b] |
|---|---|---|---|---|
| Tar River spinymussel | Elliptio steinstansana | E | 5/5/1992 | RF(1) |
| Triangular kidneyshell | Ptychobranchus greenii | E | 11/17/2000 | F |
| Tubercled blossom (pearlymussel) | Epioblasma torulosa torulosa | E;XN | 1/25/1985 | F |
| Turgid blossom (pearlymussel) | Epioblasma turgidula | E;XN | 1/25/1985 | F |
| Upland combshell | Epioblasma metastriata | E | 11/17/2000 | F |
| White catspaw (pearlymussel) | Epioblasma obliquata perobliqua | E | 1/25/1990 | F |
| White wartyback (pearlymussel) | Plethobasus cicatricosus | E;XN | 9/19/1984 | F |
| Winged mapleleaf | Quadrula fragosa | E;XN | 6/25/1997 | F |
| Yellow blossom (pearlymussel) | Epioblasma florentina florentina | E;XN | 1/25/1985 | F |

[a]E = Endangered; T = Threatened; XN = Experimental Population, Non-Essential.
[b]Recovery plan stages: F = Final; D = Draft; RF = Final Revision.

SOURCE: Adapted from "Listed FWS/Joint FWS and NMFS Species and Populations with Recovery Plans (Sorted by Listed Entity)" and "Listed U.S. Species by Taxonomic Group," in *USFWS Threatened and Endangered Species System (TESS)*, U.S. Department of the Interior, U.S. Fish and Wildlife Service, February 4, 2008, http://ecos.fws.gov/tess_public/SpeciesRecovery.do?sort=1 and http://ecos.fws.gov/tess_public/SpeciesReport.do?kingdom=V&listing Type=L (accessed February 4, 2008)

## TABLE 5.2

### Endangered and threatened crustacean species, February 2008

| Common name | Scientific name | Listing status[a] | Recovery plan date | Recovery plan stage[b] |
|---|---|---|---|---|
| Alabama cave shrimp | Palaemonias alabamae | E | 9/4/1997 | F |
| California freshwater shrimp | Syncaris pacifica | E | 7/31/1998 | F |
| Cave crayfish | Cambarus zophonastes | E | 10/30/1996 | F |
| Cave crayfish | Cambarus aculabrum | E | 10/30/1996 | F |
| Conservancy fairy shrimp | Branchinecta conservatio | E | 12/15/2005 | F |
| Hay's Spring amphipod | Stygobromus hayi | E | Exempt | — |
| Illinois cave amphipod | Gammarus acherondytes | E | 9/20/2002 | F |
| Kauai cave amphipod | Spelaeorchestia koloana | E | 7/19/2006 | F |
| Kentucky cave shrimp | Palaemonias ganteri | E | 10/7/1988 | F |
| Lee County cave isopod | Lirceus usdagalun | E | 9/30/1997 | F |
| Longhorn fairy shrimp | Branchinecta longiantenna | E | 12/15/2005 | F |
| Madison Cave isopod | Antrolana lira | T | 9/30/1996 | F |
| Nashville crayfish | Orconectes shoupi | E | 2/8/1989 | RF(1) |
| Noel's amphipod | Gammarus desperatus | E | None | — |
| Peck's cave amphipod | Stygobromus (=Stygonectes) pecki | E | None | — |
| Riverside fairy shrimp | Streptocephalus woottoni | E | 9/3/1998 | F |
| San Diego fairy shrimp | Branchinecta sandiegonensis | E | 9/3/1998 | F |
| Shasta crayfish | Pacifastacus fortis | E | 8/28/1998 | F |
| Socorro isopod | Thermosphaeroma thermophilus | E | 2/16/1982 | F |
| Squirrel Chimney Cave shrimp | Palaemonetes cummingi | T | Exempt | — |
| Vernal pool fairy shrimp | Branchinecta lynchi | T | 12/15/2005 | F |
| Vernal pool tadpole shrimp | Lepidurus packardi | E | 12/15/2005 | F |

[a]E = Endangered; T = Threatened.
[b]Recovery plan stages: F = Final; RF = Final Revision.

SOURCE: Adapted from "Listed FWS/Joint FWS and NMFS Species and Populations with Recovery Plans (Sorted by Listed Entity)" and "Listed U.S. Species by Taxonomic Group," in *USFWS Threatened and Endangered Species System (TESS)*, U.S. Department of the Interior, U.S. Fish and Wildlife Service, February 4, 2008, http://ecos.fws.gov/tess_public/SpeciesRecovery.do?sort=1 and http://ecos.fws.gov/tess_public/SpeciesReport.do?kingdom=V&listing Type=L (accessed February 4, 2008)

In 1976 the Higgins' eye pearlymussel was listed as an endangered species under the ESA. More than a century of scavenging by humans had severely depleted the species. Dams, navigational structures, and water quality problems in the upper Mississippi River system were contributing factors to its decline. In 1983 the USFWS published its first recovery plan for the Higgins' eye. The plan identified areas deemed essential habitat for the species and called for limits on construction and harvesting in these areas.

Since 2000 scientists have collected and relocated hundreds of Higgins' eye pearlymussels. Fish raised in hatcheries have been artificially infested with glochidia and released into rivers to enhance the spread of the mussel.

In 2004 the USFWS published *Higgins Eye Pearlymussel Recovery Plan: First Revision* (May 2004, http://ecos.fws.gov/docs/recovery_plans/2004/040714.pdf). The new plan examines more recent threats to species' survival, primarily the pervasive spread of zebra mussels. It acknowledges that there

**TABLE 5.3**

**Clam, snail, crustacean, and coral species with the highest expenditures under the Endangered Species Act, fiscal year 2006**

| Ranking | Species | Category | Expenditure |
|---|---|---|---|
| 1 | Vernal pool fairy shrimp | Crustacean | $1,377,963 |
| 2 | Higgins eye (pearlymussel) | Clam | $1,057,719 |
| 3 | Vernal pool tadpole shrimp | Crustacean | $744,717 |
| 4 | Oahu tree snails | Snail | $485,128 |
| 5 | Winged mapleleaf (mussel) | Clam | $408,897 |
| 6 | Utah valvata snail | Snail | $363,987 |
| 7 | Carolina heelsplitter (mussel) | Clam | $360,976 |
| 8 | Idaho springsnail | Snail | $333,516 |
| 9 | Bliss Rapids snail | Snail | $327,442 |
| 10 | Pink mucket (mussel) | Clam | $324,880 |

SOURCE: Adapted from "Table 2. Species Ranked in Descending Order of Total FY 2006 Reported Expenditures, Not Including Land Acquisition Costs," in *Federal and State Endangered and Threatened Species Expenditures: Fiscal Year 2006*, U.S. Department of the Interior, U.S. Fish and Wildlife Service, draft, 2008

is no currently feasible way to eliminate zebra mussels to the extent needed to benefit the Higgins' eye. Instead, the plan focuses on development of methods to prevent new zebra mussel infestations and working to lessen the impacts of already infested populations.

ZEBRA AND QUAGGA MUSSELS—AN INFESTATION. In 1988 an unwelcomed visitor was discovered in the waters of Lake St. Clair, Michigan: a zebra mussel (*Dreissena polymorpha*). The zebra mussel is native to eastern Europe. It is smaller than the freshwater mussels found in the United States and has a different method for spreading its young. The larva of zebra mussels do not require a fish host to develop into babies. They can attach to any hard surface under the water. This allows zebra mussels to spread much easier and quicker than their American counterparts.

It is believed that the first zebra mussels migrated to the United States in the ballast water of ships. This is water held in large tanks below deck to improve the stability and control of ships. Ballast water is pumped in and out as needed during a journey. Zebra mussels have also been found clinging to the hulls of small fishing and recreation boats. These boats are hauled overland on trailers, and this allows the creatures to travel great distances between inland water bodies.

Figure 5.1 shows a USGS map of zebra mussel distribution around the country as of January 2008. Since 1988 this invasive species has spread dramatically from the Great Lakes south to the Gulf of Mexico and east to New England. Zebra mussels have been found on boat hulls as far west as California. Throughout waterways in the Midwest, colonies of zebra mussels have clogged pipes and other structures used for municipal and industrial water supply. In addition, the pests have significantly degraded native mussel colonies by competing for available food, space, and resources.

Another foreign invader of concern is the quagga mussel (*Dreissena bugensis*), a native of Ukraine in eastern Europe. In 1989 the mussel was first sighted in the United States in Lake Erie. By the mid-1990s it had spread to other lakes in the upper Midwest. In 2007 the mussel was discovered in lakes in Nevada, Arizona, and southern California. This finding is particularly troubling to scientists, because of the large concentration of imperiled aquatic species in southwestern water bodies. There is also concern that quagga and zebra mussels will begin interbreeding (an act proved possible in laboratory experiments) and spread even more prodigiously.

CLAM AND MUSSEL RECOVERY PLANS. As of February 2008, all seventy species of clams and mussels listed under the ESA had recovery plans in draft or final form. (See Table 5.1.) Conservation efforts for freshwater mussels include the captive breeding and reintroduction of some species, as well as measures to restore damaged habitats.

## Snails

Snails belong to the class Gastropoda of mollusks. Snails typically have an external spiral-shaped shell and a distinct head that includes sensory organs. Snails inhabit terrestrial (land), marine, and freshwater environments. Most land snails prefer moist, heavily vegetated locations. Snails are found throughout the United States. Most imperiled species are located in the West (including Hawaii) and the Southeast (primarily Alabama).

As of February 2008, there were thirty-five U.S. species of snails and one foreign species listed under the ESA. (See Table 5.4 for a list of the U.S. species.) One of the U.S. species—the Oahu tree snail—has forty-one subspecies listed as endangered under the ESA. Over $485,000 was spent under the ESA during FY 2006 to conserve Oahu tree snails. (See Table 5.3.) Another $364,000 was spent on Utah valvata snails.

OAHU TREE SNAILS. Oahu tree snails belong to the genus *Achatinella* and are endemic to the Oahu island of Hawaii. All forty-one species in the genus are imperiled and are collectively known as Oahu tree snails. These snails were listed as endangered under the ESA in 1981. The snails live in mountainous forests and shrublands and feed on fungi growing on the leaves of native plants. The spread of nonnative vegetation and invasive carnivorous (meat-eating) snails has seriously depleted populations of Oahu tree snails. They are also preyed on by rats.

In 1992 the USFWS released a final recovery plan for the surviving species of *Achatinella* in Oahu. The plan designated areas of essential habitat and called for captive propagation of the snails.

UTAH VALVATA SNAILS. Utah valvata snails were listed as endangered under the ESA in 1992. They are one of five species known as the Snake River snails that inhabit the middle portion of the Snake River in southern Idaho.

FIGURE 5.1

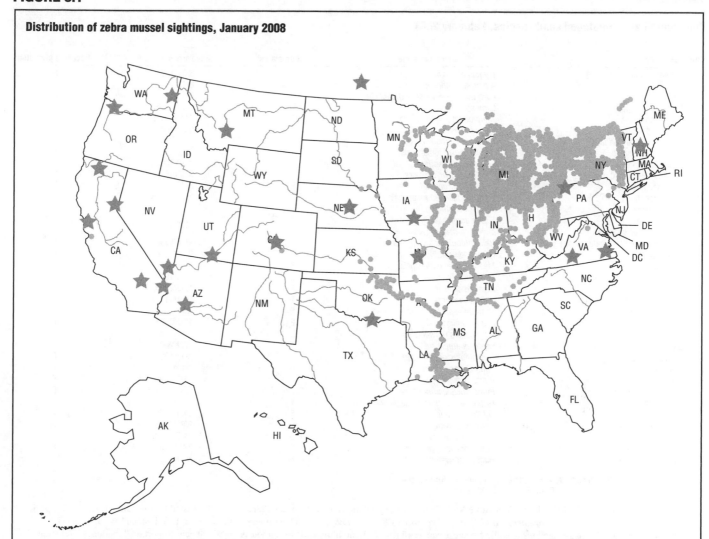

**Distribution of zebra mussel sightings, January 2008**

Note: Dots represent confirmed collections or observations of adults, juveniles, or veligers, but not always established populations. Stars represent the discovery of the overland transport of zebra mussels on trailered boats.

SOURCE: "Progression of the Zebra Mussel (<it>Dreissena Polymorpha</it>) Distribution in North America, 2008," U.S. Department of the Interior, U.S. Geological Survey, February 8, 2008, http://cars.er.usgs.gov/Nonindigenous_Species/ZM_Progression/zm_progression.html (accessed February 18, 2008)

All five species require cold, clean flowing water with high oxygen levels and low turbidity (suspended sediment) content. However, their habitat has been changed considerably over the past few decades by the construction of hydroelectric dams on the river. These dams have altered the flow and temperature of the river waters. Surviving Utah valvata snails are found in the main stem of the Snake River and in tributaries fed by cold-water springs.

A recovery plan for the endangered snail has been in effect since 1995. The plan notes that the Utah valvata snail has a high degree of threat and a low degree of recovery potential. The restoration of habitat and water quality is indicated as the only means for saving the snail from extinction.

In late 2003 Utah valvata snails were discovered on a bridge being demolished near Firth, Idaho. Before that

that time the species had not been found that far south in the Snake River. The Idaho Transportation Department suspended the demolition project so that biologists could conduct a survey of the snails. In 2004 the USFWS announced that bridge removal could continue because it did not pose a threat to the survival of the species at that location.

RECOVERY PLANS FOR SNAILS. Table 5.4 lists the snail species for which recovery plans have been published as of February 2008. Three of the species that do not have plans—Koster's springsnail, Pecos assiminea snails, and Roswell springsnails—were listed under the ESA during 2005. In 2007 the USFWS initiated a five-year status review for the slender campeloma. The white abalone snail is under the jurisdiction of the National Marine Fisheries Service (NMFS). It is a

TABLE 5.4

**Endangered and threatened snail species, February 2008**

| Common name | Scientific name | Listing status[a] | Recovery plan date | Recovery plan stage[b] |
|---|---|---|---|---|
| Alamosa springsnail | Tryonia alamosae | E | 8/31/1994 | F |
| Anthony's riversnail | Athearnia anthonyi | E; XN | 8/13/1997 | F |
| Armored snail | Pyrgulopsis (=Marstonia) pachyta | E | 7/1/1994 | D |
| Banbury Springs limpet | Lanx sp. | E | 11/26/1995 | F |
| Bliss Rapids snail | Taylorconcha serpenticola | T | 11/26/1995 | F |
| Bruneau hot springsnail | Pyrgulopsis bruneauensis | E | 9/30/2002 | F |
| Chittenango ovate amber snail | Succinea chittenangoensis | T | 7/11/2006 | RF(1) |
| Cylindrical lioplax (snail) | Lioplax cyclostomaformis | E | 12/2/2005 | F |
| Flat pebblesnail | Lepyrium showalteri | E | 12/2/2005 | F |
| Flat-spired three-toothed snail | Triodopsis platysayoides | T | 5/9/1983 | F |
| Iowa Pleistocene snail | Discus macclintocki | E | 3/22/1984 | F |
| Kanab ambersnail | Oxyloma haydeni kanabensis | E | 10/12/1995 | F |
| Koster's springsnail | Juturnia kosteri | E | None | — |
| Lacy elimia (snail) | Elimia crenatella | T | 12/2/2005 | F |
| Magazine Mountain shagreen | Mesodon magazinensis | T | 2/1/1994 | F |
| Morro shoulderband (=banded dune) snail | Helminthoglypta walkeriana | E | 9/28/1998 | F |
| Newcomb's snail | Erinna newcombi | T | 9/18/2006 | F |
| Noonday snail | Mesodon clarki nantahala | T | 9/7/1984 | F |
| Oahu tree snail (41 subspecies) | Achatinella spp. | E | 6/30/1992 | F |
| Painted rocksnail | Leptoxis taeniata | T | 12/2/2005 | F |
| Painted snake coiled forest snail | Anguispira picta | T | 10/14/1982 | F |
| Pecos assiminea snail | Assiminea pecos | E | None | — |
| Plicate rocksnail | Leptoxis plicata | E | 12/2/2005 | F |
| Roswell springsnail | Pyrgulopsis roswellensis | E | None | — |
| Round rocksnail | Leptoxis ampla | T | 12/2/2005 | F |
| Royal marstonia (snail) | Pyrgulopsis ogmorhaphe | E | 8/11/1995 | F |
| Slender campeloma | Campeloma decampi | E | None | — |
| Snake River physa snail | Physa natricina | E | 11/26/1995 | F |
| Socorro springsnail | Pyrgulopsis neomexicana | E | 8/31/1994 | F |
| Stock Island tree snail | Orthalicus reses (not incl. nesodryas) | T | 5/18/1999 | F |
| Tulotoma snail | Tulotoma magnifica | E | 11/17/2000 | F |
| Tumbling Creek cavesnail | Antrobia culveri | E | 9/22/2003 | F |
| Utah valvata snail | Valvata utahensis | E | 11/26/1995 | F |
| Virginia fringed mountain snail | Polygyriscus virginianus | E | 5/9/1983 | F |
| White abalone | Haliotis sorenseni | E | None | — |

[a]E = Endangered; T = Threatened; XN = Experimental Population, Non-Essential.
[b]Recovery plan stages: F = Final; D = Draft; RF = Final Revision.

SOURCE: Adapted from "Listed FWS/Joint FWS and NMFS Species and Populations with Recovery Plans (Sorted by Listed Entity)" and "Listed U.S. Species by Taxonomic Group," in *USFWS Threatened and Endangered Species System (TESS)*, U.S. Department of the Interior, U.S. Fish and Wildlife Service, February 4, 2008, http://ecos.fws.gov/tess_public/SpeciesRecovery.do?sort=1 and http://ecos.fws.gov/tess_public/SpeciesReport.do?kingdom=V&listing Type=L (accessed February 4, 2008)

marine snail that inhabits deep waters off the coast of Southern California.

## Crustaceans

Crustaceans are a large class of mandibulate (jawed) creatures in the phylum Arthropoda. They are mostly aquatic and inhabit marine and freshwaters. As of February 2008, there were twenty-two U.S. species listed as endangered or threatened under the ESA. (See Table 5.2.) Even though they are found throughout the United States, California is home to more imperiled crustacean species than any other state. Nearly $1.4 million was spent under the ESA during FY 2006 on the vernal pool fairy shrimp. (See Table 5.3.)

**VERNAL POOL FAIRY SHRIMP.** The vernal pool fairy shrimp was listed under the ESA as threatened in 1994. It is found in California and Oregon. Vernal is from the Latin word for "spring." This species inhabits temporary small ponds and pools of water that appear in the spring-

time and dry up after a time. The shrimp lay their eggs in these pools when they contain water. The eggs can go dormant in the dirt when the pools become dry. Baby shrimp hatch only when exposed to water at less than approximately 50°F (10°C). Adults typically reach 0.4 to 1 inch (1 to 2.5 cm) in length. The shrimp have a lifetime of two to five months.

In 2003 critical habitat was designated for the vernal pool fairy shrimp along with several other species of vernal pool shrimp. In 2005 the USFWS published *Recovery Plan for Vernal Pool Ecosystems of California and Southern Oregon* (December 15, 2005, http://ecos.fws.gov/docs/recovery_plan/060614.pdf), a recovery plan that covers dozens of imperiled plant and animal species that inhabit vernal pool ecosystems in California and southern Oregon. The plan notes that vernal pool life forms are threatened by urban and agricultural development and by invasion of non-native species. The recovery of vernal pool species will require an ecosystem-wide approach. The USFWS proposes establishing conservation areas and reserves to protect primary vernal pool habitat.

**CRUSTACEAN RECOVERY PLANS.** Nearly all endangered and threatened species of crustaceans found in the United States had recovery plans as of February 2008. (See Table 5.2.) Most plans were in final form. Two listed species—Hay's spring amphipod and squirrel chimney cave shrimp—are exempt from the requirement for a recovery plan.

## Imperiled Mollusks and Crustaceans around the World

In *2007 Red List of Threatened Species* (2007, http://www.iucnredlist.org/), the International Union for the Conservation of Nature and Natural Resources (IUCN) lists 978 species of mollusks and 460 species of crustaceans as threatened. For mollusks, this number encompasses 44% of the 2,212 species evaluated. The IUCN reports that approximately eighty-one thousand mollusk species are known. Only 553 crustacean species were evaluated for the 2007 report. Threatened species comprise 83% of this total. However, the IUCN notes that there are approximately forty thousand known species of crustaceans.

## CORALS

Corals are one of the most unusual members of the animal kingdom. They are invertebrate marine creatures of the phylum Cnidaria, along with jellyfish and anemones. Many people are familiar with coral reefs—vast and colorful undersea structures that are popular with scuba divers and snorkelers. (See Figure 5.2.) Most coral reefs are composed of many hundreds or thousands of individual coral organisms called polyps. Figure 5.3

**FIGURE 5.3**

**A coral polyp**

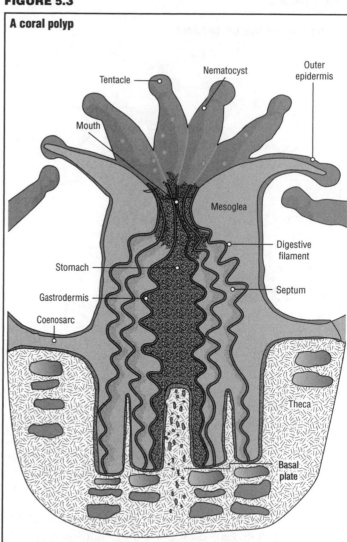

SOURCE: "Polyp," in *Education Kits: Corals*, U.S. Department of Commerce, National Oceanic and Atmospheric Administration, National Ocean Service, December 2, 2004, http://oceanservice.noaa.gov/education/kits/corals/media/supp_coral01a.html (accessed February 15, 2008)

**FIGURE 5.2**

Coral reefs are among the most diverse ecosystems in the world. They are also immediately threatened by global warming, which has caused unprecedented episodes of coral bleaching in recent years. *AP/Wide World Photos*

shows a coral polyp with its common parts labeled. The polyp has an opening (or mouth) surrounded by tentacles that capture sea creatures for food. Following digestion in the polyp's stomach, waste materials are expelled out through the mouth.

Most reef-building coral polyps have a symbiotic (mutually beneficial) relationship with algae (tiny plant cells) called zooxanthellae. The algae perform photosynthesis, which creates oxygen and provides nutrients to the coral polyps, allowing them to grow and spread. Reef-building corals secrete calcium carbonate, a hard mineral compound that forms the reef skeleton. Zooxanthellae are also responsible for the bright and varied colors found in coral reefs. Without the algae, coral polyps are naturally translucent. Scientists believe that zooxanthellae serve as sort of a "sunscreen" for warm-water corals, protecting them from the harsh ultraviolet rays of the sun.

**FIGURE 5.4**

**Locations of tropical coral reefs**

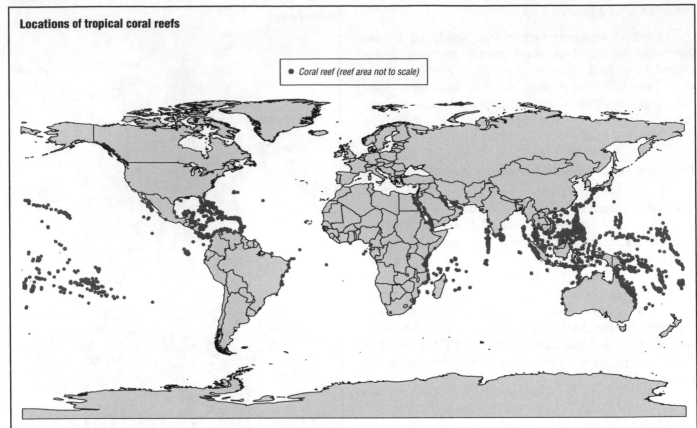

● *Coral reef (reef area not to scale)*

SOURCE: "Figure 21.1. Tropical Waters Are Home to the Majority of Known Reefs," in *An Ocean Blueprint for the 21st Century. Final Report*, U.S. Commission on Ocean Policy, 2004, http://www.oceancommission.gov/documents/full_color_rpt/000_ocean_full_report.pdf (accessed January 23, 2008)

Coral reefs are the largest living structures on Earth. They are primarily found in coastal, tropical waters. (See Figure 5.4.) These reefs are located in relatively shallow waters, making them more susceptible to human activities. The U.S. Commission on Ocean Policy states in *An Ocean Blueprint for the 21st Century: Final Report* (2004, http://www.oceancommission .gov/documents/full_color_rpt/000_ocean_full_report.pdf) that only 1% to 2% of warm-water corals are found in U.S. waters. Most warm-water corals are located in the waters of the South Pacific and around Indonesia. In addition, there are many cold-water reefs around the world that scientists are just beginning to study. These reefs are found in cold deep waters from depths of 100 feet (30.5 m) to more than three miles (4.8 km).

**General Threats to Corals**

In *An Ocean Blueprint for the 21st Century*, the Commission on Ocean Policy explains that one-third of coral reefs around the world are severely damaged and that all U.S. warm-water reefs have been damaged to some degree. Coral reefs are imperiled by diseases and coastal development that spurs the growth of unfriendly algae. Coastal development also increases the danger of the reefs being trampled by divers and boat anchors.

Other serious threats to reef ecosystems include marine pollution, blast fishing, and cyanide fishing. The collection of tropical reef specimens for the aquarium trade has also damaged a number of species.

Perhaps the greatest immediate threat to coral reefs is rising water temperature due to global climate change. Overly warm water causes zooxanthellae to leave or be expelled from coral polyps. The resulting loss of color is known as coral bleaching. Bleached coral suffers from a lack of nutrients, becoming weak and lackluster and more susceptible to disease and other environmental stressors. Long-term zooxanthellae deficiencies can cause the coral to die.

According to the National Oceanic and Atmospheric Administration (NOAA), in "What Is Coral Bleaching?" (December 12, 2006, http://celebrating200years.noaa .gov/foundations/coral/side3.html), a seawater surface temperature increase as small as 1.8°F (1°C) above the usual maximum temperature for a week or more can trigger coral bleaching. The phenomenon is believed to be aggravated by other factors, including excessive exposure of the coral to ultraviolet radiation or pollution and associated water chemistry changes.

## Imperiled U.S. Corals

As of February 2008, there were two U.S. species of coral listed as threatened under the ESA. (See Table 1.2.) The corals are Elkhorn coral (*Acropora palmata*) and Staghorn coral (*Acropora cervicornis*). Both species are branching corals found in the Caribbean, including the coastal waters of Florida, Puerto Rico, and the U.S. Virgin Islands. Their range extends to many tropical countries of Central and South America. Both species were listed under the ESA effective June 8, 2006.

As marine creatures, they are under the jurisdiction of the NMFS. According to NMFS listing documents (http://www .epa.gov/EPA-SPECIES/2007/December/Day-14/e24211 .htm), the corals are primarily threatened by disease, hur- ricanes, and elevated sea surface temperatures. The agency notes that these threats "are severe, unpredictable, and likely to increase in the foreseeable future." However, because of the wide distribution of the corals and their sexual reproduction mechanisms, they are not believed to be at risk of extinction throughout all or a significant part of their range. Thus, they are afforded a "threatened," rather than "endangered" ranking.

## Imperiled Corals around the World

The IUCN lists in *2007 Red List of Threatened Species* five species of corals as threatened. This number comprises 38% of the thirteen species evaluated. Approximately 2,175 coral species are known to scientists.

# CHAPTER 6
# AMPHIBIANS AND REPTILES

Amphibians and reptiles are collectively known by biologists as herpetofauna. In *2007 Red List of Threatened Species* (2007, http://www.iucnredlist.org/), the International Union for Conservation of Nature and Natural Resources (IUCN) notes that there are 6,199 described amphibian species and 8,240 described reptile species. New species in both these groups are being discovered every year, particularly in remote tropical regions that are only now being explored.

Most of the herpetofauna native to the United States are found in wetlands and riparian habitat (the banks and immediate areas around water bodies, such as rivers and streams). Biologists say that amphibians and reptiles play a crucial role in these ecosystems by controlling insects, processing dead organic matter into a form that is edible by smaller creatures, and providing an important link in the food chain.

Many herpetofauna species are under threat, primarily due to declines and degradation in their habitats in recent decades.

## AMPHIBIANS

Amphibians are vertebrate animals in the taxonomic class Amphibia. They represent the most ancient group of terrestrial vertebrates. The earliest amphibians are known from fossils and date from the early Devonian era, some four hundred million years ago. The three groups of amphibians that have survived to the present day are salamanders, frogs (and toads), and caecilians.

Salamanders belong to the orders Caudata or Urodela. They have moist smooth skin, slender bodies, four short legs, and long tails. This category includes the amphibians commonly known as newts (land-dwelling salamanders) and sirens (salamanders with lungs besides gills). According to the IUCN, in *2007 Red List of Threatened Species*, there are 535 salamander species

worldwide, and 185 species in the United States. Most salamanders are fairly small in size, most often 6 inches (15 cm) long or less. The Chinese and Japanese giant salamanders, which grow to be as large as 5 feet (1.5 m) in length, are the largest of all amphibians.

Frogs and toads are in the order Anura. These amphibians do not have tails as adults. They have small bodies with two short front legs and two long hind legs. Their feet are webbed, and they are good jumpers and hoppers. True frogs belong to the family Ranidae, whereas true toads belong to the family Bufonidae. There are many other families in this order whose members are commonly described as tree frogs, tailed frogs, spadefoot toads, horned toads, clawed frogs, Surinam toads, narrow-mouth frogs, or poison dart toads. Many of the species go through a swimming tadpole stage before metamorphosing into an adult. However, in some species eggs hatch directly as juvenile froglets, which are miniature versions of the adults. Tadpoles are most often herbivorous, although there are some carnivorous tadpoles, including cannibalistic species. Adults are carnivorous and catch prey with their sticky tongues. The IUCN notes that there are over fifty-two hundred known frog and toad species, but only ninety of these species are found in the United States.

Caecilians belong to the orders Gymnophiona or Apoda and share a common ancestor with the other amphibians, but look much different. They are often mistaken for worms or snakes. They have long slender bodies with no limbs and are found primarily in the tropics. According to the IUCN, there are approximately 172 species of Caecilians worldwide, but none are native to the United States.

*Amphi* means "both," and amphibians get their name from the fact that many species occupy both aquatic and terrestrial habitats. In particular, many amphibian species undergo a dramatic change called metamorphosis, in which individuals move from an aquatic larval stage to

TABLE 6.1

**Endangered and threatened amphibian species, February 2008**

| Common name | Scientific name | Listing status[a] | Recovery plan date | Recovery plan status[b] |
|---|---|---|---|---|
| Arroyo (=arroyo southwestern) toad | *Bufo californicus (=microscaphus)* | E | 7/24/1999 | F |
| Barton Springs salamander | *Eurycea sosorum* | E | 9/21/2005 | F |
| California red-legged frog | *Rana aurora draytonii* | T | 5/28/2002 | F |
| California tiger salamander | *Ambystoma californiense* | E;T | None | — |
| Cheat Mountain salamander | *Plethodon nettingi* | T | 7/25/1991 | F |
| Chiricahua leopard frog | *Rana chiricahuensis* | T | 6/4/2007 | D |
| Desert slender salamander | *Batrachoseps aridus* | E | 8/12/1982 | F |
| Flatwoods salamander | *Ambystoma cingulatum* | T | None | — |
| Golden coqui | *Eleutherodactylus jasperi* | T | 4/19/1984 | F |
| Guajon | *Eleutherodactylus cooki* | T | 9/24/2004 | F |
| Houston toad | *Bufo houstonensis* | E | 9/17/1984 | F |
| Mississippi gopher frog | *Rana capito sevosa* | E | None | — |
| Mountain yellow-legged frog | *Rana muscosa* | E | None | — |
| Puerto Rican crested toad | *Peltophryne lemur* | T | 8/7/1992 | F |
| Red Hills salamander | *Phaeognathus hubrichti* | T | 11/23/1983 | F |
| San Marcos salamander | *Eurycea nana* | T | 2/14/1996 | RF(1) |
| Santa Cruz long-toed salamander | *Ambystoma macrodactylum croceum* | E | 7/2/1999 | RD(2) |
| Shenandoah salamander | *Plethodon shenandoah* | E | 9/29/1994 | F |
| Sonora tiger salamander | *Ambystoma tigrinum stebbinsi* | E | 9/24/2002 | F |
| Texas blind salamander | *Typhlomolge rathbuni* | E | 2/14/1996 | RF(1) |
| Wyoming toad | *Bufo baxteri (=hemiophrys)* | E | 9/11/1991 | F |

[a]E = Endangered; T = Threatened.
[b]Recovery plan stages: F = Final; D = Draft; RF = Final Revision; RD = Draft Under Revision.

SOURCE: Adapted from "Listed FWS/Joint FWS and NMFS Species and Populations with Recovery Plans (Sorted by Listed Entity)" and "Listed U.S. Species by Taxonomic Group," in *USFWS Threatened and Endangered Species System (TESS)*, U.S. Department of the Interior, U.S. Fish and Wildlife Service, February 5, 2008, http://ecos.fws.gov/tess_public/SpeciesRecovery.do?sort=1 and http://ecos.fws.gov/tess_public/SpeciesReport.do?kingdom=V&listing Type=L (accessed February 5, 2008)

a terrestrial adult stage. For example, in many frog species aquatic swimming tadpoles metamorphose into terrestrial jumping frogs. In the process, they lose their muscular swimming tails and acquire forelimbs and hind limbs. Many amphibian species occupy terrestrial habitats through most of the year, but migrate to ponds to breed. However, there are also species that are either entirely aquatic or entirely terrestrial. Whatever their habitat, amphibians generally require some moisture to survive. This is because amphibians pass some oxygen and other chemicals in and out of their body directly through their skin, using processes that require water to function.

Many amphibian species are in serious decline due to factors such as habitat loss, pollution, and climate change. Amphibians are particularly vulnerable to pollution because their skin readily absorbs water and other substances from the environment. For this reason, amphibians are frequently considered biological indicator species, meaning that their presence, condition, and numbers are monitored as a gauge of the overall well-being of their habitat.

## THREATENED AND ENDANGERED SPECIES OF AMPHIBIANS

As of February 2008, there were twenty-one U.S. amphibian species listed as threatened or endangered under the Endangered Species Act (ESA). (See Table 6.1.)

**TABLE 6.2**

**Amphibian species with the highest expenditures under the Endangered Species Act, fiscal year 2006**

| Ranking | Species | Expenditure |
|---|---|---|
| 1 | California red-legged frog | $2,236,288 |
| 2 | Flatwoods salamander | $1,814,300 |
| 3 | California tiger salamander | $1,131,470 |
| 4 | Chiricahua leopard frog | $723,813 |
| 5 | Red Hills salamander | $624,257 |
| 6 | Mountain yellow-legged frog | $607,657 |
| 7 | Arroyo toad | $351,908 |
| 8 | Houston toad | $266,015 |
| 9 | Texas blind salamander | $177,516 |
| 10 | Guajon | $124,250 |

SOURCE: Adapted from "Table 2. Species Ranked in Descending Order of Total FY 2006 Reported Expenditures, Not Including Land Acquisition Costs," in *Federal and State Endangered and Threatened Species Expenditures: Fiscal Year 2006*, U.S. Department of the Interior, U.S. Fish and Wildlife Service, draft, 2008

The list contains eleven species of salamander and ten species of frogs and toads (including the golden coqui and the guajón, which are Puerto Rican frogs). Most of the listed species are endangered and nearly all have recovery plans in place. Geographically, the list is dominated by western states, where thirteen of the imperiled species are found, primarily in California and Texas.

Table 6.2 shows the ten amphibian species with the highest expenditures under the ESA during fiscal year 2006.

## FIGURE 6.1

The Texas blind salamander lives in underground caves and has only vestigial eyes, found below the skin. *U.S. Fish and Wildlife Service*

## Imperiled Salamanders in the United States

Of the eleven salamanders listed in Table 6.1, only four species are found outside the western states. The primary ranges of all species are:

- Texas—Barton Springs, San Marcos, and Texas blind salamanders (See Figure 6.1)

- California—California tiger, Desert slender, and Santa Cruz long-toed salamanders

- Arizona—Sonora tiger salamander

- Alabama—Red Hills salamander

- Virginia—Shenandoah salamander

- West Virginia—Cheat Mountain salamander

The Flatwoods salamander is found in the coastal plain areas of Florida, Georgia, and South Carolina.

Some endangered salamanders, including many cave species, have highly restricted habitats. The Barton Springs salamander is only found in and around spring-fed pools in Zilker Park in Austin, Texas. The species was first listed as endangered in 1997. Urban development has contributed to degradation of the local groundwater that feeds the spring. In addition, flows from the spring have decreased due to increasing human use of groundwater from the aquifer. Finally, the Barton Springs salamander has been the subject of contentious debate between conservationists and those who wish to expand development around the area of the pools.

In 2005 the U.S. Fish and Wildlife Service (USFWS) published *Barton Springs Salamander Recovery Plan* (September 2005, http://www.fws.gov/southwest/es/Documents/ R2ES/Barton_Springs_Salamander_FINAL_Recovery_Plan .pdf) and began a five-year review of its listing status.

The review was completed the following year and recommended no change to the endangered listing for the species.

## Imperiled Frogs and Toads in the United States

The ten species of imperiled frogs and toads found in the United States are geographically diverse. Their habitats are located in the West, Southeast, and Puerto Rico. California is home to the California red-legged frog, the arroyo toad, and the mountain yellow-legged frog (which also lives in Nevada). Arizona and New Mexico provide habitat for the Chiricahua leopard frog. The Houston toad and Wyoming toad are found in Texas and Wyoming, respectively. The Mississippi gopher frog is native to the southeastern United States. Three imperiled amphibians are found in Puerto Rico: golden coqui, guajón, and Puerto Rican crested toad.

**CALIFORNIA RED-LEGGED FROGS.** The California red-legged frog is the largest native frog in the western United States. The frog was made famous by Mark Twain's (1835–1910) short story "The Celebrated Jumping Frog of Calaveras County" (1865). The species experienced a significant decline during the mid-twentieth century. According to Environmental Defense Fund, in "California Red-Legged Frog" (August 17, 2007, http:// www.edf.org/page.cfm?tagid=7766), by 1960 California red-legged frogs had disappeared altogether from the state's Central Valley, probably due to the loss of most of their habitat. In 1996 the species was listed as threatened under the ESA.

California red-legged frogs require riverside habitats covered by vegetation and close to deep-water pools. They are extremely sensitive to habitat disturbance and water pollution—tadpoles are particularly sensitive to varying oxygen levels and siltation (mud and other natural impurities) during metamorphosis. The frogs require three to four years to reach maturity and have a normal life span of eight to ten years.

Water reservoir construction and agricultural or residential development are the primary factors in the decline of this species. Biologists have shown that California red-legged frogs generally disappear from habitats within five years of a reservoir or water diversion project. The removal of vegetation associated with flood control and the use of herbicides and restructuring of landscapes further degrade remaining habitat. Finally, nonnative species have also attacked red-legged frog populations. These include alien fish predators as well as competing species such as bullfrogs.

In 2002 the USFWS published *Recovery Plan for the California Red-Legged Frog* (2002, http://ecos.fws.gov/ docs/recovery_plans/2002/020528.pdf). It calls for eliminating threats in current habitats, restoring damaged habitats, and reintroducing populations into the historic range of the species. The U.S. National Park Service (NPS)

TABLE 6.3

**Foreign endangered and threatened amphibian species, February 2008**

| Common name | Scientific name | Listing status* | U.S. and/or foreign listed | Foreign range |
|---|---|---|---|---|
| African viviparous toads | *Nectophrynoides spp.* | E | Foreign | Tanzania, Guinea, Ivory Coast, Cameroon, Liberia, Ethiopia |
| Arroyo (=arroyo southwestern) toad | *Bufo californicus (=microscaphus)* | E | US/foreign | Mexico |
| California red-legged frog | *Rana aurora draytonii* | T | US/foreign | Mexico |
| Cameroon toad | *Bufo superciliaris* | E | Foreign | Equatorial Africa |
| Chinese giant salamander | *Andrias davidianus (=davidianus d.)* | E | Foreign | Western China |
| Chiricahua leopard frog | *Rana chiricahuensis* | T | US/foreign | Mexico |
| Goliath frog | *Conraua goliath* | T | Foreign | Cameroon, Equatorial Guinea, Gabon |
| Israel painted frog | *Discoglossus nigriventer* | E | Foreign | Israel |
| Japanese giant salamander | *Andrias japonicus (=davidianus j.)* | E | Foreign | Japan |
| Monte Verde golden toad | *Bufo periglenes* | E | Foreign | Costa Rica |
| Panamanian golden frog | *Atelopus varius zeteki* | E | Foreign | Panama |
| Puerto Rican crested toad | *Peltophryne lemur* | T | US/foreign | British Virgin Islands |
| Sonora tiger salamander | *Ambystoma tigrinum stebbinsi* | E | US/foreign | Mexico |
| Stephen Island frog | *Leiopelma hamiltoni* | E | Foreign | New Zealand |

*E = Endangered; T = Threatened.

SOURCE: Adapted from "Listed FWS/Joint FWS and NMFS Species and Populations with Recovery Plans (Sorted by Listed Entity)" and "Listed U.S. Species by Taxonomic Group," in *USFWS Threatened and Endangered Species System (TESS)*, U.S. Department of the Interior, U.S. Fish and Wildlife Service, February 5, 2008, http://ecos.fws.gov/tess_public/SpeciesRecovery.do?sort=1 and http://ecos.fws.gov/tess_public/SpeciesReport.do?kingdom=V&listing Type=L (accessed February 5, 2008)

helped preserve one current frog habitat by altering water flow in the Piru Creek connection between Lake Piru and Pyramid Lake, located in the Los Angeles and Los Padres National Forests about 60 miles (97 km) northwest of Los Angeles. This also benefited another threatened species: the arroyo southwestern toad.

The USFWS has taken measures to preserve habitat in the foothills of the Sierra Nevada, in the central coastal mountains near San Francisco, along the Pacific Coast near Los Angeles, and in the Tehachapi Mountains. Protected frog habitats have also been established in Marin and Sonoma counties.

**GUAJÓN.** The guajón is a cave-dwelling species endemic to Puerto Rico. It grows to be about 3 inches (7.5 cm) long and is primarily brown, but sometimes has yellow markings. The frog has large protruding eyes that are rimmed in white, giving it an unusual appearance that some observers consider spooky. Because of its appearance, it has been nicknamed the "demon of Puerto Rico."

Its decline has resulted largely from introductions of alien species such as mongooses, rats, and cats, all of which eat unhatched guajón eggs. In addition, the species has experienced habitat loss from garbage dumping in caves and deforestation for agriculture, roads, and dams. Deforestation also creates the potential for future environmental disasters such as flash floods, which drown adult frogs and destroy nests. Encroaching agriculture causes pollution from fertilizer runoff. Finally, the guajón, is frequently killed by superstitious local residents who believe the mere sight of the animal can bring disaster.

**Foreign Amphibians in Danger**

As of February 2008, there were fourteen foreign amphibian species listed as threatened or endangered

under the ESA. (See Table 6.3.) This includes five species found both in the United States and foreign countries and nine completely foreign species. The latter comprises seven frog and toad species and two salamander species.

The IUCN reports in *2007 Red List of Threatened Species* that 1,808 amphibian species are threatened. This represents 29% of the 6,199 described amphibian species, the highest percentage for any group of animals.

**GIANT SALAMANDERS.** There are two species of giant salamanders: the Chinese giant salamander and the Japanese giant salamander. These are by far the largest living amphibian species, reaching lengths of up to 5 feet (1.5 m). Both are listed under the ESA and are highly endangered. Giant salamanders are aquatic and have folded and wrinkled skin that allows them to absorb oxygen from their watery habitats. The Chinese giant salamander is found in fast mountain streams in western China. Despite official protection, the species is endangered partly because of hunting for food and medicine. The Chinese giant salamander is also harmed by loss of habitat and aquatic pollution. Its close relative, the Japanese giant salamander, is also endangered and protected. This species inhabits cold, fast mountain streams in northern Kyushu Island and western Honshu in Japan. Japanese giant salamanders have been successfully bred in captivity.

**GASTRIC-BROODING FROGS.** There were two species of gastric-brooding frogs, both found in Australia. Gastric-brooding frogs were described as timid and were often found hiding under rocks in water. These species were only discovered in the 1970s and became extinct only a decade after their discovery. Gastric-brooding frogs got their name from their unusual reproductive strategy: females brooded their young in their stomachs. During brooding, the mother did not eat and did not produce stomach acids. The gestation period lasted about eight weeks, and as many as thirty tadpoles were in the brood. Juveniles eventually emerged as miniature froglets from the mother's mouth. Even though it is not certain what led to the extinction of gastric-brooding frogs, one hypothesis is that populations were killed off by the chytrid fungus, which is also responsible for the decline of other frog species.

CAECILIANS. Little is known about most species of caecilians. Some species are aquatic, but most of these elusive animals are underground burrowers that are difficult to locate and study. Caecilians generally have poor eyesight because of their underground habitat—some have no eyes at all or are nearly blind. Because so little is known about this group, it is difficult for environmentalists to assess the level of endangerment of these animals. The loss of tropical habitats worldwide suggests that many caecilians are likely imperiled.

## WORLDWIDE THREATS TO AMPHIBIANS

At the end of the twentieth century, biologists uncovered growing evidence of a global decline in amphibian populations. AmphibiaWeb, a conservation organization that monitors amphibian species worldwide, reports in "Worldwide Amphibian Declines: How Big Is the Problem, What Are the Causes and What Can Be Done?" (March 12, 2008, http://amphibiaweb.org/declines/declines.html) that 168 species have become extinct in recent decades and that at least 2,469 other species are declining in population. Amphibian declines have been documented worldwide, though the degree of decline varies across regions. Areas that have been hardest hit include Central America and Australia. In the United States amphibian declines have been concentrated in California, the Rocky Mountains, the Southwest, and Puerto Rico. Particularly disturbing is the loss of many populations within protected and relatively pristine wildlife refuges.

Scientists are concerned, because many amphibian species—particularly frogs—have become extinct over a very short period. Other species are either declining or showing high levels of gross deformities, such as extra limbs.

The golden toad, named for its unusual and striking orange color, is a prime example of the global amphibian decline. In "The Extinction of the Golden Toad (*Bufo periglenes*)—Symptom of a Worldwide Crisis" (May 12, 2005, http://jrscience.wcp.muohio.edu/fieldcourses05/PapersCostaRicaArticles/TheExtinctionoftheGoldenT.html), Britton Windeler explains that over a three-year period golden toads disappeared inexplicably from their only known habitat in the Monteverde Cloud Forest Reserve in Costa Rica. In 1987 herpetologists observed an appa-

rently healthy golden toad population estimated at fifteen hundred adults along with a new generation of tadpoles. The following year, in 1988, there were only eleven toads. In 1989 only a single surviving toad was found. It was the last individual on record for the species.

### Habitat Destruction

Recent amphibian declines appear to result from a combination of causes. Loss of habitat is a major factor in the decline of many amphibian species, as it is for many endangered species. The destruction of tropical forests and wetlands, ecosystems that are rich with amphibians, has done particular damage to populations. In the United States, deforestation is blamed for the loss or decline of salamander species in the Pacific Northwest and the Appalachian hardwood forests. In addition, some amphibians have lost appropriate aquatic breeding habitats, particularly small bodies of water such as ponds. These aquatic habitats are often developed or filled in by humans, because they appear to be less biologically valuable than larger aquatic habitats.

Finally, habitat fragmentation may be particularly harmful to amphibian species that migrate during the breeding season. These species require not only that both breeding and nonbreeding habitats remain undisturbed but also that there be intact habitat along migration routes.

### Pollution

Pollution is a second major factor in global amphibian declines. Because amphibians absorb water directly through skin and into their body, they are particularly vulnerable to water pollution from pesticides or fertilizer runoff.

Furthermore, air pollution by substances such as chlorofluorocarbons has reduced the amount of protective ozone in Earth's atmosphere. This has resulted in increased levels of ultraviolet (UV) radiation striking Earth's surface. UV radiation has wavelengths of 290 to 400 nanometers (nm). Wavelengths between 290 and 315 nm are called UV-B radiation and are the most dangerous, because they can damage deoxyribonucleic acid by producing chemicals called cyclobutane pyrimidine dimers. (See Figure 6.2.) Exposure to UV-B radiation causes genetic mutations that can prevent normal development or kill eggs. Increased UV-B levels particularly affect the many frog species whose eggs lack shells and float on the exposed surfaces of ponds. Tadpoles and adults are also at risk, because of their thin delicate skins.

### Invasive Species

Many amphibian species have also been affected by the introduction of nonnative species that either compete with them or prey on them. These include fish, crayfish,

## FIGURE 6.2

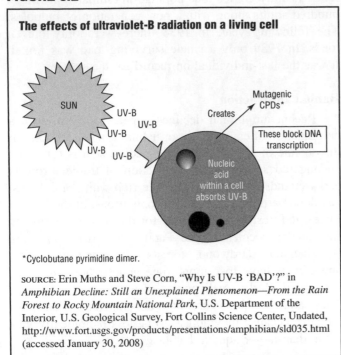

**The effects of ultraviolet-B radiation on a living cell**

*Cyclobutane pyrimidine dimer.

SOURCE: Erin Muths and Steve Corn, "Why Is UV-B 'BAD'?" in *Amphibian Decline: Still an Unexplained Phenomenon—From the Rain Forest to Rocky Mountain National Park*, U.S. Department of the Interior, U.S. Geological Survey, Fort Collins Science Center, Undated, http://www.fort.usgs.gov/products/presentations/amphibian/sld035.html (accessed January 30, 2008)

and other amphibians. The bullfrog, the cane toad (a large frog species), and the African clawed frog (a species often used in biological research) are some of the invasive species believed to have affected amphibian populations. In addition, introduced trout are blamed for the extinction of several species of harlequin frogs in Costa Rica. It is hypothesized that trout consume tadpoles. Similarly, introduced salmon have affected native frog populations in California.

### Disease

Amphibian diseases caused variously by bacteria, viruses, and fungi have devastated certain populations. Of particular importance in recent years is the chytrid fungus, which was first identified in 1998 in diseased amphibians. This fungus attacks skin, and even though there are often no symptoms initially, affected individuals eventually begin to shed skin and die. The precise cause of death is not known, though damage to the skin can interfere with respiration. The chytrid fungus is believed to be responsible for the demise of many species in Australia and Panama. In 2000 it was also documented in populations of the Chiricahua leopard frog in Arizona and the boreal toad in the Rocky Mountains. In the press release "Chytrid Fungus Discovered in Western Toads in Klondike Gold Rush National Historical Park, Skagway, Alaska" (May 16, 2006, http://www.nps.gov/applications/digest/printheadline.cfm?type=Announcements&id=4457), the NPS reports that five of the nine western toads evaluated in the Klondike Gold Rush National Historic Park during the summer of 2005 had tested positive for the fungus. The disease was being aggressively investi-

gated as a cause of a decline in the toad population in southern Alaska during recent years.

### Global Warming

Global warming is blamed for destroying unique habitats such as cloud forests (forests containing large amounts of water mists) in tropical regions, resulting in the loss of some amphibian species.

Quirin Schiermeier explains in "The Costs of Global Warming" (*Nature*, vol. 439, January 26, 2006) that global warming is also aggravating infectious diseases in the frog populations of Central and South America. Scientists have found that warmer temperatures are associated with increased cloud cover over tropical mountain areas. These conditions are conducive to increased growth of the deadly chytrid fungus.

### Human Collection

Many amphibian species are vigorously hunted for food, the pet trade, or as medical research specimens.

### Amphibian Deformities

Amphibian deformities first hit the spotlight in 1995, when middle school students discovered large numbers of deformed frogs in a pond in Minnesota. By 2000 scientists had documented malformed frogs in forty-four states and fifty-seven species. In "Amphibian Declines & Malformations" (2008, http://frogweb.nbii.gov/index.html), FrogWeb, an online service of the National Biological Information Infrastructure, indicates that rates of deformity as high as 60% have been documented in some local populations.

The high incidence of amphibian deformities in U.S. species appears to have multiple causes, as no single hypothesis accounts for all the different types of deformities seen. The most common deformities include missing hind limbs and toes, missing feet, misshapen feet, missing eyes, deformed front legs, and extra legs. Some of these malformations are believed to be related to a parasitic trematode, or flatworm, which in experiments causes the development of additional limbs. Aquatic trematodes have increased in number due to human activity, via a complicated chain of events. First, fertilizer runoff increases nutrient levels in ponds, allowing more algae to grow. An increase in algae results in a larger population of algae-eating snails, and snails host juvenile parasitic trematodes. Trematodes move on to frogs when they mature, forming cysts in the vicinity of developing frog legs. Chemical pollution and UV radiation may account for some of the other observed deformities.

The U.S. Geological Survey (USGS) set up a system whereby members of the public can report observations of deformed amphibians. The North American Reporting Center for Amphibian Malformations (NARCAM; http://

frogweb.nbii.gov/narcam/) is managed by the USGS National Biological Information Infrastructure and the University of Georgia's Savannah River Ecology Lab. NARCAM maintains an online database of thousands of reported frog deformities around the country. Listings can be searched by state, county, or deformity type (e.g., multiple hind limbs).

## REPTILES

Reptiles belong to the class Reptilia. Even though they may appear similar, reptiles differ from amphibians in that their skin is cornified—that is, made of dead cells. All reptiles obtain oxygen from the air using lungs. Most reptiles lay shelled eggs, although some species, particularly lizards and snakes, give birth to live young. According to the IUCN, in *2007 Red List of Threatened Species*, 8,240 species of reptiles have been described. The organization relies on data compiled by the Institute for Genomic Research (http://www.reptile-database.org/).

Reptiles include turtles, snakes, lizards, and crocodilians. Birds are also technically reptiles (birds and crocodiles are actually close relatives), but have historically been treated separately.

There are four taxonomic orders of reptiles:

- Squamata—more than eight thousand species of lizards, anoles, iguanas, gila monsters, monitors, skinks, geckos, chameleons, snakes (including asps, boas, pythons, and vipers), racerunners, whiptails, and amphisbaenians (worm lizards)

- Testudines—approximately three hundred species of turtles, terrapins, and tortoises

- Crocodilia—around twenty-three species, including alligators, caimans, crocodiles, and gavials (gharials)

- Rhynchocephalia—two species of tuataras found only in New Zealand

There are approximately thirty-one hundred species of snakes and fifty-one hundred species of lizards. Together, they represent the largest group of reptiles. Most lizards are carnivorous, although there are some herbivorous species as well, including the iguanas. Snakes are elongate reptiles that have, during the course of evolution, lost their limbs. All species are carnivorous. Most snakes are adapted to eating relatively large prey and have highly mobile jaws that allow them to swallow large prey. In some species the jaw can be unhinged to accommodate prey. Several groups of snakes are also characterized by a poisonous venom that they use to kill prey.

Many reptiles are in serious decline. Several species are endangered due to habitat loss or degradation. In addition, humans hunt reptile species for their skins,

shells, or meat. Global climate change has affected some reptile species, particularly turtles, in ominous ways—this is because in some reptiles, ambient temperatures determine whether males or females are produced. Even a small increase in temperature can result in few or no males being born. Natural disasters, such as hurricanes, can also affect reptiles by killing the animals or damaging their habitat.

## THREATENED AND ENDANGERED REPTILES

As of February 2008, there were thirty-seven U.S. reptiles listed as threatened or endangered under the ESA. (See Table 6.4.) Some species have dual status, because they have separate populations in the United States. In addition, a handful of reptiles are listed as T(S/A), which means threatened due to similarity of appearance. This listing is applied to animals, such as the American alligator, which closely resemble imperiled species—in this case the American crocodile.

Except for the sea turtles, many of the imperiled reptiles are geographically clustered as follows: California (six species), Puerto Rico (six species), and Florida (four species). Sea turtles spend most of their life at sea, only coming onto land to nest and lay young. Because there are many potential nesting sites along the U.S. coasts, the sea turtles are listed in many states.

The following is a breakdown of imperiled U.S. reptiles by taxonomic order:

- Squamata—twenty-one species

- Testudines—fourteen species (six sea turtles, two tortoises [land-dwelling turtles], and six other turtle species)

- Crocodilia—two species

The ten reptile species with the highest expenditures under the ESA during fiscal year 2006 are shown in Table 6.5. The list is dominated by tortoise and sea turtle species.

### Imperiled Tortoises in the United States

GOPHER TORTOISES. In 1987 the western population of the gopher tortoise was listed as threatened under the ESA. This population is found west of the Tombigbee and Mobile rivers in Alabama and across Mississippi and Louisiana. Gopher tortoises are land-dwelling turtles that prefer habitat in longleaf pine ecosystems with sandy soils. The tortoises spend much of their time in sandy burrows that often provide shelter for other animals, such as snakes and frogs. A recovery plan for the gopher tortoise was completed in 1990. At that time the primary threats to the species were habitat degradation and illegal taking.

**TABLE 6.4**

## Endangered and threatened reptile species, February 2008

| Common name | Scientific name | Listing status[a] | Recovery plan date | Recovery plan status[b] |
|---|---|---|---|---|
| Alabama red-belly turtle | Pseudemys alabamensis | E | 1/8/1990 | F |
| Alameda whipsnake (=striped racer) | Masticophis lateralis euryxanthus | T | 4/7/2003 | D |
| American alligator | Alligator mississippiensis | T(S/A) | None | — |
| American crocodile | Crocodylus acutus | E;T | 5/18/1999 | F |
| Atlantic salt marsh snake | Nerodia clarkii taeniata | T | 12/15/1993 | F |
| Bluetail mole skink | Eumeces egregius lividus | T | 5/18/1999 | F |
| Blunt-nosed leopard lizard | Gambelia silus | E | 9/30/1998 | F |
| Bog (=Muhlenberg) turtle | Clemmys muhlenbergii | T;T(S/A) | 5/15/2001 | F |
| Coachella Valley fringe-toed lizard | Uma inornata | T | 9/11/1985 | F |
| Concho water snake | Nerodia paucimaculata | T | 9/27/1993 | F |
| Copperbelly water snake | Nerodia erythrogaster neglecta | T | 9/6/2007 | D |
| Culebra Island giant anole | Anolis roosevelti | E | 1/28/1983 | F |
| Desert tortoise | Gopherus agassizii | T;T(S/A) | 6/28/1994 | F |
| Eastern indigo snake | Drymarchon corais couperi | T | 4/22/1982 | F |
| Flattened musk turtle | Sternotherus depressus | T | 2/26/1990 | F |
| Giant garter snake | Thamnophis gigas | T | 7/2/1999 | D |
| Gopher tortoise | Gopherus polyphemus | T | 12/26/1990 | F |
| Green sea turtle | Chelonia mydas | E;T | 1/12/1998 | RF(1) |
| Hawksbill sea turtle | Eretmochelys imbricata | E | 12/15/1993 | RF(1) |
| Island night lizard | Xantusia riversiana | T | 1/26/1984 | F |
| Kemp's ridley sea turtle | Lepidochelys kempii | E | 8/21/1992 | RF(1) |
| Lake Erie water snake | Nerodia sipedon insularum | T | 9/25/2003 | F |
| Leatherback sea turtle | Dermochelys coriacea | E | 1/12/1998 | RF(1) |
| Loggerhead sea turtle | Caretta caretta | T | 1/12/1998 | RF(1) |
| Mona boa | Epicrates monensis monensis | T | 4/19/1984 | F |
| Mona ground iguana | Cyclura cornuta stejnegeri | T | 4/19/1984 | F |
| Monito gecko | Sphaerodactylus micropithecus | E | 3/27/1986 | F |
| New Mexico ridge-nosed rattlesnake | Crotalus willardi obscurus | T | 3/22/1985 | F |
| Olive ridley sea turtle | Lepidochelys olivacea | E;T | 1/12/1998 | RF(1) |
| Plymouth red-bellied turtle | Pseudemys rubriventris bangsi | E | 5/6/1994 | RF(2) |
| Puerto Rican boa | Epicrates inornatus | E | 3/27/1986 | F |
| Ringed map turtle | Graptemys oculifera | T | 4/8/1988 | F |
| San Francisco garter snake | Thamnophis sirtalis tetrataenia | E | 9/11/1985 | F |
| Sand skink | Neoseps reynoldsi | T | 5/18/1999 | F |
| St. Croix ground lizard | Ameiva polops | E | 3/29/1984 | F |
| Virgin Islands tree boa | Epicrates monensis granti | E | 3/27/1986 | F |
| Yellow-blotched map turtle | Graptemys flavimaculata | T | 3/15/1993 | F |

[a]E = Endangered; T = Threatened; T(S/A) = Threatened Due to Similarity of Appearance.
[b]Recovery plan stages: F = Final; D = Draft; RF = Final Revision.

SOURCE: Adapted from "Listed FWS/Joint FWS and NMFS Species and Populations with Recovery Plans (Sorted by Listed Entity)" and "Listed U.S. Species by Taxonomic Group," in *USFWS Threatened and Endangered Species System (TESS)*, U.S. Department of the Interior, U.S. Fish and Wildlife Service, February 5, 2008, http://ecos.fws.gov/tess_public/SpeciesRecovery.do?sort=1 and http://ecos.fws.gov/tess_public/SpeciesReport.do?kingdom=V&listing Type=L (accessed February 5, 2008)

**TABLE 6.5**

## Reptile species with the highest expenditures under the Endangered Species Act, fiscal year 2006

| Ranking | Species | Expenditure |
|---|---|---|
| 1 | Gopher tortoise | $13,348,459 |
| 2 | Desert tortoise | $10,890,015 |
| 3 | Leatherback sea turtle | $6,824,249 |
| 4 | Loggerhead sea turtle | $6,791,863 |
| 5 | Green sea turtle | $4,161,684 |
| 6 | Kemp's ridley sea turtle | $3,753,258 |
| 7 | Hawksbill sea turtle | $2,102,828 |
| 8 | Giant garter snake | $1,465,861 |
| 9 | Eastern indigo snake | $1,460,331 |
| 10 | American alligator | $857,807 |

SOURCE: Adapted from "Table 2. Species Ranked in Descending Order of Total FY 2006 Reported Expenditures, Not Including Land Acquisition Costs," in *Federal and State Endangered and Threatened Species Expenditures: Fiscal Year 2006*, U.S. Department of the Interior, U.S. Fish and Wildlife Service, draft, 2008

Coastal longleaf pine forests in the Southeast have been highly degraded by centuries of land development. As this habitat has become more fragmented, isolated pockets of the species have resulted in poor reproduction rates. Scientists fear that genetic drift and interbreeding are already occurring within the population. During the Great Depression of the 1930s gopher tortoises were a highly prized meat source. Since that time their numbers have been further reduced by road strikes and collection for the pet trade. Natural predators include raccoons, foxes, snakes, and fire ants that prey on eggs or hatchlings.

In *Gopher Tortoise Recovery Plan* (December 1990, http://ecos.fws.gov/docs/recovery_plan/901226.pdf), the USFWS notes that better management of government-owned forests in the region could help the survival status of the gopher tortoise. However, most lands with suitable habitat are privately owned and have already undergone,

**FIGURE 6.3**

The desert tortoise is threatened due to habitat destruction, livestock grazing, invasion of non-native plant species, collection, and predation by ravens. *U.S. Fish and Wildlife Service*

**FIGURE 6.4**

**Sea turtles that nest on U.S. coasts**

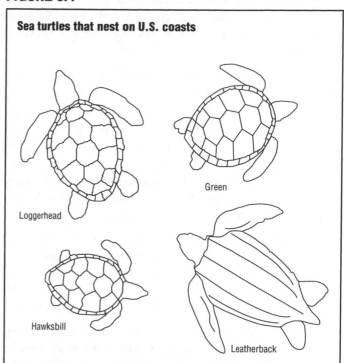

SOURCE: Adapted from "Diagrams," in *You Can Help Protect Sea Turtles*, U.S. Department of the Interior, U.S. Fish and Wildlife Service, North Florida Field Office, Undated, http://www.fws.gov/northflorida/ SeaTurtles/SeaTurtleBrochure.pdf (accessed January 30, 2008)

or are likely to undergo, development for agricultural, residential, or commercial purposes.

In 2001 the USFWS, in conjunction with the Mobile Area Water and Sewer System (MAWSS) and the conservation organizations Environmental Defense Fund and Southeastern Natural Resources, created a 222-acre (90-ha) gopher tortoise conservation bank near Big Creek Lake in Mobile, Alabama. Property owners can relocate gopher tortoises from their land to the conservation bank, which will remain undeveloped. As of April 2008, the MAWSS charged $3,500 per gopher tortoise admitted to the bank. This money is used to manage the habitat. Each bank tortoise is also equipped with a radio collar, so that the USFWS can monitor its movement.

DESERT TORTOISES. The desert tortoise (see Figure 6.3) was listed in 1990 as threatened in most of its range in the Mojave and Sonoran deserts in California, Arizona, Nevada, and Utah. Decline of this species has resulted from collection by humans, predation of young turtles by ravens, off-road vehicles, invasive plant species, and habitat destruction due to development for agriculture, mining, and livestock grazing. Livestock grazing is particularly harmful to tortoises because it results in competition for food and in the trampling of young tortoises, eggs, or tortoise burrows. Invasive plant species have caused declines in the native plants that serve as food for tortoises. Off-road vehicles destroy vegetation and sometimes hit tortoises.

Desert tortoise populations are constrained by the fact that females do not reproduce until they are fifteen to twenty years of age (individuals can live eighty to one hundred years) and by small clutch sizes, with only three to fourteen eggs per clutch. Juvenile mortality is also extremely high, with only 2% to 3% surviving to adulthood. About half this mortality is due to predation by

ravens, whose populations in the desert tortoise's habitat have increased with increasing urbanization of desert areas—human garbage provides food for ravens and power lines provide perches.

Protected habitat for the desert tortoise includes areas within Joshua Tree National Park and Lake Mead National Recreation Area in Nevada and Arizona. There is also a Desert Tortoise Research Natural Area on a Bureau of Land Management habitat in California. A Habitat Conservation Plan for the area around Las Vegas requires developers to pay fees for tortoise conservation.

## Imperiled Sea Turtles in the United States

Sea (or marine) turtles are excellent swimmers and spend nearly their entire life in water. They feed on a wide array of food items, including mollusks, vegetation, and crustaceans. Some sea turtles are migratory, swimming thousands of miles between feeding and nesting areas. Individuals are exposed to a variety of both natural and human threats. As a result, only an estimated one out of ten thousand sea turtles survives to adulthood.

There are seven species of sea turtles that exist worldwide. One species, the flatback turtle, occurs near Australia. The other six species spend part or all their life in U.S. territorial waters. The green sea turtle, hawksbill sea turtle, leatherback sea turtle, and loggerhead sea turtle also nest on U.S. lands. (See Figure 6.4.) The Kemp's ridley sea turtle and olive ridley sea turtle nest in other countries.

Imperiled sea turtles fall under the jurisdiction of the USFWS while they are on U.S. land, and under the jurisdiction of the National Marine Fisheries Service (NMFS) while they are at sea.

Information on the distribution of each imperiled sea turtle species is provided below:

- Green sea turtles—found in U.S. waters around Hawaii, the U.S. Virgin Islands, Puerto Rico, and along the mainland coast from Texas to Massachusetts and from Southern California to Alaska. Key feeding grounds are in Florida coastal waters. Primary nesting sites are the Florida east coast, the U.S. Virgin Islands, Puerto Rico, and a remote atoll in Hawaii.

- Hawksbill sea turtles—found in U.S. waters primarily around Hawaii, the U.S. Virgin Islands, Puerto Rico, and along the Gulf and southeast Florida coasts. Key nesting sites are in Puerto Rico, the U.S. Virgin Islands, Hawaii, and the southeast coast and keys of Florida.

- Kemp's ridley sea turtles—found in U.S. waters along the Gulf and New England coasts. Primary nesting sites are in Mexico and Texas along the Gulf Coast.

- Leatherback sea turtles—found in U.S. waters around Hawaii, the U.S. Virgin Islands, Puerto Rico, and along the entire Atlantic Coast. Major nesting locations are in the U.S. Virgin Islands and Georgia.

- Loggerhead sea turtles—found in U.S. waters along the entire Atlantic and Pacific coasts. Primary nesting sites occur on the Gulf and east coast of Florida and in Georgia, South Carolina, and North Carolina.

- Olive ridley sea turtles—found occasionally in southwestern U.S. waters. Major nesting sites are in Mexico along the Pacific Coast and in other tropical locations.

**THREATS TO NESTING TURTLES.** Sea turtles bury their eggs in nests on sandy beaches. The building of beachfront resorts and homes has destroyed a large proportion of nesting habitat. Artificial lighting associated with coastal development also poses a problem—lights discourage females from nesting and cause hatchlings to become disoriented and wander inland instead of out to sea. Finally, beach nourishment (the human practice of rebuilding eroded beach soil) creates unusually compacted sand on which turtles are unable to nest.

**SHRIMP NET CASUALTIES.** Shrimp trawling is recognized as one of the most deadly human activities for sea turtles in the Gulf of Mexico and the Caribbean. During the late 1970s the NMFS began developing turtle excluder devices (TEDs), which allow sea turtles to escape from shrimp nets. In "Turtle Excluder Device (TED) Chronology" (April 7, 2008, http://www.dnr.sc.gov/seaturtle/teds.htm), the South Carolina Department of Natural Resources (SCDNR) states that by the early 1980s the NMFS had developed a TED estimated to

**FIGURE 6.5**

A bycatch reduction device designed to protect sea turtles

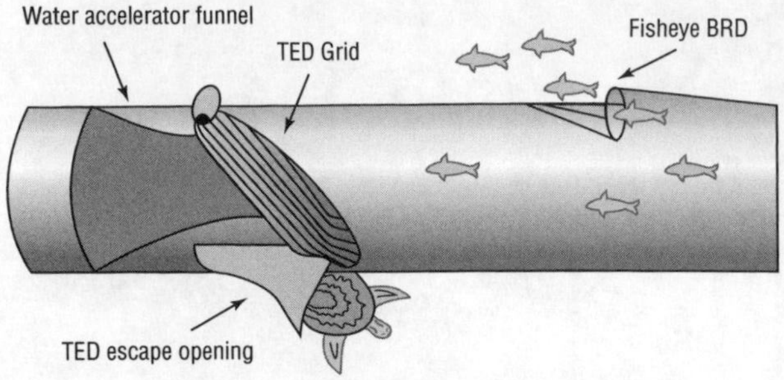

Notes: TED=turtle excluder device. BRD=bycatch reduction device.

SOURCE: Richard K. Wallace and Kristen M. Fletcher, "Figure 9," in *Understanding Fisheries Management: A Manual for Understanding the Federal Fisheries Management Process, Including Analysis of the 1996 Sustainable Fisheries Act*, 2nd ed., U.S. Department of Commerce, National Oceanic and Atmospheric Administration, National Sea Grant Office, Mississippi Alabama Sea Grant Consortium, 2001, http://nsgl.gso.uri.edu/masgc/masgch00001.pdf (accessed January 30, 2008)

exclude 97% of turtles from shrimp nets, while allowing no shrimp to escape. (See Figure 6.5.) At that time the NMFS estimated that shrimp trawling killed more than twelve thousand sea turtles annually.

The SCDNR reports that during the early 1980s the NMFS asked for voluntary use of the devices by the shrimping industry, but this request was widely ignored. By 1986 less than 2% of the U.S. shrimp fleet was using TEDs. In 1987 federal regulations were published requiring TED usage in certain fisheries during specified seasons. The result was a bitter fight between the federal government and many shrimpers and the southeastern states in which they were based. The regulations were challenged in court by the states of North Carolina and Louisiana and by shrimp industry groups that believed that the federal government was infringing upon their due process and equal protection rights. Clifford D. May reports in "Vietnamese Join U.S. Shrimp Fishermen in Protest" (*New York Times*, March 29, 1987) that shrimpers said that the devices were too expensive (approximately $400 each), posed a safety hazard to their crews, reduced their catches, and were unnecessary, because few turtles were actually caught in shrimping nets. In addition, the industry complained that the regulations unfairly burdened U.S. shrimpers, making it difficult for them to compete against foreign shrimpers.

Many lawsuits and administrative problems delayed federal enforcement of TED usage until July 20, 1989. Enforcement implementation set off a two-day revolt among Gulf Coast shrimpers. They reportedly "blockaded harbors, disrupted navigation, and engaged in other forms of violence to protest the TED regulations." On

July 24, 1989, the federal government backed down, issuing a forty-five-day reprieve in TED enforcement while other options for turtle protection were considered. The next day a coalition of environmental groups sued the federal government for failing to enforce the TED regulations and eventually won their case. By 1991 year-round TED use was required for U.S. shrimpers.

On November 21, 1989, Public Law 101-162, Section 609, was enacted in the United States banning the import of shrimp from countries that use harvesting methods deemed harmful to sea turtles. The law was challenged by India, Malaysia, Pakistan, and Thailand as violating commerce agreements under the World Trade Organization (WTO). In 1998 a WTO commission found that the United States was not implementing the law consistently with all countries. In return the United States agreed to change its implementation procedures and offer technical assistance to those countries that requested it.

Each year by May 1 the U.S. Department of State issues a list of nations certified to import shrimp into the United States. Certification is based, in part, on the results of inspections conducted by the Department of State and the NMFS. In the press release "Sea Turtle Conservation and Shrimp Imports" (May 3, 2007, http://www.state.gov/r/pa/prs/ps/2007/may/84238.htm), the Department of State lists sixteen nations that were certified in May 2007 for shrimp imports under Section 609: Belize, Colombia, Costa Rica, Ecuador, El Salvador, Guatemala, Guyana, Honduras, Madagascar, Mexico, Nicaragua, Nigeria, Pakistan, Panama, Suriname, and Venezuela. Certification means that the shrimp were obtained using TEDs or in some other manner that does not endanger sea turtles. Shrimp imports are allowed from noncertified countries on a shipment-by-shipment basis if the respective governments can show that the shrimp were harvested in a manner not harmful to sea turtles.

KEMP'S RIDLEY TURTLES. Kemp's ridley turtle is the smallest sea turtle, with individuals measuring about 3 feet (1 m) in length and weighing less than 100 pounds (45.3 kg). Kemp's ridley is also the most endangered of the sea turtle species. It has two major nesting sites: Rancho Nuevo, Mexico (the primary nesting location), and the Texas Gulf Coast.

The decline of the Kemp's ridley sea turtle is due primarily to human activities such as egg collecting, fishing for juveniles and adults, and killing of adults for meat or other products. In addition, the turtles have historically been subject to high levels of incidental take by shrimp trawlers. They are also affected by pollution from oil wells and by floating debris in the Gulf of Mexico, which can choke or entangle turtles. Now under strict protection, the population appears to be in the earliest stages of recovery. In 2001 the Texas Parks and Wildlife Depart-

ment enacted restrictions on shrimp trawling within Gulf waters near nesting sea turtle populations. The NPS reports in "The 2007 Sea Turtle Nesting Season" (September 17, 2007, http://www.nps.gov/pais/naturescience/2007-season.htm) that a record 128 Kemp's ridley nests along the Texas coast were found during the 2007 nesting season (April to July). Laid eggs were collected and incubated by the NPS, and the hatchlings were released onto beaches at Padre Island National Seashore.

## Imperiled Snakes and Lizards

As of February 2008, there were twelve snakes (including whip snakes and boas) and nine lizards (including skinks, anoles, and geckos) listed as endangered or threatened under the ESA. (See Table 6.4.) Some notable species are discussed in the following sections.

GIANT GARTER SNAKES. In 1993 the giant garter snake was listed as threatened under the ESA. This species is found only in California. It prefers agricultural wetlands (such as rice fields), canals, ponds, streams, and other small water bodies. Extensive land development in the Central Valley of the state has severely depleted the snake's habitat. Other threats to their survival include invasive predatory fishes, water pollution, and flood control activities. In 1999 the USFWS published *Draft Recovery Plan for the Giant Garter Snake* (1999, http://www.fws.gov/pacific/news/1999/garter.pdf), and in 2007 the agency initiated a five-year status review of the species to determine if its listing is still appropriate.

SAN FRANCISCO GARTER SNAKES. The San Francisco garter snake is one of the most endangered reptiles in the United States. It was one of the first species to be listed under the ESA. The decline of this species can be attributed primarily to habitat loss resulting from urbanization. Most of the snake's habitat was lost when the Skyline Ponds, located along Skyline Boulevard south of San Francisco County along the San Andreas Fault, were drained in 1966 for development. In addition, the building of the San Francisco International Airport and the Bay Area Rapid Transit regional commuter network destroyed additional snake habitat. Pollution and illegal collection have also contributed to the species' decline. Most San Francisco garter snakes today inhabit areas in San Mateo County, south of San Francisco. The species lives close to streams or ponds and feeds mainly on frogs, including Pacific tree frogs, small bullfrogs, and California red-legged frogs, which are also endangered.

LAKE ERIE WATER SNAKES. The Lake Erie water snake inhabits portions of the Ohio mainland and several small islands in Lake Erie. Its population has declined primarily due to habitat loss and human persecution, among other factors. The Lake Erie water snake is now extinct on three islands that it previously inhabited. The species was listed as threatened in 1999, and in 2003 the USFWS published *Lake Erie Watersnake Recovery Plan* (September 2003, http://www.fws.gov/midwest/endangered/reptiles/lews-fnl-rpla-sm.pdf).

MONITO GECKOS. The endangered Monito gecko is a small lizard less than 2 inches (5 cm) long. This species exists only on the 38-acre (15-ha) Monito Island off the Puerto Rican coast. Endangerment of the Monito gecko has resulted from human activity and habitat destruction. After World War II (1939–1945) the U.S. military used Monito Island as a site for bombing exercises, causing large-scale habitat destruction. In 1982 the USFWS observed only twenty-four Monito geckos on Monito Island. In 1985 Monito Island was designated critical habitat for the species. The Commonwealth of Puerto Rico is now managing the island for the gecko and as a refuge for seabirds; unauthorized human visitation is prohibited.

HORNED LIZARDS. Horned lizards are native to the deserts of North America. There are fourteen species of horned lizards. All species have flat, broad torsos and spiny scales and feed largely on ants. Even though all horned lizards are reptiles, they are often referred to as horny toads because they bear some resemblance to toads in size and shape.

The Texas horned lizard was once abundant in the state of Texas and was designated the official state reptile in 1992. It has declined largely as a result of pesticide pollution, the spread of invasive fire ants across the state, and habitat loss. It is protected by state law in Texas.

Ted J. Case, Robert N. Fisher, and Andrew V. Suarez of the University of California, San Diego, indicate in "Spatial Patterns in the Abundance of the Coastal Horned Lizard" (*Conservation Biology*, vol. 16, no. 1, February 2002) that besides habitat loss, California coastal horned lizards have been negatively affected by the proliferation of tiny black and dark brown Argentine ants, which have displaced the larger native ants on which the horned lizards depend for much of their food. Because the smaller, faster Argentine ants are more difficult to catch, coastal horned lizards from the Mexican border up to Los Angeles have experienced a sharp decline.

## Imperiled Crocodilians

Crocodilians play a crucial role in their habitat. They control fish populations and dig water holes, which are important to many species in times of drought. The disappearance of alligators and crocodiles has a profound effect on the biological communities these animals occupy. There are two imperiled crocodilian species in the United States: the American alligator and the American crocodile. They are similar in appearance with only slight differences. The crocodile has a narrower more pointed snout and an indentation in its upper jaw that allows a tooth to be seen when its mouth is closed.

The American alligator has a unique history under the ESA. It was on the first list of endangered species published in 1967. During the 1970s and 1980s populations of the species in many states rebounded in abundance and could have been delisted. Instead, it was reclassified as threatened. This measure was taken, in part, because federal officials acknowledged a certain amount of "public hostility" toward the creatures and feared that delisting would open the population to excessive hunting. Also, it was feared that the American alligator was so similar in appearance to the highly endangered American crocodile that delisting the alligator might lead to accidental taking of the crocodile species. By 1987 the alligator was considered fully recovered in the United States. As of February 2008, the alligator was listed as threatened due to similarity of appearance to other crocodilians throughout its entire range.

The American crocodile is another success story of the ESA. When the species was originally listed as endangered in 1975, less than three hundred individuals existed. Over the next three decades the species thrived and expanded its nesting range to new locations on the east and west coasts of Florida. In 2005 the USFWS initiated a five-year status review of the species. In 2007 the western distinct population segment of the species in Florida was downlisted from endangered to threatened. At that time an estimated two thousand American crocodiles lived in the state, not including hatchlings.

## Threatened and Endangered Foreign Reptile Species

As of February 2008, there were ninety-five foreign reptile species listed under the ESA. (See Table 6.6.) A handful are found both in the United States and foreign countries.

The IUCN reports in *2007 Red List of Threatened Species* that 422 reptile species are threatened. This represents nearly a third (30%) of the 1,385 reptile species evaluated, but only 5% of all described species (8,240).

FOREIGN LIZARDS AND TURTLES. Monitor lizards are among the largest lizard species in existence. The Komodo dragon, native to only a few islands in Indonesia, is the world's largest lizard. It reaches lengths of as much as 10 feet (3 m) and weighs up to 300 pounds (136 kg). Even though the Komodo dragon is protected under Appendix I of the Convention on International Trade in Endangered Species of Wild Fauna and Flora (CITES), one of the greatest threats to this species is illegal trade.

Gray's Monitor, a species found in forested low mountain habitats of the Philippine Islands, is also prized in illegal trade. Gray's Monitor is also protected under

**TABLE 6.6**

**Foreign endangered and threatened reptile species, February 2008**

| Common name | Scientific name | Listing status* | U.S. and/or foreign listed | Foreign range |
|---|---|---|---|---|
| Acklins ground iguana | Cyclura rileyi nuchalis | T | Foreign | West Indies - Bahamas |
| African dwarf crocodile | Osteolaemus tetraspis tetraspis | E | Foreign | West Africa |
| African slender-snouted crocodile | Crocodylus cataphractus | E | Foreign | Western and Central Africa |
| Allen's Cay iguana | Cyclura cychlura inornata | T | Foreign | West Indies - Bahamas |
| American crocodile | Crocodylus acutus | E;T | US/foreign | Mexico, Caribbean, Central and South America |
| Andros Island ground iguana | Cyclura cychlura cychlura | T | Foreign | West Indies - Bahamas |
| Anegada ground iguana | Cyclura pinguis | E | Foreign | West Indies - British Virgin Islands (Anegada Island) |
| Angulated tortoise | Geochelone yniphora | E | Foreign | Malagasy Republic (=Madagascar) |
| Apaporis River caiman | Caiman crocodilus apaporiensis | E | Foreign | Colombia |
| Aquatic box turtle | Terrapene coahuila | E | Foreign | Mexico |
| Aruba Island rattlesnake | Crotalus unicolor | T | Foreign | Aruba Island (Netherland Antilles) |
| Barrington land iguana | Conolophus pallidus | E | Foreign | Ecuador (Galapagos Islands) |
| Black caiman | Melanosuchus niger | E | Foreign | Amazon Basin |
| Black softshell turtle | Trionyx nigricans | E | Foreign | Bangladesh |
| Bolson tortoise | Gopherus flavomarginatus | E | Foreign | Mexico |
| Brazilian sideneck turtle | Phrynops hogei | E | Foreign | Brazil |
| Broad-snouted caiman | Caiman latirostris | E | Foreign | Brazil, Argentina, Paraguay, Uruguay |
| Brother's Island tuatara | Sphenodon guntheri | E | Foreign | New Zealand (N. Brother's Island) |
| Brown caiman | Caiman crocodilus fuscus (includes Caiman crocodilus chiapasius) | T(S/A) | Foreign | Mexico, Central America, Colombia, Ecuador, Venezuela, Peru |
| Burmese peacock turtle | Morenia ocellata | E | Foreign | Burma |
| Cat Island turtle | Trachemys terrapen | E | Foreign | West Indies - Jamaica, Bahamas |
| Cayman Brac ground iguana | Cyclura nubila caymanensis | T | Foreign | West Indies - Cayman Islands |
| Central American river turtle | Dermatemys mawii | E | Foreign | Mexico, Belize, Guatemala |
| Ceylon mugger crocodile | Crocodylus palustris kimbula | E | Foreign | Sri Lanka |
| Chinese alligator | Alligator sinensis | E | Foreign | China |
| Common caiman | Caiman crocodilus crocodilus | T(S/A) | Foreign | Brazil, Colombia, Ecuador, French Guiana, Guyana, Suriname, Venezuela, Bolivia, Peru |
| Congo dwarf crocodile | Osteolaemus tetraspis osborni | E | Foreign | Congo River drainage |
| Cuatro Cienegas softshell turtle | Trionyx ater | E | Foreign | Mexico |
| Cuban crocodile | Crocodylus rhombifer | E | Foreign | Cuba |
| Cuban ground iguana | Cyclura nubila nubila | T | Foreign | Cuba |
| Day gecko | Phelsuma edwardnewtoni | E | Foreign | Indian Ocean - Mauritius |
| Desert monitor | Varanus griseus | E | Foreign | North Africa to Aral Sea, through Central Asia to Pakistan, Northwest India |
| Desert tortoise | Gopherus agassizii | T;T(S/A) | US/foreign | Mexico |
| Exuma Island iguana | Cyclura cychlura figginsi | T | Foreign | West Indies - Bahamas |
| Fiji banded iguana | Brachylophus fasciatus | E | Foreign | Pacific - Fiji, Tonga |
| Fiji crested iguana | Brachylophus vitiensis | E | Foreign | Pacific - Fiji |
| Galapagos tortoise | Geochelone nigra (=elephantopus) | E | Foreign | Ecuador (Galapagos Islands) |
| Gavial | Gavialis gangeticus | E | Foreign | Pakistan, Burma, Bangladesh, India, Nepal |
| Geometric turtle | Psammobates geometricus | E | Foreign | South Africa |
| Grand Cayman ground iguana | Cyclura nubila lewisi | E | Foreign | West Indies - Cayman Islands |
| Green sea turtle | Chelonia mydas | E;T | US/foreign | Circumglobal in tropical and temperate seas and oceans |
| Hawksbill sea turtle | Eretmochelys imbricata | E | US/foreign | Tropical seas |
| Hierro giant lizard | Gallotia simonyi simonyi | E | Foreign | Spain (Canary Islands) |
| Ibiza wall lizard | Podarcis pityusensis | T | Foreign | Spain (Balearic Islands) |
| Inagua Island turtle | Trachemys stejnegeri malonei | E | Foreign | West Indies - Bahamas (Great Inagua Island) |
| Indian (=Bengal) monitor | Varanus bengalensis | E | Foreign | Iran, Iraq, India, Sri Lanka, Malaysia, Afghanistan, Burma, Vietnam, Thailand |
| Indian python | Python molurus molurus | E | Foreign | Sri Lanka and India |
| Indian sawback turtle | Kachuga tecta tecta | E | Foreign | India |
| Indian softshell turtle | Trionyx gangeticus | E | Foreign | Pakistan, India |
| Jamaican boa | Epicrates subflavus | E | Foreign | Jamaica |
| Jamaican iguana | Cyclura collei | E | Foreign | West Indies - Jamaica |
| Kemp's ridley sea turtle | Lepidochelys kempii | E | US/foreign | Tropical and temperate seas in Atlantic Basin, incl. Gulf of Mexico |
| Komodo Island monitor | Varanus komodoensis | E | Foreign | Indonesia (Komodo, Rintja, Padar, and western Flores Island) |

CITES Appendix I. Many turtles are highly imperiled, particularly in Asia, where they are hunted for both food and medicine.

**FOREIGN CROCODILIANS.** Illegal trade poses one of the greatest threats to crocodilians, despite CITES restrictions. Conservation efforts include enforcement of trade restrictions and habitat restoration. Captive breeding programs are also under way for several species.

The Chinese alligator is one of many species listed in CITES Appendix I. However, this species is among those most prized by collectors. The false gavial, a crocodilian that grows to 13 feet (4 m) in length and is native to

**TABLE 6.6**

**Foreign endangered and threatened reptile species, February 2008** [CONTINUED]

| Common name | Scientific name | Listing status* | U.S. and/or foreign listed | Foreign range |
|---|---|---|---|---|
| Lake Erie water snake | Nerodia sipedon insularum | T | US/foreign | U.S.A. (OH), Canada (Ontario) |
| Lar Valley viper | Vipera latifii | E | Foreign | Iran |
| Leatherback sea turtle | Dermochelys coriacea | E | US/foreign | Tropical, temperate, and subpolar seas |
| Loggerhead sea turtle | Caretta caretta | T | US/foreign | Circumglobal in tropical and temperate seas and oceans |
| Madagascar radiated tortoise | Geochelone radiata | E | Foreign | Malagasy Republic (=Madagascar) |
| Maria Island ground lizard | Cnemidophorus vanzoi | E | Foreign | West Indies - St. Lucia (Maria Islands) |
| Maria Island snake | Liophus ornatus | E | Foreign | West Indies - St. Lucia (Maria Islands) |
| Mayaguana iguana | Cyclura carinata bartschi | T | Foreign | West Indies - Bahamas |
| Morelet's crocodile | Crocodylus moreletii | E | Foreign | Mexico, Belize, Guatemala |
| Mugger crocodile | Crocodylus palustris palustris | E | Foreign | India, Pakistan, Iran, Bangladesh |
| New Mexican ridge-nosed rattlesnake | Crotalus willardi obscurus | T | US/foreign | Mexico |
| Nile crocodile | Crocodylus niloticus | T | Foreign | Africa, Middle East |
| Olive ridley sea turtle | Lepidochelys olivacea | E;T | US/foreign | Circumglobal in tropical and temperate seas |
| Orinoco crocodile | Crocodylus intermedius | E | Foreign | South America - Orinoco River Basin |
| Peacock softshell turtle | Trionyx hurum | E | Foreign | India, Bangladesh |
| Philippine crocodile | Crocodylus novaeguineae mindorensis | E | Foreign | Philippine Islands |
| River terrapin | Batagur baska | E | Foreign | Malaysia, Bangladesh, Burma, India, Indonesia |
| Round Island bolyeria boa | Bolyeria multocarinata | E | Foreign | Indian Ocean - Mauritius |
| Round Island casarea boa | Casarea dussumieri | E | Foreign | Indian Ocean - Mauritius |
| Round Island day gecko | Phelsuma guentheri | E | Foreign | Indian Ocean - Mauritius |
| Round Island skink | Leiolopisma telfairi | T | Foreign | Indian Ocean - Mauritius |
| Saltwater crocodile | Crocodylus porosus | E;T | Foreign | Southeast Asia, Australia, Papua New Guinea, Islands of the West Pacific Ocean |
| San Esteban Island chuckwalla | Sauromalus varius | E | Foreign | Mexico |
| Serpent Island gecko | Cyrtodactylus serpensinsula | T | Foreign | Indian Ocean - Mauritius |
| Short-necked or western swamp turtle | Pseudemydura umbrina | E | Foreign | Australia |
| Siamese crocodile | Crocodylus siamensis | E | Foreign | Southeast Asia, Malay Peninsula |
| South American red-lined turtle | Trachemys scripta callirostris | E | Foreign | Colombia, Venezuela |
| Spotted pond turtle | Geoclemys hamiltonii | E | Foreign | North India, Pakistan |
| Tartaruga | Podocnemis expansa | E | Foreign | South America - Orinoco River and Amazon River Basins |
| Three-keeled Asian turtle | Melanochelys tricarinata | E | Foreign | Central India to Bangladesh and Burma |
| Tomistoma | Tomistoma schlegelii | E | Foreign | Malaysia, Indonesia |
| Tracaja | Podocnemis unifilis | E | Foreign | South America - Orinoco River and Amazon River Basins |
| Tuatara | Sphenodon punctatus | E | Foreign | New Zealand |
| Turks and Caicos iguana | Cyclura carinata carinata | T | Foreign | West Indies - Turks and Caicos Islands |
| Virgin Islands tree boa | Epicrates monensis granti | E | US/foreign | British Virgin Islands |
| Watling Island ground iguana | Cyclura rileyi rileyi | E | Foreign | West Indies - Bahamas |
| White Cay ground iguana | Cyclura rileyi cristata | T | Foreign | West Indies - Bahamas |
| Yacare caiman | Caiman yacare | T | Foreign | Bolivia, Argentina, Peru, Brazil |
| Yellow monitor | Varanus flavescens | E | Foreign | West Pakistan through India to Bangladesh |

*E = Endangered; T = Threatened; T(S/A) = Threatened Due to Similarity of Appearance.

SOURCE: Adapted from "Listed FWS/Joint FWS and NMFS Species and Populations with Recovery Plans (Sorted by Listed Entity)" and "Listed U.S. Species by Taxonomic Group," in *USFWS Threatened and Endangered Species System (TESS)*, U.S. Department of the Interior, U.S. Fish and Wildlife Service, February 5, 2008, http://ecos.fws.gov/tess_public/SpeciesRecovery.do?sort=1 and http://ecos.fws.gov/tess_public/SpeciesReport.do?kingdom=V&listing Type=L (accessed February 5, 2008)

Indonesia, is also threatened by illegal collection. Like the Chinese alligator, the false gavial is protected under CITES Appendix I.

**FOREIGN TUATARAS.** The 2-foot (0.6-m) long, lizard-like tuatara is sometimes called a living fossil, being the sole existing representative of a once diverse group, the Sphenodontia, which coexisted with dinosaurs. Tuataras are native to New Zealand and the Cook Strait. Like many other reptiles, tuataras are valued by collectors. They are protected by CITES under Appendix I.

# CHAPTER 7

# TERRESTRIAL MAMMALS

Terrestrial animals are animals that inhabit the land. Mammals are warm blooded, breathe air, have hair at some point in their life, give birth to live young (as opposed to laying eggs), and nourish their young by secreting milk.

The biggest cause of terrestrial mammalian decline and extinction in the twenty-first century is habitat loss and degradation. As humans convert forests, grasslands, rivers, and wetlands for various uses, they relegate many species to precarious existences in small, fragmented habitat patches. In addition, some terrestrial mammals have been purposely eliminated by humans. For example, bison (buffalo), elk, and beaver stocks were severely depleted in the United States following colonization by European settlers. All three species were nearly hunted to extinction by the end of the 1800s. The disappearance of native large game had consequences on other species. Wolves and other predators began preying on livestock and became the target of massive kill-offs by humans.

Some terrestrial mammal species have been imperiled, in part, because they are considered dangerous to human life. This has been the case for many bears, wolves, and mountain lions. Changing attitudes have led to interest in preserving all species, and conservation measures have allowed several terrestrial mammals to recover.

## ENDANGERED AND THREATENED U.S. SPECIES

As of February 2008, there were sixty-seven species of terrestrial mammals in the United States listed under the Endangered Species Act (ESA) as endangered or threatened. (See Table 7.1.) Nearly all have an endangered listing, meaning that they are at risk of extinction, and most have recovery plans in place.

The imperiled species fall into nine broad categories:

- Bats

- Bears

- Canines—foxes and wolves

- Deer, caribou, pronghorns, and bighorn sheep

- Felines—jaguars, jaguarundis, lynx, ocelots, panthers, and pumas

- Ferrets

- Rabbits

- Rodents—beavers, mice, prairie dogs, rats, squirrels, and voles

- Shrews

Table 7.2 shows the ten terrestrial mammal species with the highest expenditures under the ESA during fiscal year (FY) 2006. The gray wolf was the most expensive ($8.3 million), followed by the grizzly bear ($7.5 million) and the Indiana bat ($4.2 million).

### Bats

Bats belong to the taxonomic order Chiroptera, which means "hand-wing." They are the only true flying mammals. According to the International Union for Conservation of Nature and Natural Resources (IUCN), in *2007 Red List of Threatened Species* (2007, http://www.iucnredlist .org/), there are 1,024 species of bats worldwide; however, most are found in warm tropical regions. Only about four-dozen species inhabit the United States. They typically weigh less than two ounces and have wingspans of less than 20 inches (51 cm). Most are insectivores, meaning that insects are their primary food source. Bats prefer to sleep during the day and feed after dusk. Biologists believe that bats are vastly underappreciated for their role in controlling nighttime insect populations.

# TABLE 7.1

**Endangered and threatened terrestrial mammal species, February 2008**

| Common name | Scientific name | Listing status[a] | Recovery plan date | Recovery plan stage[b] |
|---|---|---|---|---|
| Alabama beach mouse | Peromyscus polionotus ammobates | E | 8/12/1987 | F |
| Amargosa vole | Microtus californicus scirpensis | E | 9/15/1997 | F |
| American black bear | Ursus americanus | T(S/A) | None | — |
| Anastasia Island beach mouse | Peromyscus polionotus phasma | E | 9/23/1993 | F |
| Bighorn sheep | Ovis canadensis | E | 10/25/2000 | F |
| Black-footed ferret | Mustela nigripes | E;XN | 8/8/1988 | RF(1) |
| Buena Vista Lake ornate shrew | Sorex ornatus relictus | E | 9/30/1998 | F |
| Canada lynx | Lynx canadensis | T | None | — |
| Carolina northern flying squirrel | Glaucomys sabrinus coloratus | E | 9/24/1990 | F |
| Choctawhatchee beach mouse | Peromyscus polionotus allophrys | E | 8/12/1987 | F |
| Columbian white-tailed deer | Odocoileus virginianus leucurus | E | 6/14/1983 | RF(1) |
| Delmarva Peninsula fox squirrel | Sciurus niger cinereus | E;XN | 6/8/1993 | RF(2) |
| Eastern puma (=cougar) | Puma (=Felis) concolor cougar | E | 8/2/1982 | F |
| Florida panther | Puma (=Felis) concolor coryi | E | 5/18/1999 | F |
| Florida salt marsh vole | Microtus pennsylvanicus dukecampbelli | E | 9/30/1997 | F |
| Fresno kangaroo rat | Dipodomys nitratoides exilis | E | 9/30/1998 | F |
| Giant kangaroo rat | Dipodomys ingens | E | 9/30/1998 | F |
| Gray bat | Myotis grisescens | E | 7/8/1982 | F |
| Gray wolf | Canis lupus | E;XN | 8/3/1987 | RF(1) |
| Grizzly bear | Ursus arctos horribilis | T;XN | Various | RF(1) |
| Gulf Coast jaguarundi | Herpailurus (=Felis) yagouaroundi cacomitli | E | 8/22/1990 | F |
| Hawaiian hoary bat | Lasiurus cinereus semotus | E | 5/11/1998 | F |
| Hualapai Mexican vole | Microtus mexicanus hualpaiensis | E | 8/19/1991 | F |
| Indiana bat | Myotis sodalis | E | 4/13/2007 | F |
| Jaguar | Panthera onca | E | 8/22/1990 | F |
| Key deer | Odocoileus virginianus clavium | E | 5/18/1999 | F |
| Key Largo cotton mouse | Peromyscus gossypinus allapaticola | E | 5/18/1999 | F |
| Key Largo woodrat | Neotoma floridana smalli | E | 5/18/1999 | F |
| Lesser long-nosed bat | Leptonycteris curasoae yerbabuenae | E | 3/4/1997 | F |
| Little Mariana fruit bat | Pteropus tokudae | E | 11/2/1990 | F |
| Louisiana black bear | Ursus americanus luteolus | T | 9/27/1995 | F |
| Lower Keys marsh rabbit | Sylvilagus palustris hefneri | E | 5/18/1999 | F |
| Mariana fruit bat (=Mariana flying fox) | Pteropus mariannus mariannus | T | None | — |
| Mexican long-nosed bat | Leptonycteris nivalis | E | 9/8/1994 | F |
| Morro Bay kangaroo rat | Dipodomys heermanni morroensis | E | 1/25/2000 | RD(1) |
| Mount Graham red squirrel | Tamiasciurus hudsonicus grahamensis | E | 5/3/1993 | F |
| Northern Idaho ground squirrel | Spermophilus brunneus brunneus | T | 9/16/2003 | F |
| Ocelot | Leopardus (=Felis) pardalis | E | 8/22/1990 | F |
| Ozark big-eared bat | Corynorhinus (=Plecotus) townsendii ingens | E | 3/28/1995 | RF(1) |
| Pacific pocket mouse | Perognathus longimembris pacificus | E | 9/28/1998 | F |
| Perdido Key beach mouse | Peromyscus polionotus trissyllepsis | E | 8/12/1987 | F |
| Point Arena mountain beaver | Aplodontia rufa nigra | E | 6/2/1998 | F |
| Preble's meadow jumping mouse | Zapus hudsonius preblei | T | None | — |
| Puma (=mountain lion) | Puma (=Felis) concolor (all subsp. except coryi) | T(S/A) | None | — |
| Pygmy rabbit | Brachylagus idahoensis | E | 9/7/2007 | D |
| Red wolf | Canis rufus | E;XN | 10/26/1990 | RF(2) |
| Rice rat | Oryzomys palustris natator | E | 5/18/1999 | F |
| Riparian brush rabbit | Sylvilagus bachmani riparius | E | 9/30/1998 | F |
| Riparian woodrat (=San Joaquin Valley) | Neotoma fuscipes riparia | E | 9/30/1998 | F |
| Salt marsh harvest mouse | Reithrodontomys raviventris | E | 11/16/1984 | F |
| San Bernardino Merriam's kangaroo rat | Dipodomys merriami parvus | E | None | — |
| San Joaquin kit fox | Vulpes macrotis mutica | E | 9/30/1998 | F |
| San Miguel Island fox | Urocyon littoralis littoralis | E | None | — |
| Santa Catalina Island fox | Urocyon littoralis catalinae | E | None | — |
| Santa Cruz Island fox | Urocyon littoralis santacruzae | E | None | — |
| Santa Rosa Island fox | Urocyon littoralis santarosae | E | None | — |
| Sierra Nevada bighorn sheep | Ovis canadensis californiana | E | 7/30/2003 | D |
| Sinaloan jaguarundi | Herpailurus (=Felis) yagouaroundi tolteca | E | Exempt | Exempt |
| Sonoran pronghorn | Antilocapra americana sonoriensis | E | 12/3/1998 | RF(1) |
| Southeastern beach mouse | Peromyscus polionotus niveiventris | T | 9/23/1993 | F |
| St. Andrew beach mouse | Peromyscus polionotus peninsularis | E | None | — |
| Stephens' kangaroo rat | Dipodomys stephensi (incl. D. cascus) | E | 6/23/1997 | D |
| Tipton kangaroo rat | Dipodomys nitratoides nitratoides | E | 9/30/1998 | F |
| Utah prairie dog | Cynomys parvidens | T | 9/30/1991 | F |

As of February 2008, there were nine bat species in the United States listed by the U.S. Fish and Wildlife Service (USFWS) as endangered or threatened:

- Gray bat
- Hawaiian hoary bat
- Indiana bat
- Lesser long-nosed bat
- Little Mariana fruit bat
- Mariana fruit bat

## TABLE 7.1

### Endangered and threatened terrestrial mammal species, February 2008 [CONTINUED]

| Common name | Scientific name | Listing status[a] | Recovery plan date | Recovery plan stage[b] |
|---|---|---|---|---|
| Virginia big-eared bat | *Corynorhinus (=Plecotus) townsendii virginianus* | E | 5/8/1984 | F |
| Virginia northern flying squirrel | *Glaucomys sabrinus fuscus* | E | 9/24/1990 | F |
| Woodland caribou | *Rangifer tarandus caribou* | E | 3/4/1994 | RF(2) |

[a]E = Endangered; T = Threatened; T(S/A) = Threatened Due to Similarity in Appearance; XN = Experimental Population, Non-Essential.
[b]Recovery plan stages: F = Final; D = Draft; RD = Draft Under Revision; RF = Final Revision.

SOURCE: Adapted from "Listed FWS/Joint FWS and NMFS Species and Populations with Recovery Plans (Sorted by Listed Entity)" and "Listed U.S. Species by Taxonomic Group," in *USFWS Threatened and Endangered Species System (TESS)*, U.S. Department of the Interior, U.S. Fish and Wildlife Service, February 5, 2008, http://ecos.fws.gov/tess_public/SpeciesRecovery.do?sort=1 and http://ecos.fws.gov/tess_public/SpeciesReport.do?kingdom=V&listing Type=L (accessed February 5, 2008)

## TABLE 7.2

### Terrestrial mammal species with the highest expenditures under the Endangered Species Act, fiscal year 2006

| Ranking | Species | Expenditure |
|---|---|---|
| 1 | Gray wolf | $8,337,507 |
| 2 | Grizzly bear | $7,472,950 |
| 3 | Indiana bat | $4,179,484 |
| 4 | Canada lynx | $4,057,162 |
| 5 | Florida panther | $2,864,132 |
| 6 | Black-footed ferret | $2,277,798 |
| 7 | Sonoran pronghorn | $1,483,432 |
| 8 | Red wolf | $1,159,040 |
| 9 | Gray bat | $1,020,123 |
| 10 | San Joaquin kit fox | $946,767 |

SOURCE: Adapted from "Table 2. Species Ranked in Descending Order of Total FY 2006 Reported Expenditures, Not Including Land Acquisition Costs," in *Federal and State Endangered and Threatened Species Expenditures: Fiscal Year 2006*, U.S. Department of the Interior, U.S. Fish and Wildlife Service, draft, 2008

- Mexican long-nosed bat
- Ozark big-eared bat
- Virginia big-eared bat

Bats are imperiled for a variety of reasons, including habitat degradation, disturbance of hibernating and maternity colonies, direct extermination by humans, and the indirect effects of pesticide use on insects.

INDIANA BATS. The Indiana bat is a medium-sized, brown-colored bat found throughout a region encompassing the mid-Atlantic states and into the Midwest. The bats spend their winters in hibernation spots (or hibernacula) consisting primarily of large caves and abandoned mines. The bats are extremely sensitive to any disturbances during hibernation. If they are awakened, they become agitated and waste precious energy flying around frantically. This can leave them too weak and malnourished to survive the remainder of the winter. In the springtime, adult females move to wooded areas near agricultural crops and form maternity colonies. The loss of suitable habitat due to deforestation has disrupted this

natural process. In addition, the bats have a low reproductive rate, producing only one baby per year. This makes it difficult for their populations to grow.

During the 1800s some hibernacula became popular winter visiting spots for tourists, cave explorers, bat fanciers, and well-meaning researchers. These disturbances, along with the removal of suitable maternity habitat, led to decreased numbers of Indiana bats. In 2002 winter tours were discontinued at the Wyandotte Cave in Indiana, a prime hibernacula for the bats. Biologists report that this measure has resulted in increased bat numbers in the cave.

In 2007 the USFWS published *Indiana Bat Draft Recovery Plan: First Revision* (April 2007, http://ecos.fws.gov/docs/recovery_plan/070416.pdf). The USFWS estimates that there were 883,300 Indiana bats in the United States in 1965. By 2001 this number had dropped to 381,156. Since that time the population estimate has risen, reaching 457,374 individuals in 2005. Scientists believe the species may be fully recovered by the 2020s.

### Bears

Bears belong to the family Ursidae. Their furry bodies are large and heavy, with powerful arms and legs and short tails. For the most part, they feed on fruits and insects, but they also eat meat.

As of February 2008, there were three bear species listed as endangered or threatened in the United States: the American black bear, the Louisiana black bear, and the grizzly bear. Many bears are endangered due to habitat loss. Some bears have been hunted because they are considered predatory or threatening, whereas others are hunted for sport.

According to the USFWS, in *Federal and State Endangered and Threatened Species Expenditures: Fiscal Year 2006* (draft, 2008), over $8 million was spent under the ESA on imperiled bear species during FY 2006.

The vast majority of this money (nearly $7.5 million) was devoted to the grizzly bear. (See Table 7.2.)

**GRIZZLY BEARS.** Grizzly bears are large animals, standing 4 feet (1.2 m) high at the shoulder when on four paws, and as tall as 7 feet (2 m) when upright. Males weigh 500 pounds (227 kg) on average but are sometimes as large as 900 pounds (408 kg). Females weigh 350 pounds (159 kg) on average. Grizzlies have a distinctive shoulder hump, which actually represents a massive digging muscle. Their claws are 2 to 4 inches (5 to 12.5 cm) long.

The grizzly bear was originally found throughout the continental United States, but has now been eliminated from all but a handful of western habitats. The first recovery plan for grizzly bears was published by the USFWS in 1982. A revised recovery plan was published in 1993. At that time the species was found in a few western ecosystems; however, the populations were considered distinct from one another. The grizzly bear has declined primarily due to aggressive hunting and habitat loss. It is listed as threatened under the ESA, except in nonessential experimental populations in parts of Idaho and Montana.

The federal government has established recovery zones for the grizzly bear in Yellowstone National Park, the North Continental Divide, the Selkirk and Bitterroot Mountains in Idaho, the North Cascades, the San Juan Mountains in Colorado, and the Cabinet/Yaak area on the Canadian border. Recovery plans for this species are coordinated under the Interagency Grizzly Bear Committee (http://www.igbconline.org/), which was created in 1983.

In 2007 the USFWS delisted the distinct population segment (DPS) of the grizzly bear in the Yellowstone National Park. Biologists reported that the population had grown from only two hundred to three hundred individuals in the 1970s to more than six hundred bears.

## Canines

Canine is the common term used to describe a member of the Canidae family of carnivorous animals. This family includes wolves, foxes, coyotes, jackals, and domestic dogs.

As of February 2008, there were five fox species and two wolf species listed under the ESA in the United States:

- San Joaquin kit fox
- San Miguel Island fox
- Santa Catalina Island fox
- Santa Cruz Island fox
- Santa Rosa Island fox
- Gray wolf
- Red wolf

In *Federal and State Endangered and Threatened Species Expenditures*, the USFWS notes that approximately $11 million was spent under the ESA during FY 2006 on endangered canines. This included $8.3 million for the gray wolf, nearly $1.2 million for the red wolf, and $947,000 for the San Joaquin kit fox. (See Table 7.2.)

**WOLVES.** Wolves were once among the most widely distributed mammals on Earth. Before European settlement, wolves ranged over most of North America, from central Mexico to the Arctic Ocean. Their decline has largely resulted from hunting. In 1914 Congress authorized funding for the removal of all large predators, including wolves, from federal lands. By the 1940s wolves had been eliminated from most of the contiguous United States. In 1967 the wolf, which had all but disappeared, was on the first list of endangered species issued by the USFWS. Two species of wolves exist in North America today: the gray wolf and the red wolf, and both are imperiled.

In 1991 Congress instructed the USFWS to prepare an environmental impact report on the possibility of reintroducing wolves to habitats in the United States. Reintroductions began in 1995. Over a two-year period sixty-six gray wolves from southwestern Canada were introduced to Yellowstone National Park and central Idaho.

Wolf reintroductions were not greeted with universal enthusiasm. Ranchers in particular were concerned that wolves would attack livestock. They were also worried that their land would be open to government restrictions as a result of the wolves' presence. Several measures were adopted to address the ranchers' concerns. The most significant was that ranchers would be reimbursed for livestock losses from a compensation fund maintained by the Defenders of Wildlife, a private conservation group based in Washington, D.C. In "The Bailey Wildlife Foundation Wolf Compensation Trust" (2008, http://www.defenders.org/programs_and_policy/wildlife_conservation/solutions/wolf_compensation_trust/index.php), the Defenders of Wildlife states that between 1987 and February 2008 the fund had paid out $1,047,738 to 738 ranchers, covering the losses of 2,079 sheep, 1,084 cattle, and 84 other animals killed by wolves.

Wolf introductions were legally challenged in 1997, when the American Farm Bureau Federation initiated a lawsuit calling for the removal of wolves from Yellowstone. The farm coalition scored an initial victory, but in 2000 the Tenth Circuit Court of Appeals in Denver overturned the decision on appeal by the U.S. Department of the Interior, the World Wildlife Fund, and other conservation groups.

The USFWS issues an annual report on the status of gray wolf populations in the Northern Rocky Mountain states (Idaho, Montana, and Wyoming). The most recent report is *Rocky Mountain Wolf Recovery 2006 Interagency Annual Report* (2007, http://www.fws.gov/mountain-prairie/species/mammals/wolf/annualrpt06/2006_annual_report.pdf). It places the population of gray wolves at around thirteen hundred individuals. Gray wolves in central Idaho and the greater Yellowstone Park area have been quite successful. Recovery has been more challenging in the northwestern Montana recovery area. In 2003 the northwestern Montana gray wolf population was reclassified from endangered to threatened. However, the decision was reversed in 2005 following a court challenge.

As of February 2008, the gray wolf was listed under the ESA as endangered throughout the lower forty-eight states, with the following exceptions:

- Minnesota—delisted in 2007 due to recovery

- Portions of Wyoming, Idaho, and Montana—experimental population, nonessential (listed 1994)

- Mexican gray wolf in portions of Arizona, New Mexico, and Texas—experimental population, nonessential (listed 1998)

- Western Great Lakes DPS—delisted in 2007 due to recovery

In July 2007 the USFWS proposed delisting the Northern Rocky Mountain Gray Wolf DPS outside of federal and tribal lands. The proposal was approved, and delisting became effective as of March 2008.

The red wolf was once found throughout the eastern United States, but declined as a result of habitat loss and aggressive hunting by humans. (See Figure 7.1.) The species was first listed as endangered in 1967. The red wolf is a smaller species than its relative, the gray wolf, and, despite its name, may have any of several coat colors including black, brown, gray, and yellow. In 1975, to prevent the immediate extinction of this species, the USFWS captured the twenty-some remaining individuals and began a captive breeding program. The red wolf reintroduction program began in 1987, marking the first reintroduction of a species extinct in the wild.

Red wolves now inhabit an area covering about 1 million acres (405,000 ha) in North Carolina and Tennessee, including three national wildlife refuges, a U.S. Department of Defense bombing range, some state-owned lands, and private property (with the permission and cooperation of landowners). These wolves are classified as nonessential experimental populations. Through-

**FIGURE 7.1**

The red wolf is found in the eastern United States. *U.S. Fish and Wildlife Service*

out the remainder of the lower forty-eight states, the red wolf is still considered endangered.

## Deer, Caribou, Pronghorns, and Bighorn Sheep

Deer and caribou are members of the Cervidae family, along with elk and moose. Pronghorn are the last surviving members of the Antilocapridae family and are often confused with antelopes. Bighorn sheep belong to the large Bovidae family, which also contains antelopes, bison, gazelles, and domesticated sheep, cattle, and goats. Even though these species are diverse in taxonomy, the wild populations share a common threat: they are popular big-game animals for hunters.

As of February 2008, there were five species of big game listed under the ESA:

- Woodland caribou

- Columbian white-tailed deer

- Key deer

- Sonoran pronghorn

- Bighorn sheep

According to the USFWS, in *Federal and State Endangered and Threatened Species Expenditures*, approximately $2.8 million was spent under the ESA during FY 2006 to preserve imperiled big game species. About half of the funds were devoted to the Sonoran pronghorn ($1.5 million), which is found only in Arizona. (See Table 7.2.)

**SONORAN PRONGHORNS.** The Sonoran pronghorn is one of five subspecies of pronghorn, all of which were severely depleted in the United States by the end of the nineteenth century. It is an antelope-like creature that stands approximately 3 feet (1 m) tall when fully grown. It is the fastest mammal on land in North America. The species is found in the broad valleys of the Sonoran Desert in southern Arizona, and its diet consists primarily of cacti.

The Sonoran pronghorn was on the first list of endangered species issued by the USFWS in 1967. The first recovery plan was dated 1982, and it was replaced in 1998. At that time the USFWS estimated that less than three hundred individuals of the species remained in the United States. Another two hundred to five hundred individuals were believed living in Mexico.

A variety of reasons are blamed for the imperiled status of the species. These include insufficient food and/or water, drought, predation, illegal hunting, and degradation and fragmentation of habitat due to development, primarily for livestock ranching. Pronghorn are not jumpers; hence, they are prevented from foraging by fencing. Historically, the species has been dependent on the Gila River to provide a "greenbelt" of scrubby vegetation on which the animals survived when other food sources became scarce. Agricultural and residential development has dramatically reduced river flows and is believed to be a major factor in the species' endangered status.

## Felines

*Feline* is the common term used for a member of the Felidae family. This diverse family includes bobcats, cheetahs, cougars, jaguars, jaguarundis, leopards, lions, lynx, panthers, pumas, tigers, and domesticated cats. All the wild species are under threat as development has left them with less and less natural habitat in which to live.

As of February 2008, there were seven wild feline species listed as endangered or threatened under the ESA in the United States:

- Jaguar
- Gulf Coast jaguarundi
- Sinaloan jaguarundi
- Canada lynx
- Ocelot
- Florida panther
- Puma

The USFWS notes in *Federal and State Endangered and Threatened Species Expenditures* that nearly $7 million was spent under the ESA to preserve these species during FY 2006. Most of the money was devoted to the Canada lynx ($4.1 million) and the Florida panther ($2.9 million). (See Table 7.2.)

CANADA LYNXES. The Canada lynx is a medium-sized feline; adults average 30 to 35 inches (76 to 89 cm) in length and weigh about 20 pounds (9 kg). The animal has tufted ears, a short tail, long legs, and large flat paws that allow it to walk on top of the snow. Canada lynx inhabit cold, moist northern forests dominated by coniferous trees. Their primary food source is the snowshoe hare. Habitat modification, chiefly forest fragmentation due to timber harvesting, forest fire suppression, and human development, is blamed for imperiling both the snowshoe hare and the Canada lynx.

In 1982 the USFWS designated the Canada lynx as a candidate species for listing. However, no action was taken on listing until 1994, when the agency decided to list the species as threatened. This decision was challenged in court by a group of conservation organizations led by the Defenders of Wildlife. This began a protracted legal battle that resulted in a 2004 court order forcing the USFWS to set critical habitat for the Canada lynx. Originally, approximately 18,000 square miles (46,620 sq km) were proposed for this purpose. This area was substantially reduced to approximately 1,800 square miles (4,662 sq km) when the final designation was made in 2006.

In 2007 the USFWS initiated a five-year status review to determine the appropriateness of the threatened listing for the species. As of April 2008, the Canada lynx was listed as threatened under the ESA in fourteen states (Colorado, Idaho, Maine, Michigan, Minnesota, Montana, New Hampshire, New York, Oregon, Utah, Vermont, Washington, Wisconsin, and Wyoming).

MOUNTAIN LIONS AND FLORIDA PANTHERS. Mountain lions are large felines that can weigh between 70 and 170 pounds (32 to 77 kg). The twenty-seven subspecies of mountain lion were once found from southern Argentina to northern British Columbia, making them one of the most widely distributed terrestrial species in the Americas. Mountain lions are regionally known as panthers, pumas, or cougars. They prey on large game animals, particularly deer, and wild hogs, rabbits, and rodents. They require large home ranges for securing food. By 1900 mountain lions were nearly extinct due to habitat loss and hunting. Until the 1960s many states offered monetary rewards for the killing of mountain lions. Mountain lions are now found primarily in mountainous, unpopulated areas, particularly in the West. In most of the eastern United States, however, mountain lions have long been presumed extinct. If they are present, they are extremely rare.

The Florida panther is a subspecies of mountain lion that has been considered endangered since 1967. The species has declined due to loss of habitat from urbanization and development, water contamination, and highway traffic. Its population became so small that many of these panthers began suffering from genetic disorders due to inbreeding. In 1994 and 1995 scientists and wildlife managers introduced Texas cougars, the Florida panthers' closest relatives, into habitats in Florida. Eight female Texas cougars were released. Biologists hoped that interbreeding would strengthen and diversify the Florida panther gene pool. In fact, Florida panthers and Texas cougars once formed a single, interbreeding population that ranged freely throughout the southeastern United States. They were eventually isolated from each other by human encroachment a little more than a hundred years ago.

Florida Fish and Wildlife Conservation Commission (FFWCC) biologists have been tracking subsequent generations of Texas-Florida crossbreeds as part of a genetic restoration project. The scientists hope to develop a long-term management plan that will ensure the survival of the Florida panther as a species. In 2007 the agency released *Annual Report on the Research and Management of the Florida Panther: 2006–2007* (http://myfwc.com/panther/news/pdf/FWC_Florida_Panther_Annual_Report_2006_2007.pdf), which details species protection measures. The FFWCC estimates that less than one hundred adult individuals make up the Florida panther population. More than twenty of the animals were reported killed between 2006 and 2007, most by vehicular collisions. Five of the Texas cougars released into Florida during the mid-1990s produced at least twenty offspring that began interbreeding with Florida panthers. The FFWCC notes that none of the original Texas females are still alive in Florida.

As a result of the Florida panther's plight and public affection for the animal, in 1982 Florida declared the panther its state animal. The state's National Hockey League is named the Florida Panthers.

## Ferrets

The ferret is a member of the Mustelidae family along with muskrats, badgers, otters, mink, skunks, and weasels. Ferrets are small, furry creatures with long, skinny bodies typically less than 2 feet (0.5 m) long. They have short legs and elongated necks with small heads. Ferrets are carnivores; in the wild they feed on rodents, rabbits, reptiles, and insects.

As of February 2008, there was one U.S. species of ferret listed under the ESA: the black-footed ferret, which was listed as endangered, except in nonessential experimental populations in portions of Arizona, Colorado, Montana, South Dakota, Utah, and Wyoming.

BLACK-FOOTED FERRETS. The black-footed ferret is a small, furrow-digging mammal. It is a nocturnal creature and helps control populations of snakes and rodents, including its primary prey: black-tailed prairie dogs. Black-footed ferrets once ranged over eleven Rocky Mountain states and parts of Canada. They have declined drastically because of the large-scale conversion of prairie habitats to farmland and because their main prey, prairie dogs, have been nearly exterminated by humans.

Prairie dogs are considered pests because they dig holes and tunnels just beneath the ground surface. These can cause serious injury to horses or other large animals that step into them. (Some municipalities also poison prairie dogs in city parks, where burrow holes can trip and injure humans.) Poisons used to kill prairie dogs may also kill some ferrets.

Black-footed ferret populations had declined so greatly that the species was put on the Endangered Species List in 1973. However, prairie dog poisonings continued, and by 1979 it was believed that the black-footed ferret was extinct. In 1981 a ferret was sighted in Wyoming and discovered to be part of a remnant population. Rewards were offered for more sightings, and by the end of the year a few black-footed ferret populations had been located. These typically existed in close proximity to prairie dog populations in areas characterized by heavy sagebrush. In 1985 ferret populations were struck by disease, and by 1987 only eighteen black-footed ferrets were in existence. These individuals were captured and entered into a captive breeding program.

The captive breeding of ferrets has been markedly successful. By 1998 more than twenty-six hundred ferrets had been produced in captivity. In 1996 the Black-Footed Ferret Recovery Implementation Team (BFFRIT; http://www.blackfootedferret.org/) was created to integrate the efforts of dozens of agencies and nonprofit organizations working to save the species. In "Ten Captive-Bred Black-Footed Ferrets Released Near Vernal" (December 13, 2007, http://www.blackfootedferret.org/pdf/SLT121307.pdf), the BFFRIT reports that approximately 300 to 350 black-footed ferrets are born each year into the captive breeding program. Hundreds of the animals have been released to the wild after being injected with computer chips to aid in identification. Surveys conducted during the 2000s indicate an increasing population of unchipped (thus, wild-born) ferrets, buoying hopes that the species can be recovered.

In 1988 the USFWS published *Black-Footed Ferret Recovery Plan* (August 1998, http://ecos.fws.gov/docs/recovery_plans/1988/880808.pdf). At that time it was hoped the species could be moved from endangered to threatened status by 2010. This would require that fifteen hundred breeding adults exist in the wild in a minimum of ten separate locations, with a minimum of thirty breeding adults included in each population.

## Rabbits

Rabbits are members of the Leporidae family, along with hares. Rabbits are generally smaller than hares and have somewhat shorter ears. Both species have tall slender ears and short bodies with long limbs and thick soft fur. Domesticated rabbits are all descended from European species.

As of February 2008, there were three rabbit species listed as endangered under the ESA in the United States. The species and their primary locations are:

- Lower Keys marsh rabbit—Florida

- Pygmy rabbit—western states

- Riparian brush rabbit—California

According to the USFWS, in *Federal and State Endangered and Threatened Species Expenditures*, approximately $1 million was spent under the ESA to preserve imperiled rabbit species during FY 2006. The funds were nearly evenly split between the three imperiled species.

**PYGMY RABBITS.** The pygmy rabbit is the smallest species in the Leporidae family. Adults weigh up to 1 pound (0.4 kg) and can be up to 1 foot (30.5 cm) in length. The animals have relatively short rounded ears and small tails. Their only habitat is underneath sagebrush, a rough scrubby bush found in dry alkaline soils in the western United States. Sagebrush provides shelter and most of their food source, particularly during the winter. Pygmy rabbits are burrowers and prefer deep loose soils.

Historically, the pygmy rabbit was found throughout the semiarid regions of California, Idaho, Montana, Nevada, Utah, Washington, and Wyoming. There is a DPS located in the Columbia River basin, an area extending from northern Oregon through eastern Washington. This DPS is considered to be distinct from other populations within the historic range. The pygmy rabbits in the DPS became a candidate species in 1991. A decade later the USFWS was forced to issue an emergency endangered listing for the DPS to settle litigation filed by a number of conservation groups. In 2003 a final listing of endangered was made for the Columbia Basin DPS of the pygmy rabbit. At that time the USFWS reported that fewer than thirty individuals made up the DPS.

Since 2001 the Washington Department of Fish and Wildlife and the Oregon Zoo have operated a captive propagation project for the endangered pygmy rabbits. It is hoped that the captive animals can be returned to their native habitat at some point in the future.

## Rodents

Rodents are members of the order Rodentia, the single largest group of mammals. This order includes mice, rats, beavers, chipmunks, squirrels, prairie dogs, voles, and many other species. The IUCN indicates in *2007 Red List of Threatened Species* that there are 2,040 rodent species. Rodents are characterized by their distinctive teeth, particularly a pair of chisel-shaped incisors in each jaw. Even though most rodents are plant eaters, some species include insects in their diets.

As of February 2008, there were twenty-eight rodent species listed under the ESA as endangered or threatened:

**FIGURE 7.2**

**The prairie dog**

SOURCE: Bob Savannah, artist, "Prairie Dogs," in *Bob Savannah Line Art*, U.S. Department of the Interior, U.S. Fish and Wildlife Service, Undated, http://www.fws.gov/pictures/lineart/bobsavannah/prairiedogs.html (accessed January 30, 2008)

- Kangaroo rat—six species

- Mountain beaver—one species

- Mouse—ten species

- Prairie dog—one species

- Rat—three species

- Squirrel—four species

- Vole—three species

In *Federal and State Endangered and Threatened Species Expenditures*, the USFWS states that over $4 million was spent under the ESA to conserve imperiled rodents in the United States during FY 2006. The highest expenditures were for the Delmarva peninsula fox squirrel ($730,391) and the Alabama beach mouse ($619,830). Another rodent species of particular interest is the Utah prairie dog. Just over $300,000 was spent on this controversial species under the ESA in FY 2006.

**UTAH PRAIRIE DOGS.** Prairie dogs are members of the Sciuridae family, along with chipmunks and squirrels. (See Figure 7.2.) They are endemic to the United States and inhabit mostly arid grasslands. They are found from

Montana and North Dakota south to Texas. The nineteenth-century explorers Meriwether Lewis (1774–1809) and William Clark (1770–1838) allegedly named the animals prairie dogs because of their barklike calls.

Before settlers moved into the West, it is believed that millions of prairie dogs inhabited the area. Prairie dogs are burrowing creatures and live in colonies. They produce holes, tunnels, and dirt mounds that can be damaging to land used for agriculture. The holes also pose a tripping hazard to horses. As a result, ranchers of the late 1800s and early 1900s tried to eradicate the prairie dog using poison on a large scale. They were assisted in their efforts by the federal government.

The Utah prairie dog is a small furry creature that reaches 12 to 14 inches (30.5 to 36 cm) in length when fully grown. It is reddish brown in color and has a short, white-tipped tail. Before the control programs of the 1920s, approximately one hundred thousand of the animals lived in Utah. By 1972 the population had been reduced to about three thousand individuals. Massive poisoning by humans, disease (a form of plague), and loss of suitable habitat are blamed for the population decline. In 1973 the USFWS listed the Utah prairie dog as endangered under the ESA. Over the next decade conservation efforts began to pay off. Over thirty-five hundred of the animals were counted during a 1982 census. However, angry farmers began reporting massive crop damage caused by the creatures, particularly to summer alfalfa crops, a favorite food source for the prairie dogs. The state of Utah petitioned the USFWS to downlist the species from endangered to threatened; this reclassification took place in 1984.

The USFWS recognized that Utah farmers were not going to tolerate continuing threats to their crops from the prairie dogs. In a unique action, the agency established a special regulation allowing the Utah Division of Wildlife Resources to issue permits to private landowners who wished to kill Utah prairie dogs on their property. A maximum of five thousand of the "nuisance" animals could be taken annually in specific portions of the state. In 1991 the maximum allowable take was raised to six thousand animals per year, and the area of allowed take was expanded to include all private lands within the species' range. In addition, the USFWS began relocating Utah prairie dogs from private lands to lands under control of the federal government.

In 2003 a coalition of conservation organizations petitioned the USFWS to reclassify the Utah prairie dog as endangered. After failing to issue a ninety-day finding on the petition, the USFWS was sued by the coalition. In 2006 a settlement agreement was reached that culminated in a decision by the agency that the reclassification was not warranted. The USFWS also initiated a five-year review of the species' listing status.

## Shrews

Shrews are members of the order Insectivora, along with moles and hedgehogs. Shrews are small furry creatures with long, pointed snouts. As of February 2008, there was one shrew species listed as endangered under the ESA: the Buena Vista Lake shrew, which is endemic to California. In *Federal and State Endangered and Threatened Species Expenditures*, the USFWS states that over $16,000 was spent on this species under the ESA in FY 2006.

The Buena Vista Lake shrew is one of nine subspecies of the ornate shrew. Adult animals reach only about 4 inches (10 cm) in length and weigh around a quarter of an ounce. Historically, the subspecies was found throughout freshwater wetlands near Buena Vista Lake in south-central California. Much of this area has been converted to agricultural purposes, and many of the wetlands have been drained or filled. As a result, populations of the subspecies are believed to be severely depleted.

In 1996 the Buena Vista Lake shrew was designated a candidate species by the USFWS. In 2002 the agency was forced under court order to make a listing determination for the animal; it was listed as endangered. Following additional litigation the USFWS was ordered to make a final critical habitat determination by 2005. In 2005 the agency designated 84 acres (34 ha) in Kern County, California, as critical habitat for the Buena Vista Lake shrew.

## IMPERILED TERRESTRIAL MAMMALS AROUND THE WORLD

As of February 2008, the USFWS listed 272 foreign species of terrestrial mammals as endangered or threatened under the ESA. (See Table 7.3.) Many of the species are from groups also imperiled in the United States, such as bats, bears, big game, canines, felines, rabbits, and rodents. In addition, there are exotic animals not native to this country, particularly elephants, pandas, primates, and rhinoceroses.

In *2007 Red List of Threatened Species*, the IUCN lists 1,094 mammals as threatened. Approximately 960 of these mammals could be considered terrestrial mammals. Orders with large numbers of listed animals are:

- Rodentia (rodents)—315 species

- Chiroptera (bats)—248 species

- Primates—114 species

- Soricomorpha (shrews and moles)—97 species

- Carnivora (bears, big cats, etc.)—79 species

- Artiodactyla (big game, camels, hippos, etc.)—75 species

- Diprotodontia (kangaroos, koala bears, etc.)—34 species

Together, these orders comprise 87.9% of the threatened terrestrial mammals on the Red List. Among the

**TABLE 7.3**

**Foreign endangered and threatened terrestrial mammal species, February 2008**

| Common name | Scientific name | Listing status* | U.S. and/or foreign listed | Foreign range |
|---|---|---|---|---|
| Addax | Addax nasomaculatus | E | Foreign | North Africa |
| African elephant | Loxodonta africana | T | Foreign | Africa |
| African wild ass | Equus asinus | E | Foreign | Somalia, Sudan, Ethiopia |
| African wild dog | Lycaon pictus | E | Foreign | Sub-Saharan Africa |
| Andean cat | Felis jacobita | E | Foreign | Chile, Peru, Bolivia, Argentina |
| Apennine chamois | Rupicapra rupicapra ornata | E | Foreign | Italy |
| Arabian gazelle | Gazella gazella | E | Foreign | Arabian Peninsula, Palestine, Sinai |
| Arabian oryx | Oryx leucoryx | E | Foreign | Arabian Peninsula |
| Arabian tahr | Hemitragus jayakari | E | Foreign | Oman |
| Argali | Ovis ammon | E;T | Foreign | Afganistan, China, India, Kazakhstan, Kyrgyzstan, Mongolia, Nepal, Pakistan, Russia, Tajikistan, Uzbekistan |
| Asian elephant | Elephas maximus | E | Foreign | South-Central and Southeastern Asia |
| Asian golden (=Temmnick's) cat | Catopuma (=Felis) temminckii | E | Foreign | Nepal, China, Southeast Asia, Indonesia (Sumatra) |
| Asian tapir | Tapirus indicus | E | Foreign | Burma, Laos, Cambodia, Vietnam, Malaysia, Indonesia, Thailand |
| Asian wild ass | Equus hemionus | E | Foreign | Southwestern and Central Asia |
| Asiatic lion | Panthera leo persica | E | Foreign | Turkey to India |
| Australian native mouse | Notomys aquilo | E | Foreign | Australia |
| Australian native mouse | Zyzomys pedunculatus | E | Foreign | Australia |
| Avahi | Avahi laniger (entire genus) | E | Foreign | Malagasy Republic (=Madagascar) |
| Aye-aye | Daubentonia madagascariensis | E | Foreign | Malagasy Republic (=Madagascar) |
| Babirusa | Babyrousa babyrussa | E | Foreign | Indonesia |
| Bactrian camel | Camelus bactrianus | E | Foreign | Mongolia, China |
| Bactrian deer | Cervus elaphus bactrianus | E | Foreign | Tajikistan, Uzbekistan, Afghanistan |
| Baluchistan bear | Ursus thibetanus gedrosianus | E | Foreign | Iran, Pakistan |
| Banded hare wallaby | Lagostrophus fasciatus | E | Foreign | Australia |
| Banteng | Bos javanicus | E | Foreign | Southeast Asia |
| Barbary deer | Cervus elaphus barbarus | E | Foreign | Morocco, Tunisia, Algeria |
| Barbary hyena | Hyaena hyaena barbara | E | Foreign | Morocco, Algeria, Tunisia |
| Barbary serval | Leptailurus (=Felis) serval constantina | E | Foreign | Algeria |
| Barbary stag | Cervus elaphus barbarus | E | Foreign | Tunisia, Algeria |
| Barred bandicoot | Perameles bougainville | E | Foreign | Australia |
| Beaver (Mongolian) | Castor fiber birulai | E | Foreign | Mongolia |
| Bighorn sheep | Ovis canadensis | E | US/foreign | Canada, Mexico |
| Black colobus monkey | Colobus satanas | E | Foreign | Equatorial Guinea, People's Republic of Congo, Cameroon, Gabon |
| Black howler monkey | Alouatta pigra | T | Foreign | Mexico, Guatemala, Belize |
| Black rhinoceros | Diceros bicornis | E | Foreign | Sub-Saharan Africa |
| Black-faced impala | Aepyceros melampus petersi | E | Foreign | Namibia, Angola |
| Black-footed cat | Felis nigripes | E | Foreign | Southern Africa |
| Black-footed ferret | Mustela nigripes | E;XN | US/foreign | Chihuahua, Mexico. Presumed to be extirpated in other states of range and Canada |
| Black-footed ferret | Mustela nigripes | E;XN | US/foreign | Canada |
| Bontebok | Damaliscus pygarus (=dorcas) dorcas | E | Foreign | South Africa |
| Brazilian three-toed sloth | Bradypus torquatus | E | Foreign | Brazil |
| Brindled nail-tailed wallaby | Onychogalea fraenata | E | Foreign | Australia |
| Brown bear | Ursus arctos arctos | E | Foreign | Palearctic |
| Brown bear | Ursus arctos pruinosus | E | Foreign | China (Tibet) |
| Brown hyena | Parahyaena (=Hyaena) brunnea | E | Foreign | Southern Africa |
| Brush-tailed rat-kangaroo | Bettongia penicillata | E | Foreign | Australia |
| Buff-headed marmoset | Callithrix flaviceps | E | Foreign | Brazil |
| Bulmer's fruit bat (=flying fox) | Aproteles bulmerae | E | Foreign | Papua New Guinea |
| Bumblebee bat | Craseonycteris thonglongyai | E | Foreign | Thailand |
| Cabrera's hutia | Capromys angelcabrerai | E | Foreign | Cuba |
| Calamianes (=Philippine) deer | Axis porcinus calamianensis | E | Foreign | Philippines (Calamian Islands) |
| Canada lynx | Lynx canadensis | T | US/foreign | Canada |
| Capped langur | Trachypithecus (=Presbytis) pileatus | E | Foreign | India, Burma, Bangladesh |
| Cedros Island mule deer | Odocoileus hemionus cerrosensis | E | Foreign | Mexico (Cedros Island) |

remaining listed species are some animals that garner high levels of public interest, such as elephants and rhinoceroses.

## Big Cats

Wild tigers are found exclusively in Asia, from India to Siberia. Even though the world tiger population surpassed one hundred thousand in the nineteenth century, experts fear that fewer than ten thousand remained in the early 2000s. Besides habitat loss, countless tigers fall victim to the illegal wildlife trade every year. Many tiger body parts are used as ingredients in traditional Chinese medicine, and the big cats are also prized in the exotic pet industry.

**TABLE 7.3**

**Foreign endangered and threatened terrestrial mammal species, February 2008** [CONTINUED]

| Common name | Scientific name | Listing status* | U.S. and/or foreign listed | Foreign range |
|---|---|---|---|---|
| Central American tapir | *Tapirus bairdii* | E | Foreign | Southern Mexico to Colombia and Ecuador |
| Cheetah | *Acinonyx jubatus* | E | Foreign | Africa to India |
| Chiltan (=wild goat) markhor | *Capra falconeri (=aegragrus) chiltanensis* | E | Foreign | Chiltan Range of West-Central Pakistan |
| Chimpanzee | *Pan troglodytes* | E;T | Foreign | Africa |
| Chinchilla | *Chinchilla brevicaudata boliviana* | E | Foreign | Bolivia |
| Clark's gazelle | *Ammodorcas clarkei* | E | Foreign | Somalia, Ethiopia |
| Clouded leopard | *Neofelis nebulosa* | E | Foreign | Southeastern and South-Central Asia, Taiwan |
| Corsican red deer | *Cervus elaphus corsicanus* | E | Foreign | Corsica, Sardinia |
| Costa Rican puma | *Puma (= Felis) concolor costaricensis* | E | Foreign | Nicaragua, Panama, Costa Rica |
| Cotton-top marmoset | *Saguinus oedipus* | E | Foreign | Costa Rica to Colombia |
| Crescent nail-tailed wallaby | *Onychogalea lunata* | E | Foreign | Australia |
| Cuban solenodon | *Solenodon cubanus* | E | Foreign | Cuba |
| Dama gazelle | *Gazella dama* | E | Foreign | North Africa |
| Desert (=plain) rat-kangaroo | *Caloprymnus campestris* | E | Foreign | Australia |
| Desert bandicoot | *Perameles eremiana* | E | Foreign | Australia |
| Dhole | *Cuon alpinus* | E | Foreign | Commonwealth of Independent States, Korea, China, India, Southeast Asia |
| Diana monkey | *Cercopithecus diana* | E | Foreign | Coastal West Africa |
| Dibbler | *Antechinus apicalis* | E | Foreign | Australia |
| Douc langur | *Pygathrix nemaeus* | E | Foreign | Cambodia, Laos, Vietnam |
| Drill | *Mandrillus (=Papio) leucophaeus* | E | Foreign | Equatorial West Africa |
| Dwarf hutia | *Capromys nana* | E | Foreign | Cuba |
| Eastern jerboa marsupial | *Antechinomys laniger* | E | Foreign | Australia |
| Eastern native-cat | *Dasyurus viverrinus* | E | Foreign | Australia |
| Eastern puma (=cougar) | *Puma (= Felis) concolor couguar* | E | US/foreign | Eastern North America |
| Eld's brow-antlered deer | *Cervus eldi* | E | Foreign | India to Southeast Asia |
| False water rat | *Xeromys myoides* | E | Foreign | Australia |
| Fea's muntjac | *Muntiacus feae* | E | Foreign | Northern Thailand, Burma |
| Field's mouse | *Pseudomys fieldi* | E | Foreign | Australia |
| Flat-headed cat | *Prionailurus (= Felis) planiceps* | E | Foreign | Malaysia, Indonesia |
| Formosan rock macaque | *Macaca cyclopis* | T | Foreign | Taiwan |
| Formosan sika deer | *Cervus nippon taiouanus* | E | Foreign | Taiwan |
| Formosan yellow-throated marten | *Martes flavigula chrysospila* | E | Foreign | Taiwan |
| Francois' langur | *Trachypithecus (= Presbytis) francoisi* | E | Foreign | China (Kwangsi), Indochina |
| Gaimard's rat-kangaroo | *Bettongia gaimardi* | E | Foreign | Australia |
| Gelada baboon | *Theropithecus gelada* | T | Foreign | Ethiopia |
| Giant armadillo | *Priodontes maximus* | E | Foreign | Venezuela and Guyana to Argentina |
| Giant panda | *Ailuropoda melanoleuca* | E | Foreign | China |
| Giant sable antelope | *Hippotragus niger variani* | E | Foreign | Angola |
| Gibbons | *Hylobates spp. (including Nomascus)* | E | Foreign | China, India, Southeast Asia |
| Goeldi's marmoset | *Callimico goeldii* | E | Foreign | Brazil, Colombia, Ecuador, Peru, Bolivia |
| Golden langur | *Trachypithecus (= Presbytis) geei* | E | Foreign | India (Assam), Bhutan |
| Golden-rumped tamarin | *Leontopithecus spp.* | E | Foreign | Brazil |
| Goral | *Naemorhedus goral* | E | Foreign | East Asia |
| Gorilla | *Gorilla gorilla* | E | Foreign | Central and Western Africa |
| Gould's mouse | *Pseudomys gouldii* | E | Foreign | Australia |
| Gray (=entellus) langur | *Semnopithecus (= Presbytis) entellus* | E | Foreign | China (Tibet), India, Pakistan, Kashmir, Sri Lanka, Sikkim, Bangladesh |
| Gray wolf | *Canis lupus* | E;XN | US/foreign | Holarctic |
| Great Indian rhinoceros | *Rhinoceros unicornis* | E | Foreign | India, Nepal |
| Grevy's zebra | *Equus grevyi* | T | Foreign | Kenya, Ethiopia, Somalia |
| Guatemalan jaguarundi | *Herpailurus (= Felis) yagouaroundi fossata* | E | Foreign | Mexico, Nicaragua |
| Guizhou snub-nosed monkey | *Rhinopithecus brelichi* | E | Foreign | China |
| Gulf Coast jaguarundi | *Herpailurus (= Felis) yagouaroundi cacomitli* | E | US/foreign | Mexico |
| Haitian solenodon | *Solenodon paradoxus* | E | Foreign | Dominican Republic, Haiti |
| Hartmann's mountain zebra | *Equus zebra hartmannae* | T | Foreign | Namibia, Angola |
| Hispid hare | *Caprolagus hispidus* | E | Foreign | India, Nepal, Bhutan |
| Indochina hog deer | *Axis porcinus annamiticus* | E | Foreign | Thailand, Indochina |
| Indri | *Indri indri (entire genus)* | E | Foreign | Malagasy Republic (=Madagascar) |
| Iriomote cat | *Prionailurus (= Felis) bengalensis iriomotensis* | E | Foreign | Japan (Iriomote Island, Ryukyu Islands) |
| Jaguar | *Panthera onca* | E | US/foreign | Mexico, Central and South America |
| Japanese macaque | *Macaca fuscata* | T | Foreign | Japan (Shikoku, Kyushu and Honshu Islands) |
| Javan rhinoceros | *Rhinoceros sondaicus* | E | Foreign | Indonesia, Indochina, Burma, Thailand, Sikkim, Bangladesh, Malaysia |

In 1999 the Wildlife Conservation Society reported a rebound in the world tiger population, in part because of a worldwide moratorium on tiger hunting imposed by listing in the Convention on International Trade in Endangered Species of Wild Fauna and Flora (CITES). However, ecologists warn that tigers, which hunt deer, wild pigs, cattle, antelope, and other large mammals, are seriously threatened by loss of prey, much of which consists of nonprotected species being eliminated by hunters.

**SIBERIAN TIGERS.** The Siberian tiger is the largest cat in the world and one of the world's most endangered

| Common name | Scientific name | Listing status* | U.S. and/or foreign listed | Foreign range |
|---|---|---|---|---|
| Jentink's duiker | *Cephalophus jentinki* | E | Foreign | Sierra Leone, Liberia, Ivory Coast |
| Kabul markhor | *Capra falconeri megaceros* | E | Foreign | Afghanistan, Pakistan |
| Kashmir stag | *Cervus elaphus hanglu* | E | Foreign | Kashmir |
| Koala | *Phascolarctos cinereus* | T | Foreign | Australia |
| Kouprey | *Bos sauveli* | E | Foreign | Vietnam, Laos, Cambodia, Thailand |
| Kuhl's (=Bawean) deer | *Axis porcinus kuhli* | E | Foreign | Indonesia |
| L'hoest's monkey | *Cercopithecus lhoesti* | E | Foreign | Upper Eastern Congo River Basin, Cameroon |
| Large desert marsupial-mouse | *Sminthopsis psammophila* | E | Foreign | Australia |
| Large-eared hutia | *Capromys auritus* | E | Foreign | Cuba |
| Leadbeater's possum | *Gymnobelideus leadbeateri* | E | Foreign | Australia |
| Lemurs | *Lemuridae (incl. genera Lemur, Phaner, Hapalemur, Lepilemur, Microcebus, Allocebus, Cheirogaleus, Varecia)* | E | Foreign | Malagasy Republic (=Madagascar) |
| Leopard | *Panthera pardus* | E;T | Foreign | Africa, Asia |
| Leopard cat | *Prionailurus (=Felis) bengalensis bengalensis* | E | Foreign | India, Southeast Asia |
| Lesser long-nosed bat | *Leptonycteris curasoae yerbabuenae* | E | US/foreign | Mexico, Central America |
| Lesser rabbit bandicoot | *Macrotis leucura* | E | Foreign | Australia |
| Lesser slow loris | *Nycticebus pygmaeus* | T | Foreign | Indochina |
| Lesuer's rat-kangaroo | *Bettongia lesueur* | E | Foreign | Australia |
| Lion-tailed macaque | *Macaca silenus* | E | Foreign | India |
| Little earth hutia | *Capromys sanfelipensis* | E | Foreign | Cuba |
| Little planigale | *Planigale ingrami subtilissima* | E | Foreign | Australia |
| Long-tailed langur | *Presbytis potenziani* | T | Foreign | Indonesia |
| Long-tailed marsupial-mouse | *Sminthopsis longicaudata* | E | Foreign | Australia |
| Lowland anoa | *Bubalus depressicornis* | E | Foreign | Indonesia |
| Malabar large-spotted civet | *Viverra civettina (=megaspila c.)* | E | Foreign | India |
| Mandrill | *Mandrillus (=Papio) sphinx* | E | Foreign | Equatorial West Africa |
| Maned wolf | *Chrysocyon brachyurus* | E | Foreign | Argentina, Bolivia, Brazil, Paraguay, Uruguay |
| Mantled howler monkey | *Alouatta palliata* | E | Foreign | Mexico to South America |
| Marbled cat | *Pardofelis (=Felis) marmorata* | E | Foreign | Nepal, Southeast Asia, Indonesia |
| Margay | *Leopardus (=Felis) wiedii* | E | Foreign | U.S.A. (TX), Central and South America |
| Marsh deer | *Blastocerus dichotomus* | E | Foreign | Argentina, Uruguay, Paraguay, Bolivia, Brazil |
| McNeill's deer | *Cervus elaphus macneilii* | E | Foreign | China (Sinkiang, Tibet) |
| Mexican bobcat | *Lynx (=Felis) rufus escuinapae* | E | Foreign | Central Mexico |
| Mexican grizzly bear | *Ursus arctos* | E | Foreign | Holarctic |
| Mexican long-nosed bat | *Leptonycteris nivalis* | E | US/foreign | Mexico, Central America |
| Mexican prairie dog | *Cynomys mexicanus* | E | Foreign | Mexico |
| Mhorr gazelle | *Gazella dama mhorr* | E | Foreign | Morocco |
| Mongolian saiga (antelope) | *Saiga tatarica mongolica* | E | Foreign | Mongolia |
| Moroccan gazelle | *Gazella dorcas massaesyla* | E | Foreign | Morocco, Algeria, Tunisia |
| Mountain (=Cuvier's) gazelle | *Gazella cuvieri* | E | Foreign | Morocco, Algeria, Tunisia |
| Mountain anoa | *Bubalus quarlesi* | E | Foreign | Indonesia |
| Mountain pygmy possum | *Burramys parvus* | E | Foreign | Australia |
| Mountain tapir | *Tapirus pinchaque* | E | Foreign | Colombia, Ecuador and possibly Peru and Venezuela |
| Mountain zebra | *Equus zebra zebra* | E | Foreign | South Africa |
| Musk deer | *Moschus spp. (all species)* | E | Foreign | Central and Eastern Asia |
| New Holland mouse | *Pseudomys novaehollandiae* | E | Foreign | Australia |
| North Andean huemul | *Hippocamelus antisensis* | E | Foreign | Ecuador, Peru, Chile, Bolivia, Argentina |
| North China sika deer | *Cervus nippon mandarinus* | E | Foreign | China (Shantung and Chihli Provinces) |
| Northern swift fox | *Vulpes velox hebes* | E | Foreign | U.S.A. (northern plains), Canada |
| Northern white rhinoceros | *Ceratotherium simum cottoni* | E | Foreign | Zaire, Sudan, Uganda, Central African Republic |
| Numbat | *Myrmecobius fasciatus* | E | Foreign | Australia |
| Ocelot | *Leopardus (=Felis) pardalis* | E | US/foreign | U.S.A. (AZ, TX) to Central and South America |
| Orangutan | *Pongo pygmaeus* | E | Foreign | Borneo, Sumatra |
| Pagi Island langur | *Nasalis concolor* | E | Foreign | Indonesia |
| Pakistan sand cat | *Felis margarita scheffeli* | E | Foreign | Pakistan |
| Pampas deer | *Ozotoceros bezoarticus* | E | Foreign | Brazil, Argentina, Uruguay, Bolivia, Paraguay |
| Panamanian jaguarundi | *Herpailurus (=Felis) yagouaroundi panamensis* | E | Foreign | Nicaragua, Costa Rica, Panama |
| Parma wallaby | *Macropus parma* | E | Foreign | Australia |
| Pelzeln's gazelle | *Gazella dorcas pelzelni* | E | Foreign | Somalia |
| Peninsular pronghorn | *Antilocapra americana peninsularis* | E | Foreign | Mexico (Baja California) |
| Persian fallow deer | *Dama mesopotamica (=dama m.)* | E | Foreign | Iraq, Iran |
| Philippine tarsier | *Tarsius syrichta* | T | Foreign | Philippines |
| Pied tamarin | *Saguinus bicolor* | E | Foreign | Brazil |

species, with only approximately six hundred individuals estimated to exist in the wild. (See Figure 7.3.) There are also several hundred Siberian tigers in captivity. The Siberian tiger, also known as the Amur tiger, once occupied mixed deciduous and coniferous forest habitats in the Amur-Ussuri area in Siberia and in northern China and Korea. It is now believed to be extinct, or nearly extinct, in China and Korea.

Populations have suffered greatly from habitat loss caused by logging and deforestation, and from illegal trade. The Siberian tiger is sought for its skin, bones,

| Common name | Scientific name | Listing status* | U.S. and/or foreign listed | Foreign range |
|---|---|---|---|---|
| Pig-footed bandicoot | Chaeropus ecaudatus | E | Foreign | Australia |
| Pink fairy armadillo | Chlamyphorus truncatus | E | Foreign | Argentina |
| Preuss' red colobus monkey | Procolobus (=Colobus) preussi (=badius p.) | E | Foreign | Cameroon |
| Proboscis monkey | Nasalis larvatus | E | Foreign | Borneo |
| Przewalski's horse | Equus przewalskii | E | Foreign | Mongolia, China |
| Pudu | Pudu pudu | E | Foreign | Southern South America |
| Purple-faced langur | Presbytis senex | T | Foreign | Sri Lanka |
| Pygmy chimpanzee | Pan paniscus | E | Foreign | Zaire |
| Pygmy hog | Sus salvanius | E | Foreign | India, Nepal, Bhutan, Sikkim |
| Pyrenean ibex | Capra pyrenaica pyrenaica | E | Foreign | Spain |
| Queensland hairy-nosed wombat (incl. Barnard's) | Lasiorhinus krefftii (formerly L. barnardi and L. gillespiei) | E | Foreign | Australia |
| Queensland rat-kangaroo | Bettongia tropica | E | Foreign | Australia |
| Quokka | Setonix brachyurus | E | Foreign | Australia |
| Rabbit bandicoot | Macrotis lagotis | E | Foreign | Australia |
| Red lechwe | Kobus leche | T | Foreign | Southern Africa |
| Red-backed squirrel monkey | Saimiri oerstedii | E | Foreign | Costa Rica, Panama |
| Red-bellied monkey | Cercopithecus erythrogaster | E | Foreign | Western Nigeria |
| Red-eared nose-spotted monkey | Cercopithecus erythrotis | E | Foreign | Nigeria, Cameroon, Fernando Po |
| Rio de Oro Dama gazelle | Gazella dama lozanoi | E | Foreign | Western Sahara |
| Rodrigues fruit bat (=flying fox) | Pteropus rodricensis | E | Foreign | Indian Ocean - Rodrigues Island |
| Ryukyu rabbit | Pentalagus furnessi | E | Foreign | Japan (Ryukyu Islands) |
| Ryukyu sika deer | Cervus nippon keramae | E | Foreign | Japan (Ryukyu Islands) |
| Sand gazelle | Gazella subgutturosa marica | E | Foreign | Jordan, Arabian Peninsula |
| Saudi Arabian gazelle | Gazella dorcas saudiya | E | Foreign | Israel, Iraq, Jordan, Syria, Arabian Peninsula |
| Scaly-tailed possum | Wyulda squamicaudata | E | Foreign | Australia |
| Scimitar-horned oryx | Oryx dammah | E | Foreign | North Africa |
| Seledang | Bos gaurus | E | Foreign | Bangladesh, Southeast Asia, India |
| Serow | Naemorhedus (=Capricornis) sumatraensis | E | Foreign | East Asia, Sumatra |
| Shansi sika deer | Cervus nippon grassianus | E | Foreign | China (Shansi Province) |
| Shapo | Ovis vignei vignei | E | Foreign | Kashmir |
| Shark Bay mouse | Pseudomys praeconis | E | Foreign | Australia |
| Shortridge's mouse | Pseudomys shortridgei | E | Foreign | Australia |
| Shou | Cervus elaphus wallichi | E | Foreign | Tibet, Bhutan |
| Siamang | Symphalangus syndactylus | E | Foreign | Malaysia, Indonesia |
| Sichuan snub-nosed monkey | Rhinopithecus roxellana | E | Foreign | China |
| Sifakas | Propithecus spp. | E | Foreign | Malagasy Republic (=Madagascar) |
| Simien fox | Canis simensis | E | Foreign | Ethiopia |
| Sinaloan jaguarundi | Herpailurus (=Felis) yagouaroundi tolteca | E | US/foreign | Mexico |
| Singapore roundleaf horseshoe bat | Hipposideros ridleyi | E | Foreign | Malaysia |
| Slender-horned gazelle | Gazella leptoceros | E | Foreign | Sudan, Egypt, Algeria, Libya |
| Smoky mouse | Pseudomys fumeus | E | Foreign | Australia |
| Snow leopard | Uncia (=Panthera) uncia | E | Foreign | Central Asia |
| Sonoran pronghorn | Antilocapra americana sonoriensis | E | US/foreign | Mexico |
| South American (=Brazilian) tapir | Tapirus terrestris | E | Foreign | Colombia and Venezuela south to Paraguay and Argentina |
| South Andean huemul | Hippocamelus bisulcus | E | Foreign | Chile, Argentina |
| South China sika deer | Cervus nippon kopschi | E | Foreign | Southern China |
| Southern bearded saki | Chiropotes satanas satanas | E | Foreign | Brazil |
| Southern planigale | Planigale tenuirostris | E | Foreign | Australia |
| Spanish lynx | Felis pardina | E | Foreign | Spain, Portugal |
| Spider monkey | Ateles geoffroyi panamensis | E | Foreign | Costa Rica, Panama |
| Spider monkey | Ateles geoffroyi frontatus | E | Foreign | Costa Rica, Nicaragua |
| Spotted linsang | Prionodon pardicolor | E | Foreign | Nepal, Assam, Vietnam, Cambodia, Laos, Burma |
| Stick-nest rat | Leporillus conditor | E | Foreign | Australia |
| Straight-horned markhor | Capra falconeri jerdoni | E | Foreign | Afghanistan, Pakistan |
| Stump-tailed macaque | Macaca arctoides | T | Foreign | India (Assam) to southern China |
| Sumatran rhinoceros | Dicerorhinus sumatrensis | E | Foreign | Bangladesh to Vietnam to Indonesia (Borneo) |
| Swamp deer | Cervus duvauceli | E | Foreign | India, Nepal |
| Swayne's hartebeest | Alcelaphus buselaphus swaynei | E | Foreign | Ethiopia, Somalia |
| Tamaraw | Bubalus mindorensis | E | Foreign | Philippines |
| Tana River mangabey | Cercocebus galeritus galeritus | E | Foreign | Kenya |
| Tana River red colobus monkey | Procolobus (=Colobus) rufomitratus (=badius r.) | E | Foreign | Kenya |
| Tasmanian forester kangaroo | Macropus giganteus tasmaniensis | E | Foreign | Australia (Tasmania) |

eyes, whiskers, teeth, internal organs, and genitals. These are used for everything from skin cures to tooth medicine. Like the Florida panther, the Siberian tiger has also been weakened by inbreeding, which increases the possibility of reproductive problems and birth defects.

**CHEETAHS.** The cheetah is the fastest land animal on Earth, able to sprint at speeds up to 70 miles (113 km) per hour. Cheetahs occupy grassland, shrubland, and woodland habitats. Their range once extended through most of Africa and southwestern Asia. Currently, cheetahs are found only in a few areas in Iran, North Africa, and

TABLE 7.3

**Foreign endangered and threatened terrestrial mammal species, February 2008** [CONTINUED]

| Common name | Scientific name | Listing status* | U.S. and/or foreign listed | Foreign range |
|---|---|---|---|---|
| Tasmanian tiger | *Thylacinus cynocephalus* | E | Foreign | Australia |
| Temnick's ground pangolin | *Manis temminckii* | E | Foreign | Africa |
| Thin-spined porcupine | *Chaetomys subspinosus* | E | Foreign | Brazil |
| Tibetan antelope | *Pantholops hodgsonii* | E | Foreign | China, India, Nepal |
| Tiger | *Panthera tigris* | E | Foreign | Temperate and tropical Asia |
| Tiger cat | *Leopardus (=Felis) tigrinus* | E | Foreign | Costa Rica to Northern Argentina |
| Tonkin snub-nosed monkey | *Rhinopithecus avunculus* | E | Foreign | Vietnam |
| Toque macaque | *Macaca sinica* | T | Foreign | Sri Lanka |
| Tora hartebeest | *Alcelaphus buselaphus tora* | E | Foreign | Ethiopia, Sudan, Egypt |
| Uakari (all species) | *Cacajao spp.* | E | Foreign | Peru, Brazil, Ecuador, Colombia, Venezuela |
| Urial | *Ovis musimon ophion* | E | Foreign | Cyprus |
| Vancouver Island marmot | *Marmota vancouverensis* | E | Foreign | Canada (Vancouver Island) |
| Vicuna | *Vicugna vicugna* | E | Foreign | South America (Andes) |
| Visayan deer | *Cervus alfredi* | E | Foreign | Philippines |
| Volcano rabbit | *Romerolagus diazi* | E | Foreign | Mexico |
| Walia ibex | *Capra walie* | E | Foreign | Ethiopia |
| Western giant eland | *Taurotragus derbianus derbianus* | E | Foreign | Senegal to Ivory Coast |
| Western hare wallaby | *Lagorchestes hirsutus* | E | Foreign | Australia |
| Western mouse | *Pseudomys occidentalis* | E | Foreign | Australia |
| White-collared mangabey | *Cercocebus torquatus* | E | Foreign | Senegal to Ghana; Nigeria to Gabon |
| White-eared (=buffy tufted-ear) marmoset | *Callithrix aurita (=jacchus a.)* | E | Foreign | Brazil |
| White-footed tamarin | *Saguinus leucopus* | T | Foreign | Colombia |
| White-nosed saki | *Chiropotes albinasus* | E | Foreign | Brazil |
| Wild yak | *Bos mutus (=grunniens m.)* | E | Foreign | China (Tibet), India |
| Wood bison | *Bison bison athabascae* | E | Foreign | Canada |
| Woodland caribou | *Rangifer tarandus caribou* | E | US/foreign | Canada |
| Woolly spider monkey | *Brachyteles arachnoides* | E | Foreign | Brazil |
| Yarkand deer | *Cervus elaphus yarkandensis* | E | Foreign | China (Sinkiang) |
| Yellow-footed rock wallaby | *Petrogale xanthopus* | E | Foreign | Australia |
| Yellow-tailed woolly monkey | *Lagothrix flavicauda* | E | Foreign | Andes of Northern Peru |
| Yunnan snub-nosed monkey | *Rhinopithecus bieti* | E | Foreign | China |
| Zanzibar red colobus monkey | *Procolobus (=Colobus) pennantii (=kirki) kirki* | E | Foreign | Tanzania |
| Zanzibar suni | *Neotragus moschatus moschatus* | E | Foreign | Zanzibar (and nearby islands) |

*E = Endangered; T = Threatened; XN = Experimental Population, Non-Essential.

SOURCE: Adapted from "Listed FWS/Joint FWS and NMFS Species and Populations with Recovery Plans (Sorted by Listed Entity)" and "Listed U.S. Species by Taxonomic Group," in *USFWS Threatened and Endangered Species System (TESS)*, U.S. Department of the Interior, U.S. Fish and Wildlife Service, February 5, 2008, http://ecos.fws.gov/tess_public/SpeciesRecovery.do?sort=1 and http://ecos.fws.gov/tess_public/SpeciesReport.do?kingdom=V&listing Type=L (accessed February 5, 2008)

**FIGURE 7.3**

The Siberian tiger is one of the most endangered species in the world. It now occupies forest habitats in the Amur-Ussuri region of Siberia. *Field Mark Publications*

sub-Saharan Africa. Cheetahs hunt small prey, particularly Thomson's gazelle. The cheetah has been listed in CITES Appendix I since 1975. According to the Cheetah Conservation Fund (2008, http://www.cheetah.org/?nd=42), in 2008 there were an estimated ten thousand to fifteen thousand cheetahs in the wild.

Cheetah populations have declined for many reasons. Much of the species' habitat has been developed for agricultural or ranching use, and many of the cats are shot by farmers who wish to protect their livestock. In addition, because of their declining numbers and loss of habitat, cheetahs are badly inbred, and many individuals are infertile. Cheetahs are also smaller and less aggressive than other predators that share their environment (including lions and leopards) and often have their food kills stolen or their cubs killed. Conservation biologists have determined that to save the cheetah, human assistance in the form of habitat protection, protection from competitor species, and measures to improve the genetic diversity of the species are required.

## Elephants

Elephants are the largest land animals on Earth. They are frequently described as the "architects" of the savanna habitats in which they live. Elephants dig water holes, keep forest growth in check, and open up grasslands that support other species, including the livestock of African herders. Elephants are highly intelligent, emotional animals and form socially complex herds. There are two species of elephants: African elephants and Asian elephants, both of which are highly endangered. The African elephant, which sometimes weighs as much as six tons, is the larger species. (See Figure 7.4.) The World Wildlife Fund explains in "Elephant Ivory Trade" (2008, http://www.worldwildlife.org/trade/faqs_elephant .cfm) that in 2008 an estimated five hundred thousand African elephants and between thirty-five thousand and fifty thousand Asian elephants remained in the wild.

Elephants have huge protruding teeth (tusks) made of ivory. Ivory is valued by humans for several reasons, particularly for use in making jewelry and figurines. Piano keys were also once made almost exclusively of ivory; however, this practice has ceased. The market for ivory has had tragic consequences for African elephants. In "Africa's Environment in Crisis" (2002, http://diglib1 .amnh.org/articles/Africa/Africa_environment.html), Gordy Slack of the American Museum of Natural History states that their numbers dropped from between five million and ten million individuals in 1930 to only six hundred thousand in 1989. As a result of this decline, CITES banned worldwide commerce in ivory and other elephant products in 1990. However, like rhinoceros horns, elephant tusks continue to be illegally traded. Many elephants are poached each year. Despite continued poaching, elephant populations have recovered somewhat since receiving CITES protection.

Even though the ivory trade has always been the largest threat to elephants, conflicts between humans and elephants are an increasing issue. The ranges of many elephant herds now extend outside protected refuges, and elephants frequently come into contact with farmers, eating or otherwise destroying crops. Increasing human settlement in areas inhabited by elephants will likely result in more conflicts over time.

### Pandas

Few creatures have engendered more human affection than the giant panda, with its roly-poly character, small ears, and black eye patches on a snow-white face. Giant pandas are highly endangered. According to the National Zoo (2008, http://nationalzoo.si.edu/Animals/ GiantPandas/PandaFacts/default.cfm), in 2008 there were approximately 1,600 pandas in the wild and about 160 individuals in captivity. Pandas are endemic to portions of southwestern China, where they inhabit a few fragmentary areas of high-altitude bamboo forest. Unlike other bear species, to which they are closely related, pandas have a vegetarian diet that consists entirely of

**FIGURE 7.4**

Elephants are highly intelligent and social animals. Once on the verge of extinction, elephants have recovered somewhat after a worldwide ban on the ivory trade. *Field Mark Publications*

bamboo. Pandas also have a sixth digit that functions like a thumb and that they use to peel tender bamboo leaves from their stalks.

Pandas have become star attractions at many zoos, where they draw scores of visitors. Despite tremendous efforts, pandas have proven notoriously difficult to breed in captivity. The birth of a giant panda cub, named Hua Mei, at the San Diego Zoo in 1999 was a major event, with millions of people following the cub's progress online and in the papers through her first days of life. Hua Mei was the first panda born in captivity outside of China.

Zoos typically pay China millions of dollars for the loan of adult pandas. These funds are used to support panda conservation efforts in China, including the purchase of land for refuges as well as the development of habitat corridors to link protected areas.

**RED PANDAS.** The red panda is also called the lesser panda because it is significantly smaller than the giant panda, with a length of about 42 inches (107 cm) and a weight of only seven to fourteen pounds (3 to 6 kg). Red pandas are not related to bears—they are actually raccoon relatives. Red pandas are virtually extinct in the wild, mostly due to habitat loss and degradation. Red pandas occupy temperate forests in the foothills of the Himalayas in Nepal, Burma, and southwestern China at altitudes between 5,000 and 13,000 feet (1,524 and 3,962 m). They are solitary creatures, occupying nonoverlapping home ranges of approximately 1 square mile (2.6 sq km) for females and 2 square miles (5.2 sq km) for males. Like giant pandas, red pandas eat bamboo, focusing on the tenderest leaves. Because bamboo is not very nutritious, red pandas spend as much as thirteen hours each day eating to acquire the nutrients they need. Red pandas have difficulty recovering from population declines due to a slow rate of reproduction. A captive breeding effort for red pandas is under way at zoos across the world to prevent the complete extinction of this species.

## Big Game

Most big game species are members of the Artiodactyla order. This order contains a variety of ungulates (hoofed animals), including antelopes, bison, buffalo, camels, deer, goats, hartebeests, hippos, gazelles, impalas, and sheep. Many of the wild species have been overhunted for their meat, bones, or horns. Horns are used in traditional Chinese medicine and are popular trophies for big-game hunters. The argali is the largest of the wild sheep and is highly prized for its large curved horns.

Big game species also face threats from domesticated livestock due to competition for habitat and food resources.

## Primates

The IUCN reports in *2007 Red List of Threatened Species* that the 296 examined species of primates (excluding humans) are among the most endangered mammals. Twenty-one species are listed as critically endangered, forty-seven species as endangered, and forty-six species as vulnerable. Critically endangered primate species include the Roloway monkey (lowland tropical rain forest in Ghana and Côte d'Ivoire), the Mentawai macaque (Indonesia), Sclater's black lemur (lowland tropical rain forest, Madagascar), the red-handed howling monkey (Brazil), and the black lion tamarin (lowland tropical rain forest, Brazil), among others. Much of the endangerment of primate species is due to loss of habitat and overhunting. Primates are dependent on large expanses of tropical forests, a habitat under siege worldwide.

Countries with large numbers of primate species include Brazil, Indonesia, the Democratic Republic of Congo, and Madagascar. Many of the most endangered primate species are found on Madagascar, which has a diverse and unique primate fauna. Most of Madagascar's

FIGURE 7.5

The orangutan is highly endangered, along with the majority of the world's primate species. *Field Mark Publications*

primate species are endemic—that is, they are found nowhere else on Earth.

Habitat loss, especially the fragmentation and conversion of tropical forests for road building and agriculture, contributes to the decline of nearly all IUCN-listed primates. For example, in Indonesia and Borneo, which are home to most of the world's orangutans, deforestation has dramatically shrunk orangutan habitat. (See Figure 7.5.) Logging and extensive burning have caused many orangutans to flee the forests for villages, where they have been killed or captured by humans.

Some threatened primates also face pressures from excessive hunting and poaching. As of 2008, almost all countries have either banned or strictly regulated the trade of primates, but these laws are often hard to enforce. Primates are also used in medical research because of their close biological relationship with humans.

## Rhinoceros

Rhinoceros are among the largest land mammals. They weigh up to 8,000 pounds (3,629 kg)—as much as fifty average-sized men—and are herbivorous grazers. The name rhinoceros consists of two Greek words meaning "nose" and "horn," and rhinos are in fact the only animals on Earth that have horns on their noses. Figure 7.6 shows an African white rhinoceros with two horns. The female may be identified by her longer, more slender primary horn.

Rhinoceros have roamed Earth for more than forty million years, but in less than a century, humans—their only predators—have reduced populations to dangerously low levels. There are five species of rhinoceros: black rhino (African), white rhino (African), Sumatran rhino (found in Borneo, Malaysia, and Sumatra), Javan rhino (found in Indonesia and Vietnam), and Indian rhino

**FIGURE 7.6**

The white rhinoceros is native to Africa and can weigh up to 8,000 pounds. *U.S. Fish and Wildlife Service*

(found in India and Nepal). Certain rhino species can be divided into distinct subspecies. For example, the Javan rhino has two subspecies, one found in Vietnam and the other in Indonesia.

Hunting has been the primary cause of rhinoceros decline. Rhinoceros horn is highly prized as an aphrodisiac, as well as an ingredient in Chinese medicine (although its potency has never been shown). Rhinos were first listed by CITES in 1976. This banned international trade in the species and their products. In 1992 CITES also started requiring the destruction of horn caches confiscated from poachers. Nonetheless, people continue to buy and consume rhinoceros horn, and many poachers are willing to risk death to acquire it.

# CHAPTER 8
# BIRDS

Birds belong to the class Aves, which contains dozens of orders. Birds are warm-blooded vertebrates with wings, feathers, and light hollow bones. The vast majority of birds are capable of flight. In *2007 Red List of Threatened Species* (2007, http://www.iucnredlist.org/), the International Union for Conservation of Nature and Natural Resources (IUCN) states that 9,956 species of birds have been identified around the world. According to the U.S. Fish and Wildlife Service (USFWS; 2008, http://www.fws.gov/birds/), over eight hundred of these species spend all or part of their life in the United States.

Besides taxonomy, birds are broadly classified by their physical characteristics (such as feet or beak structure), eating habits, primary habitats, or migratory habits. For example, raptors (birds of prey) have curved beaks and talons well suited for catching prey. This category includes eagles, vultures, hawks, buzzards, and owls. Perching birds have a unique foot structure with three toes in front and one large flexible toe to the rear. Ducks and geese are known as open-water or swimming birds and have webbed feet. Habitat categories include seabirds, shore birds, and arboreal (tree-dwelling) birds. Some birds migrate over long distances and others, such as turkeys and quail, do not migrate at all.

The IUCN notes that 139 bird species have gone extinct during the course of human history. Bird species have died out due to habitat destruction, hunting and collection, pollution, and predation by nonnative species. The extinction rate of bird species is alarming not only because of the irrevocable loss of each species but also because of implications for the health of entire ecosystems.

## ENDANGERED AND THREATENED U.S. SPECIES

As of February 2008, there were eighty-seven bird species listed under the Endangered Species Act (ESA) as endangered or threatened in the United States. (See Table 8.1.) The vast majority have an endangered listing, meaning that they are at risk of extinction. Nearly all have recovery plans in place.

The imperiled birds come from many different genera (plural of genus) and represent a variety of habitats. Most are perching birds, seabirds, or shore birds. There are also a handful of other bird types, including woodpeckers and raptors, such as the Puerto Rican broadwinged hawk and the northern spotted owl.

Table 8.2 shows the ten bird species with the highest expenditures under the ESA during fiscal year 2006. The three most expensive species were the southwestern willow flycatcher ($14.7 million), the red-cockaded woodpecker ($13.9 million), and the bald eagle in the lower forty-eight states ($12.3 million).

The following sections describe the categories of birds that are found on the list of endangered and threatened species.

### Woodpeckers

Woodpeckers belong to the order Piciformes and the family Picidae. They are characterized by their physiology. They have hard chisel-like beaks and a unique foot structure with two toes pointing forward and two toes pointing backward. This allows them to take a firm grip on tree trunks and extend horizontally from vertical surfaces. Woodpeckers prefer arboreal habitats, primarily dead trees in old-growth forests. The birds hammer away at the bark on the trees to dig out insects living there. They often form deep cavities in the tree to use as roosting and nesting holes.

RED-COCKADED WOODPECKERS. The red-cockaded woodpecker is shown in Figure 8.1. The bird is named for the red patches, or cockades, of feathers on the head of the male. This species is found in old pine forests in the southeastern United States, where family

TABLE 8.1

**Endangered and threatened bird species, February 2008**

| Common name | Scientific name | Listing status[a] | Recovery plan date | Recovery plan stage[b] |
|---|---|---|---|---|
| Akiapola àu (honeycreeper) | Hemignathus munroi | E | 9/22/2006 | RF(1) |
| Attwater's greater prairie-chicken | Tympanuchus cupido attwateri | E | 11/19/2007 | RF(1) |
| Audubon's crested caracara | Polyborus plancus audubonii | T | 5/18/1999 | F |
| Bachman's warbler (=wood) | Vermivora bachmanii | E | Exempt | — |
| Black-capped vireo | Vireo atricapilla | E | 9/30/1991 | F |
| Bridled white-eye | Zosterops conspicillatus conspicillatus | E | 9/28/1990 | F |
| Brown pelican | Pelecanus occidentalis | E | 2/3/1983 | F |
| California clapper rail | Rallus longirostris obsoletus | E | 11/16/1984 | F |
| California condor | Gymnogyps californianus | E;XN | 4/25/1996 | RF(3) |
| California least tern | Sterna antillarum browni | E | 9/27/1985 | RF(1) |
| Cape Sable seaside sparrow | Ammodramus maritimus mirabilis | E | 5/18/1999 | F |
| Coastal California gnatcatcher | Polioptila californica californica | T | Exempt | — |
| Crested honeycreeper | Palmeria dolei | E | 9/22/2006 | RF(1) |
| Eskimo curlew | Numenius borealis | E | Exempt | — |
| Everglade snail kite | Rostrhamus sociabilis plumbeus | E | 5/18/1999 | F |
| Florida grasshopper sparrow | Ammodramus savannarum floridanus | E | 5/18/1999 | F |
| Florida scrub jay | Aphelocoma coerulescens | T | 5/9/1990 | F |
| Golden-cheeked warbler (=wood) | Dendroica chrysoparia | E | 9/30/1992 | F |
| Guam Micronesian kingfisher | Halcyon cinnamomina cinnamomina | E | 4/28/2004 | RD(1) |
| Guam rail | Rallus owstoni | E;XN | 9/28/1990 | F |
| Hawaii akepa (honeycreeper) | Loxops coccineus coccineus | E | 9/22/2006 | RF(1) |
| Hawaii creeper | Oreomystis mana | E | 9/22/2006 | RF(1) |
| Hawaiian (='alala) crow | Corvus hawaiiensis | E | 12/18/2003 | RD(1) |
| Hawaiian (='Io) hawk | Buteo solitarius | E | 5/9/1984 | F |
| Hawaiian (=koloa) duck | Anas wyvilliana | E | 8/24/2005 | RD(3) |
| Hawaiian common moorhen | Gallinula chloropus sandvicensis | E | 8/24/2005 | RD(3) |
| Hawaiian coot | Fulica americana alai | E | 8/24/2005 | RD(3) |
| Hawaiian dark-rumped petrel | Pterodroma phaeopygia sandwichensis | E | 4/25/1983 | F |
| Hawaiian goose | Branta (=Nesochen) sandvicensis | E | 9/24/2004 | RD(1) |
| Hawaiian stilt | Himantopus mexicanus knudseni | E | 8/24/2005 | RD(3) |
| Inyo California towhee | Pipilo crissalis eremophilus | T | 4/10/1998 | F |
| Ivory-billed woodpecker | Campephilus principalis | E | 8/22/2007 | D |
| Kauai akialoa (honeycreeper) | Hemignathus procerus | E | 9/22/2006 | RF(1) |
| Kauai òò (honeyeater) | Moho braccatus | E | 9/22/2006 | RF(1) |
| Kirtland's warbler (=wood) | Dendroica kirtlandii | E | 8/11/1978 | F |
| Large Kauai (=kamao) thrush | Myadestes myadestinus | E | 9/22/2006 | RF(1) |
| Laysan duck | Anas laysanensis | E | 11/4/2004 | RD(1) |
| Laysan finch (honeycreeper) | Telespyza cantans | E | 10/4/1984 | F |
| Least Bell's vireo | Vireo bellii pusillus | E | 5/6/1998 | D |
| Least tern | Sterna antillarum | E | 9/19/1990 | F |
| Light-footed clapper rail | Rallus longirostris levipes | E | 6/24/1985 | RF(1) |
| Marbled murrelet | Brachyramphus marmoratus | T | 9/24/1997 | F |
| Mariana (=aga) crow | Corvus kubaryi | E | 1/11/2006 | RD(1) |
| Mariana common moorhen | Gallinula chloropus guami | E | 9/30/1991 | F |
| Mariana gray swiftlet | Aerodramus vanikorensis bartschi | E | 9/30/1991 | F |
| Masked bobwhite (quail) | Colinus virginianus ridgwayi | E | 4/21/1995 | RF(2) |
| Maui akepa (honeycreeper) | Loxops coccineus ochraceus | E | 9/22/2006 | RF(1) |
| Maui parrotbill (honeycreeper) | Pseudonestor xanthophrys | E | 9/22/2006 | RF(1) |
| Mexican spotted owl | Strix occidentalis lucida | T | 10/16/1995 | F |
| Micronesian megapode | Megapodius laperouse | E | 4/10/1998 | F |
| Mississippi sandhill crane | Grus canadensis pulla | E | 9/6/1991 | RF(3) |
| Molokai creeper | Paroreomyza flammea | E | 9/22/2006 | RF(1) |
| Molokai thrush | Myadestes lanaiensis rutha | E | 9/22/2006 | RF(1) |
| Newell's Townsend's shearwater | Puffinus auricularis newelli | T | 4/25/1983 | F |
| Nightingale reed warbler (old world warbler) | Acrocephalus luscinia | E | 4/10/1998 | F |
| Nihoa finch (honeycreeper) | Telespyza ultima | E | 10/4/1984 | F |
| Nihoa millerbird (old world warbler) | Acrocephalus familiaris kingi | E | 10/4/1984 | F |
| Northern aplomado falcon | Falco femoralis septentrionalis | E;XN | 6/8/1990 | F |
| Northern spotted owl | Strix occidentalis caurina | T | None | — |
| Nukupuù (honeycreeper) | Hemignathus lucidus | E | 9/22/2006 | RF(1) |
| Oahu creeper | Paroreomyza maculata | E | 9/22/2006 | RF(1) |
| Oahu elepaio | Chasiempis sandwichensis ibidis | E | 9/22/2006 | RF(1) |

groups—consisting of a breeding male and female as well as several helpers—nest within self-dug cavities in pine trees. Tree cavities serve as nesting sites and provide protection from predators. Because red-cockaded woodpeckers rarely nest in trees less than eighty years old, heavy logging has destroyed much of their former habitat. The red-cockaded woodpecker was first placed on the Endangered Species List in 1970. It is currently found in fragmented populations in the southeastern seaboard westward into Texas. In 2003 the USFWS published *Red-Cockaded Woodpecker Recovery Plan* (January 2003, http://www.fws.gov/rcwrecovery/finalrecoveryplan.pdf) and estimated that approximately fourteen thousand of the birds still exist in the wild.

TABLE 8.1

**Endangered and threatened bird species, February 2008** [CONTINUED]

| Common name | Scientific name | Listing status[a] | Recovery plan date | Recovery plan stage[b] |
|---|---|---|---|---|
| Palila (honeycreeper) | *Loxioides bailleui* | E | 9/22/2006 | RF(1) |
| Piping plover | *Charadrius melodus* | E;T | 9/16/2003 | F |
| Poòuli (honeycreeper) | *Melamprosops phaeosoma* | E | 9/22/2006 | RF(1) |
| Puerto Rican broad-winged hawk | *Buteo platypterus brunnescens* | E | 9/8/1997 | F |
| Puerto Rican nightjar | *Caprimulgus noctitherus* | E | 4/19/1984 | F |
| Puerto Rican parrot | *Amazona vittata* | E | 4/30/1999 | RD(2) |
| Puerto Rican plain pigeon | *Columba inornata wetmorei* | E | 10/14/1982 | F |
| Puerto Rican sharp-shinned hawk | *Accipiter striatus venator* | E | 9/8/1997 | F |
| Red-cockaded woodpecker | *Picoides borealis* | E | 3/20/2003 | RF(2) |
| Roseate tern | *Sterna dougallii dougallii* | E;T | 9/24/1993 | F |
| Rota bridled white-eye | *Zosterops rotensis* | E | 10/19/2007 | D |
| San Clemente loggerhead shrike | *Lanius ludovicianus mearnsi* | E | 1/26/1984 | F |
| San Clemente sage sparrow | *Amphispiza belli clementeae* | T | 1/26/1984 | F |
| Short-tailed albatross | *Phoebastria (=Diomedea) albatrus* | E | 10/27/2005 | D |
| Small Kauai (=puaiohi) thrush | *Myadestes palmeri* | E | 9/22/2006 | RF(1) |
| Southwestern willow flycatcher | *Empidonax traillii extimus* | E | 8/30/2002 | F |
| Spectacled eider | *Somateria fischeri* | T | 8/12/1996 | F |
| Steller's eider | *Polysticta stelleri* | T | 9/30/2002 | F |
| Western snowy plover | *Charadrius alexandrinus nivosus* | T | 9/20/2007 | D |
| White-necked crow | *Corvus leucognaphalus* | E | None | — |
| Whooping crane | *Grus americana* | E;XN | 5/29/2007 | RF(3) |
| Wood stork | *Mycteria americana* | E | 1/27/1997 | RF(1) |
| Yellow-shouldered blackbird | *Agelaius xanthomus* | E | 11/12/1996 | RF(1) |
| Yuma clapper rail | *Rallus longirostris yumanensis* | E | 2/4/1983 | F |
| Òù (honeycreeper) | *Psittirostra psittacea* | E | 9/22/2006 | RF(1) |

[a]E = Endangered; T = Threatened; XN = Experimental Population, Non-Essential.
[b]Recovery plan stages: F = Final; D = Draft; RD = Draft Under Revision; RF = Final Revision.

SOURCE: Adapted from "Listed FWS/Joint FWS and NMFS Species and Populations with Recovery Plans (Sorted by Listed Entity)" and "Listed U.S. Species by Taxonomic Group," in *USFWS Threatened and Endangered Species System (TESS)*, U.S. Department of the Interior, U.S. Fish and Wildlife Service, February 5, 2008, http://ecos.fws.gov/tess_public/SpeciesRecovery.do?sort=1 and http://ecos.fws.gov/tess_public/SpeciesReport.do?kingdom=V&listing Type=L (accessed February 5, 2008)

In March 2001 the USFWS rescued several red-cockaded woodpeckers from habitat areas in Daniel Boone National Forest in Kentucky. Fifteen woodpeckers in six family groups were relocated to the Carolina Sandhills National Wildlife Refuge in South Carolina and the Ouachita National Forest in Arkansas. Daniel Boone National Forest had become uninhabitable for the woodpeckers after a 1999 infestation of southern pine beetles. The beetles quickly destroyed 90% of local woodpecker habitat despite efforts by U.S. Forest Service officials and volunteers to control the beetles' spread. The removal of this red-cockaded woodpecker population from Kentucky means that the species is now absent from the state. The bird is also believed extirpated (wiped out) in Maryland, Missouri, New Jersey, and Tennessee.

In *Red-Cockaded Woodpecker Five-Year Review: Summary and Evaluation* (October 2006, http://ecos.fws.gov/docs/five_year_review/doc787.pdf), the USFWS concludes that the endangered status listing is still appropriate for the species. The agency reports that over six thousand active clusters (occupied territories) of the bird had been documented, up from around forty-seven hundred active clusters reported in the early 1990s. However, the USFWS believes the bird still faces significant threats from the loss, degradation, and fragmentation of nesting and foraging habitat.

**TABLE 8.2**

**Bird species with the highest expenditures under the Endangered Species Act, fiscal year 2006**

| Ranking | Species | Expenditure |
|---|---|---|
| 1 | Southwestern willow flycatcher | $14,668,834 |
| 2 | Red-cockaded woodpecker | $13,875,377 |
| 3 | Bald eagle | $12,309,254 |
| 4 | Piping plover | $8,295,377 |
| 5 | Whooping crane | $6,796,708 |
| 6 | Least tern | $6,577,825 |
| 7 | Northern spotted owl | $6,109,964 |
| 8 | Wood stork | $3,005,638 |
| 9 | Western snowy plover | $2,897,722 |
| 10 | Florida scrub jay | $2,587,062 |

SOURCE: Adapted from "Table 2. Species Ranked in Descending Order of Total FY 2006 Reported Expenditures, Not Including Land Acquisition Costs," in *Federal and State Endangered and Threatened Species Expenditures: Fiscal Year 2006*, U.S. Department of the Interior, U.S. Fish and Wildlife Service, draft, 2008

**IVORY-BILLED WOODPECKERS.** The ivory-billed woodpecker is the largest woodpecker species in the United States, with a wingspan up to 30 inches (76 cm) and a body nearly 20 inches (51 cm) long. The birds have a striking black and white pattern on their body and an ivory-colored beak. The males have a brilliant red crest. In the nineteenth century the species was found throughout

**FIGURE 8.1**

**The red cockaded woodpecker**

SOURCE: Bob Savannah, artist, "Red Cockaded Woodpeckers," in *Bob Savannah Line Art*, U.S. Department of the Interior, U.S. Fish and Wildlife Service, Undated, http://www.fws.gov/pictures/lineart/bobsavannah/redcockadedwoodpeckers.html (accessed January 30, 2008)

the southeastern United States and in Cuba. Intense logging and loss of habitat are believed to have driven the birds extinct sometime in the 1940s. Occasional unconfirmed sightings continued to occur over the following decades. John W. Fitzpatrick et al. report in "Ivory-Billed Woodpecker (*Campephilus Principalis*) Persists in Continental North America" (*Science*, vol. 308, no. 5727, June 3, 2005) that scientists at Cornell University had confirmed sightings and a videotape taken of ivory-billed woodpeckers in the Big Woods region of Arkansas. This area is home to the Cache River National Wildlife Refuge. Conservationists are excited that an apparently lost species has been rediscovered.

Since the discovery, surveys for the bird have been conducted by a coalition of government agencies, universities, and conservation groups in Arkansas, Florida, Louisiana, Alabama, Georgia, South Carolina, and Texas. As of April 2008, no additional sightings of the bird had been confirmed.

The USFWS outlines in *Draft Recovery Plan for the Ivory-Billed Woodpecker* (August 2007, http://www.fws.gov/ivorybill/IBWDraftRecoveryPlan.pdf) the steps necessary to reliably determine the current distribution of the bird and ensure its survival. The agency estimates it could cost $27.8 million to recover the species by 2075.

## Passerines

Just over half of all bird species belong to the order Passeriformes and are called passerines. They are informally known as perching birds or songbirds, although not all passerines are truly songbirds. According to the Integrated Taxonomic Information System (April 28, 2008, http://www.itis.gov/servlet/SingleRpt/SingleRpt?search_topic=TSN&search_value=178265), a taxonomic tracking system operated by various North American government agencies, there are more than eighty families in this order, and they include many well-known species, such as robins, bluebirds, larks, blue jays, mockingbirds, finches, wrens, sparrows, swallows, starlings, cardinals, blackbirds, and crows. More than a third of the U.S. species of endangered and threatened birds are passerine (perching) birds.

**SOUTHWESTERN WILLOW FLYCATCHERS.** The southwestern willow flycatcher is a subspecies of the willow flycatcher. This small bird has a grayish-green back and wings with a pale yellow belly and a white-colored throat. It was first listed as endangered in 1995, when less than six hundred individuals were believed to be in existence. The bird is found in portions of Arizona, California, Colorado, New Mexico, Nevada, Texas, and Utah. It migrates to Mexico and Central and South America for the winter. The bird feeds on insects and prefers riparian areas (dense vegetation near rivers or streams) for its habitat. It is endangered primarily due to loss of riparian vegetation. In ranching areas, this vegetation is often stripped by grazing livestock. Another factor in its decline is harm from brood parasites—bird species that lay their eggs in the nests of other species. Brown-headed cowbirds are brood parasites that threaten southwestern willow flycatchers. They lay their eggs in the flycatchers' nests, and the unsuspecting flycatchers raise the cowbirds' young as their own.

In 1997 the USFWS designated critical habitat for the bird in compliance with a court order resulting from a lawsuit filed against the agency by the Southwest Center for Biological Diversity. The critical habitat covered nearly 600 miles (966 km) of streams and rivers in California, Arizona, and New Mexico. A recovery plan for the bird was finalized in 2002 that includes six recovery units. (See Figure 8.2.) In 2005 the USFWS designated new critical habitat for the southwestern willow flycatcher covering 737 miles (1,186 km) of waterways in California, Arizona, Nevada, Utah, and New Mexico. The new designation was made in response to a court order.

**BLACK-CAPPED VIREOS AND GOLDEN-CHEEKED WARBLERS.** The black-capped vireo and golden-cheeked warbler are among the threatened songbirds listed under the ESA. Both species nest in central Texas and other locations in the United States and winter in Mexico and Central America. Both species have declined largely due

## FIGURE 8.2

### Recovery areas for the Southwestern willow flycatcher

[By management unit name within state and recovery unit boundaries.]

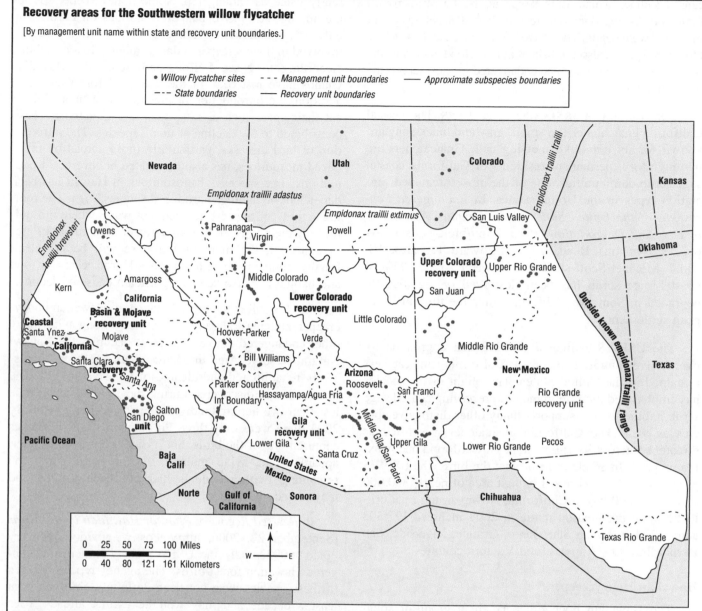

SOURCE: "Figure 4. Recovery and Management Units for the Southwestern Willow Flycatcher," in *Southwestern Willow Flycatcher Recovery Plan*, U.S. Department of the Interior, U.S. Fish and Wildlife Service, August 2002, http://ecos.fws.gov/docs/recovery_plans/2002/020830c.pdf (accessed February 21, 2008)

to loss of habitat caused by land clearing for development and invasion of brown-headed cowbirds. In certain areas, more than half the black-capped vireo nests contain brown-headed cowbird eggs. The black-capped vireo was placed on the Endangered Species List in 1987; the golden-cheeked warbler was listed in 1990.

Much of the critical nesting habitat for black-capped vireos and golden-cheeked warblers lies in the Hill Country of central Texas. In an effort to balance development with wildlife preservation, the city of Austin, Texas, invited the Nature Conservancy to formulate a plan to protect Hill Country habitats while enabling some development. The result was the Balcones Canyonlands Conservation Plan

(http://www.co.travis.tx.us/tnr/bccp/default.asp), which includes a 75,000-acre (33,350-ha) preserve in the Texas Hill Country.

Fort Hood, Texas, a heavy artillery training site for the U.S. Army, was designated an essential nesting habitat for the black-capped vireo and golden-cheeked warbler in 1993. With the help of the Nature Conservancy, the army currently manages some 66,000 acres (27,000 ha) of habitat for these species. Control of brown-headed cowbird populations has been a major part of the conservation effort. Vincent Muehter of the Audubon explains in "Cowbirds and Conservation" (January 5, 2005, http://www.audubon.org/bird/research/) that brown-headed cowbirds parasitize the nests of over 220 species of songbirds and have caused declines in many of these species. Nest parasitism rates for the black-capped vireo were as high as 90% before control measures were begun. They have been reduced to 22%. Many other bird species also use habitat at Fort Hood, including the bald eagle and threatened and endangered species, such as the whooping crane.

COASTAL CALIFORNIA GNATCATCHERS. The coastal California gnatcatcher is a small, gray and black songbird known for its kittenlike mewing call. Gnatcatchers are nonmigratory, permanent residents of California coastal sage scrub communities, one of the most threatened vegetation types in the United States. In *Endangered Ecosystems of the United States: A Preliminary Assessment of Loss and Degradation* (1995, http://biology.usgs.gov/pubs/ecosys.htm), Reed F. Noss, Edward T. LaRoe III, and J. Michael Scott state that between 70% to 90% of coastal sage scrub has been destroyed or significantly degraded in Southern California since the time of European settlement.

The USFWS estimated in 1993 that approximately twenty-five hundred pairs of California gnatcatchers remained in the United States. The plight of the species has emphasized the importance of preserving coastal sage scrub habitat, which supports many other distinctive species as well. The California gnatcatcher was listed as threatened across its entire range in California and Mexico in 1993. In an effort to protect the birds, the USFWS proposed in 2003 a critical habitat area of nearly 300,000 acres (121,000 ha) in California. However, the final critical habitat designation made in 2007 included 197,303 acres (79,846 ha) in San Diego, Orange, Riverside, San Bernardino, Los Angeles, and Ventura counties.

## Hawaiian Honeycreepers

The Hawaiian honeycreepers are a group of songbirds endemic to Hawaii—that is, this species is found there and nowhere else on Earth. Hawaiian honeycreepers are believed to have radiated (formed many separate species, each adapted to a particular lifestyle) from a single species that colonized the Hawaiian Islands thousands of years ago. The honeycreepers are named for the characteristic creeping behavior some species exhibit as they search for nectar. The Hawaiian honeycreepers are extremely diverse in their diet—different species are insect, nectar, or seed eaters. Species also differ in the shapes of their beaks and in plumage coloration. Hawaiian honeycreepers are found in forest habitats at high elevations. According to Daniel Harrington, in "Native and Endangered Species of the Hawaiian Islands" (2007, http://www.hawaiianencyclopedia.com/native-and-endangered-species.asp) there were approximately fifty Hawaiian honeycreeper species and subspecies originally, but twenty-one of them are already extinct.

Twelve species of Hawaiian honeycreepers are currently listed as endangered. Some honeycreeper species are among the most endangered animals on Earth, with only a few individuals left. One of the primary factors involved in honeycreeper endangerment is loss of habitat. According to Noss, LaRoe, and Scott, the Hawaiian Islands have lost 67% of their original forest cover. In addition, the introduction of predators that hunt birds or eat their eggs, such as rats, cats, and mongooses, have contributed to the decline of many species. The introduction of bird diseases, particularly those spread by introduced mosquitoes, has also decimated honeycreeper populations. The success of mosquitoes in Hawaii has been dependent on another introduced species: pigs. The rooting activity of pigs creates pools of water where mosquitoes lay their eggs. In fact, the greater the number of pigs in a habitat, the more bird disease will be prevalent. Finally, competition with introduced bird species for food and habitat has also been a significant cause of decline.

The Po'ouli is the most endangered Hawaiian honeycreeper and may already be extinct. Along with many other endangered native species, it occupies the Hanawi Natural Reserve Area in Maui, which has been aggressively rehabilitated and cleared of invasive species. The bird was only discovered during the 1970s. At that time less than two hundred individuals existed in the wild. By 2004 there were only three Po'ouli birds left. Scientists captured one of the birds, but it died a few months later, apparently of avian malaria. As of April 2008, the remaining two individuals had not been located and may already have died.

In *Revised Recovery Plan for Hawaiian Forest Birds* (September 22, 2006, http://ecos.fws.gov/docs/recovery_plan/060922a.pdf), the USFWS covers nineteen endangered Hawaiian forest birds. The agency reports that ten of these species have not been definitely observed in at least a decade and may well be extinct already. (See Table 8.3.) Most of these species are native to rain forests at elevations above 4,000 feet (1,220 m) on the islands of Hawaii (Big Island), Maui, and Kauai. Major threats to endangered forest species include habitat loss and modification, other human activity, disease, and predation. Of particular importance are nonnative plants, which have converted native plant communities to alien ecosystems unsuitable as habitat.

## Migratory Songbirds

In the fact sheet "Neotropical Migratory Bird Basics" (2008, http://nationalzoo.si.edu/ConservationAndScience/MigratoryBirds/Fact_Sheets/default.cfm?fxsht=9), Mary Deinlein of the Smithsonian Migratory Bird Center states that there are more than two hundred species of songbirds known as neotropical migrators. Every year these birds migrate between the United States and tropical areas in Mexico, the Caribbean, and Central and South America.

## TABLE 8.3

**Hawaiian forest birds covered by a recovery plan, 2006**

| Species (common name, scientific name) | Estimated number or last observation |
|---|---|
| O`ahu `elepaio, *Chasiempis sandwichensis ibidis* | 1,980 |
| Kāma`o (large Kaua`i thrush), *Myadestes myadestinus* | Last detected in 1989 |
| Oloma`o (Moloka`i thrush), *Myadestes lanaiensis rutha* | Last detected in 1988 |
| Puaiohi (small Kaua`i thrush), *Myadestes palmeri* | 300 |
| `Ō`ō `ā`ā (Kaua `i `ō`ō), *Moho braccatus* | Last detected in 1987 |
| `Ō`ū, *Psittirostra psittacea* | Last detected in 1989 |
| Palila, *Loxioides bailleui* | 3,390 (16-year average) |
| Maui parrotbill, *Pseudonestor xanthophrys* | 500 |
| Kaua`i `akialoa, *Hemignathus procerus* | Last detected in late 1960s |
| Kaua`i nukupu`u, *Hemignathus lucidus hanapepe* | Last confirmed detection in 1987 |
| Maui nukupu`u, *Hemignathus lucidus affinis* | Last detected in 1996 |
| `Akiapōlā`au, *Hemignathus munroi* | 1,163 |
| Hawai`i creeper, *Oreomystis mana* | 12,500 |
| O`ahu `alauahio (O`ahu creeper), *Paroreomyza maculata* | Last confirmed detection in 1985 |
| Kākāwahie (Moloka`i creeper), *Paroreomyza flammea* | Last detected in 1963 |
| Hawai`iākepa, *Loxops coccineus coccineus* | 14,000 |
| Maui `ākepa, *Loxops coccineus ochraceus,* | Last confirmed detection in 1970 |
| `Ākohekohe (crested honeycreeper), *Palmeria dolei* | 3,800 |
| Po`ouli, *Melamprosops phaeosoma* | Last 2 known birds not seen since 2004 |

SOURCE: Adapted from "Table 1. Federally Listed Endangered Species of Hawaiian Forest Birds Addressed in This Recovery Plan, Their Estimated Population Size or Date Last Observed, Listing Date, Federal Recovery Priority Number, and International Union for the Conservation of Nature Species Status (IUCN 1994)," in *Revised Recovery Plan for Hawaiian Forest Birds*, U.S. Fish and Wildlife Service, 2006, http://ecos.fws.gov/docs/recovery_plans/2006/060922a_docs/doc761.pdf (accessed February 21, 2008)

Even though some songbirds are appreciated by humans for their beautiful songs and colorful plumage, migratory songbirds also play a vital role in many ecosystems. For example, during spring migration in the Ozarks dozens of migratory bird species arrive and feed on the insects that inhabit oak trees, thereby helping control insect populations.

Migratory species are particularly vulnerable because they are dependent on suitable habitat in both their winter and spring ranges. In North America, real estate development has eliminated many forest habitats. Migratory songbird habitats are also jeopardized in Central and South America, where farmers and ranchers have been burning and clearing tropical forests to plant crops and graze livestock. Some countries, including Belize, Costa Rica, Guatemala, and Mexico, have set up preserves for songbirds, but improved forest management is needed to save them.

### Raptors

The term *raptor* is derived from the Latin word *raptores*, which was once the order on the taxonomy table to which birds of prey were assigned. Eventually, scientists split the birds into three orders:

- Accipitriformes—includes hawks, eagles, and buzzards
- Falconiformes—falcons
- Strigiformes—owls

As of February 2008, there were less than a dozen raptors listed as endangered or threatened in the United States. (See Table 8.1.) Species of note include the northern spotted owl and the California condor.

**NORTHERN SPOTTED OWLS.** The northern spotted owl occupies old-growth forests in the Pacific Northwest, where it nests in the cavities of trees two hundred years old or older. It does not seem afraid of humans and in fact appears to be curious about humans and human activity. Its primary prey includes the nocturnal northern flying squirrel, mice, and other rodents and reptiles. According to the Sierra Club (2008, http://www.sierraclub.org/lewisandclark/species/owl.asp), owl pairs may forage across areas as large as 2,200 acres (890 ha).

Northern spotted owl populations have declined primarily due to habitat loss. Most of the private lands in its range have been heavily logged, leaving only public lands, such as national forests and national parks, for habitat. Because logging has also been permitted in many old-growth national forest areas, the Sierra Club (2008, http://www.sierraclub.org/lewisandclark/species/owl2.asp#owl2) indicates that the species has lost approximately 90% of its original habitat. In 1990 the USFWS placed the northern spotted owl on its list of threatened species. Court battles began over continued logging in national forest habitats. In 1991 a U.S. Federal District Court ruled in favor of the Seattle Audubon Society and against the Forest Service, declaring that the Forest Service was not meeting its obligation to "maintain viable populations." The Forest Service had argued that the USFWS was responsible for the management and recovery of this species. However, the court pointed out that the Forest Service had its own distinct obligations to protect species under the ESA and that courts had already reprimanded the USFWS for failing to designate critical habitat for the northern spotted owl.

In 1992 the USFWS set aside 7 million acres (3 million ha) as critical habitat for the species and published a recovery plan. A year later the Northwest Forest Plan (http://www.fs.fed.us/r6/nwfp.htm) was established. It reduced logging in thirteen national forests by about 85% to protect northern spotted owl habitats. However, populations of the northern spotted owl continued to decline—this despite the unanticipated discovery of fifty pairs of nesting adults in California's Marin County, just north of the Golden Gate Bridge.

In 2004 the USFWS published *Northern Spotted Owl Five-Year Review: Summary and Evaluation* (November 2004, http://ecos.fws.gov/docs/five_year_review/doc743.pdf). The review was conducted in response to a lawsuit filed by the Western Council of Industrial Workers. The agency concluded that the bird should continue to have a threatened listing under the ESA. The USFWS found that habitat loss on federal lands has been minimized since the species was originally listed. This success is attributed to the Northwest Forest Plan. However, the agency noted that the population of northern spotted owls in Washington, Oregon, and California has continued to decline and that the species faces emerging threats from forest fires, West Nile virus, Sudden Oak Death (a plant disease that has killed hundreds of thousands of trees in California and Oregon), and competition for habitat from barred owls.

In 2007 the USFWS issued *Draft Recovery Plan for the Northern Spotted Owl* (April 2007, http://ecos.fws.gov/docs/recovery_plan/070426.pdf). A former draft recovery plan that was issued in 1992 was never finalized by the agency. The new plan cites competition from the barred owl as the most important threat facing the spotted owl. Other threats include lost and degraded habitat due to past actions and ongoing and expected future habitat losses due to fire, logging, and human development. In June 2007 the USFWS proposed revised critical habitat covering approximately 5.4 million acres (2.2 million ha) of federal lands in California, Oregon, and Washington. This represents 1.5 million less acres (607,000 ha) than were originally designated in 1992.

CALIFORNIA CONDORS. The California condor has a wingspan of more than 9 feet (2.8 m) and is among the continent's most impressive birds. Ten thousand years ago, this species soared over most of North America. However, its range contracted at the end of the Ice Age, and eventually individuals were found only along the Pacific Coast. Like other vulture species, the California condor is a carrion eater and feeds on the carcasses of deer, sheep, and smaller species such as rodents. Random shooting, egg collection, poisoning, and loss of habitat devastated the condor population. The species was listed as endangered in 1967. In the press release "California Condor Chick Takes Flight in Southern California" (November 15, 2006, http://www.fws.gov/news/News Releases/showNews.cfm?newsId=EEBC36AD-E3FC-17D3-F1EEEF6BCD8C7611), the USFWS states that by late 1984 only fifteen condors remained in the wild. After seven of these birds died, the agency decided to capture the remaining population.

An intense captive breeding program for the California condor was initiated in 1987. (See Figure 8.3.) The first chick hatched in 1988. The breeding program was successful enough that California condors were released into the wild beginning in 1992. Four years later a release

## FIGURE 8.3

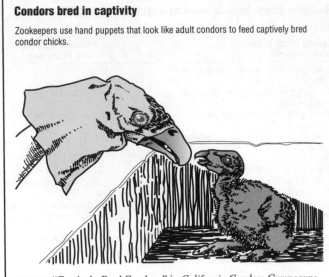

**Condors bred in captivity**

Zookeepers use hand puppets that look like adult condors to feed captively bred condor chicks.

SOURCE: "Captively-Bred Condors," in *California Condor: Gymnogyps Californianus*, U.S. Fish and Wildlife Service, August 1998, http://training.fws.gov/library/Pubs/condor.pdf (accessed January 30, 2008)

took place near the Grand Canyon, providing the public opportunities to view the largest bird in North America. The introduced birds in parts of Arizona, Nevada, and Utah were designated a nonessential experimental population. The California condor is listed as endangered in the remainder of Arizona and all of California and Oregon.

In April 2002, for the first time in eighteen years, a condor egg laid in the wild hatched in the wild. The parents of this chick had been captive-bred at the Los Angeles Zoo and the San Diego Wild Animal Park, respectively, and released into the wild in 1995 at the age of one. The San Diego Zoo reports in "Milestones in California Condor Conservation" (April 2008, http://cres.sandiegozoo.org/projects/sp_condors_milestones.html) that in 2008 there were 299 condors in the United States, with 147 living in the wild.

### Water Birds

Water birds live in and around bodies of water. Some prefer marine (ocean) habitats and others are found only near freshwater. Many species inhabit swamps and wetlands. These areas may be inland or intertidal (along the sea coast).

As of February 2008, there were more than two dozen water birds listed as endangered or threatened in the United States. (See Table 8.1.) They include a variety of species from many different taxonomic orders.

MIGRATORY SHORE BIRDS. Migratory shore birds are found most often in marshes, mudflats, estuaries, and other wetland areas where the sea meets freshwater. This category includes plovers, stilts, snipes, oystercatchers, avocets, shearwaters, and sandpipers. These birds vary greatly in size and color, but nearly all migrate over long distances. Most of them breed near the North Pole in the spring and spend their winters anywhere from the southern United States to South America. During their annual migrations, the birds stop to rest and feed at specific locations, known as staging areas, in the United States. Major staging areas include Delaware Bay, the Copper River Delta in Alaska, Cheyenne Bottoms in Kansas, San Francisco Bay, and the Great Salt Lake in Utah.

SEABIRDS. Seabirds spend most of their time out at sea, but nest on land. They are also known as pelagic birds, because pelagic means oceanic (associated with the open seas). Seabird species include gulls, terns, albatrosses, puffins and penguins, kittiwakes, petrels, murres and murrelets, auks and auklets, and cormorants.

The marbled murrelet is one of a handful of seabirds listed under the ESA. The bird was first listed in 1992 and is designated as threatened in California, Oregon, and Washington. The marbled murrelet is about 9 inches (23 cm) long and has a distinctive two-tone pattern of dark and light markings. The species prefers to nest in the trees of old-growth forests along the northwest Pacific coastline. Logging and other causes of habitat degradation have resulted in population declines.

In 2004 the USFWS completed a five-year status review for the marbled murrelet. The agency concluded that the population living in Oregon, Washington, and California did not qualify for a listing as a distinct population segment under the ESA and that the species should retain its listing as threatened. The status review was performed in response to a lawsuit filed by the American Forest Resources Council and other parties.

WADING BIRDS. Wading birds are unusual birds characterized by long skinny legs and extended necks and beaks. They wade in shallow waters of swamps, wetlands, and bays, where they feed on aquatic life forms. Wading birds include species of egret, crane, stork, and ibis. As of February 2008, there were two wading birds of note listed under the ESA: the wood stork and the whooping crane.

The wood stork weighs only about 5 pounds (2.3 kg), but stands up to 3 feet (1 m) tall with a 5-foot (1.5-m) wingspan. (See Figure 8.4.) At one time tens of thousands of the birds inhabited the southeastern coastline. In 1984 the species was listed under the ESA as endangered in Alabama, Florida, Georgia, and South Carolina. A recovery plan for the bird was published in 1999. At that time about five thousand breeding pairs lived in the wild. Populations have declined in the Everglades in southern Florida, but increased in coastal areas farther north.

FIGURE 8.4

The wood stork is a wading bird

SOURCE: "The Wood Stork Is an Indicator," in *Wood Stork: Everglades National Park*, U.S. Department of the Interior, National Park Service, Everglades National Park, November 17, 1997, http://www.nps.gov/ever/eco/wdstork.htm (accessed January 30, 2008)

Standing 5 feet (1.5 m) tall, the whooping crane is North America's tallest bird and among the best-known endangered species in the United States. (See Figure 8.5.) Its name comes from its loud and distinctive call, which can be heard for miles. Historically, whooping cranes lived in the Great Plains and along the southeastern coast of the United States. The birds were once heavily hunted, for meat as well as for their beautiful, long white feathers. In addition, the heavy loss of wetland areas in the United States deprived whooping cranes of much of their original habitat. In 1937 it was discovered that fewer than twenty whooping cranes were left in the wild in two small populations: a migratory population that nested in Canada and wintered on the Texas coast and a nonmigratory population living in Louisiana.

Each year the migratory whooping cranes fly 2,500 miles (4,023 km) from nesting grounds in Wood Buffalo, Canada, to Aransas, Texas, for the winter before returning north in March to breed. Whooping cranes return to the same nesting site each year with the same mate. In 1937 the Aransas Wildlife Refuge was established in southern Texas to protect the species' wintering habitat. Conservation efforts for the whooping crane are coordinated with the Canadian government, which manages the birds' breeding areas.

The whooping crane is listed under the ESA as endangered in Colorado, Kansas, Montana, North Dakota, Nebraska, Oklahoma, South Dakota, and Texas. Nonessential experimental populations were designated in 1993 and 2001 in dozens of states from Wyoming to Florida. In 2001 the first introduced cranes in Wisconsin were led to their Florida wintering grounds along the

## FIGURE 8.5

The whooping crane is highly endangered. Each year whooping cranes migrate from breeding grounds in Canada to wintering grounds in south Texas. *Field Mark Publications*

migration route by ultralight aircraft. The birds successfully made the return trip on their own in following years.

**OTHER BIRDS.** Other birds listed under the ESA include nonmigratory shore birds, such as the clapper rail and the Guam rail (a flightless bird); swimming birds, including coots, ducks, eiders, and geese; ground-dwelling birds, such as the prairie chicken; and coastal dwellers, such as the brown pelican.

## GENERAL THREATS TO U.S. BIRD SPECIES

The U.S. government has long recognized the importance of bird biodiversity and promoted habitat conservation under the Migratory Bird Conservation Act, passed by Congress in 1929. This law established the Migratory Bird Conservation Commission, which works with the secretary of the interior to designate and fund avian wildlife refuge areas. The USFWS is responsible for acquiring necessary lands through direct purchase, lease, or easement (agreement with landowners). The agency has procured over 4 million acres (1.6 million ha) of land for bird refuges. Other domestic laws and international conventions from 1900 to 2001 concerning migratory birds are listed in Table 8.4.

### Habitat Loss and Environmental Decline

The driving force behind current declines in many bird species is the destruction, degradation, and fragmentation of habitat due to increasing human population size and the wasteful consumption of resources. The leading cause of habitat destruction in the United States is agricultural development. Large corporate farms cause environmental damage by clearing out native plant species, planting only one or a few crops, and draining wetlands.

## TABLE 8.4

**Major international conventions and U.S. legislation devoted to migratory bird conservation, 1900–2001**

| Year | Authority |
| --- | --- |
| 1900 | Lacey Act (amended 1981) |
| 1913 | Weeks-McLean Law (Migratory Bird Conservation Act 1913) |
| 1916 | Convention for the Protection of Migratory Birds (Canada) |
| 1918 | Migratory Bird Treaty Act |
| 1929 | Migratory Bird Conservation Act |
| 1934 | Migratory Bird Hunting and Conservation Stamp Act (Duck Stamp Act) |
| 1936 | Migratory Bird Convention with Mexico (amended 1972) |
| 1940 | Pan American (or Western Hemisphere) Convention |
| 1940 | Bald Eagle Protection Act |
| 1956 | Waterfowl Depredations Prevention Act |
| 1961 | Wetlands Loan Act of 1961 (amended 1969, 1976) |
| 1972 | Migratory Bird Convention with Japan |
| 1972 | Convention on Wetlands of International Importance especially as waterfowl habitats (RAMSAR) |
| 1973 | Endangered Species Act (ESA) |
| 1973 | Convention on International Trade in Endangered Species of Wild Fauna and Flora (CITES) |
| 1976 | Migratory Bird Convention with the Union of Soviet Socialist Republics |
| 1978 | Antarctic Conservation Act |
| 1980 | Fish and Wildlife Conservation Act (amended 1988, 1989) |
| 1982 | Convention on Conservation of Antarctic Living Marine Resources |
| 1986 | Emergency Wetlands Resources Act |
| 1987 | Driftnet Impact Monitoring, Assessment, and Control Act of 1987 |
| 1989 | North American Wetlands Conservation Act (NAWCA) |
| 1990 | Coastal Wetlands Planning, Protection and Restoration Act |
| 1992 | Wild Bird Conservation Act |
| 2000 | Neotropical Migratory Bird Conservation Act |
| 2001 | Responsibilities of Federal Agencies to Protect Migratory Birds (executive order 13186) |

SOURCE: "Appendix 3. Primary International Conventions and Major Domestic Legislation for the Conservation of Migratory Birds and Their Habitats in the United States," in *A Blueprint for the Future of Migratory Birds: Migratory Bird Program Strategic Plan 2004–2014*, U.S. Department of the Interior, U.S. Fish and Wildlife Service, 2004, http://www.fws.gov/migratorybirds/mbstratplan/MBStratPlanTOC.htm (accessed February 21, 2008)

Natural habitats are also lost to urban sprawl, logging, mining, and road building.

### Pesticides

During the latter half of the twentieth century, pesticides and other toxic chemicals were recognized as a major cause of avian mortality and a primary factor in the endangerment of several species, including the bald eagle and the peregrine falcon. Even though the U.S. Environmental Protection Agency regulates the manufacture and use of toxic chemicals nationwide, the USFWS (under the Federal Insecticide, Fungicide, and Rodenticide Act) is responsible for preventing and punishing the misuse of chemicals that affect wildlife.

Many chemicals harmful to birds, such as the pesticide dichlorodiphenyltrichloroethane (DDT) and toxaphene, have been banned. Other chemicals, such as endrin, the most toxic of the chlorinated hydrocarbon pesticides, are still legal for some uses.

**FIGURE 8.6**

A bird is cleaned of oil after the disastrous Exxon Valdez spill in Prince William Sound, Alaska, in 1989. *AP/Wide World Photos*

## Oil Spills

Oil spills constitute a major threat to birds. (See Figure 8.6.) One of the worst and most infamous spills in history occurred on March 24, 1989, when the *Exxon Valdez* tanker released eleven million tons of crude oil into Alaska's Prince William Sound. To many Americans, it still exemplifies the disastrous effects oil spills have on wildlife. Thousands of birds died immediately after coming in contact with the oil, either from losing the insulation of their feathers or by ingesting lethal amounts of oil when they tried to clean themselves. Exxon personnel burned untold piles of birds; other birds were saved in cold storage under orders from the USFWS. A complete count was never obtained, but the USFWS (July 2, 2004, http://alaska.fws.gov/fisheries/contaminants/exxon.htm) estimates that 250,000 seabirds died as a result of the accident.

In "Biological and Ecotoxicological Characteristics of Terrestrial Vertebrate Species Residing in Estuaries" (August 1, 2003, http://www.pwrc.usgs.gov/bioeco/cmurre.htm), the U.S. Geological Survey indicates that approximately 185,000 common murres were eventually killed by the *Exxon Valdez* spill. The yellow-billed loon population was also seriously depleted, as was the population of Kittlitz's murrelet, a species found almost exclusively in Prince William Sound. Other affected bird species included the bald eagle, black oystercatcher, common loon, harlequin duck, marbled murrelet, pigeon guillemot, and the pelagic, red-faced, and double-crested cormorants.

The detergents used to clean up oil spills can also be deadly to waterfowl—detergents destroy feathers, which leads to fatal chills or trauma. Research shows that even after careful rehabilitation, birds that have been returned to nature after a spill often die in a matter of months.

Daniel W. Anderson, Franklin Gress, and D. Michael Fry find in "Survival and Dispersal of Oiled Brown Pelicans after Rehabilitation and Release" (*Marine Pollution Bulletin*, vol. 32, 10, October 1996) that only 12% to 15% of rehabilitated pelicans survive for two years, compared to the 80% to 90% of pelicans not exposed to oil. For many ornithologists (zoologists who study the lives and behaviors of birds), these dismal results raise the issue of whether avian rescue efforts are worthwhile. Could money spent on rehabilitation be better used for spill prevention and habitat restoration? In "Post-release Survival of Oiled, Cleaned Seabirds in North America" (*Ibis*, vol. 138, no. 2, April 1996), Brian E. Sharp argues that the cleanup effort might ease the conscience of the public and of politicians, but in reality it does little to benefit birds. Under the Clean Water Act, the oil industry pays a tax that helps fund cleanups after spills.

## Domestic Cats

Studies in the United States and Britain show that house cats kill millions of small birds and mammals every year, a death toll that contributes to declines of rare species in some areas. Many cat victims are plentiful urban species, but the USFWS explains in "Migratory Bird Mortality: Many Human-Caused Threats Afflict Our Bird Populations" (January 2002, http://www.fws.gov/birds/mortality-fact-sheet.pdf) that cats also kill hundreds of millions of migratory songbirds annually. In addition, cats have devastated bird fauna on some islands and are believed to have contributed to the declines of several grassland species in the United States.

## Trade in Exotic Birds

Birds are among the most popular pets in U.S. homes. According to the American Pet Products Manufacturers Association, in *2007/2008 National Pet Owners Survey* (2008, http://www.appma.org/press_industrytrends.asp), sixteen million birds are kept as pets in the United States. Many of these are common finches, canaries, or parakeets, all of which are raised in captivity in the United States. However, wild birds are owned and traded as well, including many species of passerines (songbirds) and psittacines (parrots and their relatives).

The most commonly traded passerines include warblers, buntings, weavers, finches, starlings, flycatchers, and sparrows. Passerines are regarded as low-value birds, and few passerines are endangered due to trade.

The psittacines, however, are generally rarer and thus much more valuable than passerines. The most commonly traded psittacines are macaws, amazons, cockatoos, lovebirds, lories, and parakeets. Besides their vivid colors and pleasant songs, many of these birds possess the ability to "talk," which makes them particularly appealing to some owners. Bird dealers have created demand for an ever-increasing variety of birds, including parrots, macaws, cockatoos, parakeets, mynahs, toucans, tanagers, and other tropical species.

## Invasive Species—The Case of Guam

Invasive species have damaged bird populations in some parts of the world, particularly those that occupy islands. Guam's unique bird fauna has been all but wiped out by the brown tree snake, an invasive species. Earl William Campbell III of the USFWS explains in "Brown Treesnake Fact Sheet" (May 3, 2004, http://www.hear.org/cgaps/pdfs/cgaps_btsfactsheet.pdf) that the brown tree snake was probably introduced from New Guinea via ship cargo in the late 1940s. The snake population thrived on the island, because of the absence of natural enemies and the presence of plentiful prey in the form of forest birds. According to the National Zoo, in the fact sheet "Where Have the Birds of Guam Gone?" (2008, http://nationalzoo.si.edu/Animals/Birds/Facts/FactSheets/fact-guambirds.cfm), there are believed to be as many as fourteen thousand snakes in a single square mile (2.6 sq km) in some Guam forest habitats. Nine out of eighteen bird species have already gone extinct on Guam, including the Guam flycatcher, the Rufus fantail, the white-throated ground dove, and the cardinal honey-eater. Several other Guam bird species are close to extinction. Many of these birds are or were unique to Guam. Measures have been implemented to try to keep this destructive snake from invading other islands, including careful inspection of all cargo arriving from Guam. The removal of the brown tree snake in select habitat areas on Guam (which is a high effort project, requiring the constant trapping of snakes) allowed the reintroduction of one bird, the flightless Guam rail, in 1998. The Guam rail had gone extinct in the wild, but a population is maintained in captivity.

Other particularly destructive invasive species include several associated with humans, including cats, dogs, and rats, which often prey on birds and their eggs.

## BACK FROM THE BRINK: SUCCESS STORIES
## Bald Eagles

The bald eagle is a raptor with special emphasis in the United States. (See Figure 8.7.) A symbol of honor, courage, nobility, and independence (eagles do not fly in flocks), the bald eagle is found only in North America, and its image is engraved on the official seal of the United States of America. John G. Herron of the USFWS notes in "Bald Eagle (*Haliaeetus leucocephalus*)" (June 2007, http://www.fws.gov/species/species_accounts/bio_eagl.html) that when the nation was founded, there were an estimated one hundred thousand bald eagles in the country in the late eighteenth century.

FIGURE 8.7

The bald eagle was once endangered due to habitat destruction and pollution by pesticides, such as DDT. Its populations have recovered with protection and a ban on DDT. *Field Mark Publications*

The bald eagle nests over most of the United States and Canada, building its aerie, or nest, in mature conifer forests or on top of rocks or cliffs. Its nest is of such a grand size—sometimes as large as a small car—that a huge rock or tree is necessary to secure it. The birds use the same nest year after year, adding to it each nesting season. It is believed that eagles mate for life. Bald eagles prey primarily on fish, water birds, and turtles.

Bald eagles came dangerously close to extinction in the twentieth century, largely due to DDT, which was introduced in 1947. Like other carnivorous species, bald eagles ingested large amounts of DDT by eating prey that had been exposed to it. DDT either prevents birds from laying eggs or causes the eggshells to be so thin that they are unable to protect the eggs until they hatch. The Bald Eagle Protection Act of 1940, which made it a federal offense to kill bald eagles, helped protect the species. However, numbers continued to dwindle. Herron indicates that by 1963 there were 417 breeding pairs of the bird. The bald eagle was listed as endangered in 1967.

Bald eagle populations started to recover with the banning of DDT in 1972. The species also benefited from habitat protection and attempts to clean up water pollution. In 1995 the bald eagle was moved from endangered to threatened status on the Endangered Species List. In 1999 the species was proposed for delisting. A year later all delisting criteria contained in species recovery plans were achieved. However, the USFWS was slow to complete the delisting process. In June 2007 the bald eagle was finally delisted due to recovery. Herron states that at that time the USFWS estimated there were 9,789 breeding pairs of the bird in the United States.

## Peregrine Falcons

Many falcon species have declined with the spread of humans. Like other predatory species, falcons were often hunted, either for sport or because they were considered a threat to chickens or livestock.

In the fact sheet "Peregrine Falcon (*Falco peregrinus*)" (May 2006, http://www.fws.gov/endangered/pdfs/peregrin/Peregrinefactsheet.pdf), the USFWS states that the peregrine falcon is the fastest bird on Earth. It can achieve diving speeds of over 200 miles per hour (322 kph). Like the bald eagle, much of the species' decline was due to DDT. Populations sank to approximately fifteen hundred nesting pairs during the 1930s and 1940s. In 1970 the American peregrine falcon and the Arctic peregrine falcon were listed as endangered. Both subspecies ranged throughout the United States.

The recovery of the peregrine falcon was made possible by the banning of DDT and by the establishment of special captive breeding centers on several continents. The USFWS reports in the press release "The Peregrine Falcon Is Back! Babbitt Announces Removal of World's Fastest Bird from Endangered Species List" (August 20, 1999, http://www.fws.gov/news/NewsReleases/R9/A11C3CFD-AC20-11D4-A179009027B6B5D3.html) that between 1974 and 1999 over six thousand of the birds were released into the wild. Federal and state agencies contributed to the conservation effort, as did private organizations such as the Peregrine Fund, the Santa Cruz Predatory Bird Research Group, and the Midwestern Peregrine Falcon Restoration Project.

The Arctic peregrine falcon and the American peregrine falcon were delisted in 1994 and 1999, respectively. In 2003 the USFWS conducted the first of five postdelisting surveys to ascertain the condition of the species. At that time three thousand breeding pairs were counted in the United States, Canada, and Mexico. Another survey was completed in 2006. As of April 2008, those results had not been published.

## Aleutian Canada Geese

Brian Anderson of the Alaska Department of Fish and Game notes in "Aleutian Canada Goose (*Branta canadensis leucopareia*)" (February 15, 2008, http://www.adfg.state.ak.us/special/esa/canada_goose/ac_goose

.php) that the Aleutian Canada goose was first placed on the Endangered Species List in 1967, when there were an estimated eight hundred individuals. The species had been thought extinct for several decades until a remnant population was discovered in 1962 by USFWS biologists on a remote Aleutian island. Deterioration of habitat and the introduction of predators such as Arctic foxes and red foxes were blamed for the animal's decline. According to Anderson, by February 2008 the goose population had rebounded to fifteen thousand. Conservation efforts included captive breeding, removal of foxes, and relocation and reintroduction of geese to unoccupied islands. The Aleutian Canada goose was officially delisted in 2001.

## Brown Pelicans

The brown pelican is a coastal bird found in the United States along the Atlantic Coast from Virginia southward, along the Gulf Coast in Alabama, Louisiana, and Texas, and along the Pacific Coast. The bird prefers the most southern parts of this range for its nesting areas. Pelicans are social birds that congregate and nest in large colonies. They weigh 8 to 10 pounds (3.6 to 4.5 kg) when fully grown and have a wingspan of up to 7.5 feet (2.3 m). Their brownish gray feathers were highly sought after for women's hats during the late 1800s and early 1900s. As a result the species underwent a dramatic decline. Their numbers were further decimated following World War I (1914–1918), when fishermen killed thousands of the birds, claiming they were competing for food fish. The use of DDT over the following decades took a huge toll on the birds by causing severe weakening of the shells of their eggs.

In 1970 the brown pelican was listed as endangered throughout its range. By the mid-1980s DDT restrictions and conservation efforts had allowed the Atlantic Coast population of the species to rebound. In 1985 that population was delisted due to recovery. In "Brown Pelican (*Pelecanus occidentalis*)" (January 2008, http://www.fws.gov/species/species_accounts/bio_plcn.html), the USFWS states that it proposed delisting the Gulf Coast population in 2007. At that time the agency estimated that nearly twelve thousand breeding pairs of the birds existed across Alabama, Louisiana, and Texas. The Pacific Coast population was also improving dramatically and is expected to be proposed for delisting sometime in the future.

## FOREIGN SPECIES OF ENDANGERED AND THREATENED BIRDS

As of February 2008, there were 206 foreign species of birds listed under the ESA. (See Table 8.5.) Categories include several endangered species, such as cranes, eagles, owls, parakeets, parrots, pheasants, pigeons, and warblers.

**TABLE 8.5**

## Foreign endangered and threatened bird species, February 2008

| Common name | Scientific name | Listing status* | U.S. and/or foreign listed | Foreign range |
|---|---|---|---|---|
| Abbott's booby | Papasula (= Sula) abbotti | E | Foreign | Indian Ocean - Christmas Island |
| Alaotra grebe | Tachybaptus rufolavatus | E | Foreign | Madagascar |
| Aldabra warbler (old world warbler) | Nesillas aldabranus | E | Foreign | Indian Ocean - Seychelles (Aldabra Island) |
| Algerian nuthatch | Sitta ledanti | E | Foreign | Algeria |
| Amsterdam albatross | Diomedia amsterdamensis | E | Foreign | Indian Ocean - Amsterdam Island |
| Andean condor | Vultur gryphus | E | Foreign | Colombia to Chile and Argentina |
| Andrew's frigatebird | Fregata andrewsi | E | Foreign | East Indian Ocean |
| Anjouan Island sparrowhawk | Accipiter francesii pusillus | E | Foreign | Indian Ocean - Comoro Islands |
| Anjouan scops owl | Otus rutilus capnodes | E | Foreign | Indian Ocean - Comoro Islands |
| Arabian ostrich | Struthio camelus syriacus | E | Foreign | Jordan, Saudi Arabia |
| Atitlan grebe | Podilymbus gigas | E | Foreign | Guatemala |
| Audouin's gull | Larus audouinii | E | Foreign | Mediterranean Sea |
| Aukland Island rail | Rallus pectoralis muelleri | E | Foreign | New Zealand |
| Azores wood pigeon | Columba palumbus azorica | E | Foreign | East Atlantic Ocean - Azores |
| Bachman's warbler (=wood) | Vermivora bachmanii | E | US/foreign | Cuba |
| Bahaman or Cuban parrot | Amazona leucocephala | E | Foreign | West Indies - Cuba, Bahamas, Caymans |
| Banded cotinga | Cotinga maculata | E | Foreign | Brazil |
| Banded wattle-eye | Platysteira laticincta | E | Foreign | Cameroon |
| Bannerman's turaco | Tauraco bannermani | E | Foreign | Cameroon |
| Bar-tailed pheasant | Syrmaticus humaie | E | Foreign | Burma, China |
| Barbados yellow warbler (=wood) | Dendroica petechia petechia | E | Foreign | West Indies - Barbados |
| Black-capped vireo | Vireo atricapilla | E | US/foreign | Mexico |
| Black-fronted piping-guan | Pipile jacutinga | E | Foreign | Argentina |
| Black-necked crane | Grus nigricollis | E | Foreign | China (Tibet) |
| Blue-throated (=ochre-marked) parakeet | Pyrrhura cruentata | E | Foreign | Brazil |
| Blyth's tragopan pheasant | Tragopan blythii | E | Foreign | Burma, China, India |
| Brown eared pheasant | Crossoptilon mantchuricum | E | Foreign | China |
| Brown pelican | Pelecanus occidentalis | E | US/foreign | West Indies, coastal Central and South America |
| Brown pelican | Pelecanus occidentalis | E | US/foreign | West Indies, coastal Central and South America |
| Cabot's tragopan pheasant | Tragopan caboti | E | Foreign | China |
| Cahow | Pterodroma cahow | E | Foreign | Entire |
| California least tern | Sterna antillarum browni | E | US/foreign | Mexico |
| Campbell Island flightless teal | Anas aucklandica nesiotis | E | Foreign | New Zealand (Campbell Island) |
| Canarian black oystercatcher | Haematopus meadewaldoi | E | Foreign | Atlantic Ocean - Canary Islands |
| Cebu black shama (thrush) | Copsychus niger cebuensis | E | Foreign | Philippines |
| Chatham Island pigeon | Hemiphaga novaeseelandiae chathamensis | E | Foreign | New Zealand |
| Chatham Island robin | Petroica traversi | E | Foreign | New Zealand |
| Cheer pheasant | Catreus wallichii | E | Foreign | India, Nepal, Pakistan |
| Chinese egret | Egretta eulophotes | E | Foreign | China, Korea |
| Chinese monal pheasant | Lophophorus lhuysii | E | Foreign | China |
| Christmas Island goshawk | Accipiter fasciatus natalis | E | Foreign | Indian Ocean - Christmas Island |
| Clarke's weaver | Ploceus golandi | E | Foreign | Kenya |
| Cloven-feathered dove | Drepanoptila holosericea | E | Foreign | Southwest Pacific Ocean - New Caledonia |
| Coastal California gnatcatcher | Polioptila californica californica | T | US/foreign | Mexico |
| Cuba hook-billed kite | Chondrohierax uncinatus wilsonii | E | Foreign | West Indies - Cuba |
| Cuba sandhill crane | Grus canadensis nesiotes | E | Foreign | West Indies - Cuba |
| Dappled mountain robin | Arcanator orostruthus | T | Foreign | Mozambique, Tanzania |
| Djibouti francolin | Francolinus ochropectus | E | Foreign | Djibouti |
| Edward's pheasant | Lophura edwardsi | E | Foreign | Vietnam |
| Elliot's pheasant | Syrmaticus ellioti | E | Foreign | China |
| Eskimo curlew | Numenius borealis | E | US/foreign | Alaska and Northern Canada to Argentina |
| Euler's flycatcher | Empidonax euleri johnstonei | E | Foreign | West Indies - Grenada |
| Eurasian peregrine falcon | Falco peregrinus peregrinus | E | Foreign | Europe, Eurasia south to Africa and Mideast |
| Eyrean grasswren (flycatcher) | Amytornis goyderi | E | Foreign | Australia |
| Forbes' parakeet | Cyanoramphus auriceps forbesi | E | Foreign | New Zealand |
| Freira | Pterodroma madeira | E | Foreign | Atlantic Ocean - Madeira Island |
| Galapagos hawk | Buteo galapagoensis | E | Foreign | Ecuador (Galapagos Islands) |
| Galapagos penguin | Spheniscus mendiculus | E | Foreign | Ecuador (Galapagos Islands) |
| Giant scops owl | Mimizuku (= Otus) gurneyi | E | Foreign | Philippines - Marinduque and Mindanao Island |
| Glaucous macaw | Anodorhynchus glaucus | E | Foreign | Paraguay, Uruguay, Brazil |
| Golden parakeet | Aratinga guarouba | E | Foreign | Brazil |
| Golden-cheeked warbler (=wood) | Dendroica chrysoparia | E | US/foreign | Mexico, Guatemala, Honduras, Nicaragua, Belize |
| Golden-shouldered parakeet | Psephotus chrysopterygius | E | Foreign | Australia |

The IUCN indicates in *2007 Red List of Threatened Species* that a total of 1,217 bird species are considered threatened out of 9,956 species evaluated (all known species). Certain groups of birds have declined particularly. All albatross species are considered threatened largely due to deaths from long-line fishing. Many Arctic

## TABLE 8.5

**Foreign endangered and threatened bird species, February 2008** [CONTINUED]

| Common name | Scientific name | Listing status* | U.S. and/or foreign listed | Foreign range |
|---|---|---|---|---|
| Great Indian bustard | *Ardeotis (= Choriotis) nigriceps* | E | Foreign | India, Pakistan |
| Greenland white-tailed eagle | *Haliaeetus albicilla groenlandicus* | E | Foreign | Greenland and adjacent Atlantic islands |
| Grenada gray-fronted dove | *Leptotila rufaxilla wellsi* | E | Foreign | West Indies - Grenada |
| Grenada hook-billed kite | *Chondrohierax uncinatus mirus* | E | Foreign | West Indies - Grenada |
| Grey-necked rockfowl | *Picathartes oreas* | E | Foreign | Cameroon, Gabon |
| Ground parrot | *Pezoporus wallicus* | E | Foreign | Australia |
| Guadeloupe house wren | *Troglodytes aedon guadeloupensis* | E | Foreign | West Indies - Guadeloupe |
| Harpy eagle | *Harpia harpyja* | E | Foreign | Mexico south to Argentina |
| Helmeted honeyeater | *Lichenostomus melanops cassidix (= Meliphaga c.)* | E | Foreign | Australia |
| Helmeted hornbill | *Buceros (= Rhinoplax) vigil* | E | Foreign | Thailand, Malaysia |
| Hooded crane | *Grus monacha* | E | Foreign | Japan, Russia |
| Hook-billed hermit (hummingbird) | *Ramphodon (= Glaucis) dohrnii* | E | Foreign | Brazil |
| Horned guan | *Oreophasis derbianus* | E | Foreign | Guatemala, Mexico |
| Ibadan malimbe | *Malimbus ibadanensis* | E | Foreign | Nigeria |
| Imperial parrot | *Amazona imperialis* | E | Foreign | West Indies - Dominica |
| Imperial pheasant | *Lophura imperialis* | E | Foreign | Vietnam |
| Imperial woodpecker | *Campephilus imperialis* | E | Foreign | Mexico |
| Indigo macaw | *Anodorhynchus leari* | E | Foreign | Brazil |
| Ivory-billed woodpecker | *Campephilus principalis* | E | US/foreign | Cuba |
| Japanese crane | *Grus japonensis* | E | Foreign | China, Japan, Korea, Russia |
| Japanese crested ibis | *Nipponia nippon* | E | Foreign | China, Japan, Russia, Korea |
| Kagu | *Rhynochetos jubatus* | E | Foreign | South Pacific Ocean - New Caledonia |
| Kakapo | *Strigops habroptilus* | E | Foreign | New Zealand |
| Kirtland's warbler (=wood) | *Dendroica kirtlandii* | E | US/foreign | Canada, West Indies - Bahama Islands |
| Koch's pitta | *Pitta kochi* | E | Foreign | Philippines |
| Kokako (wattlebird) | *Callaeas cinerea* | E | Foreign | New Zealand |
| Least Bell's vireo | *Vireo bellii pusillus* | E | US/foreign | Mexico |
| Lesser rhea (incl. Darwin's) | *Rhea (= Pterocnemia) pennata* | E | Foreign | Argentina, Bolivia, Peru, Uruguay |
| Little blue macaw | *Cyanopsitta spixii* | E | Foreign | Brazil |
| Long-tailed ground roller | *Uratelornis chimaera* | E | Foreign | Malagasy Republic (=Madagascar) |
| Lord Howe wood rail | *Gallirallus (= Tricholimnas) sylvestris* | E | Foreign | Australia (Lord Howe Island) |
| Madagascar pochard | *Aythya innotata* | E | Foreign | Madagascar |
| Madagascar red owl | *Tyto soumagnei* | E | Foreign | Madagascar |
| Madagascar sea eagle | *Haliaeetus vociferoides* | E | Foreign | Madagascar |
| Madagascar serpent eagle | *Eutriorchis astur* | E | Foreign | Madagascar |
| Maleo megapode | *Macrocephalon maleo* | E | Foreign | Indonesia (Celebes) |
| Marbled murrelet | *Brachyramphus marmoratus* | T | US/foreign | Canada |
| Martinique trembler (thrasher) | *Cinclocerthia ruficauda gutturalis* | E | Foreign | West Indies - Martinique |
| Marungu sunbird | *Nectarinia prigoginei* | E | Foreign | Zaire |
| Mascarene black petrel | *Pterodroma aterrima* | E | Foreign | Indian Ocean - Mauritius (Reunion Island) |
| Masked bobwhite (quail) | *Colinus virginianus ridgwayi* | E | US/foreign | Mexico |
| Mauritius cuckoo-shrike | *Coquus typicus* | E | Foreign | Indian Ocean - Mauritius |
| Mauritius fody | *Foudia rubra* | E | Foreign | Indian Ocean - Mauritius |
| Mauritius kestrel | *Falco punctatus* | E | Foreign | Indian Ocean - Mauritius |
| Mauritius olivaceous bulbul | *Hypsipetes borbonicus olivaceus* | E | Foreign | Indian Ocean - Mauritius |
| Mauritius parakeet | *Psittacula echo* | E | Foreign | Indian Ocean - Mauritius |
| Merriam's Montezuma quail | *Cyrtonyx montezumae merriami* | E | Foreign | Mexico (Vera Cruz) |
| Mexican spotted owl | *Strix occidentalis lucida* | T | US/foreign | Mexico |
| Micronesian megapode | *Megapodius laperouse* | E | US/foreign | West Pacific Ocean - Palau Islands |
| Mikado pheasant | *Syrmaticus mikado* | E | Foreign | Taiwan |
| Mindoro imperial (=zone-tailed) pigeon | *Ducula mindorensis* | E | Foreign | Philippines |
| Morden's owlet | *Otus ireneae* | E | Foreign | Kenya |
| New Zealand bushwren | *Xenicus longipes* | E | Foreign | New Zealand |
| New Zealand shore plover | *Thinornis novaeseelandiae* | E | Foreign | New Zealand |
| New Zealand thrush (wattlebird) | *Turnagra capensis* | E | Foreign | New Zealand |
| Night (=Australian) parrot | *Geopsittacus occidentalis* | E | Foreign | Australia |
| Noisy scrub-bird | *Atrichornis clamosus* | E | Foreign | Australia |
| Nordmann's greenshank | *Tringa guttifer* | E | Foreign | Russia, Japan, south to Malaya, Borneo |
| Norfolk Island parakeet | *Cyanoramphus cookii (= novaezelandiae c.)* | E | Foreign | Australia (Norfolk Island) |

bird species are threatened by habitat loss due to global warming. Tropical bird species are threatened by large-scale deforestation worldwide. Rapid deforestation in Southeast Asian rain forests has increased the number of threatened doves, parrots, and perching birds. The illegal bird trade has severely harmed many threatened species, particularly in Central and South America.

The largest numbers of endangered birds are found in Indonesia, the Philippines, Brazil, Colombia, China, Peru, India, and Tanzania. Island species are particularly vulnerable to habitat destruction because their ranges are usually very small. In addition, because many island birds evolved in the absence of predators, there are many flightless species—these are highly vulnerable to hunting

TABLE 8.5

**Foreign endangered and threatened bird species, February 2008** [CONTINUED]

| Common name | Scientific name | Listing status* | U.S. and/or foreign listed | Foreign range |
|---|---|---|---|---|
| Norfolk Island white-eye | Zosterops albogularis | E | Foreign | Indian Ocean - Norfolk Islands |
| Northern aplomado falcon | Falco femoralis septentrionalis | E;XN | US/foreign | Guatamala, Mexico |
| Northern bald ibis | Geronticus eremita | E | Foreign | Southern Europe, Southwestern Asia, Northern Africa |
| Northern spotted owl | Strix occidentalis caurina | T | US/foreign | Canada |
| Orange-bellied parakeet | Neophema chrysogaster | E | Foreign | Australia |
| Oriental white stork | Ciconia boyciana (=ciconia b.) | E | Foreign | China, Japan, Korea, Russia |
| Palawan peacock pheasant | Polyplectron emphanum | E | Foreign | Philippines |
| Paradise parakeet | Psephotus pulcherrimus | E | Foreign | Australia |
| Philippine eagle | Pithecophaga jefferyi | E | Foreign | Philippines |
| Pink pigeon | Columba mayeri | E | Foreign | Indian Ocean - Mauritius |
| Pink-headed duck | Rhodonessa caryophyllacea | E | Foreign | India |
| Piping plover | Charadrius melodus | E;T | US/foreign | Canada, Mexico, Bahamas, West Indies |
| Plain wanderer (=collared-hemipode) | Pedionomous torquatus | E | Foreign | Australia |
| Pollen's vanga | Xenopirostris polleni | T | Foreign | Madagascar |
| Ponape greater white-eye | Rukia longirostra | E | Foreign | West Pacific Ocean - Federated States of Micronesia |
| Ponape mountain starling | Aplonis pelzelni | E | Foreign | West Pacific Ocean - Federated States of Micronesia |
| Raso lark | Alauda razae | E | Foreign | Atlantic Ocean - Raso Island (Cape Verde) |
| Razor-billed curassow | Mitu mitu mitu | E | Foreign | Brazil (Eastern) |
| Red siskin | Carduelis cucullata | E | Foreign | South America |
| Red-billed curassow | Crax blumenbachii | E | Foreign | Brazil |
| Red-browed parrot | Amazona rhodocorytha | E | Foreign | Brazil |
| Red-capped parrot | Pionopsitta pileata | E | Foreign | Brazil |
| Red-faced malkoha (cuckoo) | Phaenicophaeus pyrrhocephalus | E | Foreign | Sri Lanka (=Ceylon) |
| Red-necked parrot | Amazona arausiaca | E | Foreign | West Indies - Dominica |
| Red-spectacled parrot | Amazona pretrei pretrei | E | Foreign | Brazil, Argentina |
| Red-tailed parrot | Amazona brasiliensis | E | Foreign | Brazil |
| Relict gull | Larus relictus | E | Foreign | India, China |
| Resplendent quetzel | Pharomachrus mocinno | E | Foreign | Mexico to Panama |
| Reunion cuckoo-shrike | Coquus newtoni | E | Foreign | Indian Ocean - Reunion |
| Rodrigues fody | Foudia flavicans | E | Foreign | Indian Ocean - Rodrigues Island (Mauritius) |
| Rodrigues warbler (old world warbler) | Bebrornis rodericanus | E | Foreign | Mauritius (Rodrigues Islands) |
| Roseate tern | Sterna dougallii dougallii | E;T | US/foreign | Tropical and temperate coasts of Atlantic Basin and East Africa |
| Rothschild's starling (myna) | Leucopsar rothschildi | E | Foreign | Indonesia (Bali) |
| Sao Miguel bullfinch (finch) | Pyrrhula pyrrhula murina | E | Foreign | Eastern Atlantic Ocean - Azores |
| Scarlet-breasted robin (flycatcher) | Petroica multicolor multicolor | E | Foreign | Australia (Norfolk Island) |
| Scarlet-chested parakeet | Neophema splendida | E | Foreign | Australia |
| Sclater's monal pheasant | Lophophorus sclateri | E | Foreign | Burma, China, India |
| Semper's warbler (=wood) | Leucopeza semperi | E | Foreign | West Indies - St. Lucia |
| Seychelles fody (weaver-finch) | Foudia sechellarum | E | Foreign | Indian Ocean - Seychelles |
| Seychelles kestrel | Falco araea | E | Foreign | Indian Ocean - Seychelles Islands |
| Seychelles lesser vasa parrot | Coracopsis nigra barklyi | E | Foreign | Indian Ocean - Seychelles (Praslin Island) |
| Seychelles magpie-robin (thrush) | Copsychus sechellarum | E | Foreign | Indian Ocean - Seychelles Islands |
| Seychelles paradise flycatcher | Terpsiphone corvina | E | Foreign | Indian Ocean - Seychelles |
| Seychelles scops owl | Otus magicus (=insularis) insularis | E | Foreign | Indian Ocean - Seychelles Islands |
| Seychelles turtle dove | Streptopelia picturata rostrata | E | Foreign | Indian Ocean - Seychelles |
| Seychelles warbler (old world warbler) | Bebrornis sechellensis | E | Foreign | Indian Ocean - Seychelles Island |
| Seychelles white-eye | Zosterops modesta | E | Foreign | Indian Ocean - Seychelles |
| Short-tailed albatross | Phoebastria (=Diomedea) albatrus | E | US/foreign | North Pacific Ocean and Bering Sea-Canada, China, Japan, Mexico, Russia, Taiwan |
| Siberian white crane | Grus leucogeranus | E | Foreign | Commwealth of Independent States (Siberia) to India, including Iran and China |
| Slender-billed grackle | Quisicalus palustris | E | Foreign | Mexico |
| Solitary tinamou | Tinamus solitarius | E | Foreign | Brazil, Paraguay, Argentina |
| Southwestern willow flycatcher | Empidonax traillii extimus | E | US/foreign | Mexico |
| Spanish imperial eagle | Aquila heliaca adalberti | E | Foreign | Spain, Morocco, Algeria |
| Spectacled eider | Somateria fischeri | T | US/foreign | Russia |
| St Vincent parrot | Amazona guildingii | E | Foreign | West Indies - St. Vincent |
| St. Lucia house wren | Troglodytes aedon mesoleucus | E | Foreign | West Indies - St. Lucia |

or predation by introduced species, including humans, cats, dogs, and rats. In fact, the IUCN reports that invasive species represent the single most frequent cause of bird extinctions since 1800.

**TABLE 8.5**

**Foreign endangered and threatened bird species, February 2008** [CONTINUED]

| Common name | Scientific name | Listing status* | U.S. and/or foreign listed | Foreign range |
|---|---|---|---|---|
| St. Lucia parrot | *Amazona versicolor* | E | Foreign | West Indies - St. Lucia |
| Swinhoe's pheasant | *Lophura swinhoii* | E | Foreign | Taiwan |
| Tahiti flycatcher | *Pomarea nigra* | E | Foreign | South Pacific Ocean - Tahiti |
| Taita thrush | *Turdus olivaceus helleri* | E | Foreign | Kenya |
| Thick-billed parrot | *Rhynchopsitta pachyrhyncha* | E | Foreign | Mexico |
| Thyolo alethe | *Alethe choloensis* | E | Foreign | Malawi, Mozambique |
| Trinidad white-headed curassow | *Pipile pipile pipile* | E | Foreign | West Indies - Trinidad |
| Tristam's woodpecker | *Dryocopus javensis richardsi* | E | Foreign | Korea |
| Turquoise parakeet | *Neophema pulchella* | E | Foreign | Australia |
| Ulugura bush-shrike | *Malaconotus alius* | T | Foreign | Tanzania |
| Van Dam's vanga | *Xenopirostris damii* | T | Foreign | Madagascar |
| Vinaceous-breasted parrot | *Amazona vinacea* | E | Foreign | Brazil |
| West African ostrich | *Struthio camelus spatzi* | E | Foreign | Spanish Sahara |
| Western bristlebird | *Dasyornis longirostris (=brachypterus l.)* | E | Foreign | Australia |
| Western rufous bristlebird | *Dasyornis broadbenti littoralis* | E | Foreign | Australia |
| Western snowy plover | *Charadrius alexandrinus nivosus* | T | US/foreign | Mexico |
| Western tragopan pheasant | *Tragopan melanocephalus* | E | Foreign | India, Pakistan |
| Western whipbird | *Psophodes nigrogularis* | E | Foreign | Australia |
| White-eared pheasant | *Crossoptilon crossoptilon* | E | Foreign | China (Tibet), India |
| White-breasted guineafowl | *Agelastes meleagrides* | T | Foreign | West Africa |
| White-breasted thrasher | *Ramphocinclus brachyurus* | E | Foreign | West Indies - St. Lucia, Martinique |
| White-naped crane | *Grus vipio* | E | Foreign | Mongolia |
| White-necked rockfowl | *Picathartes gymnocephalus* | E | Foreign | Africa - Togo to Sierra Leone |
| White-tailed laurel pigeon | *Columba junoniae* | T | Foreign | Atlantic Ocean - Canary Islands |
| White-winged cotinga | *Xipholena atropurpurea* | E | Foreign | Brazil |
| White-winged guan | *Penelope albipennis* | E | Foreign | Peru |
| White-winged wood duck | *Cairina scutulata* | E | Foreign | India, Malaysia, Indonesia, Thailand |
| Whooping crane | *Grus americana* | E;XN | US/foreign | Canada, Mexico |

*E = Endangered; T = Threatened; XN = Experimental Population, Non-Essential.

SOURCE: Adapted from "Listed FWS/Joint FWS and NMFS Species and Populations with Recovery Plans (Sorted by Listed Entity)" and "Listed U.S. Species by Taxonomic Group," in *USFWS Threatened and Endangered Species System (TESS)*, U.S. Department of the Interior, U.S. Fish and Wildlife Service, February 5, 2008, http://ecos.fws.gov/tess_public/SpeciesRecovery.do?sort=1 and http://ecos.fws.gov/tess_public/SpeciesReport.do?kingdom=V&listing Type=L (accessed February 5, 2008)

## CHAPTER 9
# INSECTS AND SPIDERS

Insects are members of the Animalia kingdom and belong to the phylum Arthropoda, along with crustaceans. There are many classes of arthropods, including the insects and arachnids. Both are invertebrates, but insects have six legs, whereas arachnids have eight legs. The arachnids include spiders, mites, ticks, scorpions, and harvestmen.

Insects are the most diverse group in the animal kingdom. Scientists are not certain of the total number of insect species; estimates range as high as thirty million species. The International Union for Conservation of Nature and Natural Resources (IUCN) indicates in *2007 Red List of Threatened Species* (2007, http://www.iucn redlist.org/) that 950,000 of the species have been described. Insects have not been nearly as thoroughly studied as the vertebrate groups, and so there are likely to be many endangered insects whose state is unknown.

Insects and arachnids, like many other species, suffer from diminished habitat as a result of encroaching development, industrialization, changing land use patterns, and invasive species.

## THREATENED AND ENDANGERED INSECT SPECIES IN THE UNITED STATES

As of February 2008, there were fifty-seven U.S. insect entities listed under the Endangered Species Act (ESA). (See Table 9.1.) They represent forty-two different species. There are two subspecies of ground beetle, twelve subspecies of pomace fly, and four subspecies of tiger beetle.

Predominant species types listed under the ESA include butterflies (nineteen species), pomace flies (twelve subspecies), and beetles (eleven species). The remaining insects are an assortment of types including a dragonfly, a fly, a grasshopper, two ground beetles, two moths, a naucorid (see Figure 9.1), three skippers, and four tiger bee-

tles. Most of the listed insects are endangered, and nearly all have recovery plans in place.

According to the U.S. Fish and Wildlife Service (USFWS), most of the imperiled insects are found exclusively in one of three states: California (twenty species), Hawaii (two species, one including twelve subspecies), and Texas (seven species). The remainder of the species are scattered across the country.

Table 9.2 shows the ten insect species with the highest expenditures under the ESA during fiscal year (FY) 2006. The list is dominated by butterflies and skippers. Nearly $2.3 million was devoted to the valley elderberry longhorn beetle of California. Over $821,000 was spent on the Karner blue butterfly, which inhabits midwestern states.

### Butterflies, Skippers, and Moths

Butterflies, skippers, and moths are flying insects that belong to the order Lepidoptera. Scientists believe there could be several hundred thousand species in this order. Skippers have stockier bodies than butterflies, but are also structurally different from moths. They are considered intermediate between butterflies and moths.

Like amphibians, many butterflies and moths are considered indicator species (meaning that their well-being gives scientists a good indication of the general health of their habitat) because they are particularly sensitive to environmental degradation. The decline of these species serves as a warning to human beings about the condition of the environment. Part of the reason butterflies are sensitive to many aspects of the environment is that these species undergo a drastic metamorphosis, or change, from larva to adult as a natural part of their life cycle. Butterfly larvae are generally crawling, herbivorous caterpillars, whereas butterfly adults fly and are eat nectar. Butterflies can thrive only when intact habitats are

# TABLE 9.1

## Endangered and threatened insect species, February 2008

| Common name | Scientific name | Listing status[a] | Recovery plan date | Recovery plan stage[b] |
|---|---|---|---|---|
| Beetle, American burying | Nicrophorus americanus | E | 9/27/1991 | F |
| Beetle, Coffin Cave mold | Batrisodes texanus | E | 8/25/1994 | F |
| Beetle, Comal Springs dryopid | Stygoparnus comalensis | E | None | — |
| Beetle, Comal Springs riffle | Heterelmis comalensis | E | None | — |
| Beetle, delta green ground | Elaphrus viridis | T | 12/15/2005 | F |
| Beetle, Helotes mold | Batrisodes venyivi | E | None | — |
| Beetle, Hungerford's crawling water | Brychius hungerfordi | E | 9/28/2006 | F |
| Beetle, Kretschmarr Cave mold | Texamaurops reddelli | E | 8/25/1994 | F |
| Beetle, Mount Hermon June | Polyphylla barbata | E | 9/28/1998 | F |
| Beetle, Tooth Cave ground | Rhadine persephone | E | 8/25/1994 | F |
| Beetle, valley elderberry longhorn | Desmocerus californicus dimorphus | T | 6/28/1984 | F |
| Butterfly, bay checkerspot | Euphydryas editha bayensis | T | 9/30/1998 | F |
| Butterfly, Behren's silverspot | Speyeria zerene behrensii | E | 1/20/2004 | D |
| Butterfly, callippe silverspot | Speyeria callippe callippe | E | None | — |
| Butterfly, El Segundo blue | Euphilotes battoides allyni | E | 9/28/1998 | F |
| Butterfly, Fender's blue | Icaricia icarioides fenderi | E | None | — |
| Butterfly, Karner blue | Lycaeides melissa samuelis | E | 9/19/2003 | F |
| Butterfly, Lange's metalmark | Apodemia mormo langei | E | 4/25/1984 | RF(1) |
| Butterfly, lotis blue | Lycaeides argyrognomon lotis | E | 12/26/1985 | F |
| Butterfly, mission blue | Icaricia icarioides missionensis | E | 10/10/1984 | F |
| Butterfly, Mitchell's satyr | Neonympha mitchellii mitchellii | E | 4/2/1998 | F |
| Butterfly, Myrtle's silverspot | Speyeria zerene myrtleae | E | 9/29/1998 | F |
| Butterfly, Oregon silverspot | Speyeria zerene hippolyta | T | 8/22/2001 | RF(1) |
| Butterfly, Palos Verdes blue | Glaucopsyche lygdamus palosverdesensis | E | 1/19/1984 | F |
| Butterfly, Quino checkerspot | Euphydryas editha quino (=E. e. wrighti) | E | 9/17/2003 | F |
| Butterfly, Saint Francis' satyr | Neonympha mitchellii francisci | E | 4/23/1996 | F |
| Butterfly, San Bruno elfin | Callophrys mossii bayensis | E | 10/10/1984 | F |
| Butterfly, Schaus swallowtail | Heraclides aristodemus ponceanus | E | 5/18/1999 | F |
| Butterfly, Smith's blue | Euphilotes enoptes smithi | E | 11/9/1984 | F |
| Butterfly, Uncompahgre fritillary | Boloria acrocnema | E | 3/17/1994 | F |
| Dragonfly, Hine's emerald | Somatochlora hineana | E | 9/27/2001 | F |
| Fly, Delhi Sands flower-loving | Rhaphiomidas terminatus abdominalis | E | 9/14/1997 | F |
| Grasshopper, Zayante band-winged | Trimerotropis infantilis | E | 9/28/1998 | F |
| Ground beetle, [unnamed] | Rhadine exilis | E | None | — |
| Ground beetle, [unnamed] | Rhadine infernalis | E | None | — |
| Moth, Blackburn's sphinx | Manduca blackburni | E | 8/26/2005 | F |
| Moth, Kern primrose sphinx | Euproserpinus euterpe | T | 2/8/1984 | F |
| Naucorid, Ash Meadows | Ambrysus amargosus | T | 9/28/1990 | F |
| Pomace fly, [unnamed] | Drosophila aglaia | E | None | — |
| Pomace fly, [unnamed] | Drosophila differens | E | None | — |
| Pomace fly, [unnamed] | Drosophila hemipeza | E | None | — |
| Pomace fly, [unnamed] | Drosophila heteroneura | E | None | — |
| Pomace fly, [unnamed] | Drosophila montgomeryi | E | None | — |
| Pomace fly, [unnamed] | Drosophila mulli | T | None | — |
| Pomace fly, [unnamed] | Drosophila musaphila | E | None | — |
| Pomace fly, [unnamed] | Drosophila neoclavisetae | E | None | — |
| Pomace fly, [unnamed] | Drosophila obatai | E | None | — |
| Pomace fly, [unnamed] | Drosophila ochrobasis | E | None | — |
| Pomace fly, [unnamed] | Drosophila substenoptera | E | None | — |
| Pomace fly, [unnamed] | Drosophila tarphytrichia | E | None | — |
| Skipper, Carson wandering | Pseudocopaeodes eunus obscurus | E | 9/13/2007 | D |
| Skipper, Laguna Mountains | Pyrgus ruralis lagunae | E | None | — |
| Skipper, Pawnee montane | Hesperia leonardus montana | T | 9/21/1998 | F |
| Tiger beetle, northeastern beach | Cicindela dorsalis dorsalis | T | 9/29/1994 | F |
| Tiger beetle, Ohlone | Cicindela ohlone | E | None | — |
| Tiger beetle, Puritan | Cicindela puritana | T | 9/29/1993 | F |
| Tiger beetle, Salt Creek | Cicindela nevadica lincolniana | E | None | — |

[a]E=Endangered; T=Threatened.
[b]Recovery plan stages: F=Final; D=Draft; RF=Final Revision.

SOURCE: Adapted from "Listed FWS/Joint FWS and NMFS Species and Populations with Recovery Plans (Sorted by Listed Entity)" and "Listed U.S. Species by Taxonomic Group," in *USFWS Threatened and Endangered Species System (TESS)*, U.S. Department of the Interior, U.S. Fish and Wildlife Service, February 5, 2008, http://ecos.fws.gov/tess_public/SpeciesRecovery.do?sort=1 and http://ecos.fws.gov/tess_public/SpeciesReport.do?kingdom=V&listing Type=L (accessed February 5, 2008)

available for both caterpillars and adults. Consequently, healthy butterfly populations tend to occur in areas with healthy ecosystems. Because many species are extremely sensitive to changing environmental conditions, moths and butterflies are carefully monitored by scientists and conservationists around the world.

## FIGURE 9.1

**The ash meadows naucorid**

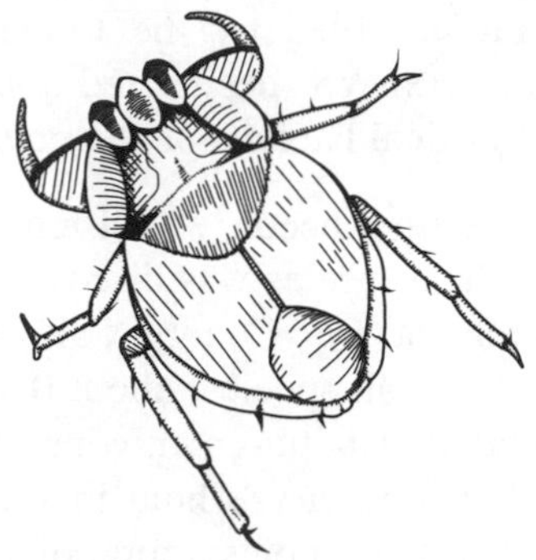

SOURCE: E. Tobin, illustrator, "Ash Meadows Naucorid *Pelecorus shoshone*," in *Planning Update 1: Ash Meadows National Wildlife Refuge*, U.S. Department of the Interior, U.S. Fish and Wildlife Service, January 1999, http://www.fws.gov/pacific/planning/am_pu1.pdf (accessed February 21, 2008)

## TABLE 9.2

**Insect species with the highest expenditures under the Endangered Species Act, fiscal year 2006**

| Ranking | Species | Expenditure |
|---|---|---|
| 1 | Valley elderberry longhorn beetle | $2,298,612 |
| 2 | Karner blue butterfly | $821,498 |
| 3 | Schaus swallowtail butterfly | $460,327 |
| 4 | Fender's blue butterfly | $404,249 |
| 5 | Hine's emerald dragonfly | $382,167 |
| 6 | American burying beetle | $369,329 |
| 7 | Mission blue butterfly | $318,513 |
| 8 | Oregon silverspot butterfly | $309,817 |
| 9 | Saint Francis' satyr butterfly | $294,008 |
| 10 | Carson wandering skipper | $211,855 |

SOURCE: Adapted from "Table 2. Species Ranked in Descending Order of Total FY 2006 Reported Expenditures, Not Including Land Acquisition Costs," in *Federal and State Endangered and Threatened Species Expenditures: Fiscal Year 2006*, U.S. Department of the Interior, U.S. Fish and Wildlife Service, draft, 2008

Butterflies and moths have alerted scientists to many habitat changes. For example, in southern Florida the sharp decline of swallowtail butterflies alerted biologists to the harm caused by mosquito sprays, as well as to the fact that pesticides had contaminated the water. In "Parallel Rise and Fall of Melanic Peppered Moths in America and Britain" (*Journal of Heredity*, vol. 87, no. 5, 1996), Bruce S. Grant, Denis F. Owen, and Cyril A. Clarke note that in 1996 scientists in Michigan and England reported that during the 1960s darker-colored moths began to predominate over light, white-and-black-flecked moths in polluted areas. This was seen in both England and the United States and was probably because darker moths were better able to blend into the dingy environment and hide from predators. In both countries, clean air laws were passed and decreases in pollution resulted. Now, in both countries, lighter-colored moths are again predominant. Carol Kaesuk Yoon reports in "Parallel Plots in Classic of Evolution" (*New York Times*, November 12, 1996) that Douglas Futuyma of the State University of New York, Stony Brook, found that other insect species show increases in the proportion of darker-colored individuals in industrialized areas, a phenomenon called industrial melanism. In those species, as well, the proportion of dark specimens drops as air quality improves.

In many cases butterflies also help conservationists decide where to locate parks and nature refuges. Generally, the more varieties of butterflies that exist in an area, the more species of other animals and plants will live there as well. However, many butterfly species are disappearing around the world.

The major threats to butterflies include:

- Habitat destruction
- Mowing of pastures, ditches, and highway rights-of-way
- Collisions with moving automobiles
- Insecticides

**KARNER BLUE BUTTERFLIES.** The Karner blue butterfly was listed as endangered in 1992. Historically, it occupied habitats in the eastern United States from Minnesota to Maine as well as in Ontario, Canada. However, the species is now found only in portions of Minnesota, Wisconsin, Indiana, Michigan, New York, New Hampshire, and Ohio. Most Karner blue butterfly populations are extremely small and in danger of extinction.

The caterpillars of the Karner blue butterfly feed on a species of lupine that is now found primarily on roadsides, military bases, and some forest areas. The primary reason for endangerment of the Karner blue butterfly is habitat loss due to land development for human use and forest maturation. In 2003 the USFWS published a recovery plan for the Karner blue butterfly. Figure 9.2 shows the recovery units, or populations, of the species, sites for potential recovery units, and other sites where the species has historically been found.

### California Insects

There are twenty insects found only in California on the list of endangered and threatened species. These include fourteen species of butterflies, skippers, and moths; four types of beetles; and a fly and a grasshopper.

**VALLEY ELDERBERRY LONGHORN BEETLES.** Nearly $2.3 million was spent under the ESA in FY 2006 on the valley elderberry longhorn beetle. (See Table 9.2.) This is a stout-bodied beetle that is nearly 1 inch (2.5 cm) long when fully grown. The species overwhelmingly prefers only one type of host plant: elderberry shrubs along creeks and rivers in California's Central Valley. This is an area that has undergone extensive agricultural and urban development over the last century. Long-term

## FIGURE 9.2

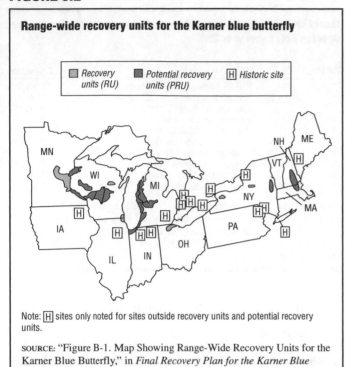

**Range-wide recovery units for the Karner blue butterfly**

Recovery units (RU) | Potential recovery units (PRU) | H Historic site

Note: H sites only noted for sites outside recovery units and potential recovery units.

SOURCE: "Figure B-1. Map Showing Range-Wide Recovery Units for the Karner Blue Butterfly," in *Final Recovery Plan for the Karner Blue Butterfly (Lycaeides Melissa Samuelis)*, U.S. Fish and Wildlife Service, 2003, http://ecos.fws.gov/docs/recovery_plans/2003/030919.pdf (accessed February 21, 2008)

destruction and fragmentation of riparian (river and stream) ecosystems has imperiled the beetle population. It was first listed under the ESA in 1980 as a threatened species. Two areas in Sacramento County were designated critical habitat. A recovery plan was finalized in 1984.

In *Valley Elderberry Longhorn Beetle Five-Year Review: Summary and Evaluation* (September 2006, http://ecos.fws.gov/docs/five_year_review/doc779.pdf), the USFWS recommends that the beetle be delisted. The agency notes that tens of thousands of acres of the riparian habitat preferred by the beetle have been given protected status and more than 5,000 acres (2,023 ha) have been restored.

SANTA CRUZ MOUNTAINS. California's Santa Cruz Mountains are home to two imperiled insect species: the Zayante band-winged grasshopper and the Ohlone tiger beetle. Factors leading to endangerment include sand mining, urban development, conversion of land to agricultural uses, recreational use (such as hiking, horseback riding, off-road vehicle use, bicycling, and camping), competition with nonnative species, fire suppression, pesticides, logging, and overcollection.

The tiny Zayante band-winged grasshopper, barely 0.5 inches (1.3 cm) long, occupies areas containing abundant high-quality silica sand, known as Zayante or Santa Margarita sand. This sand is valuable for making glass

and fiberglass products, and several businesses have entered the area in the hope of capitalizing on this. The Zayante band-winged grasshopper joined the ranks of listed endangered species in January 1997. In 2001, as a result of a lawsuit filed by the Center for Biological Diversity, the USFWS designated over 10,000 acres (4,046 ha) of critical habitat for the grasshopper.

The Ohlone tiger beetle was listed as endangered in October 2001. The species was discovered in 1987 and is found only in Santa Cruz County, California. The Ohlone tiger beetle is a small species, about 0.5 inches (1.3 cm) long, with spotted metallic-green wings and copper-green legs. Both adults and larvae hunt invertebrate prey. The Ohlone tiger beetle occupies a total of less than 20 acres (8 ha) of remnant native coastal prairie habitat on state and private land and on property belonging to the University of California, Santa Cruz. The species declined due to habitat loss and habitat fragmentation resulting from urban development, overcollection, pollution from pesticides, and the increasing encroachment of invasive plant species. The petition to list the Ohlone tiger beetle with the USFWS was originally made by a private citizen in 1997.

### Hawaiian Insects

There are thirteen Hawaiian insects listed under the ESA: twelve subspecies of pomace fly and Blackburn's sphinx moth.

POMACE FLIES. Pomace flies (also known as Hawaiian picture-wing flies) are of the genus *Drosophila*, a group commonly called fruit flies. There are more than one hundred species of *Drosophila*. They are relatively large flies with elaborate markings on their wings. The Hawaiian subspecies are renowned for their colorful wing patterns. Table 9.3 lists the twelve imperiled species in Hawaii, each of which is found on only a single island. They prefer mostly mesic (adequately moist) forest and wet forest habitats. Each fly is dependent on one or more specific host plants. This dependence is one of the factors that has imperiled the flies. All the host plants face threats to their survival due to competition with nonnative plants and trampling and ingestion by livestock and wild animals.

In May 2006 all twelve subspecies were listed by the USFWS under the ESA. All but one were designated as endangered. (See Table 9.1.) *Drosophila mulli* was designated as threatened. As of April 2008, a recovery plan had not been issued for the Hawaiian pomace flies.

BLACKBURN'S SPHINX MOTHS. Blackburn's sphinx moth was first listed as an endangered species in February 2000 and is found exclusively in Hawaii. This moth species is threatened by urban development, conversion of land for agricultural use, invasive plant species, trampling

**TABLE 9.3**

**Distribution, habitat, and primary host plant(s) of imperiled Hawaiian pomace flies, 2006**

| Species | Island | General habitat type | Primary host plant(s) |
|---|---|---|---|
| *Drosophila aglaia* | Oahu | Mesic forest | *Urera glabra* |
| *D. differens* | Molokai | Wet forest | *Clermontia sp.* |
| *D. hemipeza* | Oahu | Mesic forest | *Cyanea sp.*, *Lobelia sp.*, and *Urera kaalae* |
| *D. heteroneura* | Hawaii | Mesic to wet forest | *Cheirodendron sp.*, *Clermontia sp.*, *Delissea sp.* |
| *D. montgomeryi* | Oahu | Mesic forest | *Urera kaalae* |
| *D. mulli* | Hawaii | Wet forest | *Pritchardia beccariana* |
| *D. musaphilia* | Kauai | Mesic forest | *Acacia koa* |
| *D. neoclavisetae* | Maui | Wet forest | *Cyanea sp.* |
| *D. obatai* | Oahu | Dry to mesic forest | *Pleomele aurea* and *Pleomele forbesii* |
| *D. ochrobasis* | Hawaii | Mesic to wet forest | *Clermontia sp.*, *Marattia sp.*, and *Myrsine sp.* |
| *D. substenoptera* | Oahu | Wet forest | *Cheirodendron sp.* and *Tetraplasandra sp.* |
| *D. tarphytrichia* | Oahu | Mesic forest | *Charpentiera sp.* |

SOURCE: "Table 1. Distribution of 12 Hawaiian Picture-Wing Flies by Island, General Habit at Type, and Primary Host Plant(s)," in *Federal Register*, vol. 71, no. 89, May 9, 2006, http://a257.g.akamaitech.net/7/257/2422/01jan20061800/edocket.access.gpo.gov/2006/pdf/06-4299.pdf (accessed February 29, 2008)

of vegetation by nonnative ungulates (hoofed animals), and invasive predators and parasites.

In *Recovery Plan for the Blackburn's Sphinx Moth* (2005, http://ecos.fws.gov/docs/recovery_plans/2005/050926 .pdf), the USFWS provides several conservation recommendations, such as habitat conservation and restoration, planting of the moth's host plant in new habitats, and a captive breeding and reintroduction program. The total cost for recovery of the species is estimated at nearly $5.6 million.

### Other Insect Species of Interest

HINE'S EMERALD DRAGONFLIES. The Hine's emerald dragonfly has been listed as an endangered species since 1995 and is found in federal and state preserves and national forest lands in Illinois, Wisconsin, Michigan, and Missouri. In earlier times, its range extended through portions of Ohio, Alabama, and Indiana as well. The Hine's emerald dragonfly has a metallic-green body and emerald-green eyes. It is considered a biological indicator species because it is extremely sensitive to water pollution. The decline of this dragonfly species has resulted primarily from loss of suitable wetland habitat, such as wet prairies, marshes, sedge meadows, and fens occurring over dolomite rock. (The lakeside daisy is another species damaged by the decline of these habitats and is listed as threatened.)

Wetland habitats support dragonflies during their aquatic larval period, which lasts some three to four years. Adult dragonflies occupy open areas and forest edges near wetland habitats, where they feed on invertebrate species such as mosquitoes. Hine's emerald dragonflies also serve as prey for a variety of bird and fish species. The recovery plan for the dragonfly includes measures to protect current habitat as well as the reintroduction of the species to portions of its former range. Private companies that own land supporting dragonfly populations have aided conservation efforts by monitoring populations and preserving important habitat areas.

### THREATENED AND ENDANGERED FOREIGN SPECIES OF INSECTS

As of February 2008, there were eight foreign insects listed under the ESA. (See Table 9.4.) Four of the insects are found in the United States and foreign countries, whereas the other four are completely foreign. All are classified as endangered.

In *2007 Red List of Threatened Species*, the IUCN lists 623 species of insects as threatened. This number comprises half of the species evaluated (1,255), but less than 1% of the 950,000 described species.

### Monarch Butterflies

Among the best-known insect species, the adult monarch butterfly is characterized by orange wings with black veins and white spots at the outer margins. Historically, monarch butterflies migrated by the millions up and down the North American continent on a journey extending 3,000 miles (4,830 km). Over time, monarch butterfly populations have also become established in Australia and on the Pacific islands of Samoa and Tahiti. Other monarch populations have appeared in Hawaii and New Zealand.

For many years, naturalists sought to pinpoint the location where monarchs hibernate in January and February in preparation for their mating season and northward migration in March. In 1975, following an arduous search, a serene monarch hibernation area was located in the high altitude forests of the Michoacán Mountains in Mexico. Mexico declared the impoverished region a protected area. The inhabitants of the area turned the site into an ecotourism attraction to generate income for the economy. However, ecotourism not only failed to generate sufficient money to support the people of the area but

**TABLE 9.4**

**Foreign endangered and threatened insect species, February 2008**

| Common name | Scientific name | Listing status* | U.S. and/or foreign listed | Foreign range |
|---|---|---|---|---|
| American burying beetle | *Nicrophorus americanus* | E | US/foreign | Canada |
| Corsican swallowtail butterfly | *Papilio hospiton* | E | Foreign | Corsica, Sardinia |
| Homerus swallowtail butterfly | *Papilio homerus* | E | Foreign | Jamaica |
| Hungerford's crawling water beetle | *Brychius hungerfordi* | E | US/foreign | Canada |
| Karner blue butterfly | *Lycaeides melissa samuelis* | E | US/foreign | Canada |
| Luzon peacock swallowtail butterfly | *Papilio chikae* | E | Foreign | Philippines |
| Queen Alexandra's birdwing butterfly | *Troides (= Omithoptara) alexandrae* | E | Foreign | Papua New Guinea |
| Quino checkerspot butterfly | *Euphydryas editha quino (= E. e. wrighti)* | E | US/foreign | Mexico |

*E = Endangered.

SOURCE: Adapted from "Listed FWS/Joint FWS and NMFS Species and Populations with Recovery Plans (Sorted by Listed Entity)" and "Listed U.S. Species by Taxonomic Group," in *USFWS Threatened and Endangered Species System (TESS)*, U.S. Department of the Interior, U.S. Fish and Wildlife Service, February 5, 2008, http://ecos.fws.gov/tess_public/SpeciesRecovery.do?sort=1 and http://ecos.fws.gov/tess_public/SpeciesReport.do?kingdom=V&listing Type=L (accessed February 5, 2008)

also caused severe habitat disruption. The onslaught of tourists affected habitats by introducing excessive noise, tobacco smoke, fire, and pollution. Monarch butterflies are now considered endangered by the IUCN. The USFWS and the Mexican government have since attempted to nurture a self-sustaining economy in the monarch hibernation area by introducing fish breeding and horticulture.

## THREATENED AND ENDANGERED ARACHNID SPECIES IN THE UNITED STATES

As of February 2008, there were twelve U.S. species of arachnids listed under the ESA. (See Table 9.5.) All the arachnids have endangered status, and six of them have recovery plans in place. The imperiled arachnids fall into four species types:

- Harvestmen—three species
- Meshweaver—four species
- Pseudoscorpion—one species
- Spider—four species

Ten of the arachnids are cave-dwelling species found only in Texas. The only imperiled arachnids outside of Texas are the Kauai cave wolf spider, which inhabits Hawaii, and the spruce-fir moss spider, which is found in North Carolina and Tennessee.

In *Federal and State Endangered and Threatened Species Expenditures: Fiscal Year 2006* (draft, 2008), the USFWS notes that over $300,000 was spent under the ESA for arachnid species during FY 2006. Most of this amount ($223,560) was devoted to Madla's Cave meshweaver, a Texas species.

### Texas Cave Arachnids

Ten of the listed arachnids are found only in underground karst caves in a handful of counties in Texas. (See Figure 9.3.) Karst is a geological term referring to a type of underground terrain resulting when limestone bedrock

is exposed to mildly acidic groundwater over a long period. Eventually, the bedrock becomes a honeycomb of cracks, fissures, holes, and other openings. There are dozens of these karst caves located in Bexar, Travis, and Williamson counties in Texas. In recent decades scientists have discovered unusual invertebrate species living in these caves. The tiny cave dwellers are eyeless and have no pigment (color) to their bodies. Ten of the creatures have been added to the endangered species list. They include two true spiders, one pseudoscorpion, four meshweavers (tiny web-making arachnids), and three harvestmen (commonly known as daddy longlegs or granddaddy longlegs).

The species were listed under the ESA after a collection of conservation groups petitioned the USFWS in 1992. The creatures were listed as endangered in 2000. In 2003 approximately 1,000 acres (405 ha) were designated as critical habitat for six of the arachnids. In addition, four of the species are included in the USFWS's *Recovery Plan for Endangered Karst Invertebrates in Travis and Williamson Counties, Texas* (1994, http://ecos.fws .gov/docs/recovery_plan/940825.pdf), which also covers other imperiled invertebrate species living in the caves.

### Kauai Cave Wolf Spiders

The Kauai cave wolf spider, ranging from about 0.5 to 0.75 inches (1.3 to 1.9 cm) in length, is a blind species found only in special caves on the southern part of the island of Kauai in Hawaii. These caves are formed by young lava flows. Unlike most other spiders, which trap their prey in webs, the Kauai cave wolf spider hunts its prey directly. Its prey includes the Kauai cave amphipod, a species that is also highly endangered. The USFWS originally listed both species as endangered in January 2000. Female cave wolf spiders lay some fifteen to thirty eggs per clutch and carry young on their back after hatching. Cave species are extremely sensitive to changes in temperature and light. In 2006 the USFWS published *Recovery Plan for*

## TABLE 9.5

**Endangered and threatened spider species, February 2008**

| Common name | Scientific name | Listing status[a] | Recovery plan date | Recovery plan stage[b] |
|---|---|---|---|---|
| Bee Creek Cave harvestman | *Texella reddelli* | E | 8/25/1994 | F |
| Bone Cave harvestman | *Texella reyesi* | E | 8/25/1994 | F |
| Braken Bat Cave meshweaver | *Cicurina venii* | E | None | — |
| Cokendolpher Cave harvestman | *Texella cokendolpheri* | E | None | — |
| Government Canyon Bat Cave meshweaver | *Cicurina vespera* | E | None | — |
| Government Canyon Bat Cave spider | *Neoleptoneta microps* | E | None | — |
| Kauai cave wolf or pe'e pe'e maka 'ole spider | *Adelocosa anops* | E | 7/19/2006 | F |
| Madla's Cave meshweaver | *Cicurina madla* | E | None | — |
| Robber Baron Cave meshweaver | *Cicurina baronia* | E | None | — |
| Spruce-fir moss spider | *Microhexura montivaga* | E | 9/11/1998 | F |
| Tooth Cave pseudoscorpion | *Tartarocreagris texana* | E | 8/25/1994 | F |
| Tooth Cave spider | *Leptoneta myopica* | E | 8/25/1994 | F |

[a]E = Endangered.
[b]Recovery plan stages: F = Final.

SOURCE: Adapted from "Listed FWS/Joint FWS and NMFS Species and Populations with Recovery Plans (Sorted by Listed Entity)" and "Listed U.S. Species by Taxonomic Group," in *USFWS Threatened and Endangered Species System (TESS)*, U.S. Department of the Interior, U.S. Fish and Wildlife Service, February 5, 2008, http://ecos.fws.gov/tess_public/SpeciesRecovery.do?sort=1 and http://ecos.fws.gov/tess_public/SpeciesReport.do?kingdom=V&listingType=L (accessed February 5, 2008)

## FIGURE 9.3

**A karst cave provides habitat for endangered invertebrates**

SOURCE: Lisa O'Donnell, William R. Elliott, and Ruth A.Stanford, "Front Cover," in *Recovery Plan for Endangered Karst Invertebrates in Travis and Williamson Counties, Texas*, U.S. Department of the Interior, U.S. Fish and Wildlife Service, 1994, http://ecos.fws.gov/docs/recovery_plans/1994/940825.pdf (accessed February 21, 2008)

the Kauai Cave Arthropods: The Kauai Cave Wolf Spider and the Kauai Cave Amphipod (http://ecos.fws.gov/docs/recovery_plan/060719.pdf). The critical habitat established for the species includes fourteen units totaling 272 acres (110 ha) in the southern part of the island.

## Spruce-Fir Moss Spiders

The spruce-fir moss spider is an endangered spider related to the tarantula. It was placed on the Endangered Species List in 1995. Spruce-fir moss spiders live in moss mats found only in the vicinity of Fraser fir trees. Its populations have declined largely due to the introduction in the United States of an invasive European insect species, the balsam-woolly adelgid. The balsam-woolly adelgid infests Fraser fir trees, causing them to die within two to seven years. With the death of many fir trees, other forest trees can also be blown over. The resulting increase in light level and temperature causes the moss mats on the forest floor to dry up.

In 2001 the USFWS designated critical habitat for the species, including areas in the Great Smoky Mountains National Park and the Pisgah and Cherokee National Forests, as well as a preserve managed by the Nature Conservancy. This designation of critical habitat followed a lawsuit against the USFWS, which had previously deemed designating critical habitat "not prudent" because it believed the spider would be more vulnerable to collectors.

## THREATENED AND ENDANGERED FOREIGN SPECIES OF SPIDERS

As of February 2008, there were no foreign spiders listed under the ESA. The IUCN lists in *2007 Red List of Threatened Species* ten species of spiders as threatened. This number comprises more than half of the species evaluated (eighteen), but less than 1% of the more then sixty thousand described arachnid species.

# CHAPTER 10
# PLANTS

Plants belong to the Plantae kingdom. According to the International Union for Conservation of Nature and Natural Resources (IUCN), in *2007 Red List of Threatened Species* (2007, http://www.iucnredlist.org/), there are 297,326 species making up this kingdom. In general, there are two types of land-growing plants: vascular and nonvascular. Vascular plants have specially developed organs similar to veins that move liquids through their system. This category includes the trees, shrubs, flowers, and grasses. Nonvascular plants are mosses, liverworts, and hornworts. The vast majority of plant species on Earth are vascular plants that reproduce through their flowers.

In science, plants are more often identified by their scientific name than are animals. Plant species are so abundant and diverse that many plants have multiple common names. However, there are plants that have no common names because they are rare or are geographically remote. To avoid confusion, this chapter will include the scientific name for any specific common name given.

Many factors contribute to the endangerment of plant species. Many species are the victims of habitat loss due to land and agricultural development. Others have declined due to pollution or habitat damage, or as a result of competition with invasive species. Table 10.1 lists dozens of invasive plants found in the United States. Still other imperiled plants have succumbed to introduced or unknown plant diseases. Finally, collectors or dealers often illegally seek rare, showy, or unusual plants and have depleted populations through overcollection.

The preservation of plant species is important for many reasons. Not only are plants of aesthetic value but also they are crucial components of every ecosystem on Earth. Furthermore, plants serve several functions directly beneficial to humans. First, they provide genetic variation that is used in the breeding of new crop varieties—native plants pro-

vide genes that allow for adaptation to local environments and resistance to pests, disease, or drought. In addition, plants are the source of many human medicines.

## AMERICAN CHESTNUT TREE—MAKING A COMEBACK?

During the 1800s the American chestnut (*Castanea dentata*) was the predominant tree of many forests in the eastern United States. Its range extended from Maine to Mississippi. (See Figure 10.1.) The heaviest concentrations were in the southern Appalachian Mountains, where the tree made up more than a third of the overstory trees (the topmost layer of foliage in a forest). Mature trees reached 3 to 5 feet (1 to 1.5 m) in diameter and rose to 90 feet (27 m) in height with a huge canopy. The species was fast growing and produced light, durable wood that was extremely popular for firewood and for making furniture, shingles, caskets, telephone poles, railroad ties, and other products. The trees were also valued for their chestnuts and tannin content. Tannin is an extract used in the leather industry.

In 1904 observers in New York City reported that an unknown blight (disease) was killing American chestnut trees at the Bronx Zoo. By 1940 the blight had spread through the entire range of the species, leaving all the trees dead or dying. The tree structure was not damaged by the disease, so harvesting continued of dead trees for several more decades. Even though sprouts would grow from the stumps left behind, they eventually succumbed to the blight. By the 1970s the American chestnut had been virtually eliminated. More than three billion trees had been killed. The culprit was a fungus originally called *Endothia parasitica*, but later renamed *Cryphonectria parasitica*. Scientists believe the disease came into the United States with ornamental chestnut trees imported from Japan or China. Oriental trees could carry

**TABLE 10.1**

**Invasive plants**

| Species | Common name |
|---|---|
| *Acer platanoides* | Norway maple |
| *Acroptilon repens* | Russian knapweed |
| *Agropyron cristatum* | Crested wheatgrass |
| *Agropyron desertorum* | Desert wheatgrass |
| *Agrostis gigantea* | Redtop |
| *Ailanthus altissima* | Tree-of-heaven |
| *Alliaria petiolata* | Garlic mustard |
| *Amaranthus retroflexus* | Rough pigweed |
| *Arundo donax* | Giant reed |
| *Bromus hordeaceus* | Soft chess |
| *Bromus inermis* | Smooth brome |
| *Bromus japonicus* | Japanese brome |
| *Bromus madritensis* | Foxtail chess |
| *Bromus rubens* | Red brome |
| *Bromus tectorum* | Cheatgrass |
| *Calluna vulgaris* | Heather |
| *Cardaria chalapensis* | Lens-podded hoary cress |
| *Cardaria draba* | Heart-podded hoary cress |
| *Cardaria pubescens* | Globe-podded hoary cress |
| *Carduus nutans* | Musk thistle |
| *Casuarina cunninghamiana* | River sheoak |
| *Casuarina equisetifolia* | Australian-pine |
| *Casuarina glauca* | Gray sheoak |
| *Celastrus orbiculatus* | Oriental bittersweet |
| *Centaurea diffusa* | Diffuse knapweed |
| *Centaurea maculosa* | Spotted knapweed |
| *Centaurea solstitialis* | Yellow starthistle |
| *Chondrilla juncea* | Rush skeletonweed |
| *Cirsium arvense* | Canada thistle |
| *Cirsium vulgare* | Bull thistle |
| *Convolvulus arvensis* | Field bindweed |
| *Cynodon dactylon* | Bermuda grass |
| *Cynoglossum officinale* | Houndstongue |
| *Cytisus scoparius* | Scotch broom |
| *Cytisus striatus* | Portuguese broom |
| *Dactylis glomerata* | Orchard grass |
| *Descurainia sophia* | Flixweed tansymustard |
| *Echinochloa crus-galli* | Barnyard grass |
| *Elaeagnus angustifolia* | Russian-olive |
| *Elaeagnus umbellata* | Autumn-olive |
| *Elytrigia repens* | Quackgrass |
| *Eragrostis curvula* | Weeping lovegrass |
| *Eragrostis lehmanniana* | Lehmann lovegrass |
| *Eremochloa ophiuroides* | Centipede grass |
| *Erodium cicutarium* | Cutleaf filaree |
| *Eucalyptus globulus* | Bluegum eucalyptus |
| *Euphorbia esula* | Leafy spurge |
| *Genista monspessulana* | French broom |
| *Halogeton glomeratus* | Halogeton |
| *Hypericum perforatum* | St Johnswort |
| *Imperata brasiliensis* | Brazilian satintail |
| *Imperata cylindrica* | Cogon grass |
| *Kochia scoparia* | Summer-cypress |
| *Lepidium latifolium* | Perennial pepperweed |
| *Lespedeza bicolor* | Bicolor lespedeza |
| *Lespedeza cuneata* | Sericea lespedeza |
| *Lespedeza striata* | Common lespedeza |
| *Ligustrum amurense* | Amur privet |
| *Ligustrum japonicum* | Japanese privet |
| *Ligustrum sinense* | Chinese privet |
| *Ligustrum vulgare* | European privet |
| *Linaria dalmatica* | Dalmatian toadflax |
| *Linaria vulgaris* | Yellow toadflax |
| *Lolium perenne* | Perennial ryegrass |
| *Lolium multiflorum* | Italian ryegrass |
| *Lonicera* × *bella* | Bell's honeysuckle |
| *Lonicera fragantissima* | Winter honeysuckle |
| *Lonicera japonica* | Japanese honeysuckle |
| *Lonicera maackii* | Amur honeysuckle |
| *Lonicera morrowii* | Morrow's honeysuckle |
| *Lonicera tatarica* | Tatarian honeysuckle |
| *Lonicera xylosteum* | European fly honeysuckle |

**TABLE 10.1**

**Invasive plants** [CONTINUED]

| Species | Common name |
|---|---|
| *Lygodium japonicum* | Japanese climbing fern |
| *Lygodium microphyllum* | Old World climbing fern |
| *Lythrum salicaria* | Purple loosestrife |
| *Medicago sativa* | Alfalfa |
| *Melaleuca quinquenervia* | Melaleuca |
| *Melilotus alba* | White sweetclover |
| *Melilotus officinalis* | Yellow sweetclover |
| *Microstegium vimineum* | Japanese siltgrass |
| *Phalaris arundinacea* | Reed canarygrass |
| *Phleum pratense* | Timothy |
| *Poa pratensis* | Kentucky bluegrass |
| *Potentilla recta* | Sulfur cinquefoil |
| *Psathyrostachys juncea* | Russian wildrye |
| *Pueraria montana var. lobata* | Kudzu |
| *Rosa multiflora* | Multiflora rose |
| *Rubus discolor* | Himalayan blackberry |
| *Rubus laciniatus* | Evergreen blackberry |
| *Rumex acetosella* | Sheep sorrel |
| *Salsola kali* | Russian-thistle |
| *Schedonorus arundinaceus* | Tall fescue |
| *Schinus terebinthifolius* | Brazilian pepper |
| *Sisymbrium altissimum* | Tumblemustard |
| *Sonchus arvensis* | Perennial sowthistle |
| *Sorghum halepense* | Johnson grass |
| *Spartium junceum* | Spanish broom |
| *Taeniatherum caput-medusae* | Medusahead |
| *Tamarix aphylla* | Athel tamarisk |
| *Tamarix chinensis* | Saltcedar |
| *Tamarix gallica* | French tamarisk |
| *Tamarix parviflora* | Small-flowered tamarisk |
| *Tamarix ramosissima* | Saltcedar |
| *Taraxacum officinale* | Common dandelion |
| *Triadica sebifera* | Tallowtree |
| *Ulex europaeus* | Gorse |
| *Vulpia myuros* | Rattail sixweeks grass |
| *Xanthium strumarium* | Common cocklebur |

SOURCE: Adapted from "Invasive Plants List," in *Fire Effects Information System: Invasive Plants*, U.S. Department of Agriculture, U.S. Forest Service, Rocky Mountain Research Station, Fire Sciences Laboratory, Undated, http://www.fs.fed.us/database/feis/plants/weed/index.html (accessed January 21, 2008)

the disease, but not succumb to it, because they had a natural immunity to it.

During the 1920s frantic efforts began to cross the remaining American chestnut trees with the oriental species. Even though hybrid trees resulted with some resistance to the blight, they were inferior in quality to the original American species. Advances in genetic research and forestry techniques led to better hybrids by the 1980s. As of 2008 research continued by two foundations: the American Chestnut Foundation (ACF; a nonprofit organization headquartered in Vermont) and the American Chestnut Cooperators' Foundation (ACCF) at Virginia Tech University. The ACF focuses on crossing naturally blight-resistant Asiatic species with American species, whereas the ACCF produces crosses between American chestnut trees found to have some resistance to the blight in hopes of eventually producing offspring with higher resistance. Both organizations are confident that vigorous blight-resistant American chestnut trees can be developed during the twenty-first century.

**FIGURE 10.1**

**Historical distribution of the American chestnut**

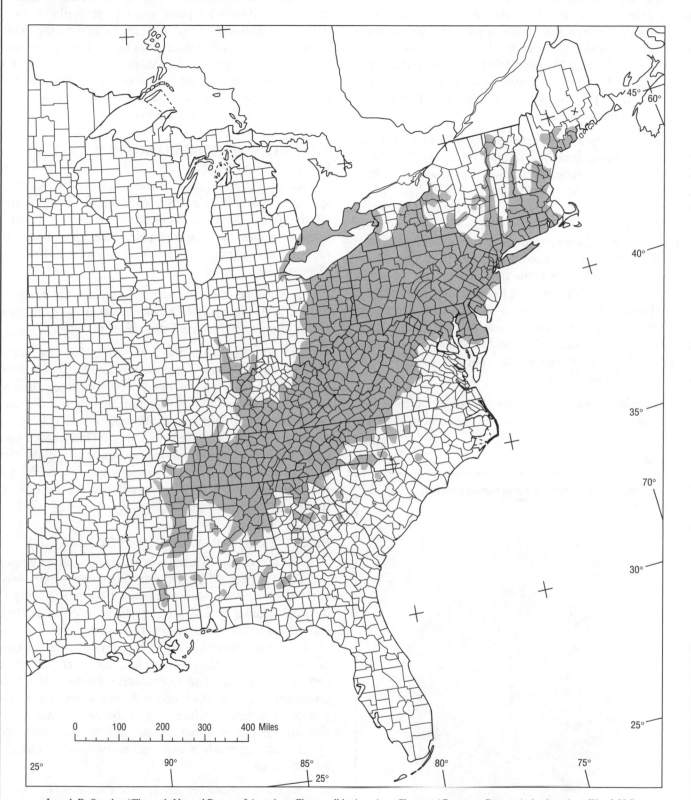

SOURCE: Joseph R. Saucier, "Figure 1. Natural Range of American Chestnut," in *American Chestnut (Castanea Dentata). An American Wood*, U.S. Department of Agriculture, U.S. Forest Service, February 1973, http://www.fpl.fs.fed.us/documnts/usda/amwood/230chest.pdf (accessed January 30, 2008)

## PROTECTION OF PLANTS UNDER THE ENDANGERED SPECIES ACT

The Endangered Species Act (ESA) of 1973 protects listed plants from deliberate destruction or vandalism. Plants also receive protection under the consultation requirements of the act—that is, all federal agencies must consult with the U.S. Fish and Wildlife Service (USFWS) to determine how best to conserve species and to ensure that no issued permits will jeopardize listed species or harm their habitat.

However, many conservationists believe that plants receive less protection than animals under the ESA. First, the ESA only protects plants that are found on federal lands. It imposes no restrictions on private landowners whose property is home to endangered plants. Critics also complain that the USFWS has been slow to list plant species and that damage to plant habitats is not addressed with the same seriousness as for animal species. However, the USFWS points out that the number of plants listed under the ESA has risen dramatically over the past three decades. In 1980 less than one hundred plants were listed as endangered or threatened. As of February 2008, this number was more than seven hundred. In fact, plants comprised 55% of all species listed under the ESA at that time. (See Figure 10.2.)

In 2000, in an effort to bolster conservation efforts for plants, the USFWS formed an agreement with the

Center for Plant Conservation, a national association of botanical gardens and arboreta. The two organizations are cooperating in developing conservation measures to help save North American plant species, particularly those listed as threatened or endangered. Central to the effort is the creation of educational programs aimed at informing the public about the importance of plant species for aesthetic, economic, biological, and medical reasons. The Center for Plant Conservation also aids in developing recovery plans for listed plant species.

## THREATENED AND ENDANGERED U.S. PLANT SPECIES

As of February 2008, there were 744 U.S. plant species listed under the ESA. (See Table 10.2.) Nearly all the plants have recovery plans in place. Because several species of imperiled plants are often found in the same ecosystem, many recovery plans cover multiple plant species.

Because the status of most plant species has not been studied in detail, many more plants are probably in danger of extinction than are listed under the ESA.

The ten plants with the highest expenditures under the ESA during fiscal year 2006 are listed in Table 10.3. All are flowering plants. Pondberry dominates the list with over $1.6 million in spending. It is a shrub found in the Southeast. American chaffseed, an herb that grows in coastal states along the Atlantic and Gulf coasts, cost more than $740,000. Johnson's seagrass is a plant that lives underwater in salty lagoons in southeastern Florida. It had more than $723,000 in spending under the ESA in fiscal year 2006.

## PLANT TAXONOMY AND CATEGORIZATION

The taxonomy of plant species can be quite complicated and is plagued by disagreements among scientists. Historically, plants were categorized by morphology—physical characteristics, such as shape or color of their leaves, fruit, bark, and so on. During the 1960s a new classification scheme emerged that groups plants based on their evolutionary similarities, for example, their chemical properties and reproductive mechanisms. This taxonomy is part of the broader science known as phylogenetic systematics, which studies the evolutionary relationships between living organisms. In the future the systematics approach is expected to be used to classify all life forms.

In general, plants are assigned to the same taxonomic levels used to classify animals. This hierarchical structure includes kingdom, phylum, class, order, family, genus, and species. Beneath the species level, plants can be classified to subspecies, just as in animal taxonomy. There is an additional classification for plants at this level called variety (abbreviated as "var."). Varieties are sub-

**FIGURE 10.2**

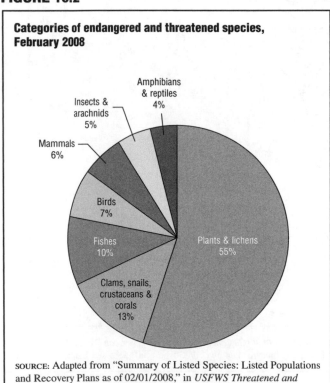

**Categories of endangered and threatened species, February 2008**

- Amphibians & reptiles 4%
- Insects & arachnids 5%
- Mammals 6%
- Birds 7%
- Fishes 10%
- Clams, snails, crustaceans & corals 13%
- Plants & lichens 55%

SOURCE: Adapted from "Summary of Listed Species: Listed Populations and Recovery Plans as of 02/01/2008," in *USFWS Threatened and Endangered Species System (TESS)*, U.S. Department of the Interior, U.S. Fish and Wildlife Service, February 1, 2008, http://ecos.fws.gov/tess_public/Boxscore.do (accessed February 1, 2008)

## TABLE 10.2

**Endangered and threatened plant species, February 2008**

| Common name | Scientific name | Listing status[a] | Recovery plan date | Recovery plan stage[b] |
|---|---|---|---|---|
| **Conifers and cycads** | | | | |
| Florida torreya | *Torreya taxifolia* | E | 9/9/1986 | F |
| Gowen cypress | *Cupressus goveniana ssp. goveniana* | T | 6/17/2005 | F |
| Santa Cruz cypress | *Cupressus abramsiana* | E | 9/26/1998 | F |
| **Ferns and allies** | | | | |
| Alabama streak-sorus fern | *Thelypteris pilosa var. alabamensis* | T | 10/25/1996 | F |
| Aleutian shield fern | *Polystichum aleuticum* | E | 9/30/1992 | F |
| American hart's-tongue fern | *Asplenium scolopendrium var. americanum* | T | 9/15/1993 | F |
| Asplenium-leaved diellia | *Diellia erecta* | E | 7/10/1999 | F |
| Black spored quillwort | *Isoetes melanospora* | E | 7/7/1993 | F |
| Elfin tree fern | *Cyathea dryopteroides* | E | 1/31/1991 | F |
| Ihi`ihi | *Marsilea villosa* | E | 4/18/1996 | F |
| Louisiana quillwort | *Isoetes louisianensis* | E | 9/30/1996 | F |
| Mat-forming quillwort | *Isoetes tegetiformans* | E | 7/7/1993 | F |
| No common name | *Adiantum vivesii* | E | 9/29/1995 | F |
| No common name | *Asplenium fragile var. insulare* | E | 9/29/1995 | F |
| No common name | *Diellia falcata* | E | 9/29/1995 | F |
| No common name | *Diellia unisora* | E | 9/29/1995 | F |
| No common name | *Diellia pallida* | E | 9/20/1995 | F |
| No common name | *Diplazium molokaiense* | E | 4/10/1998 | F |
| No common name | *Elaphoglossum serpens* | E | 1/17/1995 | F |
| No common name | *Polystichum calderonense* | E | 1/17/1995 | F |
| No common name | *Pteris lidgatei* | E | 4/10/1998 | F |
| No common name | *Tectaria estremerana* | E | 1/17/1995 | F |
| No common name | *Thelypteris inabonensis* | E | 1/17/1995 | F |
| No common name | *Thelypteris verecunda* | E | 9/29/1995 | F |
| No common name | *Thelypteris yaucoensis* | E | 1/17/1995 | F |
| Pauoa | *Ctenitis squamigera* | E | 4/10/1998 | F |
| Pendant kihi fern | *Adenophorus periens* | E | 7/10/1999 | F |
| Wawae`iole | *Huperzia mannii* | E | 7/29/1997 | F |
| Wawae`iole | *Lycopodium (=Phlegmariurus) nutans* | E | None | — |
| **Lichens** | | | | |
| Florida perforate cladonia | *Cladonia perforata* | E | 5/18/1999 | F |
| Rock gnome lichen | *Gymnoderma lineare* | E | 9/30/1997 | F |
| **Flowering plants** | | | | |
| `Ahinahina | *Argyroxiphium sandwicense ssp. macrocephalum* | T | 7/29/1997 | F |
| `Ahinahina | *Argyroxiphium sandwicense ssp. sandwicense* | E | 7/29/1997 | F |
| `Aiakeakua, popolo | *Solanum sandwicense* | E | 9/20/1995 | F |
| `Aiea | *Nothocestrum breviflorum* | E | 9/26/1996 | F |
| `Aiea | *Nothocestrum peltatum* | E | 9/26/1996 | F |
| `Akoko | *Chamaesyce celastroides var. kaenana* | E | 8/10/1998 | F |
| `Akoko | *Chamaesyce deppeana* | E | 8/10/1998 | F |
| `Akoko | *Chamaesyce herbstii* | E | 8/10/1998 | F |
| `Akoko | *Chamaesyce kuwaleana* | E | 8/10/1998 | F |
| `Akoko | *Chamaesyce rockii* | E | 8/10/1998 | F |
| `Akoko | *Euphorbia haeleeleana* | E | 8/10/1998 | F |
| `Anaunau | *Lepidium arbuscula* | E | 8/10/1998 | F |
| `Anunu | *Sicyos alba* | E | 5/11/1998 | F |
| `Awikiwiki | *Canavalia molokaiensis* | E | 9/26/1996 | F |
| `Oha wai | *Clermontia drepanomorpha* | E | 5/11/1998 | F |
| `Oha wai | *Clermontia lindseyana* | E | 5/11/1998 | F |
| `Oha wai | *Clermontia oblongifolia ssp. brevipes* | E | 5/11/1998 | F |
| `Oha wai | *Clermontia oblongifolia ssp. mauiensis* | E | 5/11/1998 | F |
| `Oha wai | *Clermontia peleana* | E | 5/11/1998 | F |
| `Oha wai | *Clermontia pyrularia* | E | 5/11/1998 | F |
| `Oha wai | *Clermontia samuelii* | E | 5/11/1998 | F |
| `Ohe`ohe | *Tetraplasandra gymnocarpa* | E | 8/10/1998 | F |
| A`e | *Zanthoxylum dipetalum var. tomentosum* | E | 5/11/1998 | F |
| A`e | *Zanthoxylum hawaiiense* | E | 5/11/1998 | F |
| Alabama leather flower | *Clematis socialis* | E | 12/27/1989 | F |
| Alani | *Melicope adscendens* | E | 7/29/1997 | F |
| Alani | *Melicope balloui* | E | 7/29/1997 | F |
| Alani | *Melicope haupuensis* | E | 7/29/1997 | Γ |
| Alani | *Melicope knudsenii* | E | 7/29/1997 | F |
| Alani | *Melicope lydgatei* | E | 7/29/1997 | F |
| Alani | *Melicope mucronulata* | E | 7/29/1997 | F |
| Alani | *Melicope munroi* | E | 7/29/1997 | F |
| Alani | *Melicope ovalis* | E | 7/29/1997 | F |

**TABLE 10.2**

| Common name | Scientific name | Listing status[a] | Recovery plan date | Recovery plan stage[b] |
|---|---|---|---|---|
| Alani | *Melicope pallida* | E | 7/29/1997 | F |
| Alani | *Melicope quadrangularis* | E | 7/29/1997 | F |
| Alani | *Melicope reflexa* | E | 7/29/1997 | F |
| Alani | *Melicope saint-johnii* | E | 7/29/1997 | F |
| Alani | *Melicope zahlbruckneri* | E | 7/29/1997 | F |
| Apalachicola rosemary | *Conradina glabra* | E | 9/27/1994 | F |
| Applegate's milk-vetch | *Astragalus applegatei* | E | 4/10/1998 | F |
| Arizona hedgehog cactus | *Echinocereus triglochidiatus var. arizonicus* | E | 9/30/1984 | D |
| Ash Meadows milk-vetch | *Astragalus phoenix* | T | 9/28/1990 | F |
| Ash Meadows sunray | *Enceliopsis nudicaulis var. corrugata* | T | 9/28/1990 | F |
| Ash-grey paintbrush | *Castilleja cinerea* | T | None | — |
| Ashy dogweed | *Thymophylla tephroleuca* | E | 7/29/1988 | F |
| Aupaka | *Isodendrion hosakae* | E | 5/23/1994 | F |
| Aupaka | *Isodendrion laurifolium* | E | 5/23/1994 | F |
| Aupaka | *Isodendrion longifolium* | T | 5/23/1994 | F |
| Avon Park harebells | *Crotalaria avonensis* | E | 5/18/1999 | F |
| Awiwi | *Centaurium sebaeoides* | E | 7/10/1999 | F |
| Awiwi | *Hedyotis cookiana* | E | 7/10/1999 | F |
| Baker's larkspur | *Delphinium bakeri* | E | None | — |
| Bariaco | *Trichilia triacantha* | E | 8/20/1991 | F |
| Bear Valley sandwort | *Arenaria ursina* | T | None | — |
| Beautiful pawpaw | *Deeringothamnus pulchellus* | E | 5/18/1999 | F |
| Ben Lomond spineflower | *Chorizanthe pungens var. hartwegiana* | E | 9/28/1998 | F |
| Ben Lomond wallflower | *Erysimum teretifolium* | E | 9/28/1998 | F |
| Big-leaved crownbeard | *Verbesina dissita* | T | None | — |
| Black lace cactus | *Echinocereus reichenbachii var. albertii* | E | 3/18/1987 | F |
| Blazingstar, Ash Meadows | *Mentzelia leucophylla* | T | None | — |
| Bluecurls, Hidden Lake | *Trichostema austromontanum ssp. compactum* | T | None | — |
| Braun's rock-cress | *Arabis perstellata* | E | 7/22/1997 | F |
| Braunton's milk-vetch | *Astragalus brauntonii* | E | 9/30/1999 | F |
| Britton's beargrass | *Nolina brittoniana* | E | 8/23/2002 | RF(1) |
| Brooksville bellflower | *Campanula robinsiae* | E | 6/20/1994 | F |
| Bunched arrowhead | *Sagittaria fasciculata* | E | 9/8/1983 | F |
| Bunched cory cactus | *Coryphantha ramillosa* | T | 4/13/1990 | F |
| Buttercup, autumn | *Ranunculus aestivalis (=acriformis)* | E | None | — |
| Cactus, Bakersfield | *Opuntia treleasei* | E | None | — |
| Cactus, Brady pincushion | *Pediocactus bradyi* | E | None | — |
| California jewelflower | *Caulanthus californicus* | E | 9/30/1998 | F |
| Calistoga allocarya | *Plagiobothrys strictus* | E | None | — |
| Capa rosa | *Callicarpa ampla* | E | 7/31/1995 | F |
| Carter's mustard | *Warea carteri* | E | 5/18/1999 | F |
| Catalina Island mountain-mahogany | *Cercocarpus traskiae* | E | None | — |
| Chaffseed, American | *Schwalbea americana* | E | None | — |
| Chinese Camp brodiaea | *Brodiaea pallida* | T | None | — |
| Chisos Mountain hedgehog Cactus | *Echinocereus chisoensis var. chisoensis* | T | 12/8/1993 | F |
| Chorro Creek bog thistle | *Cirsium fontinale var. obispoense* | E | 9/28/1998 | F |
| Chupacallos | *Pleodendron macranthum* | E | 9/11/1998 | F |
| Clara Hunt's milk-vetch | *Astragalus clarianus* | E | None | — |
| Clay-loving wild-buckwheat | *Eriogonum pelinophilum* | E | 11/10/1988 | F |
| Clay's Hibiscus | *Hibiscus clayi* | E | 9/20/1995 | F |
| Cliff-rose, Arizona | *Purshia (=Cowania) subintegra* | E | None | — |
| Coachella Valley milk-vetch | *Astragalus lentiginosus var. coachellae* | E | None | — |
| Coastal dunes milk-vetch | *Astragalus tener var. titi* | E | 6/17/2005 | F |
| Cobana negra | *Stahlia monosperma* | T | 11/1/1996 | F |
| Cochise pincushion cactus | *Coryphantha robbinsorum* | T | 9/27/1993 | F |
| Colorado Butterfly plant | *Gaura neomexicana var. coloradensis* | T | None | — |
| Conejo dudleya | *Dudleya abramsii ssp. parva* | T | 9/30/1999 | F |
| Contra Costa wallflower | *Erysimum capitatum var. angustatum* | E | 4/25/1984 | RF(1) |
| Cook's holly | *Ilex cookii* | E | 1/31/1991 | F |
| Cooley's meadowrue | *Thalictrum cooleyi* | E | 4/21/1994 | F |
| Coyote ceanothus | *Ceanothus ferrisae* | E | 9/30/1998 | F |
| Crenulate lead-plant | *Amorpha crenulata* | E | 5/18/1999 | F |
| Cumberland rosemary | *Conradina verticillata* | T | 7/12/1996 | F |
| Cumberland sandwort | *Arenaria cumberlandensis* | E | 6/20/1996 | F |
| Cushenbury buckwheat | *Eriogonum ovalifolium var. vineum* | E | 9/30/1997 | D |
| Cushenbury milk-vetch | *Astragalus albens* | E | 9/30/1997 | D |
| Davis' green pitaya | *Echinocereus viridiflorus var. davisii* | E | 9/20/1984 | F |
| Decurrent false aster | *Boltonia decurrens* | T | 9/28/1990 | F |
| Del Mar manzanita | *Arctostaphylos glandulosa ssp. crassifolia* | E | None | — |
| Deltoid spurge | *Chamaesyce deltoidea ssp. deltoidea* | E | 5/18/1999 | F |
| Deseret milk-vetch | *Astragalus desereticus* | T | None | — |
| Desert yellowhead | *Yermo xanthocephalus* | T | None | — |

TABLE 10.2

**Endangered and threatened plant species, February 2008** [CONTINUED]

| Common name | Scientific name | Listing status[a] | Recovery plan date | Recovery plan stage[b] |
|---|---|---|---|---|
| Desert-parsley, Bradshaw's | Lomatium bradshawii | E | None | — |
| Dropwort, Canby's | Oxypolis canbyi | E | None | — |
| Dudley Bluffs bladderpod | Lesquerella congesta | T | 8/13/1993 | F |
| Dwarf bear-poppy | Arctomecon humilis | E | 12/31/1985 | F |
| Dwarf iliau | Wilkesia hobdyi | E | 9/20/1995 | F |
| El Dorado bedstraw | Galium californicum ssp. sierrae | E | 8/30/2002 | F |
| Encinitas baccharis | Baccharis vanessae | T | None | — |
| Erubia | Solanum drymophilum | E | 7/9/1992 | F |
| Etonia rosemary | Conradina etonia | E | 9/27/1994 | F |
| Evening-primrose, Antioch Dunes | Oenothera deltoides ssp. howellii | E | None | — |
| Evening-primrose, Eureka Valley | Oenothera avita ssp. eurekensis | E | None | — |
| Ewa Plains Àkoko | Chamaesyce skottsbergii var. kalaeloana | E | 10/5/1993 | D |
| Fish Slough milk-vetch | Astragalus lentiginosus var. piscinensis | T | 9/30/1998 | F |
| Fleshy owl's-clover | Castilleja campestris ssp. succulenta | T | 12/15/2005 | F |
| Florida bonamia | Bonamia grandiflora | T | 6/20/1996 | RF(1) |
| Florida golden aster | Chrysopsis floridana | E | 8/29/1988 | F |
| Florida ziziphus | Ziziphus celata | E | 5/18/1999 | F |
| Fosberg's love grass | Eragrostis fosbergii | E | 8/10/1998 | F |
| Fountain thistle | Cirsium fontinale var. fontinale | E | 9/30/1998 | F |
| Four-petal pawpaw | Asimina tetramera | E | 5/18/1999 | F |
| Fragrant prickly-apple | Cereus eriophorus var. fragrans | E | 5/18/1999 | F |
| Fringed campion | Silene polypetala | E | 10/1/1996 | D |
| Garber's spurge | Chamaesyce garberi | T | 5/18/1999 | F |
| Garrett's mint | Dicerandra christmanii | E | 5/18/1999 | F |
| Gaviota tarplant | Deinandra increscens ssp. villosa | E | None | — |
| Gentner's fritillary | Fritillaria gentneri | E | 8/28/2003 | F |
| Godfrey's butterwort | Pinguicula ionantha | T | 6/22/1994 | F |
| Goetzea, beautiful | Goetzea elegans | E | None | — |
| Golden paintbrush | Castilleja levisecta | T | 8/23/2000 | F |
| Golden sedge | Carex lutea | E | None | — |
| Goldenrod, Blue Ridge | Solidago spithamaea | T | None | — |
| Goldfields, Burke's | Lasthenia burkei | E | None | — |
| Goldfields, Contra Costa | Lasthenia conjugens | E | None | — |
| Grass, Colusa | Neostapfia colusana | T | None | — |
| Grass, Eureka Dune | Swallenia alexandrae | E | None | — |
| Greene's tuctoria | Tuctoria greenei | E | 12/15/2005 | F |
| Gumplant, Ash Meadows | Grindelia fraxino-pratensis | T | None | — |
| Guthrie's (=Pyne's) ground-plum | Astragalus bibullatus | E | None | — |
| Gypsum wild-buckwheat | Eriogonum gypsophilum | T | 3/30/1984 | F |
| Ha`iwale | Cyrtandra crenata | E | 8/10/1998 | F |
| Ha`iwale | Cyrtandra dentata | E | 8/10/1998 | F |
| Ha`iwale | Cyrtandra giffardii | E | 8/10/1998 | F |
| Ha`iwale | Cyrtandra limahuliensis | T | 8/10/1998 | F |
| Ha`iwale | Cyrtandra munroi | E | 8/10/1998 | F |
| Ha`iwale | Cyrtandra polyantha | E | 8/10/1998 | F |
| Ha`iwale | Cyrtandra subumbellata | E | 8/10/1998 | F |
| Ha`iwale | Cyrtandra tintinnabula | E | 8/10/1998 | F |
| Ha`iwale | Cyrtandra viridiflora | E | 8/10/1998 | F |
| Haha | Cyanea acuminata | E | 8/10/1998 | F |
| Haha | Cyanea asarifolia | E | 8/10/1998 | F |
| Haha | Cyanea copelandii ssp. copelandii | E | 8/10/1998 | F |
| Haha | Cyanea copelandii ssp. haleakalaensis | E | 8/10/1998 | F |
| Haha | Cyanea dunbarii | E | 8/10/1998 | F |
| Haha | Cyanea glabra | E | 8/10/1998 | F |
| Haha | Cyanea grimesiana ssp. grimesiana | E | 8/10/1998 | F |
| Haha | Cyanea grimesiana ssp. obatae | E | 8/10/1998 | F |
| Haha | Cyanea hamatiflora ssp. carlsonii | E | 8/10/1998 | F |
| Haha | Cyanea hamatiflora ssp. hamatiflora | E | 8/10/1998 | F |
| Haha | Cyanea humboldtiana | E | 8/10/1998 | F |
| Haha | Cyanea koolauensis | E | 8/10/1998 | F |
| Haha | Cyanea lobata | E | 8/10/1998 | F |
| Haha | Cyanea longiflora | E | 8/10/1998 | F |
| Haha | Cyanea macrostegia ssp. gibsonii | E | 8/10/1998 | F |
| Haha | Cyanea mannii | E | 8/10/1998 | F |
| Haha | Cyanea mceldowneyi | E | 8/10/1998 | F |
| Haha | Cyanea pinnatifida | E | 8/10/1998 | F |
| Haha | Cyanea platyphylla | E | 8/10/1998 | F |
| Haha | Cyanea procera | E | 8/10/1998 | F |
| Haha | Cyanea recta | T | 8/10/1998 | F |
| Haha | Cyanea remyi | E | 8/10/1998 | F |
| Haha | Cyanea shipmannii | E | 8/10/1998 | F |
| Haha | Cyanea stictophylla | E | 8/10/1998 | F |

| Common name | Scientific name | Listing status[a] | Recovery plan date | Recovery plan stage[b] |
|---|---|---|---|---|
| Haha | Cyanea st-johnii | E | 8/10/1998 | F |
| Haha | Cyanea superba | E | 8/10/1998 | F |
| Haha | Cyanea truncata | E | 8/10/1998 | F |
| Haha | Cyanea undulata | E | 8/10/1998 | F |
| Hairy rattleweed | Baptisia arachnifera | E | 3/19/1984 | F |
| Hala pepe | Pleomele hawaiiensis | E | 5/11/1998 | F |
| Harperella | Ptilimnium nodosum | E | 3/5/1991 | F |
| Harper's beauty | Harperocallis flava | E | 9/14/1983 | F |
| Hau kuahiwi | Hibiscadelphus giffardianus | E | 5/11/1998 | F |
| Hau kuahiwi | Hibiscadelphus hualalaiensis | E | 5/11/1998 | F |
| Hau kuahiwi | Hibiscadelphus woodii | E | 5/11/1998 | F |
| Hawaiian bluegrass | Poa sandvicensis | E | 9/20/1995 | F |
| Hawaiian gardenia (=Na`u) | Gardenia brighamii | E | 9/30/1993 | F |
| Hawaiian red-flowered geranium | Geranium arboreum | E | 7/29/1997 | F |
| Hawaiian vetch | Vicia menziesii | E | 5/18/1984 | F |
| Heartleaf, dwarf-flowered | Hexastylis naniflora | T | None | — |
| Heau | Exocarpos luteolus | E | 9/20/1995 | F |
| Heliotrope milk-vetch | Astragalus montii | T | 9/27/1995 | D |
| Heller's blazingstar | Liatris helleri | T | 1/28/2000 | RF(1) |
| Hidden Lake bluecurls | Trichostema austromontanum ssp. compactum | T | None | — |
| Highlands scrub hypericum | Hypericum cumulicola | E | 5/18/1999 | F |
| Higo chumbo | Harrisia portoricensis | T | 11/12/1996 | F |
| Higuero de Sierra | Crescentia portoricensis | E | 9/23/1991 | F |
| Hoffmann's rock-cress | Arabis hoffmannii | E | 9/26/2000 | F |
| Hoffmann's slender-flowered gilia | Gilia tenuiflora ssp. hoffmannii | E | 9/26/2000 | F |
| Holei | Ochrosia kilaueaensis | E | 9/26/1996 | F |
| Holmgren milk-vetch | Astragalus holmgreniorum | E | 9/22/2006 | F |
| Honohono | Haplostachys haplostachya | E | 9/20/1993 | D |
| Hoover's spurge | Chamaesyce hooveri | T | 12/15/2005 | |
| Houghton's goldenrod | Solidago houghtonii | T | 9/17/1997 | F |
| Howell's spectacular thelypody | Thelypodium howellii spectabilis | T | 6/3/2002 | F |
| Howell's spineflower | Chorizanthe howellii | E | 9/29/1998 | F |
| Iagu, Hayun (=(Guam), Tronkon guafi (Rota)) | Serianthes nelsonii | E | None | — |
| Indian Knob Mountain balm | Eriodictyon altissimum | E | 9/28/1998 | F |
| Ione (incl. Irish Hill) buckwheat | Eriogonum apricum (incl. var. prostratum) | E | None | — |
| Ione manzanita | Arctostaphylos myrtifolia | T | None | — |
| Ipomopsis, Holy Ghost | Ipomopsis sancti-spiritus | E | None | — |
| Iris, Dwarf Lake | Iris lacustris | T | None | — |
| Ischaemum, Hilo | Ischaemum byrone | E | None | — |
| Island barberry | Berberis pinnata ssp. insularis | E | 9/26/2000 | F |
| Island bedstraw | Galium buxifolium | E | 9/26/2000 | F |
| Ivesia, Ash Meadows | Ivesia kingii var. eremica | T | None | — |
| Jacquemontia, beach | Jacquemontia reclinata | E | None | — |
| Jesup's milk-vetch | Astragalus robbinsii var. jesupi | E | 11/21/1989 | F |
| Johnston's frankenia | Frankenia johnstonii | E | 5/24/1988 | F |
| Jones cycladenia | Cycladenia jonesii (=humilis) | T | None | — |
| Kamakahala | Labordia cyrtandrae | E | 8/10/1998 | F |
| Kamakahala | Labordia lydgatei | E | 8/10/1998 | F |
| Kamakahala | Labordia tinifolia var. lanaiensis | E | 8/10/1998 | F |
| Kamakahala | Labordia tinifolia var. wahiawaensis | E | 8/10/1998 | F |
| Kamakahala | Labordia triflora | E | 8/10/1998 | F |
| Kamanomano | Cenchrus agrimonioides | E | 7/10/1999 | F |
| Kauai hau kuahiwi | Hibiscadelphus distans | E | 6/5/1996 | F |
| Kauila | Colubrina oppositifolia | E | 9/26/1996 | F |
| Kaulu | Pteralyxia kauaiensis | E | 9/20/1995 | F |
| Kearney's blue-star | Amsonia kearneyana | E | 5/24/1993 | F |
| Keck's checker-mallow | Sidalcea keckii | E | None | — |
| Kenwood Marsh checker-mallow | Sidalcea oregana ssp. valida | E | None | — |
| Kern mallow | Eremalche kernensis | E | 9/30/1998 | F |
| Key tree cactus | Pilosocereus robinii | E | 5/18/1999 | F |
| Kio`ele | Hedyotis coriacea | E | 7/29/1997 | F |
| Kiponapona | Phyllostegia racemosa | E | 5/11/1998 | F |
| Kneeland Prairie penny-cress | Thlaspi californicum | E | 8/14/2003 | F |
| Knieskern's beaked-rush | Rhynchospora knieskernii | T | 9/29/1993 | F |
| Knowlton cactus | Pediocactus knowltonii | E | 3/29/1985 | F |
| Ko`oko`olau | Bidens micrantha ssp. kalealaha | E | 7/29/1997 | F |
| Ko`oko`olau | Bidens wiebkei | E | 7/29/1997 | F |
| Ko`oloa`ula | Abutilon menziesii | E | 9/29/1995 | F |
| Kodachrome bladderpod | Lesquerella tumulosa | E | None | — |
| Kohe malama malama o kanaloa | Kanaloa kahoolawensis | E | 9/19/2002 | F |
| Koki`o | Kokia drynarioides | E | 5/6/1994 | F |
| Koki`o | Kokia kauaiensis | E | 5/6/1994 | F |

TABLE 10.2

| Common name | Scientific name | Listing status[a] | Recovery plan date | Recovery plan stage[b] |
|---|---|---|---|---|
| Koki`o ke`oke`o | *Hibiscus arnottianus ssp. immaculatus* | E | 9/26/1996 | F |
| Koki`o ke`oke`o | *Hibiscus waimeae ssp. hannerae* | E | 9/26/1996 | F |
| Koki`o, Cooke's | *Kokia cookei* | E | None | — |
| Kolea | *Myrsine juddii* | E | 8/10/1998 | F |
| Kolea | *Myrsine linearifolia* | T | 8/10/1998 | F |
| Kopa | *Hedyotis schlechtendahliana var. remyi* | E | 9/19/2002 | F |
| Kuahiwi laukahi | *Plantago hawaiensis* | E | 9/26/1996 | F |
| Kuahiwi laukahi | *Plantago princeps* | E | 9/26/1996 | F |
| Kuawawaenohu | *Alsinidendron lychnoides* | E | 8/23/1998 | F |
| Kuenzler hedgehog cactus | *Echinocereus fendleri var. kuenzleri* | E | 3/28/1985 | F |
| Kula wahine noho | *Isodendrion pyrifolium* | E | 9/26/1996 | F |
| Kulu`i | *Nototrichium humile* | E | 8/10/1998 | F |
| La Graciosa thistle | *Cirsium loncholepis* | E | None | — |
| Ladies'-tresses, Canelo Hills | *Spiranthes delitescens* | E | None | — |
| Laguna Beach liveforever | *Dudleya stolonifera* | T | None | — |
| Lakela's mint | *Dicerandra immaculata* | E | 5/18/1999 | F |
| Lakeside daisy | *Hymenoxys herbacea* | T | 9/19/1990 | F |
| Lane Mountain milk-vetch | *Astragalus jaegerianus* | E | None | — |
| Large-flowered fiddleneck | *Amsinckia grandiflora* | E | 9/29/1997 | F |
| Large-fruited sand-verbena | *Abronia macrocarpa* | E | 9/30/1992 | F |
| Last Chance townsendia | *Townsendia aprica* | T | 8/20/1993 | F |
| Lau `ehu | *Panicum niihauense* | E | 7/10/1999 | F |
| Laulihilihi | *Schiedea stellarioides* | E | 8/23/1998 | F |
| Layia, beach | *Layia carnosa* | E | None | — |
| Layne's butterweed | *Senecio layneae* | T | 8/30/2002 | F |
| Leafy prairie-clover | *Dalea foliosa* | E | 9/30/1996 | F |
| Lee pincushion cactus | *Coryphantha sneedii var. leei* | T | 3/21/1986 | F |
| Liliwai | *Acaena exigua* | E | 7/29/1997 | F |
| Little amphianthus | *Amphianthus pusillus* | T | 7/7/1993 | F |
| Lloyd's Mariposa cactus | *Echinomastus mariposensis* | T | 4/13/1990 | F |
| Lo`ulu | *Pritchardia affinis* | E | 9/26/1996 | F |
| Lo`ulu | *Pritchardia kaalae* | E | 9/26/1996 | F |
| Lo`ulu | *Pritchardia munroi* | E | 9/26/1996 | F |
| Lo`ulu | *Pritchardia napaliensis* | E | 9/26/1996 | F |
| Lo`ulu | *Pritchardia remota* | E | 9/26/1996 | F |
| Lo`ulu | *Pritchardia schattaueri* | E | 9/26/1996 | F |
| Lo`ulu | *Pritchardia viscosa* | E | 9/26/1996 | F |
| Loch Lomond coyote thistle | *Eryngium constancei* | E | 12/15/2005 | F |
| Locoweed, Fassett's | *Oxytropis campestris var. chartacea* | T | None | — |
| Lomatium, Cook's | *Lomatium cookii* | E | None | — |
| Lompoc yerba santa | *Eriodictyon capitatum* | E | None | — |
| Longspurred mint | *Dicerandra cornutissima* | E | 7/1/1987 | F |
| Lousewort, Furbish | *Pedicularis furbishiae* | E | None | — |
| Lupine, clover | *Lupinus tidestromii* | E | None | — |
| Lupine, Kincaid's | *Lupinus sulphureus (=oreganus) ssp. kincaidii (=var. kincaidii)* | T | None | — |
| Lyrate bladderpod | *Lesquerella lyrata* | T | 10/17/1996 | F |
| Ma`o hau hele (=native yellow hibiscus) | *Hibiscus brackenridgei* | E | None | — |
| Ma`oli`oli | *Schiedea apokremnos* | E | 9/20/1995 | F |
| Ma`oli`oli | *Schiedea kealiae* | E | 9/20/1995 | F |
| MacFarlane's four-o'clock | *Mirabilis macfarlanei* | T | 6/30/2000 | RF(1) |
| Maguire daisy | *Erigeron maguirei* | T | 8/15/1995 | F |
| Mahoe | *Alectryon macrococcus* | E | 7/29/1997 | F |
| Makou | *Peucedanum sandwicense* | T | 9/20/1995 | F |
| Malacothrix, island | *Malacothrix squalida* | E | None | — |
| Mancos milk-vetch | *Astragalus humillimus* | E | 12/20/1989 | F |
| Mann's bluegrass | *Poa mannii* | E | 9/20/1995 | F |
| Mapele | *Cyrtandra cyaneoides* | E | 8/23/1998 | F |
| Marcescent dudleya | *Dudleya cymosa ssp. marcescens* | T | 9/30/1999 | F |
| Marin dwarf-flax | *Hesperolinon congestum* | T | 9/30/1998 | F |
| Mariposa pussypaws | *Calyptridium pulchellum* | T | None | — |
| Marsh sandwort | *Arenaria paludicola* | E | 9/28/1998 | F |
| Mauna Loa (=Ka'u) silversword | *Argyroxiphium kauense* | E | 11/21/1995 | F |
| McDonald's rock-cress | *Arabis mcdonaldiana* | E | 2/28/1984 | F |
| Meadowfoam, Butte County | *Limnanthes floccosa ssp. californica* | E | None | — |
| Meadowfoam, large-flowered woolly | *Limnanthes floccosa ssp. grandiflora* | E | None | — |
| Mead's milkweed | *Asclepias meadii* | T | 9/22/2003 | F |
| Mehamehame | *Flueggea neowawraea* | E | 7/10/1999 | F |
| Menzies' wallflower | *Erysimum menziesii* | E | 9/29/1998 | F |
| Mesa Verde cactus | *Sclerocactus mesae-verdae* | T | 3/30/1984 | F |
| Metcalf Canyon jewelflower | *Streptanthus albidus ssp. albidus* | E | 9/30/1998 | F |
| Mexican flannelbush | *Fremontodendron mexicanum* | E | None | — |

**TABLE 10.2**

| Common name | Scientific name | Listing status[a] | Recovery plan date | Recovery plan stage[b] |
|---|---|---|---|---|
| Miccosukee gooseberry | *Ribes echinellum* | T | None | — |
| Minnesota dwarf trout lily | *Erythronium propullans* | E | 12/16/1987 | F |
| Missouri bladderpod | *Lesquerella filiformis* | T | 4/7/1988 | F |
| Mohr's Barbara button | *Marshallia mohrii* | T | 11/26/1991 | F |
| Monkey-flower, Michigan | *Mimulus glabratus var. michiganensis* | E | None | — |
| Monterey clover | *Trifolium trichocalyx* | E | 6/17/2005 | F |
| Monterey gilia | *Gilia tenuiflora ssp. arenaria* | E | 9/29/1998 | F |
| Monterey spineflower | *Chorizanthe pungens var. pungens* | T | 9/29/1998 | F |
| Morefield's leather flower | *Clematis morefieldii* | E | 5/3/1994 | F |
| Morro manzanita | *Arctostaphylos morroensis* | T | 9/28/1998 | F |
| Mountain golden heather | *Hudsonia montana* | T | 9/14/1983 | F |
| Munz's onion | *Allium munzii* | E | None | — |
| Na Pali beach hedyotis | *Hedyotis st.-johnii* | E | 9/20/1995 | F |
| Na`ena`e | *Dubautia herbstobatae* | E | 8/10/1998 | F |
| Na`ena`e | *Dubautia latifolia* | E | 8/10/1998 | F |
| Na`ena`e | *Dubautia pauciflorula* | E | 8/10/1998 | F |
| Na`ena`e | *Dubautia plantaginea ssp. humilis* | E | 8/10/1998 | F |
| Nani wai`ale`ale | *Viola kauaiensis var. wahiawaensis* | E | 8/23/1998 | F |
| Nanu | *Gardenia mannii* | E | 8/10/1998 | F |
| Napa bluegrass | *Poa napensis* | E | None | — |
| Naupaka, dwarf | *Scaevola coriacea* | E | None | — |
| Navajo sedge | *Carex specuicola* | T | 9/24/1987 | F |
| Navarretia, few-flowered | *Navarretia leucocephala ssp. pauciflora (=N. pauciflora)* | E | None | — |
| Navarretia, many-flowered | *Navarretia leucocephala ssp. plieantha* | E | None | — |
| Navasota ladies'-tresses | *Spiranthes parksii* | E | 9/21/1984 | F |
| Nehe | *Lipochaeta fauriei* | E | 9/20/1995 | F |
| Nehe | *Lipochaeta kamolensis* | E | 9/20/1995 | F |
| Nehe | *Lipochaeta lobata var. leptophylla* | E | 9/20/1995 | F |
| Nehe | *Lipochaeta micrantha* | E | 9/20/1995 | F |
| Nehe | *Lipochaeta tenuifolia* | E | 9/20/1995 | F |
| Nehe | *Lipochaeta waimeaensis* | E | 9/20/1995 | F |
| Nellie cory cactus | *Coryphantha minima* | E | 9/20/1984 | F |
| Nelson's checker-mallow | *Sidalcea nelsoniana* | T | 9/30/1998 | F |
| Nevin's barberry | *Berberis nevinii* | E | None | — |
| Nichol's Turk's head cactus | *Echinocactus horizonthalonius var. nicholii* | E | 4/14/1986 | F |
| Nioi | *Eugenia koolauensis* | E | 8/10/1998 | F |
| Nipomo Mesa lupine | *Lupinus nipomensis* | E | None | — |
| Niterwort, Amargosa | *Nitrophila mohavensis* | E | None | — |
| No common name | *Abutilon eremitopetalum* | E | 9/29/1995 | F |
| No common name | *Abutilon sandwicense* | E | 9/29/1995 | F |
| No common name | *Achyranthes mutica* | E | 9/29/1995 | F |
| No common name | *Alsinidendron obovatum* | E | 9/29/1995 | F |
| No common name | *Alsinidendron trinerve* | E | 9/29/1995 | F |
| No common name | *Alsinidendron viscosum* | E | 9/29/1995 | F |
| No common name | *Amaranthus brownii* | E | 9/29/1995 | F |
| No common name | *Aristida chaseae* | E | 9/29/1995 | F |
| No common name | *Auerodendron pauciflorum* | E | 9/29/1995 | F |
| No common name | *Bonamia menziesii* | E | 9/29/1995 | F |
| No common name | *Calyptranthes thomasiana* | E | 9/29/1995 | F |
| No common name | *Catesbaea melanocarpa* | E | 9/29/1995 | F |
| No common name | *Chamaecrista glandulosa var. mirabilis* | E | 9/29/1995 | F |
| No common name | *Chamaesyce halemanui* | E | 12/29/1995 | F |
| No common name | *Cordia bellonis* | E | 9/29/1995 | F |
| No common name | *Cranichis ricartii* | E | 11/29/1995 | F |
| No common name | *Cyanea (=Rollandia) crispa* | E | 9/29/1995 | F |
| No common name | *Daphnopsis hellerana* | E | 6/19/1995 | F |
| No common name | *Delissea rhytidosperma* | E | 9/29/1995 | F |
| No common name | *Delissea undulata* | E | 9/29/1995 | F |
| No common name | *Eugenia woodburyana* | E | 9/29/1995 | F |
| No common name | *Gahnia lanaiensis* | E | 9/29/1995 | F |
| No common name | *Geocarpon minimum* | T | 9/29/1995 | F |
| No common name | *Gesneria pauciflora* | T | 9/29/1995 | F |
| No common name | *Gouania hillebrandii* | E | 9/29/1995 | F |
| No common name | *Gouania meyenii* | E | 9/29/1995 | F |
| No common name | *Gouania vitifolia* | E | 9/29/1995 | F |
| No common name | *Hedyotis degeneri* | E | 9/29/1995 | F |
| No common name | *Hedyotis parvula* | E | 9/29/1995 | F |
| No common name | *Hesperomannia arborescens* | E | 9/29/1995 | F |
| No common name | *Hesperomannia arbuscula* | E | 9/29/1995 | F |
| No common name | *Hesperomannia lydgatei* | E | 9/29/1995 | F |
| No common name | *Ilex sintenisii* | E | 9/29/1995 | F |
| No common name | *Lepanthes eltoroensis* | E | 9/29/1995 | F |

**TABLE 10.2**

**Endangered and threatened plant species, February 2008** [CONTINUED]

| Common name | Scientific name | Listing status[a] | Recovery plan date | Recovery plan stage[b] |
|---|---|---|---|---|
| No common name | Leptocereus grantianus | E | 9/29/1995 | F |
| No common name | Lipochaeta venosa | E | 9/29/1995 | F |
| No common name | Lobelia gaudichaudii ssp. koolauensis | E | 9/29/1995 | F |
| No common name | Lobelia monostachya | E | 9/29/1995 | F |
| No common name | Lobelia niihauensis | E | 9/29/1995 | F |
| No common name | Lobelia oahuensis | E | 9/29/1995 | F |
| No common name | Lyonia truncata var. proctorii | E | 9/29/1995 | F |
| No common name | Lysimachia filifolia | E | 9/29/1995 | F |
| No common name | Lysimachia lydgatei | E | 9/29/1995 | F |
| No common name | Lysimachia maxima | E | 9/29/1995 | F |
| No common name | Mariscus fauriei | E | 9/29/1995 | F |
| No common name | Mariscus pennatiformis | E | 9/29/1995 | F |
| No common name | Mitracarpus maxwelliae | E | 9/29/1995 | F |
| No common name | Mitracarpus polycladus | E | 9/29/1995 | F |
| No common name | Munroidendron racemosum | E | 9/29/1995 | F |
| No common name | Myrcia paganii | E | 9/29/1995 | F |
| No common name | Neraudia angulata | E | 9/29/1995 | F |
| No common name | Neraudia ovata | E | 9/29/1995 | F |
| No common name | Neraudia sericea | E | 9/29/1995 | F |
| No common name | Nesogenes rotensis | E | 9/29/1995 | F |
| No common name | Osmoxylon mariannense | E | 9/29/1995 | F |
| No common name | Phyllostegia glabra var. lanaiensis | E | 9/29/1995 | F |
| No common name | Phyllostegia hirsuta | E | 9/29/1995 | F |
| No common name | Phyllostegia kaalaensis | E | 9/29/1995 | F |
| No common name | Phyllostegia knudsenii | E | 9/29/1995 | F |
| No common name | Phyllostegia mannii | E | 9/29/1995 | F |
| No common name | Phyllostegia mollis | E | 9/29/1995 | F |
| No common name | Phyllostegia parviflora | E | 9/29/1995 | F |
| No common name | Phyllostegia velutina | E | 9/29/1995 | F |
| No common name | Phyllostegia waimeae | E | 9/29/1995 | F |
| No common name | Phyllostegia warshaueri | E | 9/29/1995 | F |
| No common name | Phyllostegia wawrana | E | 9/29/1995 | F |
| No common name | Platanthera holochila | E | 9/29/1995 | F |
| No common name | Poa siphonoglossa | E | 9/29/1995 | F |
| No common name | Remya kauaiensis | E | 9/29/1995 | F |
| No common name | Remya montgomeryi | E | 9/29/1995 | F |
| No common name | Sanicula mariversa | E | 9/29/1995 | F |
| No common name | Sanicula purpurea | E | 9/29/1995 | F |
| No common name | Schiedea haleakalensis | E | 9/29/1995 | F |
| No common name | Schiedea helleri | E | 9/29/1995 | F |
| No common name | Schiedea hookeri | E | 9/29/1995 | F |
| No common name | Schiedea kaalae | E | 9/29/1995 | F |
| No common name | Schiedea kauaiensis | E | 9/29/1995 | F |
| No common name | Schiedea lydgatei | E | 9/29/1995 | F |
| No common name | Schiedea membranacea | E | 9/29/1995 | F |
| No common name | Schiedea nuttallii | E | 9/29/1995 | F |
| No common name | Schiedea sarmentosa | E | 9/29/1995 | F |
| No common name | Schiedea spergulina var. leiopoda | E | 9/29/1995 | F |
| No common name | Schiedea spergulina var. spergulina | T | 9/29/1995 | F |
| No common name | Schiedea verticillata | E | 9/29/1995 | F |
| No common name | Schoepfia arenaria | T | 9/29/1995 | F |
| No common name | Silene alexandri | E | 9/29/1995 | F |
| No common name | Silene hawaiiensis | T | 9/29/1995 | F |
| No common name | Silene lanceolata | E | 9/29/1995 | F |
| No common name | Silene perlmanii | E | 9/29/1995 | F |
| No common name | Spermolepis hawaiiensis | E | 9/29/1995 | F |
| No common name | Stenogyne angustifolia var. angustifolia | E | 9/29/1995 | F |
| No common name | Stenogyne bifida | E | 9/29/1995 | F |
| No common name | Stenogyne campanulata | E | 9/29/1995 | F |
| No common name | Stenogyne kanehoana | E | 9/29/1995 | F |
| No common name | Ternstroemia subsessilis | E | 9/29/1995 | F |
| No common name | Tetramolopium arenarium | E | 9/29/1995 | F |
| No common name | Tetramolopium filiforme | E | 9/29/1995 | F |
| No common name | Tetramolopium lepidotum ssp. lepidotum | E | 9/29/1995 | F |
| No common name | Tetramolopium remyi | E | 9/29/1995 | F |
| No common name | Tetramolopium rockii | T | 9/29/1995 | F |
| No common name | Trematolobelia singularis | E | 9/29/1995 | F |
| No common name | Vernonia proctorii | E | 9/29/1995 | F |
| No common name | Vigna o-wahuensis | E | 9/29/1995 | F |
| No common name | Viola helenae | E | 9/29/1995 | F |
| No common name | Viola lanaiensis | E | 9/29/1995 | F |
| No common name | Viola oahuensis | E | 9/29/1995 | F |

**TABLE 10.2**

| Common name | Scientific name | Listing status[a] | Recovery plan date | Recovery plan stage[b] |
|---|---|---|---|---|
| No common name | *Xylosma crenatum* | E | 9/29/1995 | F |
| Nohoanu | *Geranium multiflorum* | E | 7/29/1997 | F |
| Northeastern bulrush | *Scirpus ancistrochaetus* | E | 8/25/1993 | F |
| Northern wild monkshood | *Aconitum noveboracense* | T | 9/23/1983 | F |
| Oak, Hinckley | *Quercus hinckleyi* | T | None | — |
| Oha | *Delissea rivularis* | E | 8/23/1998 | F |
| Oha | *Delissea subcordata* | E | 8/23/1998 | F |
| Ohai | *Sesbania tomentosa* | E | 7/10/1999 | F |
| Okeechobee gourd | *Cucurbita okeechobeensis ssp. okeechobeensis* | E | 5/18/1999 | F |
| Olulu | *Brighamia insignis* | E | 9/20/1995 | F |
| Opuhe | *Urera kaalae* | E | 8/10/1998 | F |
| Orchid, eastern prairie fringed | *Platanthera leucophaea* | T | None | — |
| Orcutt grass, California | *Orcuttia californica* | E | None | — |
| Orcutt grass, hairy | *Orcuttia pilosa* | E | None | — |
| Orcutt's spineflower | *Chorizanthe orcuttiana* | E | None | — |
| Osterhout milk-vetch | *Astragalus osterhoutii* | E | 9/30/1992 | F |
| Otay mesa-mint | *Pogogyne nudiuscula* | E | 9/3/1998 | F |
| Otay tarplant | *Deinandra (=Hemizonia) conjugens* | T | 12/28/2004 | F |
| Oxytheca, cushenbury | *Oxytheca parishii var. goodmaniana* | E | None | — |
| Pallid manzanita | *Arctostaphylos pallida* | T | 4/7/2003 | D |
| Palma de Manaca | *Calyptronoma rivalis* | T | 6/25/1992 | F |
| Palmate-bracted bird's beak | *Cordylanthus palmatus* | E | 9/30/1998 | F |
| Palo Colorado | *Ternstroemia luquillensis* | E | 7/31/1995 | F |
| Palo de Jazmin | *Styrax portoricensis* | E | 7/31/1995 | F |
| Palo de Nigua | *Cornutia obovata* | E | 8/7/1992 | F |
| Palo de Ramon | *Banara vanderbiltii* | E | 3/15/1991 | F |
| Palo de Rosa | *Ottoschulzia rhodoxylon* | E | 9/20/1994 | F |
| Pamakani | *Tetramolopium capillare* | E | 7/29/1997 | F |
| Pamakani | *Viola chamissoniana ssp. chamissoniana* | E | 7/29/1997 | F |
| Panicgrass, Carter's | *Panicum fauriei var. carteri* | E | None | — |
| Parish's daisy | *Erigeron parishii* | T | 9/30/1997 | D |
| Pedate checker-mallow | *Sidalcea pedata* | E | 7/31/1998 | F |
| Peebles Navajo cactus | *Pediocactus peeblesianus peeblesianus* | E | 3/30/1984 | F |
| Peirson's milk-vetch | *Astragalus magdalenae var. peirsonii* | T | None | — |
| Pelos del diablo | *Aristida portoricensis* | E | 5/16/1994 | F |
| Penland alpine fen mustard | *Eutrema penlandii* | T | None | — |
| Penland beardtongue | *Penstemon penlandii* | E | 9/30/1992 | F |
| Pennell's bird's-beak | *Cordylanthus tenuis ssp. capillaris* | E | 9/30/1998 | F |
| Penstemon, blowout | *Penstemon haydenii* | E | None | — |
| Pentachaeta, Lyon's | *Pentachaeta lyonii* | E | None | — |
| Persistent trillium | *Trillium persistens* | E | 3/27/1984 | F |
| Peter's Mountain mallow | *Iliamna corei* | E | 9/28/1990 | F |
| Phacelia, clay | *Phacelia argillacea* | E | None | — |
| Phacelia, island | *Phacelia insularis ssp. insularis* | E | None | — |
| Phacelia, North Park | *Phacelia formosula* | E | None | — |
| Pigeon wings | *Clitoria fragrans* | T | 5/18/1999 | F |
| Pilo | *Hedyotis mannii* | E | 9/26/1996 | F |
| Pima pineapple cactus | *Coryphantha scheeri var. robustispina* | E | None | — |
| Pine Hill ceanothus | *Ceanothus roderickii* | E | 8/30/2002 | F |
| Pine Hill flannelbush | *Fremontodendron californicum ssp. decumbens* | E | 8/30/2002 | F |
| Pinkroot, gentian | *Spigelia gentianoides* | E | None | — |
| Pismo clarkia | *Clarkia speciosa ssp. immaculata* | E | 9/28/1998 | F |
| Pitcher-plant, Alabama canebrake | *Sarracenia rubra alabamensis* | E | None | — |
| Pitcher-plant, green | *Sarracenia oreophila* | E | None | — |
| Pitcher-plant, mountain sweet | *Sarracenia rubra ssp. jonesii* | E | None | — |
| Pitcher's thistle | *Cirsium pitcheri* | T | 9/20/2002 | F |
| Pitkin marsh lily | *Lilium pardalinum ssp. pitkinense* | E | None | — |
| Po`e | *Portulaca sclerocarpa* | E | 9/26/1996 | F |
| Polygala, Lewton's | *Polygala lewtonii* | E | None | — |
| Pondberry | *Lindera melissifolia* | E | 9/23/1993 | F |
| Pondweed, Little Aguja (=creek) | *Potamogeton clystocarpus* | E | None | — |
| Popolo ku mai | *Solanum incompletum* | E | 7/10/1999 | F |
| Potentilla, Hickman's | *Potentilla hickmanii* | E | None | — |
| Prairie bush-clover | *Lespedeza leptostachya* | T | 10/6/1988 | F |
| Presidio Clarkia | *Clarkia franciscana* | E | 9/30/1998 | F |
| Presidio Manzanita | *Arctostaphylos hookeri var. ravenii* | E | 10/6/2003 | F |
| Price's potato-bean | *Apios priceana* | T | 2/10/1993 | F |
| Primrose, Maguire | *Primula maguirei* | T | None | — |
| Pu`uka`a | *Cyperus trachysanthos* | E | 7/10/1999 | F |
| Pua `ala | *Brighamia rockii* | E | 9/26/1996 | F |
| Purple amole | *Chlorogalum purpureum* | T | None | — |
| Pygmy fringe-tree | *Chionanthus pygmaeus* | E | 5/18/1999 | F |

## TABLE 10.2

## Endangered and threatened plant species, February 2008 [CONTINUED]

| Common name | Scientific name | Listing status[a] | Recovery plan date | Recovery plan stage[b] |
|---|---|---|---|---|
| Red Hills vervain | Verbena californica | T | None | — |
| Reed-mustard, Barneby | Schoenocrambe barnebyi | E | None | — |
| Reed-mustard, clay | Schoenocrambe argillacea | T | None | — |
| Relict trillium | Trillium reliquum | E | 1/31/1991 | F |
| Remya, Maui | Remya mauiensis | E | None | — |
| Rhododendron, Chapman | Rhododendron chapmanii | E | None | — |
| Ridge-cress, Barneby | Lepidium barnebyanum | E | None | — |
| Roan Mountain bluet | Hedyotis purpurea var. montana | E | 5/13/1996 | F |
| Robust (incl. Scotts Valley) spineflower | Chorizanthe robusta (incl. vars. robusta and hartwegii) | E | 12/20/2004 | F |
| Roseroot, Leedy's | Sedum integrifolium ssp. leedyi | T | None | — |
| Rough popcornflower | Plagiobothrys hirtus | E | 9/25/2003 | F |
| Rough-leaved loosestrife | Lysimachia asperulaefolia | E | 4/19/1995 | F |
| Round-leaved chaff-flower | Achyranthes splendens var. rotundata | E | 10/5/1993 | D |
| Rugel's pawpaw | Deeringothamnus rugelii | E | 4/5/1988 | F |
| Running buffalo clover | Trifolium stoloniferum | E | 6/27/2007 | RD(1) |
| Rush-rose, island | Helianthemum greenei | T | None | — |
| Ruth's golden aster | Pityopsis ruthii | E | 6/11/1992 | F |
| Sacramento Mountains thistle | Cirsium vinaceum | T | 9/27/1993 | F |
| Sacramento Orcutt grass | Orcuttia viscida | E | 12/15/2005 | F |
| Sacramento prickly poppy | Argemone pleiacantha ssp. pinnatisecta | E | 8/31/1994 | F |
| Salt marsh bird's-beak | Cordylanthus maritimus ssp. maritimus | E | 12/6/1985 | F |
| San Benito evening-primrose | Camissonia benitensis | T | 9/19/2006 | F |
| San Bernardino bluegrass | Poa atropurpurea | E | None | — |
| San Bernardino Mountains bladderpod | Lesquerella kingii ssp. bernardina | E | 9/30/1997 | D |
| San Clemente Island broom | Lotus dendroideus ssp. traskiae | E | 1/26/1984 | F |
| San Clemente Island bush-mallow | Malacothamnus clementinus | E | 1/26/1984 | F |
| San Clemente Island indian paintbrush | Castilleja grisea | E | 1/26/1984 | F |
| San Clemente Island larkspur | Delphinium variegatum ssp. kinkiense | E | 1/26/1984 | F |
| San Diego ambrosia | Ambrosia pumila | E | None | — |
| San Diego button-celery | Eryngium aristulatum var. parishii | E | 9/3/1998 | F |
| San Diego mesa-mint | Pogogyne abramsii | E | 9/3/1998 | F |
| San Diego thornmint | Acanthomintha ilicifolia | T | None | — |
| San Francisco lessingia | Lessingia germanorum (=L.g. var. germanorum) | E | 10/6/2003 | F |
| San Francisco Peaks groundsel | Senecio franciscanus | T | 7/21/1987 | F |
| San Jacinto Valley crownscale | Atriplex coronata var. notatior | E | None | — |
| San Joaquin Orcutt grass | Orcuttia inaequalis | T | 12/15/2005 | F |
| San Mateo thornmint | Acanthomintha obovata ssp. duttonii | E | 9/30/1998 | F |
| San Mateo woolly sunflower | Eriophyllum latilobum | E | 9/30/1998 | F |
| San Rafael cactus | Pediocactus despainii | E | 10/2/1995 | D |
| Sandalwood, Lanai (=iliahi) | Santalum freycinetianum var. lanaiense | E | None | — |
| Sandlace | Polygonella myriophylla | E | 5/18/1999 | F |
| Sandplain gerardia | Agalinis acuta | E | 9/20/1989 | F |
| Santa Ana River woolly-star | Eriastrum densifolium ssp. sanctorum | E | None | — |
| Santa Barbara Island liveforever | Dudleya traskiae | E | 6/27/1985 | F |
| Santa Clara Valley dudleya | Dudleya setchellii | E | 9/30/1998 | F |
| Santa Cruz Island bush-mallow | Malacothamnus fasciculatus var. nesioticus | E | 9/26/2000 | F |
| Santa Cruz Island dudleya | Dudleya nesiotica | T | 9/26/2000 | F |
| Santa Cruz Island fringepod | Thysanocarpus conchuliferus | E | 9/26/2000 | F |
| Santa Cruz Island malacothrix | Malacothrix indecora | E | 9/26/2000 | F |
| Santa Cruz Island rockcress | Sibara filifolia | E | None | — |
| Santa Cruz tarplant | Holocarpha macradenia | T | None | — |
| Santa Monica Mountains dudleyea | Dudleya cymosa ssp. ovatifolia | T | 9/30/1999 | F |
| Santa Rosa Island manzanita | Arctostaphylos confertiflora | E | 9/26/2000 | F |
| Schiedea, Diamond Head | Schiedea adamantis | E | None | — |
| Scotts Valley polygonum | Polygonum hickmanii | E | None | — |
| Scrub blazingstar | Liatris ohlingerae | E | 5/18/1999 | F |
| Scrub buckwheat | Eriogonum longifolium var. gnaphalifolium | T | 8/23/2002 | RF(1) |
| Scrub lupine | Lupinus aridorum | E | 6/20/1996 | RF(1) |
| Scrub mint | Dicerandra frutescens | E | 5/18/1999 | F |
| Scrub plum | Prunus geniculata | E | 6/20/1996 | RF(1) |
| Seabeach amaranth | Amaranthus pumilus | T | 11/12/1996 | F |
| Seablite, California | Suaeda californica | E | None | — |
| Seagrass, Johnson's | Halophila johnsonii | T | None | — |
| Sebastopol meadowfoam | Limnanthes vinculans | E | None | — |
| Sensitive joint-vetch | Aeschynomene virginica | T | 9/29/1995 | F |
| Sentry milk-vetch | Astragalus cremnophylax var. cremnophylax | E | 9/28/2006 | F |
| Shale barren rock-cress | Arabis serotina | E | 8/15/1991 | F |
| Shivwits milk-vetch | Astragalus ampullarioides | E | 9/22/2006 | F |
| Short-leaved rosemary | Conradina brevifolia | E | 5/18/1999 | F |
| Short's goldenrod | Solidago shortii | E | 5/25/1988 | F |
| Showy Indian clover | Trifolium amoenum | E | None | — |
| Shrubby reed-mustard | Schoenocrambe suffrutescens | E | 9/14/1994 | F |

| Common name | Scientific name | Listing status[a] | Recovery plan date | Recovery plan stage[b] |
|---|---|---|---|---|
| Siler pincushion cactus | Pediocactus (=Echinocactus, =Utahia) sileri | T | 4/14/1986 | F |
| Skullcap, Florida | Scutellaria floridana | T | None | — |
| Skullcap, large-flowered | Scutellaria montana | T | None | — |
| Slender Orcutt grass | Orcuttia tenuis | T | 12/15/2005 | F |
| Slender rush-pea | Hoffmannseggia tenella | E | 9/13/1988 | F |
| Slender-horned spineflower | Dodecahema leptoceras | E | None | — |
| Slender-petaled mustard | Thelypodium stenopetalum | E | 7/31/1998 | F |
| Small whorled pogonia | Isotria medeoloides | T | 11/13/1992 | RF(1) |
| Small-anthered bittercress | Cardamine micranthera | E | 7/10/1991 | F |
| Small's milkpea | Galactia smallii | E | 5/18/1999 | F |
| Smooth coneflower | Echinacea laevigata | E | 4/18/1995 | F |
| Snakeroot | Eryngium cuneifolium | E | 5/18/1999 | F |
| Sneed pincushion cactus | Coryphantha sneedii var. sneedii | E | 3/21/1986 | F |
| Soft bird's-beak | Cordylanthus mollis ssp. mollis | E | None | — |
| Soft-leaved paintbrush | Castilleja mollis | E | 9/26/2000 | F |
| Solano grass | Tuctoria mucronata | E | 12/15/2005 | F |
| Sonoma alopecurus | Alopecurus aequalis var. sonomensis | E | None | — |
| Sonoma spineflower | Chorizanthe valida | E | 9/29/1998 | F |
| Sonoma sunshine | Blennosperma bakeri | E | None | — |
| South Texas ambrosia | Ambrosia cheiranthifolia | E | None | — |
| Southern Mountain wild-buckwheat | Eriogonum kennedyi var. austromontanum | T | None | — |
| Spalding's catchfly | Silene spaldingii | T | 10/12/2007 | D |
| Spreading avens | Geum radiatum | E | 4/28/1993 | F |
| Spreading navarretia | Navarretia fossalis | T | 9/3/1998 | F |
| Spring Creek bladderpod | Lesquerella perforata | E | 9/6/2006 | F |
| Spring-loving centaury | Centaurium namophilum | T | 9/28/1990 | F |
| Springville clarkia | Clarkia springvillensis | T | None | — |
| St. Thomas prickly-ash | Zanthoxylum thomasianum | E | 4/5/1988 | F |
| Star cactus | Astrophytum asterias | E | 11/6/2003 | F |
| Steamboat buckwheat | Eriogonum ovalifolium var. williamsiae | E | 9/20/1995 | F |
| Stebbins' morning-glory | Calystegia stebbinsii | E | 8/30/2002 | F |
| Stickseed, showy | Hackelia venusta | E | None | — |
| Stonecrop, Lake County | Parvisedum leiocarpum | E | None | — |
| Suisun thistle | Cirsium hydrophilum var. hydrophilum | E | None | — |
| Sumac, Michaux's | Rhus michauxii | E | None | — |
| Sunburst, Hartweg's golden | Pseudobahia bahiifolia | E | None | — |
| Sunburst, San Joaquin adobe | Pseudobahia peirsonii | T | None | — |
| Sunflower, Pecos (=puzzle, =paradox) | Helianthus paradoxus | T | None | — |
| Sunflower, Schweinitz's | Helianthus schweinitzii | E | None | — |
| Swamp pink | Helonias bullata | T | 9/30/1991 | F |
| Taraxacum, California | Taraxacum californicum | E | None | — |
| Telephus spurge | Euphorbia telephioides | T | 6/22/1994 | F |
| Tennessee purple coneflower | Echinacea tennesseensis | E | 11/14/1989 | RF(1) |
| Tennessee yellow-eyed grass | Xyris tennesseensis | E | 6/24/1994 | F |
| Terlingua Creek cat's-eye | Cryptantha crassipes | E | 4/5/1994 | F |
| Texas ayenia | Ayenia limitaris | E | None | — |
| Texas poppy-mallow | Callirhoe scabriuscula | E | 3/29/1985 | F |
| Texas prairie dawn-flower | Hymenoxys texana | E | 4/13/1990 | F |
| Texas snowbells | Styrax texanus | E | 7/31/1987 | F |
| Texas trailing phlox | Phlox nivalis ssp. texensis | E | 3/28/1995 | F |
| Texas wild-rice | Zizania texana | E | 2/14/1996 | RF(1) |
| Thread-leaved brodiaea | Brodiaea filifolia | T | 9/3/1998 | F |
| Tiburon jewelflower | Streptanthus niger | E | 9/30/1998 | F |
| Tiburon mariposa lily | Calochortus tiburonensis | T | 9/30/1998 | F |
| Tiburon paintbrush | Castilleja affinis ssp. neglecta | E | 9/30/1998 | F |
| Tiny polygala | Polygala smallii | E | 5/18/1999 | F |
| Tobusch fishhook cactus | Ancistrocactus tobuschii | E | 3/18/1987 | F |
| Todsen's pennyroyal | Hedeoma todsenii | E | 1/31/2001 | RF(2) |
| Triple-ribbed milk-vetch | Astragalus tricarinatus | E | None | — |
| Twinpod, Dudley Bluffs | Physaria obcordata | T | None | — |
| Uhiuhi | Caesalpinia kavaiense | E | 5/6/1994 | F |
| Uinta Basin hookless cactus | Sclerocactus glaucus | T | 9/27/1990 | F |
| Ute ladies'-tresses | Spiranthes diluvialis | T | 9/21/1995 | D |
| Uvillo | Eugenia haematocarpa | E | 9/11/1998 | F |
| Vahl's boxwood | Buxus vahlii | E | 4/28/1987 | F |
| Vail Lake ceanothus | Ceanothus ophiochilus | T | None | — |
| Ventura Marsh milk-vetch | Astragalus pycnostachyus var. lanosissimus | E | None | — |
| Verity's dudleya | Dudleya verityi | T | 9/30/1999 | F |
| Vine Hill clarkia | Clarkia imbricata | E | None | — |
| Virginia round-leaf birch | Betula uber | T | 9/24/1990 | RF(2) |
| Virginia sneezeweed | Helenium virginicum | T | 10/2/2000 | D |
| Virginia spiraea | Spiraea virginiana | T | 11/13/1992 | F |

TABLE 10.2

**Endangered and threatened plant species, February 2008** [CONTINUED]

| Common name | Scientific name | Listing status[a] | Recovery plan date | Recovery plan stage[b] |
|---|---|---|---|---|
| Wahane | Pritchardia aylmer-robinsonii | E | None | — |
| Walker's manioc | Manihot walkerae | E | 12/12/1993 | F |
| Water howellia | Howellia aquatilis | T | 9/24/1996 | D |
| Watercress, Gambel's | Rorippa gambellii | E | None | — |
| Water-plantain, Kral's | Sagittaria secundifolia | T | None | — |
| Water-umbel, Huachuca | Lilaeopsis schaffneriana var. recurva | E | None | — |
| Water-willow, Cooley's | Justicia cooleyi | E | None | — |
| Welsh's milkweed | Asclepias welshii | T | 9/30/1992 | F |
| Wenatchee Mountains checkermallow | Sidalcea oregana var. calva | E | 9/30/2004 | F |
| West Indian walnut (=Nogal) | Juglans jamaicensis | E | 12/9/1999 | F |
| Western lily | Lilium occidentale | E | 3/31/1998 | F |
| Western prairie fringed orchid | Platanthera praeclara | T | 9/30/1996 | F |
| Wheeler's peperomia | Peperomia wheeleri | E | 11/26/1990 | F |
| White birds-in-a-nest | Macbridea alba | T | 6/22/1994 | F |
| White bladderpod | Lesquerella pallida | E | 10/16/1992 | F |
| White irisette | Sisyrinchium dichotomum | E | 4/10/1995 | F |
| White sedge | Carex albida | E | None | — |
| White-haired goldenrod | Solidago albopilosa | T | 9/28/1993 | F |
| White-rayed pentachaeta | Pentachaeta bellidiflora | E | 9/30/1998 | F |
| Whitlow-wort, papery | Paronychia chartacea | T | None | — |
| Wide-leaf warea | Warea amplexifolia | E | 2/17/1993 | F |
| Wild-rice, Texas | Zizania texana | E | None | — |
| Willamette daisy | Erigeron decumbens var. decumbens | E | None | — |
| Willowy monardella | Monardella linoides ssp. viminea | E | None | — |
| Winkler cactus | Pediocactus winkleri | T | 10/2/1995 | D |
| Wire-lettuce, Malheur | Stephanomeria malheurensis | E | None | — |
| Wireweed | Polygonella basiramia | E | 5/18/1999 | F |
| Woodland-star, San Clemente Island | Lithophragma maximum | E | None | — |
| Wooly-threads, San Joaquin | Monolopia (=Lembertia) congdonii | E | None | — |
| Wright fishhook cactus | Sclerocactus wrightiae | E | 12/24/1985 | F |
| Yadon's piperia | Piperia yadonii | E | 6/17/2005 | F |
| Yellow larkspur | Delphinium luteum | E | None | — |
| Yreka phlox | Phlox hirsuta | E | 9/18/2006 | F |
| Zapata bladderpod | Lesquerella thamnophila | E | 8/25/2004 | F |
| Zuni fleabane | Erigeron rhizomatus | T | 9/30/1988 | F |

[a]E = Endangered; T = Threatened.
[b]Recovery plan stages: F = Final; D = Draft; RD = Draft Under Revision; RF = Final Revision.

SOURCE: Adapted from "Listed FWS/Joint FWS and NMFS Species and Populations with Recovery Plans (Sorted by Listed Entity)" and "Listed U.S. Species by Taxonomic Group," in *USFWS Threatened and Endangered Species System (TESS)*, U.S. Department of the Interior, U.S. Fish and Wildlife Service, February 5, 2008, http://ecos.fws.gov/tess_public/SpeciesRecovery.do?sort=1 and http://ecos.fws.gov/tess_public/SpeciesReport.do?kingdom=V&listingType=L (accessed February 5, 2008)

## TABLE 10.3

**Plant species with the highest expenditures under the Endangered Species Act, fiscal year 2006**

| Ranking | Species | Expenditure |
|---|---|---|
| 1 | Pondberry | $1,634,085 |
| 2 | American chaffseed | $740,749 |
| 3 | Johnson's seagrass | $723,350 |
| 4 | Gentner's fritillary | $410,100 |
| 5 | Kincaid's lupine | $405,136 |
| 6 | Golden paintbrush | $393,767 |
| 7 | Spermolepsis hawaiiensis | $371,243 |
| 8 | Ute Ladies'-tresses | $338,673 |
| 9 | Florida bonamia | $317,100 |
| 10 | Scrub buckwheat | $316,580 |

SOURCE: Adapted from "Table 2. Species Ranked in Descending Order of Total FY 2006 Reported Expenditures, Not Including Land Acquisition Costs," in *Federal and State Endangered and Threatened Species Expenditures: Fiscal Year 2006*, U.S. Department of the Interior, U.S. Fish and Wildlife Service, draft, 2008

groups with unique differences between them. For example, the invasive species known as kudzu has the scientific name *Pueraria montana*. There are two varieties: *Pueraria montana* var. *lobata* and *Pueraria montana* var. *montana*. The *lobata* variety is commonly found in the United States, whereas the *montana* variety is not.

Plant taxonomy also includes additional taxa (groups) between kingdom and phylum called subkingdom, superdivision, and division that distinguish between broad categories of plants. The subkingdom level distinguishes between vascular and nonvascular plants. Within vascular plants, there are two superdivisions: seed plants and seedless plants. Seed plants are divided into various divisions, the largest of which is flowering plants.

The USFWS uses four broad categories for plant types: conifers and cycads, ferns and allies, lichens, and flowering plants. These categories are division levels or similar groupings.

## Conifers and Cycads

Conifers are cone-bearing, woody plants. Most are trees; only a few species are shrubs. Common tree types include pine, cedar, fir, spruce, redwood, and cypress. There are only two conifers listed under the ESA. The Santa Cruz cypress (*Cupressus abramsiana*) and gowen cypress (*Cupressus goveniana*) are found only in Southern California. Both species are imperiled because they have a limited range of distribution and are threatened by alteration and loss of habitat.

Cycads are unusual plants often mistaken for palms or ferns. They have thick, soft trunks and large, leaflike crowns. Cycads are found in tropical or semitropical regions. Their rarity makes them popular with collectors. The Florida torreya (*Torreya taxifolia*) is the only cycad listed under the ESA. This scrubby tree is extremely rare and is found only on the bluffs along the Apalachicola River in the Florida panhandle. An unknown disease virtually wiped out the species in the wild during the 1950s.

## Ferns and Allies

Ferns are an abundant and diverse plant group. There are up to twenty thousand species of ferns, and they are associated mostly with tropical and subtropical regions. In general, these plants are characterized by stems with long protruding leaves called fronds. Fern allies are plants with similar life cycles to ferns, but without their stem or leaf structure. Examples of fern allies include the club mosses and horsetails.

As of February 2008, there were twenty-six fern and allied species listed under the ESA. (See Table 10.2.) Nearly all are endangered. Geographical locations with large numbers of imperiled ferns include Hawaii (twelve species) and Puerto Rico (eight species). The remaining species are found primarily in the Southeast, except for the Aleutian shield fern (*Polystichum aleuticum*), which is native to Alaska.

## Lichens

Lichens are not truly plants. Scientists place them in the fungi kingdom, instead of the plant kingdom. Lichens are plantlike life forms composed of two separate organisms: a fungus and an alga. Biologists believe there are up to four thousand lichen species in the United States. They are found in many different habitats and grow extremely slowly. Some lichens look like moss, whereas others appear more like traditional plants with a leafy or blade structure. Lichens do not have a "skin" to protect them from the atmosphere. As a result, they are highly sensitive to air contaminants and have disappeared from many urban areas, presumably because of air pollution. Lichens are most predominant in undisturbed forests, bogs, and wetlands, particularly in California, Hawaii, Florida, the Pacific Northwest, and the Appalachians. They are commonly found on rocky outcroppings. Lichens provide a foodstuff for some animals and are used by some bird species in nest building.

As of February 2008, there were two lichen species listed under the ESA: rock gnome lichen (*Gymnoderma lineare*) and Florida perforate cladonia (*Cladonia perforata*). Both are classified as endangered. During the 1970s rock gnome lichen was virtually wiped out in the Great Smoky Mountains National Park in Tennessee due to zealous collecting by scientists. Florida perforate cladonia is found only in rosemary scrub habitats in portions of Florida. It is endangered due to loss or degradation of those habitats.

## Flowering Plants

Flowering plants are vascular plants with flowers—clusters of specialized leaves that participate in reproduction. The flowers of some species are large and colorful, whereas others are extremely small and barely noticeable to humans. Biologists estimate that 80% to 90% of all plants on Earth are flowering plants.

As of February 2008, there were 713 flowering plants listed as endangered or threatened under the ESA. (See Table 10.2.) They come from a wide variety of taxonomic groups and are found in many different habitats. Some of the largest families represented are:

- Asteraceae (asters, daisies, and sunflowers)
- Campanulaceae (bellflowers)
- Fabaceae (legumes and pulses)
- Lamiaceae (mints)
- Brassicaceae (mustard and cabbage)

## GEOGRAPHICAL BREAKDOWN OF PLANTS

Most threatened and endangered plant species in the United States are concentrated in specific areas of the country. Figure 10.3 shows a breakdown of listed plants by predominant region as of February 2008. More than one-third (36%) of all listings occur in Hawaii. California is home to nearly one-fourth (24%) of all listed plants. Together, these two states account for more than half (60%) of all plants listed under the ESA. One other specific region, the Southeast, is notable for its contingent (22%) of threatened and endangered plants. The majority of the imperiled plants in this region are found in Florida. The southwestern United States is home to 8% of listed plants and Puerto Rico contains 7% of listed plants. The remaining 3% of imperiled plants are scattered across other regions of the country.

## FIGURE 10.3

**Regional distribution of listed threatened and endangered plants, February 2008**

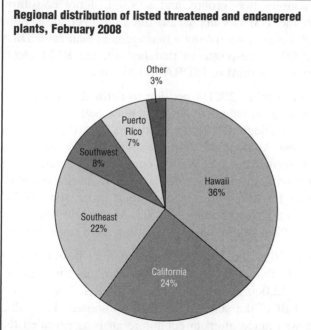

SOURCE: Adapted from "Species Counts," in *USFWS Threatened and Endangered Species System (TESS)*, U.S. Department of the Interior, U.S. Fish and Wildlife Service, February 6, 2008, http://ecos.fws.gov/tess_public/SpeciesCountReport.do (accessed February 6, 2008)

## FIGURE 10.4

**The main Hawaiian Islands**

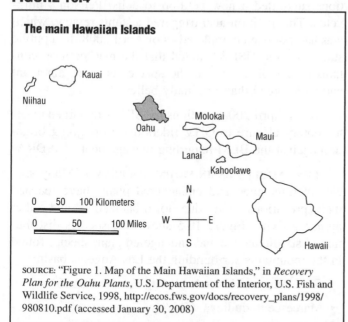

SOURCE: "Figure 1. Map of the Main Hawaiian Islands," in *Recovery Plan for the Oahu Plants*, U.S. Department of the Interior, U.S. Fish and Wildlife Service, 1998, http://ecos.fws.gov/docs/recovery_plans/1998/980810.pdf (accessed January 30, 2008)

## Hawaiian Plants

Figure 10.4 shows the eight major islands that make up the state of Hawaii. The island of Oahu is home to the state's capital Honolulu. However, Oahu is not the largest of the islands. That distinction goes to the island labeled "Hawaii," which is commonly called "the Big Island." In the following discussion, the term *Hawaii* refers to the entire state.

Because of its isolation from continental land masses, many of the species found in Hawaii exist nowhere else in the world. In fact, an estimated 90% of Hawaiian plant species are endemic. Because of large-scale deforestation and habitat destruction on the islands, Hawaii is home to more threatened and endangered plants than any other state in the nation. The USFWS notes in "Endangered and Threatened Species" (2008, http://www.fws.gov/pacificislands/wesa/endspindex.html) that in 2008 there were 294 listed plant species in Hawaii. Hawaiian plants have suffered from the introduction of invasive predators such as cows, pigs, and insects, as well as the loss of critical pollinators with the decline of many species of native birds and insects. According to Marie M. Bruegemann, in "A Plan for Hawaiian Plants and Their Ecosytems" (*Endangered Species Bulletin*, vol. 28, no. 4, July–December 2003), one hundred of Hawaii's fifteen hundred known plant species are believed to have become extinct since the islands were colonized by humans.

The USFWS has developed more than a dozen recovery plans for imperiled Hawaiian plants. Many of the plans cover multiple species found in the same ecosystem or habitat types, such as:

- *Recovery Plan for Oahu Plants* (1998, http://ecos.fws.gov/docs/recovery_plan/980810.pdf)—sixty-six species

- *Recovery Plan for the Kauai Plant Cluster* (1995, http://ecos.fws.gov/docs/recovery_plan/950920a.pdf)—thirty-seven species

- *Recovery Plan for the Big Island Plant Cluster* (1996, http://ecos.fws.gov/docs/recovery_plan/960926a.pdf)—twenty-two species

In 2003 the USFWS designated over 208,000 acres (84,000 ha) of critical habitat on the Big Island as habitat for forty-one listed plant species. The area designated was 52% smaller than originally anticipated because it excluded a large tract of U.S. Army land as well as private land held by the Queen Liliuokalani Trust and others. The U.S. Army land was excluded because of national security concerns and because the army agreed to voluntarily cooperate with the USFWS regarding activity that affects endangered species. The Queen Liliuokalani Trust land was excluded because the trust vowed to discontinue its current efforts on behalf of endangered species if its lands were included in the critical habitat designation. Finally, land near the cities of Kailua and Kona, for which housing development was planned, was excluded from critical habitat designation because the economic and social costs of inclusion were too great.

Designation of critical habitat in Hawaii was completed after a successful lawsuit brought against the USFWS by

Earthjustice, the Conservation Council for Hawaii, the Sierra Club, and the Hawaii Botanical Society.

## Californian Plants

California is home to 24% of threatened and endangered plant species in the United States. (See Figure 10.3.) More than 180 imperiled plants are found there, including several types of checker-mallow, dudleya, evening primrose, grass, jewelflower, larkspur, manzanita, milk-vetch, paintbrush, rock-cress, spineflower, and thistle.

MILK-VETCH. Milk-vetch is an herbaceous perennial flowering plant found in various parts of the world. It received its common name during the 1500s because of a belief among European farmers that the plant increased the milk yield of goats. As of February 2008, there were eleven species of milk-vetch listed as threatened or endangered in California:

- Applegate's milk-vetch (*Astragalus applegatei*)

- Braunton's milk-vetch (*Astragalus brauntonii*)

- Clara Hunt's milk-vetch (*Astragalus clarianus*)

- Coachella Valley milk-vetch (*Astragalus lentiginosus* var. *coachellae*)

- Coastal dunes milk-vetch (*Astragalus tener* var. *titi*)

- Cushenbury milk-vetch (*Astragalus albens*)

- Fish Slough milk-vetch (*Astragalus lentiginosus* var. *piscinensis*)

- Lane Mountain milk-vetch (*Astragalus jaegerianus*)

- Peirson's milk-vetch (*Astragalus magdalenae* var. *peirsonii*)

- Triple-ribbed milk-vetch (*Astragalus tricarinatus*)

- Ventura Marsh milk-vetch (*Astragalus pycnostachyus* var. *lanosissimus*)

Peirson's milk-vetch is a plant with a long history of litigation and controversy in California. It is found in only one small area of Imperial County in the southern part of the state. This area is the Imperial Sand Dunes Recreation Area (ISDRA), which is managed by the Bureau of Land Management (BLM). ISDRA has a remote and barren landscape dominated by huge rolling sand dunes—the Algodones Dunes, the largest sand dune fields in North America. ISDRA covers 185,000 acres (75,000 ha) and is a popular destination for off-highway vehicle (OHV) riders, receiving more than one million visitors annually.

In 1998 Peirson's milk-vetch was designated a threatened species by the USFWS because of the threat of destruction by OHVs and other recreational activities at ISDRA. The agency decided not to designate critical habitat at that time, fearing the remaining plants would be subject to deliberate vandalism. The BLM was sued by conservation groups and accused of not consulting with the USFWS about the threats to Peirson's milk-vetch before establishing a management plan for ISDRA. In 2000, in response to that lawsuit, the BLM closed more than a third of ISDRA to OHV use.

In October 2001 a petition to delist the species was submitted on behalf of the American Sand Association, the San Diego Off-Road Coalition, and the Off-Road Business Association. A month later two lawsuits were filed against the USFWS by conservation organizations challenging the agency's decision not to designate critical habitat for the species. Under court order, the USFWS proposed critical habitat in 2003. Meanwhile, the delisting petition submitted in 2001 triggered a status review.

In 2004 the USFWS issued a final designation of critical habitat for Peirson's milk-vetch that encompassed nearly 22,000 acres (9,000 ha) of ISDRA. This was less than half of the acreage originally proposed. The reduction was made after an economic analysis revealed that closure of ISDRA areas to OHV use would have a negative impact on local businesses. That same year the agency completed the status review triggered by the 2001 delisting proposal and found that the species should remain listed as threatened. In July 2005 the original petitioners and additional OHV and motorcycle associations submitted a new petition to delist Peirson's milk-vetch. This petition also triggered a status review, which was had not been completed as of April 2008. In a public statement, the USFWS noted that the new petition contains data indicating that the species is more abundant and widespread than originally believed.

As of April 2008, portions of ISDRA remained under temporary closure to OHV riders due to ongoing litigation against the BLM regarding management of ISDRA.

LOS ANGELES BASIN MOUNTAIN PLANTS. Many species of threatened and endangered plants have reached their precarious state due to urbanization and other human activity. Figure 10.5 shows the species distribution of six threatened and endangered plant species found in the mountains surrounding the Los Angeles basin:

- Braunton's milk-vetch (*Astragalus brauntonii*)

- Marcescent dudleya (*Dudleya cymosa* ssp. *marcescens*)

- Santa Monica Mountains dudleya (*Dudleya cymosa* ssp. *ovatifolia*)

- Conejo dudleya (*Dudleya abramsii* ssp. *parva*)

- Verity's dudleya (*Dudleya verityi*)

- Lyon's pentachaeta (*Pentachaeta lyonii*)

In *Recovery Plan for Six Plants from the Mountains Surrounding the Los Angeles Basin* (September 1999,

**FIGURE 10.5**

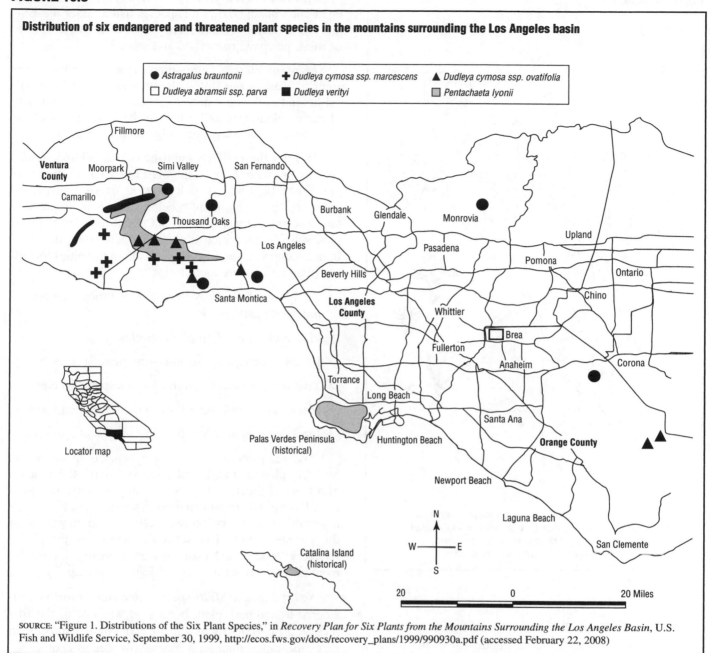

**Distribution of six endangered and threatened plant species in the mountains surrounding the Los Angeles basin**

- ● *Astragalus brauntonii*
- □ *Dudleya abramsii ssp. parva*
- ✚ *Dudleya cymosa ssp. marcescens*
- ■ *Dudleya veritiy*
- ▲ *Dudleya cymosa ssp. ovatifolia*
- ▨ *Pentachaeta lyonii*

SOURCE: "Figure 1. Distributions of the Six Plant Species," in *Recovery Plan for Six Plants from the Mountains Surrounding the Los Angeles Basin*, U.S. Fish and Wildlife Service, September 30, 1999, http://ecos.fws.gov/docs/recovery_plans/1999/990930a.pdf (accessed February 22, 2008)

http://ecos.fws.gov/docs/recovery_plans/1999/990930a.pdf), the USFWS cites threats including "urban development, recreational activities, alteration of fire cycles, fire suppression and pre-suppression (fuel modification) activities, over collecting, habitat fragmentation and degradation, and competition from invasive weeds. Several of the plants are also threatened with extinction from random events because their numbers and ranges are so limited."

## Southeastern Plants

As of February 2008, the southeastern states contained 22% of the threatened and endangered plant species listed under the ESA. (See Figure 10.3.) The most common families are the Asteraceae (asters, daisies, and sunflowers), Fabaceae (legumes and pulses), and Lamiaceae (mints).

**PONDBERRY.** Over $1.6 million was spent on pondberry (*Lindera melissifolia*) under the ESA during fiscal year 2006. (See Table 10.3.) This was the highest expenditure for any plant species that year. The plant is a member of the Lauraceae family, which includes dozens of trees and shrubs. The pondberry is a shrub that grows to be around 6 feet (2 m) tall. (See Figure 10.6.) It is deciduous (meaning it loses its leaves during some part of the year) and produces tiny red berries in late summer or fall. It prefers lowland habitats with moist soil. In "Pondberry" (October 11, 2006, http://www.dnr.sc.gov/marine/mrri/acechar/specgal/berrypon.htm), the South Carolina

## FIGURE 10.6

**Pondberry**

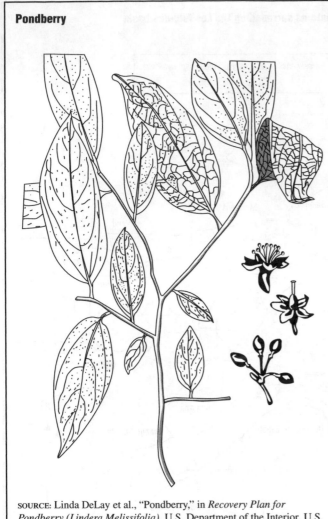

SOURCE: Linda DeLay et al., "Pondberry," in *Recovery Plan for Pondberry (Lindera Melissifolia)*, U.S. Department of the Interior, U.S. Fish and Wildlife Service, 1993, http://ecos.fws.gov/docs/recovery_plan/930923a.pdf (accessed February 8, 2008)

**FLORIDIAN PLANTS.** Approximately half of the threatened and endangered plant species listed under the ESA are found only in Florida. They include multiple species of mint, pawpaw, rosemary, and spurge.

Many of Florida's imperiled plants are found in the southern part of the state—the only subtropical ecological habitat in the continental United States. The majority of native plant species located in the bottom half of the southern Florida ecosystem originated from the tropics.

In 1999 the USFWS published *South Florida Multispecies Recovery Plan* (http://ecos.fws.gov/docs/recovery_plan/990518_1.pdf), which covered sixty-eight species, including thirty-five plant species. In 2004 an implementation schedule for many, but not all, of the species in the plan was issued, which divided the ecosystem into ecological communities. The ecological communities including plant species are as follows:

- Florida scrub/Scrubby flatwoods/Scrubby high pine—nineteen plant species

- Pine rocklands—five plant species

- Beach dune/Coastal strand—one plant species

- Tropical hardwood hammock—one plant species

- Mesic and hydric pine flatwoods—one plant species

- Freshwater marsh/Wet prairie—one plant species

The recovery and restoration tasks outlined in the recovery plan are to be implemented through the creation of a team of federal, state, and local governmental agencies; Native American tribal governments; academic representatives; industry representatives; and members of the private sector. The schedule prioritizes the plan's recovery actions and estimates costs yearly for implementing the actions in each ecological community.

*South Florida Multi-species Recovery Plan* is considered a landmark plan, because it was one of the first recovery plans to focus on an ecosystem approach to recovery, rather than on a species-by-species approach.

## THREATENED AND ENDANGERED FOREIGN SPECIES OF PLANTS

As of February 2008, the USFWS listed thirty-seven foreign species of plants as threatened or endangered. (See Table 10.4.) Thirty-four of them are found in the United States and foreign countries, whereas three are completely foreign. The latter are:

- Guatemalan fir (*Abies guatemalensis*)—threatened

- Chilean false larch (*Fitzroya cupressoides*)—threatened

- Coast Rican jatropha (*Jatropha costaricensis*)—endangered

The *1997 IUCN Red List of Threatened Plants* (http://www.iucn.org/themes/ssc/97plrl/finalra.htm) from the

Department of Natural Resources notes that "pondberry does not have any particular aesthetic value, nor are any horticultural, medicinal, or other economic uses known."

The pondberry was first listed under the ESA in 1986. A recovery plan for the species was issued in 1993. The elimination and development of lowland forests across the South contributed to its imperiled condition. According to Zoë Hoyle, in "Pondberry: Modest but Mysterious" (*Compass*, July 2006), scientists believe the pondberry has always been rare. Approximately three dozen separate populations of the species are known to exist. They are so scattered that scientists believe the plant's seeds must have been spread by floods in the distant past. Extensive flood control measures implemented across the South in recent decades have likely limited the further spread of the species. Hoyle notes that approximately $5 million was spent by various federal agencies between 2002 and 2006 to study factors that affect the plant's survival.

TABLE 10.4

**Foreign endangered and threatened plant species, February 2008**

| Common name | Scientific name | Listing status* | U.S. and/or foreign listed | Foreign range |
|---|---|---|---|---|
| American hart's-tongue fern | Asplenium scolopendrium var. americanum | T | US/foreign | Canada |
| Big-leaved crownbeard | Verbesina dissita | T | US/foreign | Mexico |
| Bunched cory cactus | Coryphantha ramillosa | T | US/foreign | Mexico |
| Chilean false larch | Fitzroya cupressoides | T | Foreign | Chile, Argentina |
| Cobana negra | Stahlia monosperma | T | US/foreign | Dominican Republic |
| Cochise pincushion cactus | Coryphantha robbinsorum | T | US/foreign | Mexico |
| Costa Rican jatropha | Jatropha costaricensis | E | Foreign | Costa Rica |
| Del Mar manzanita | Arctostaphylos glandulosa ssp. crassifolia | E | US/foreign | Mexico |
| Dwarf lake iris | Iris lacustris | T | US/foreign | Canada |
| Eastern prairie fringed orchid | Platanthera leucophaea | T | US/foreign | Canada |
| Furbish lousewort | Pedicularis furbishiae | E | US/foreign | Canada |
| Golden paintbrush | Castilleja levisecta | T | US/foreign | Canada |
| Guatemalan fir (=pinabete) | Abies guatemalensis | T | Foreign | Mexico, Guatemala, Honduras, El Salvador |
| Houghton's goldenrod | Solidago houghtonii | T | US/foreign | Canada |
| Huachuca water-umbel | Lilaeopsis schaffneriana var. recurva | E | US/foreign | Mexico |
| Johnston's frankenia | Frankenia johnstonii | E | US/foreign | Mexico |
| Key tree cactus | Pilosocereus robinii | E | US/foreign | Cuba |
| Lakeside daisy | Hymenoxys herbacea | T | US/foreign | Canada |
| Lloyd's mariposa cactus | Echinomastus mariposensis | T | US/foreign | Mexico |
| Mexican flannelbush | Fremontodendron mexicanum | E | US/foreign | Mexico |
| No common name | Calyptranthes thomasiana | E | US/foreign | British Virgin Islands |
| No common name | Mitracarpus polycladus | E | US/foreign | Saba |
| Otay mesa-mint | Pogogyne nudiuscula | E | US/foreign | Mexico |
| Otay tarplant | Deinandra (=Hemizonia) conjugens | T | US/foreign | Mexico |
| Pima pineapple cactus | Coryphantha scheeri var. robustispina | E | US/foreign | Mexico |
| Pitcher's thistle | Cirsium pitcheri | T | US/foreign | Canada |
| Salt marsh bird's-beak | Cordylanthus maritimus ssp. maritimus | E | US/foreign | Mexico |
| San Diego ambrosia | Ambrosia pumila | E | US/foreign | Mexico |
| San Diego thornmint | Acanthomintha ilicifolia | T | US/foreign | Mexico |
| Small whorled pogonia | Isotria medeoloides | T | US/foreign | Canada |
| Spreading navarretia | Navarretia fossalis | T | US/foreign | Mexico |
| Star cactus | Astrophytum asterias | E | US/foreign | Mexico |
| Texas ayenia | Ayenia limitaris | E | US/foreign | Mexico |
| Walker's manioc | Manihot walkerae | E | US/foreign | Mexico |
| West Indian walnut (=Nogal) | Juglans jamaicensis | E | US/foreign | Cuba, Hispaniola |
| Western prairie fringed orchid | Platanthera praeclara | T | US/foreign | Canada |
| Willowy monardella | Monardella linoides ssp. viminea | E | US/foreign | Mexico |

*E = Endangered; T = Threatened.

SOURCE: Adapted from "Listed FWS/Joint FWS and NMFS Species and Populations with Recovery Plans (Sorted by Listed Entity)" and "Listed U.S. Species by Taxonomic Group," in *USFWS Threatened and Endangered Species System (TESS)*, U.S. Department of the Interior, U.S. Fish and Wildlife Service, February 5, 2008, http://ecos.fws.gov/tess_public/SpeciesRecovery.do?sort=1 and http://ecos.fws.gov/tess_public/SpeciesReport.do?kingdom=V&listing Type=L (accessed February 5, 2008)

IUCN was the first global assessment of plants and was the result of over twenty years of study by botanists, conservation organizations, botanical gardens, and museums around the world. It revealed that 12.5%—one of every eight—of the world's plant species are in danger of extinction. In the United States, the figure is even higher, with 29% of the nation's sixteen thousand plant species threatened.

The IUCN also reported that the vast majority of plants at risk are extremely limited geographically; most are not found outside of their home nations, making these species particularly vulnerable to extinction. Many plant species known to have medicinal value are threatened, including many species in the yew family, a source of cancer-fighting compounds. The IUCN notes that the loss of each species causes a loss of genetic material that could be used to produce stronger, healthier crops for human and animal consumption.

The *2007 Red List of Threatened Species* currently lists 8,447 species of threatened plants. This is 70% of the 12,043 plants that have been examined. However, only 3% of plant species have been studied in sufficient detail to assess their status, and the actual number of threatened species is likely to be much higher. The IUCN notes that 297,326 plant species are known and described around the world.

The majority of IUCN-listed species are flowering plants, a diverse and well-studied group. In 2007 the IUCN reported that 7,899 flowering plants were threatened. Other IUCN-listed species include 321 gymnosperms (conifers, cycads, ginkgos, and gnetophytes), 139 ferns and allies, 79 true mosses, and 9 red algae. In addition, the 2007 list includes six species of brown algae, two lichens, and one mushroom. Habitat loss accounts at least in part for the threatened status of the vast majority of IUCN-listed plants.

# IMPORTANT NAMES AND ADDRESSES

**Alaska Fisheries Science Center**
**National Oceanic and Atmospheric**
**Administration**
7600 Sand Point Way NE, Bldg. 4
Seattle, WA 98115
(206) 526-4000
FAX: (206) 526-4004
URL: http://www.afsc.noaa.gov/

**AmphibiaWeb**
3101 Valley Life Sciences Bldg. 3160
University of California
Berkeley, CA 94720
URL: http://amphibiaweb.org/

**Biological Resources Division**
**U.S. Geological Survey**
12201 Sunrise Valley Dr.
Reston, VA 20192
(703) 648-4000
URL: http://biology.usgs.gov/

**Center for Biological Diversity**
PO Box 710
Tucson, AZ 85702-0710
(520) 623-5252
1-866-357-3349
FAX: (520) 623-9797
E-mail: center@biologicaldiversity.org
URL: http://www.biologicaldiversity.org/

**Center for the Defense of Free Enterprise**
12500 NE Tenth Place
Bellevue, WA 98005
(425) 455-5038
FAX: (425) 451-3959
URL: http://www.cdfe.org/

**Center for Plant Conservation**
PO Box 299
St. Louis, MO 63166
(314) 577-9450
FAX: (314) 577-9465
E-mail: cpc@mobot.org
URL: http://www.centerforplantconservation
.org/

**Congressional Research Service**
**Library of Congress**
101 Independence Ave. SE
Washington, DC 20540-7500
URL: http://www.loc.gov/crsinfo/

**Defenders of Wildlife**
1130 Seventeenth St. NW
Washington, DC 20036
(202) 682-9400
1-800-385-9712
E-mail: defenders@mail.defenders.org
URL: http://www.defenders.org/index.php/

**Earth System Research Laboratory**
**National Oceanic and Atmospheric**
**Administration**
325 Broadway R/GMD1
Boulder, CO 80305-3337
URL: http://www.cmdl.noaa.gov/

**Environmental Defense**
257 Park Ave. South
New York, NY 10010
(212) 505-2100
FAX: (212) 505-2375
URL: http://www.environmentaldefense
.org/home.cfm

**Goddard Institute for Space Studies**
**National Aeronautics and Space**
**Administration**
2880 Broadway
New York, NY 10025
(212) 678-5500
URL: http://www.giss.nasa.gov/

**Greenpeace U.S.A.**
702 H St. NW
Washington, DC 20001
(202) 462-1177
URL: http://www.greenpeace.org/usa/

**Heritage Foundation**
214 Massachusetts Ave. NE
Washington, DC 20002-4999

(202) 546-4400
FAX: (202) 546-8328
URL: http://www.heritage.org/

**International Union for Conservation of**
**Nature and Natural Resources**
Rue Mauverney 28
Gland, 1196, Switzerland
41-22-999-0000
FAX: 41-22-999-0002
E-mail: webmaster@iucn.org
URL: http://www.iucn.org/

**International Whaling Commission**
135 Station Rd.
Impington, CB24 9NP, United Kingdom
44-0-1223-233-971
FAX: 44-01223-232-876
E-mail: secretariat@iwcoffice.org
URL: http://www.iwcoffice.org/index.htm

**Land Trust Alliance**
1660 L St. NW, Ste. 1100
Washington, DC 20036
(202) 638-4725
E-mail: info@lta.org
URL: http://www.lta.org/

**National Audubon Society**
225 Varick St., Seventh Fl.
New York, NY 10014
(212) 979-3000
URL: http://www.audubon.org/

**National Forest Service**
**U.S. Department of Agriculture**
1400 Independence Ave. SW
Washington, DC 20250-0003
(202) 205-8333
URL: http://www.fs.fed.us

**National Marine Fisheries Service**
**National Oceanic and Atmospheric**
**Administration**
1315 East-West Highway, Ninth Fl.
Silver Spring, MD 20910

(301) 713-2379
FAX: (301) 713-2384
URL: http://www.nmfs.noaa.gov/

**National Marine Mammal Laboratory**
**National Oceanic and Atmospheric**
**Administration**
7600 Sand Point Way NE F/AKC3
Seattle, WA 98115-6349
(206) 526-4045
FAX: (206) 526-6615
URL: http://nmml.afsc.noaa.gov/

**National Park Service**
1849 C St. NW
Washington, DC 20240
(202) 208-6843
URL: http://www.nps.gov/

**National Research Council**
**National Academies**
500 Fifth St. NW
Washington, DC 20001
(202) 334-2000
URL: http://www.nas.edu/nrc/

**National Wildlife Federation**
11100 Wildlife Center Dr.
Reston, VA 20190-5362
1-800-822-9919
URL: http://www.nwf.org/

**National Wildlife Health Center**
**U.S. Geological Survey**
6006 Schroeder Rd.
Madison, WI 53711-6223
(608) 270-2400
FAX: (608) 270-2415
E-mail: NWHCweb@usgs.gov
URL: http://www.nwhc.usgs.gov/

**Natural Resources Defense Council**
40 W. Twentieth St.
New York, NY 10011
(212) 727-2700
FAX: (212) 727-1773
E-mail: nrdcinfo@nrdc.org
URL: http://www.nrdc.org/

**Nature Conservancy**
4245 N. Fairfax Dr., Ste. 100
Arlington, VA 22203-1606
(703) 841-5300
1-800-628-6860
URL: http://nature.org/

**Northeast Fisheries Science Center**
**National Oceanic and Atmospheric**
**Administration**
166 Water St.
Woods Hole, MA 02543-1026
(508) 495-2000
FAX: (508) 495-2258
URL: http://www.nefsc.noaa.gov/

**Northwest Fisheries Science Center**
**National Oceanic and Atmospheric**
**Administration**
2725 Montlake Blvd. East
Seattle, WA 98112-2097
(206) 860-3200
FAX: (206) 860-3217
URL: http://www.nwfsc.noaa.gov/

**Sierra Club**
85 Second St., Second Fl.
San Francisco, CA 94105-3441
(415) 977-5500
FAX: (415) 977-5799
URL: http://www.sierraclub.org/

**TRAFFIC North America—Regional**
**Office**
1250 Twenty-fourth St. NW
Washington, DC 20037
(202) 293-4800
FAX: (202)775-8287
E-mail: tna@wwfus.org
URL: http://www.traffic.org/

**United Nations Environment**
**Programme**
United Nations Ave., Gigiri
PO Box 30552
Nairobi, 00100 Kenya
254-20-7621234
FAX: 254-20-7624489/90
E-mail: unepinfo@unep.org
URL: http://www.unep.org/

**U.S. Bureau of Land Management**
1849 C St., Rm. 406-LS
Washington, DC 20240
(202) 452-5125
FAX: (202) 452-5124
URL: http://www.blm.gov/

**U.S. Bureau of Reclamation**
1849 C St. NW
Washington, DC 20240-0001
(202) 513-0575

FAX: (202) 513-0309
URL: http://www.usbr.gov/

**U.S. Environmental Protection Agency**
**Office of Water**
1200 Pennsylvania Ave. NW
Washington, DC 20460
(202) 566-0430
URL: http://epa.gov/waterscience

**U.S. Fish and Wildlife Service**
**Division of Endangered**
**Species**
U.S. Department of the Interior
4401 N. Fairfax Dr., Rm. 420
Arlington, VA 22203
URL: http://www.fws.gov/endangered

**U.S. Government Accountability**
**Office**
441 G St. NW
Washington, DC 20548
(202) 512-3000
URL: http://www.gao.gov/

**Western Ecological Research Center**
**U.S. Geological Survey**
3020 State University Dr. East
Modoc Hall, Rm. 3006
Sacramento, CA 95819
(916) 278-9485
FAX: (916) 278-9475
URL: http://www.werc.usgs.gov/

**Wilderness Society**
1615 M St. NW
Washington, DC 20036
1-800-843-9453
URL: http://www.wilderness.org/

**World Wildlife Fund**
1250 Twenty-fourth St. NW
Washington, DC 20090-7180
(202) 293-4800
URL: http://www.worldwildlife.org/

**Worldwatch Institute**
1776 Massachusetts Ave. NW
Washington, DC 20036-1904
(202) 452-1999
FAX: (202) 296-7365
E-mail: worldwatch@worldwatch.org
URL: http://www.worldwatch.org/

# RESOURCES

A first source of information on endangered species is the U.S. Fish and Wildlife Service (USFWS), an agency of the U.S. Department of the Interior. The USFWS oversees the Endangered Species List. Its comprehensive Web site (http://www.fws.gov/endangered/) includes news stories on threatened and endangered species, information about laws protecting endangered species, regional contacts for endangered species programs, and a searchable database called the Threatened and Endangered Species System (http://ecos.fws.gov/tess_public/StartTESS.do) with information on all listed species. Each listed species has an information page that provides details regarding the status of the species (whether it is listed as threatened or endangered and in what geographic area), federal register documents pertaining to listing, information on habitat conservation plans and national wildlife refuges pertinent to the species, and, for many species, links to descriptions of biology and natural history. Particularly informative are the recovery plans published for many listed species. These detail the background research on the natural history of endangered species and list measures that should be adopted to aid in conservation.

The USFWS also maintains updated tables of the number of threatened and endangered species by taxonomic group, as well as lists of U.S. threatened and endangered species. The agency publishes the bimonthly *Endangered Species Bulletin* (http://endangered.fws.gov/bulletin.html), which provides information on new listings, delistings, and reclassifications, besides news articles on endangered species. Finally, the USFWS prints an annual report on expenditures made under the Endangered Species Act.

The National Marine Fisheries Service (NMFS; http://www.nmfs.noaa.gov/) is responsible for the oversight of threatened and endangered marine animals and anadromous fish. The NMFS is a division of the National Oceanic and Atmospheric Administration (NOAA), which also operates the National Marine Mammal Laboratory at the Alaska Fisheries Science Center (http://nmml.afsc.noaa.gov/), the Northeast Fisheries Science Center (http://nefsc.noaa.gov/), and the Northwest Fisheries Science Center (http://www.nwfsc.noaa.gov/). The NOAA's National Ocean Service (http://oceanservice.noaa.gov/) is an excellent source of information about marine creatures.

The U.S. Geological Survey (USGS) performs research on many imperiled animal species. Data sheets on individual species are available from the USGS National Wildlife Health Center (http://www.nwhc.usgs.gov/). Other important USGS centers include the Western Ecological Research Center (http://www.werc.usgs.gov/), the Northern Prairie Wildlife Research Center (http://www.npwrc.usgs.gov/), the Nonindigenous Aquatic Species information resource at the Center for Aquatic Resource Studies (http://nas.er.usgs.gov/), the Biological Resources Division (http://biology.usgs.gov/), and the Center for Biological Informatics, which maintains the National Biological Information Infrastructure (http://www.nbii.gov/).

Information on federal lands and endangered species management can be found via the National Wildlife Refuge (http://refuges.fws.gov/), the National Park System (http://www.nps.gov/), and the National Forest Service (http://www.fs.fed.us/). National Wildlife Refuge brochures are available at http://library.fws.gov/refuges/index.html.

*Endangered Ecosystems of the United States—A Preliminary Assessment of Loss and Degradation*, a 1995 publication from the National Biological Service, is the most recent assessment of U.S. ecosystems. Information on water quality in the United States is available via the Environmental Protection Agency (http://www.epa.gov/

water). Information on wetlands can be found at the USFWS's National Wetlands Inventory (http://www.nwi.fws.gov/).

Data and information related to global warming are available from the National Aeronautics and Space Administration's Goddard Institute for Space Studies (http://data.giss.nasa.gov/) and at NOAA's Earth System Research Laboratory, Global Monitoring Division (http://www.cmdl.noaa.gov/).

Other federal agencies that proved useful for this book were the U.S. Commission on Ocean Policy, which published *An Ocean Blueprint for the 21st Century: Final Report* (2004) and the U.S. Army Corps of Engineers, which maintains the National Inventory of Dams (http://crunch.tec.army.mil/nidpublic/webpages/nid.cfm). The U.S. Department of the Interior operates the National Atlas of the United States (http://nationalatlas.gov/), an online mapping tool. The U.S. Government Accountability Office (http://www.gao.gov/) and the Congressional Research Service (http://opencrs.com/) publish a number of reports assessing the policies and effectiveness of the Endangered Species Program.

The International Union for Conservation of Nature and Natural Resources (IUCN; http://www.iucn.org/) provides news articles on a wide array of worldwide conservation issues, and maintains *2007 IUCN Red List of Threatened Species* (http://www.redlist.org/). This site includes an extensive database of information on IUCN-listed threatened species. Species information available includes Red List endangerment category, the year the species was assessed, the countries in which the species is found, a list of the habitat types the species occupies, major threats to continued existence, and current population trends. Brief descriptions of ecology and natural history and of conservation measures for protecting listed species are also available. Searches can also be performed by taxonomic group, Red List categories, country, region, or habitat.

The Convention on International Trade in Endangered Species of Wild Fauna and Flora (CITES; http://www.cites.org/) provides information on international trade in endangered species. It includes a species database of protected fauna and flora in the three CITES appendices, as well as information on the history and aims of the convention and its current programs.

Many private organizations are dedicated to the conservation of listed species and their ecosystems. Readers with interest in a particular endangered species are advised to conduct Internet searches to locate these groups. The Save the Manatee Club (http://www.savethemanatee.org/), which focuses on West Indian manatees, and the Save Our Springs Alliance (http://www.sosalliance.org/), which focuses on protection of the endangered Barton Springs salamander, are only two of many examples.

BirdLife International (http://www.birdlife.net/) provides diverse resources on global bird conservation. It is an association of nongovernmental conservation organizations that has over two million members worldwide.

AmphibiaWeb (http://amphibiaweb.org/) provides detailed information on global amphibian declines. It maintains a watch list of recently extinct and declining species, discusses potential causes of amphibian declines and deformities, and provides detailed information on amphibian biology and conservation. AmphibiaWeb also sponsors a discussion board where readers can submit questions regarding amphibians.

TRAFFIC (http://www.traffic.org/) was originally founded to help implement the CITES treaty but it now addresses diverse issues in the wildlife trade. It is a joint wildlife trade monitoring organization of the World Wildlife Fund and the IUCN. TRAFFIC publishes several periodicals and report series on wildlife trade, including the *TRAFFIC Bulletin*, *TRAFFIC Online Report Series*, and *Species in Danger Series*.

The International Whaling Commission (http://www.iwcoffice.org/) provides information on whaling regulations, whale sanctuaries, and other issues associated with whales and whaling.

The Gallup Organization provided information related to public polls conducted in recent years concerning environmental issues.

Information Plus sincerely thanks all the previously mentioned organizations for the valuable information they provided.

# INDEX

*Page references in italics refer to photographs. References with the letter* t *following them indicate the presence of a table. The letter* f *indicates a figure. If more than one table or figure appears on a particular page, the exact item number for the table or figure being referenced is provided.*

## A

ACF (American Chestnut Foundation), 140
Agriculture, 18, 103
Alaska National Interest Lands Conservation Act, 12
Alaska translocation programs, 51
Alaskan oil drilling, 12–14
Aleutian Canada geese, 125
Alligators, 92, 93–94
American chestnut, 139–140, 141f, 142
American Chestnut Foundation (ACF), 140
American crocodile, 92
American Farm Bureau, 98–99
Amphibians, 9, 81–87, 82t, 83f
Anadromous fish. *See* Marine and anadromous fish
Anthropogenic emissions, 19f
ANWR (Arctic National Wildlife Refuge), 12–14, 14f, 15f
Arachnids, 136, 138
Arctic National Wildlife Refuge (ANWR), 12–14, 14f, 15f
Asoka, 23
Atmospheric carbon dioxide levels, 19f
Australia, 20

## B

Bald Eagle Protection Act, 124
Bald eagles, 124–125, 124f
Baleen whales, 41, 42f
Bats, 95–97
Bears, 97–98
Beaufort Sea polar bear den locations, 16f

Beetles, 133–134
Bering, Vitus Jonassen, 46
Big Five mass extinctions, 3
Big game, 99–100, 110
Bighorn sheep, 99–100
Bioaccumulative contaminants, 57, 58f
Biodiversity, 2, 8
Biological indicator species, 9
Birds
    Aleutian Canada geese, 125
    bald eagles, 124–125, 124f
    brown pelicans, 125
    expenditures for, under the Endangered Species Act, 115 (t8.2)
    foreign endangered and threatened species, 126t–129t
    habitat loss and environmental decline, 122
    invasive species, 20
    listed species, 114t–115t
    major international conventions and U.S. legislation, 122t
    migratory songbirds, 118–119
    passerines, 116–118, 117f
    peregrine falcons, 125
    raptors, 119–120, 120f
    recovered species, 124–125
    threats to, 122–124
    water birds, 120–122, 121f, 122f
    woodpeckers, 113–116, 116f
Bison, 4, 4f
Blackburn's sphinx moth, 134–135
Black-capped vireos, 116–117
Black-footed ferrets, 101
Bleached coral, 78
Blight, 139–140
Blue whales, 2t
Boat strikes. *See* Ship and boat strikes
Brown pelicans, 125
Brown-headed cowbirds, 117–118

Budget issues. *See* Expenditures under the Endangered Species Act
Buena Vista Lake shrew, 103
Bull trout, 61–62, 62f
Bush, George W., 12, 14, 44
Butterflies, 131–133, 135–136
Bycatch reduction devices, 90–91, 90f

## C

Caecilians, 81, 85
California
    condors, 120, 120f
    insects, 133–134
    otters, 50
    plants, 156–157
    red-legged frogs, 83–84
Canada lynxes, 37
Canaries, 9
Candidate Conservation Agreement, 32
Candidate species, 26–27, 27f
Canines, 98–99, 99f
Captive breeding programs
    black-footed ferret, 101
    California condor, 120
    pygmy rabbits, 102
Caribou, 17f, 99–100
Cats
    big cats, 104–108
    domestic, 123
    U.S. species, 100–101
Cave wolf spiders, 136, 138
Cheetahs, 107–108
Chemical pollutants, 57–58
China, 109–110
Chinese alligators, 93–94
CITES (Convention on International Trade in Endangered Species of Wild Fauna and Flora), 15, 23
Clams, 73 (t5.1), 74t
Clark, William, 103

Classification
  blue whales, 2t
  plants, 142, 153–154
  taxonomic system, 1–2
Clinton, Bill, 12, 20
Coastal California gnatcatchers, 118
Cochito, 45
Columbia River basin, 66f
Comeback, bison, 4
Commercial fishing
  salmon, 64
  tuna, 39, 45
  whale entanglement, 43
Condors, 120, 120f
Conifers, 154
Conservation
  controversies, 6–7
  ecosystem approach to habitat
    conservation, 36
  history, 23–24
  importance of, 7–8
  U.S. land conservation, 9–15
Controversies
  Endangered Species Act, 33–34, 36–37
  environmental policy, 6–7
  federally protected lands use, 11–14
  Klamath Basin controversy, 65, 67–68
Convention on Biological Diversity, 16
Convention on International Trade in
  Endangered Species of Wild Fauna and
  Flora (CITES), 15, 23
Convention on the Conservation of Migratory
  Species of Wild Animals, 16–17
Corals, 74t, 77–79, 77f, 78f
Cowbirds, 117–118
Critical habitat, 29–30, 30t, 33
Crocodilians, 92, 93–94
Crustaceans, 71, 73 (t5.2), 74t, 76–77
Cycads, 154

**D**

Dams
  impoundment hydropower plant, 56f
  Klamath River, 68
  Missouri River, 61 (f4.5)
  problems with, 55–56
  salmon, 65
Deer, 99–100
Definitions
  endangered species, 3
  species, 24
Deformities, amphibian, 86–87
Delisting
  American alligator, 92
  bird species, 124–125
  brown pelicans, 125
  gray wolves, 99
  grizzly bears, 98
  overview, 28

Peirson's milk-vetch, 156
  recovery rate controversies, 37
  U.S. and foreign species, 29t
Desert tortoises, 89, 89 (f6.3)
Diseases, amphibian, 86
Distinct population segment (DPS), 24
Dolphins, 45
Domestic cats, 123
DPS (distinct population segment), 24
Dragonflies, 135
Dugongs, 51–52

**E**

Eagles, 124–1225, 124f
Economic issues. *See* Expenditures under
  the Endangered Species Act
Ecosystem approach to species protection, 36
Ehrlich, Paul R., 37
Elephants, 108–109, 109f
Emergency listing, 28
Endangered species
  definition, 3
  list, 1967, 24t
  numbers, by state or territory, 7f
  numbers, by year, 6f
  numbers of threatened species, 4–6, 5t,
    6f
  numbers under the management of the
    National Forest Service, 10t
  value placed on different species, 8–9
Endangered Species Act
  calls to strengthen, 37–38
  critical habitat, 29–30, 30t
  ecosystem approach, 36
  emergency listing, 28
  Enhancement of Survival Permits, 32–33
  experimental populations, 30, 31t–32t
  Habitat Conservation Plans, 32
  incidental take permits, 32
  listing priority numbers, 26t
  listing process, 25–28
  litigation, 33–34
  opposition, 36–37
  overview, 24–25
  petition process, 26f
  recovery plans, 28–29, 30, 32, 33t
  status codes, 25t
  *See also* Delisting; Expenditures under
    the Endangered Species Act
Endangered Species Conservation Act, 24
Endangered Species Preservation Act, 24
Enhancement of Survival Permits, 32–33
Entanglement in fishing gear, 43
Entrainment, 56
Environmental issues
  policy controversies, 6–7
  public opinion, 8, 8t
ESA. *See* Endangered Species Act
Exotic species, 19, 123–124

Expenditures under the Endangered Species
  Act
  amphibians, 82 (t6.2)
  birds, 115 (t8.2)
  clams, snails, crustaceans, and corals,
    74t
  fish, 60 (t4.2)
  insects and spiders, 133t
  largest expenditures, by species, 35t
  mammals, 95, 97 (t7.2)
  marine and anadromous fish, 63 (t4.4)
  overview, 34–36
  plants, 153 (t10.3)
  reptiles, 88 (t6.5)
  U.S. Fish and Wildlife Service, 34f,
    35f
Experimental populations, 30, 31t–32t
Extinction, history of, 3–4
*Exxon Valdez* oil spill, 123

**F**

Falcons, 125
False gavial, 93–94
*Federal Register*, 28
Felines, 100–101, 104–108
Ferns and allies, 154
Ferrets, 101
Fish
  bull trout, 61–62, 62f
  dams, 55–56
  endangered and threatened species,
    59t–60t
  Endangered Species Act funds, by fish
    species, 60 (t4.2)
  entrainment and impingement, 56
  foreign endangered and threatened
    species, 69t
  freshwater, 58–62
  invasive species, 58
  marine and anadromous, 62–69, 63t
  overcrowding, 58
  Pacific salmon, 64f, 65f, 66f, 67t
  pallid sturgeon, 61f
  pollution, 57–58, 58f
  sediment issues, 56–57, 57f
  steelhead, 68t
Fishing gear entanglement, 43
Flies, 134
Florida
  endangered plants, 158
  panthers, 100–101
Flowering plants, 154
Fort Hood, Texas, 117–118
Fragmentation of habitat, 18
Freshwater fish, 58–62,
  59t–60t
Freshwater mussels, 71–74
Frogs and toads, 81, 83–85,
  86–87

Fruit flies, 134
Funding. *See* Expenditures under the Endangered Species Act

## G

Geckos, 92
Genetic swamping, 20
Genus, 2
Giant salamanders, 84
Global warming
    amphibians, 86
    atmospheric carbon dioxide and anthropogenic emissions levels, 19*f*
    corals, 78
    greenhouse effect, 18*f*
    mean surface temperature anomalies, 20*f*
    overview, 18–19
    polar bears, 53–54
Golden toad, 85
Golden-cheeked warblers, 116–117
Gopher tortoises, 87–89
Grasshoppers, 134
Gray wolves, 99
Greenhouse effect, 18, 18*f*
Grizzly bears, 98
Guadalupe fur seals, 46
Guajón, 84
Guam, 124

## H

Habitat conservation, 32, 36
Habitat destruction, 17–18, 85
Habitat fragmentation, 18
Hatcheries, salmon, 64, 66*f*
Hawaii
    endangered plant species, 155–156
    honeycreepers, 118
    insects, 134–135
    main islands, 155 (*f*10.4)
    monk seals, 46
    pomace flies, 135*t*
Higgins' eye pearlymussels, 72–74
Hine's emerald dragonflies, 135
History
    species protection, 23–24
    U.S. extinctions and near-extinctions, 3–4
    U.S. land conservation, 9–11
Horned lizards, 92
Human activity
    amphibians, 86
    Chinese alligators, 93–94
    ethical choices, 1
    habitat destruction, 17–19
    mass extinction, 3
Humpback whale, 41*f*
Hunting
    bison, 4
    as contributing factor, 19
    whales, 42–43
Hydroelectric dams, 56, 56*f*, 68

## I

Identification of organisms, 1–2
Illegal trade. *See* Trade
Impingement, 56
Inbreeding, 3
Incidental take permits, 32
Indiana bats, 97
Insects and spiders
    arachnid species, 136
    butterflies, skippers, and moths, 131–133
    California, 133–134
    expenditures under the Endangered Species Act, 133*t*
    foreign species, 136*t*, 138
    Hawaii, 134–135
    Hawaiian pomace flies, 135*t*
    Karner blue butterfly, 134*f*
    listed species, 132*t*, 137*t*
    Monarch butterflies, 135–136
    naucorid, 133*f*
International Convention for the Regulation of Whaling, 42
International Dolphin Conservation Program Act, 45
International issues
    amphibians, 84, 84*t*, 85
    birds, 126*t*–129*t*
    conservation efforts, 15–17
    corals, 79
    fish, 68–69
    history of species protection, 23
    insects and spiders, 135–136, 136*t*, 138
    manatees and dugongs, 52
    numbers of endangered species, 4–6, 5*t*
    plants, 158–159, 159*t*
    reptiles, 92–94
    sea otters, 51
    whaling, 42–43
International Union for the Conservation of Nature and Natural Resources (IUCN), 3, 23
Invasive species
    amphibians, threats to, 85–86
    aquatic species, 58
    birds, threats to, 124
    overview, 20–21
    plants, 140*t*
Invasive Species Management Plan, 21
IUCN (International Union for the Conservation of Nature and Natural Resources), 3, 23
Ivory trade, 109
Ivory-billed woodpeckers, 115–116

## K

Karner blue butterflies, 133, 134*f*
Karst caves, 136, 137*f*
Kauai cave wolf spiders, 136, 138
Kemp's ridley turtle, 91

Kempthorne, Dirk, 54
Kentucky, 115
Klamath Basin controversy, 65, 67–68
Kublai Khan, 23

## L

Lake Erie water snakes, 91–92
Land conservation, 9–15, 13*f*
Land Trust Alliance, 14–15
Land use, 11–14
Lawsuits. *See* Litigation
Legislation
    Alaska National Interest Lands Conservation Act, 12
    Bald Eagle Protection Act, 124
    bird conservation, 122*t*
    Endangered Species Conservation Act, 24
    Endangered Species Preservation Act, 24
    land conservation, 9
    Marine Mammal Protection Act, 39–40
    Wilderness Act, 10
    *See also* Endangered Species Act
Lewis, Meriwether, 103
Lichens, 154
Linnaeus, Carolus, 1–2
Listed species
    anadromous fish, 63 (*t*4.3)
    aquatic mammals, 40*t*
    birds, 114*t*–115*t*
    categories, 142*f*
    clams, 72*t*–73*t*, 73 (*t*5.1)
    crustaceans, 73*t*, 73 (*t*5.2)
    foreign amphibian species, 84*t*
    foreign bird species, 126*t*–129*t*
    foreign endangered species, 104*t*–108*t*
    foreign fish species, 69*t*
    foreign insect species, 136*t*
    foreign plant species, 159*t*
    foreign terrestrial mammal species, 104*t*–108*t*
    freshwater fish, 59*t*–60*t*
    geographical distribution of endangered plant species, 155 (*f*10.3)
    insects and spiders, 132*t*
    overview, 25–28
    plants, 143*t*–153*t*
    priority numbers, 26*t*
    reptiles, 93*t*–94*t*
    salmon, 67*t*
    seals and sea lions, 49*t*
    snails, 76, 76*t*
    spiders, 137*t*
    steelhead, 67*t*
    terrestrial mammals, 96*t*–97*t*
    whales, 45*t*
Litigation
    bull trout protection, 62
    Endangered Species Act, 33–34

Klamath Basin distribution issues, 67–68
northern spotted owls protection, 119
polar bear protection, 52–53
wolf protection, 98–99
Lizards, 92–93
Logging industry
habitat destruction, 18
northern spotted owls, 119–120
Pacific Northwest, 6–7, 12
Los Angeles basin mountain plants, 156–157, 157f
Lynxes, 100

**M**

Mammals. *See* Marine mammals; Terrestrial mammals
Manatees, 51–52, 52f
Marbled murrelets, 121
Marine and anadromous fish, 62–69, 63t
Marine Mammal Protection Act (MMPA), 39–40
Marine mammals
dolphins and porpoises, 45
endangered and threatened aquatic mammals, 40 (t3.1)
Endangered Species Act, 40–41
expenditures under the Endangered Species Act, 40 (t3.2)
manatees and dugongs, 51–52, 52f
Marine Mammal Protection Act (MMPA), 39–40
polar bears, 52–53, 53f
sea otters, 48–51, 49f, 50f
seals and sea lions, 45–48, 47f, 48f, 49t
ship strikes, 44f
whales, 41–44, 43t, 45t
Mass extinction, 3
Mediterranean monk seals, 47
Mexico, 135–136
Migration, salmon, 63
Migratory species
Convention on the Conservation of Migratory Species of Wild Animals, 16–17
shore birds, 120–121
songbirds, 118–119
Missouri River alterations, 61, 61 (f4.5)
MMPA (Marine Mammal Protection Act), 39–40
Mokelumne River Programmatic Safe Harbor Agreement, 33
Monarch butterflies, 135–136
Monito geckos, 92
Moral issues, 1
Moths, 131–133, 134–135
Mountain lions, 100–101
Muir, John, 9
Mussels, 71–74

**N**

Naming of organisms, 1–2
National Forests, 10, 10t
National Inventory of Dams, 55–56
National Marine Fisheries Service (NMFS)
budget, 34–35
responsibilities, 3
whale protection, 41–44
National parks, 4, 9–10, 23
National Petroleum Reserve—Alaska (NPRA), 14f
National Wilderness Preservation System, 13f
National Wildlife Refuge System, 10, 11t–12t
Native Americans, 67, 68
Nature Conservancy, 14
Naucorid, 133f
Nest parasitism, 117–118
NMFS. *See* National Marine Fisheries Service
Northern right whales, 42, 43–44
Northern spotted owls, 6–7, 8f, 12, 119–120
Northwest Forest Plan, 7
NPRA (National Petroleum Reserve—Alaska), 14f
NWRS (National Wildlife Refuge System), 10, 11t–12t

**O**

Oahu tree snails, 74
Ohlone tiger beetles, 134
Oil drilling, 12–14
Oil spills, 123, 123f
Old-growth forests, 7, 12
Orangutans, 110f
Otters, 48–51
Overcrowding, fish, 58
Owls, 6–7, 8f, 12, 119–120

**P**

Pacific Northwest, 6–7, 12
Pacific salmon, 63–65, 64f, 65f, 66f, 67–68, 67t
PacifiCorp, 68
Pallid sturgeon, 60–61, 61f
Pandas, 109–110
Panthers, 100–101
Passenger pigeons, 3
Passerines, 116–118, 117f, 123
Pearl industry, 71, 72–73
Pearlymussels, 72–74
Pelican Island, Florida, 10
Pelicans, 125
Peregrine falcons, 125
Permits, 32–33
Pesticides, 122
Pet trade, 19
Petition process, 25–28, 26f

Plants
American chestnut, 139–140, 141f, 142
California, 156–157
expenditures for, under the Endangered Species Act, 153 (t10.3)
Florida, 158
foreign endangered and threatened species, 158–159, 159t
geographical breakdown of endangered plant species, 154, 155 (f10.3)
Hawaii, 155—156
invasive species, 140t
listed species, 142, 143t–153t
Los Angeles basin mountain plants, 157f
naming, 2
pondberry, 157–158, 158f
Southeastern United States, 157–158
taxonomy and categorization, 142, 153–154
Poaching, 109, 110, 111
Polar bears, 16f, 37, 52–54, 53f
Pollution, 19, 57–58, 85
Polo, Marco, 23
Pomace flies, 134, 135t
Pombo, Richard W., 36, 37
Pondberry, 157–158, 158f
Po'ouli, 118
Porpoises, 45
Prairie dogs, 102–103, 102f
Primates, 110, 110f
Private land conservation, 14–15
Pronghorns, 99–100
Property rights, 36, 37
Psittacines, 123–124
Public opinion, 8, 8t
Pygmy rabbits, 102

**Q**

Quagga mussels, 74

**R**

Rabbits, 101–102
Ranchers, 98
Raptors, 119–120
Recovered species. *See* Delisting
Recovery plans
bats, 97
black-footed ferrets, 101
clams and mussels, 74
crustaceans, 77
Endangered Species Act, 30, 32
Florida panthers, 101
freshwater fish, 62
gopher tortoises, 87–89
grizzly bears, 98
Hawaiian forest birds, 118, 119t
marine and anadromous fish, 68
northern spotted owls, 120
priority ranking system, U.S. Fish and Wildlife Service, 33t

seals and sea lions, 46–48
snails, 75–76
whales, 44–45
woodpeckers, 116
Recovery potential priority ranking system, 33t
Recovery rate, 37
Red knots, 28
*Red List of Threatened Species* (IUCN), 4–6
Red pandas, 109–110
Red wolves, 99, 99f
Red-cockaded woodpeckers, 113–115, 116f
Reefs, coral, 77–79, 78f
Reptiles, 87–91, 88t
Rhinoceros, 110–111, 111f
Rodents, 102–103
Roosevelt, Theodore, 9, 10

## S

Safe Harbor Agreements, 32–33
Saimaa seals, 47–48
Salamanders, 81, 83, 83f, 84
Salmon, 63–65, 65f, 66f, 67–68, 67t
San Francisco garter snakes, 91
Santa Cruz Mountains, 134
Science, 36–37, 37–38
Scientific names, 2
Sea lions, 45–48, 49t
Sea otters, 48–51, 49f, 50f
Sea turtles, 89–91, 89 (f6.4)
Seabirds, 121
Seals, 45–48, 49t
Sediment, 56–57, 57f
Ship and boat strikes, 43–44, 44f, 51–52
Shrews, 103
Shrimp net casualties, 90
Siberian tigers, 105–107, 108f
Sierra Club, 9
Siltation, 56–57, 57f
Skippers, 131–133
Snail darters, 56
Snails, 74–76, 74t, 76t
Snakes, 91–92, 124
Songbirds, 118–119
Sonoran pronghorn, 99–100
"Sound science" movement, 36–37
Southeastern United States, 157–158
Southern sea otters, 49–50, 50f
Southwestern willow flycatchers, 116, 117f
Species identification, 1–2
Spiders. *See* Insects and spiders
Spruce-fir moss spiders, 138
Statistical information
    amphibian species expenditures, 82 (t6.2)
    atmospheric carbon dioxide levels and anthropogenic emissions trend, 19f

bird species expenditures, 115 (t8.2)
candidate species, by state, 27f
clam, snail, crustacean, and coral species expenditures under the ESA, 74t
count of endangered and threatened species, 5t
critical habitat, 30t
expenditures under the Endangered Species Act, 40 (t3.2)
fish consumption advisories, contaminants blamed for, 58f
fish species expenditures, 60 (t4.2)
global mean surface temperature anomalies, 20f
insect and spider species expenditures, 133t
listed species categories, 142f
mammal species expenditures, 97 (t7.2)
manatee mortality causes, 52f
marine and anadromous fish species expenditures, 63 (t4.4)
Missouri River alterations effects, 61 (f4.5)
National Forest Service management, species under, 10t
numbers of endangered and threatened species, 6f
plant species expenditures, 153 (t10.3)
public opinion on the greatest environmental problems, 8t
reptile species expenditures, 88 (t6.5)
sea otters, 50 (f)
southern sea otter mortality causes, 50 (f3.9)
Steller sea lion populations, 48f
U.S. Fish and Wildlife Service budget, 34f, 35f
whale species, 45t
whales, incidents involving, 43t
Status review, 25–26
Steelhead, 68, 68t
Steller, Georg Wilhelm, 46
Steller sea lions, 46–47, 47f, 48f
Stocks, salmon, 63
Stray cats, 20
Subspecies, 1–2

## T

Taxonomy
    blue whales, 2t
    classification system, 1–2
    plants, 142, 153–154
Tellico Dam, 56
Terrestrial mammals
    bats, 95–97
    bears, 97–98
    big cats, 104–108
    big game, 110
    Canada lynxes, 100
    cheetahs, 107–108

deer, caribou, pronghorns, and bighorn sheep, 99–100
    elephants, 108–109, 109f
    expenditures for species under the ESA, 97 (t7.2)
    ferrets, 101
    Florida panthers, 100–101
    foreign listed species, 103–104, 104t–108t
    lynxes, 100
    mountain lions, 100–101
    pandas, 109–110
    prairie dogs, 102–103, 102f
    primates, 110, 110f
    rabbits, 101–102
    rhinoceros, 110–111, 111f
    rodents, 102–103
    shrews, 103
    tigers, 104–107, 108f
    wolves, 98–99, 99f
Texas
    birds, 117–118
    cave arachnids, 136
    horned lizard, 92
    karst caves, 137f
Threatened species definition, 3
Tigers, 104–107, 108f
Toads. *See* Frogs and toads
Tortoises, 87–89, 89 (f6.3)
Toxic pollutant advisories, 57–58, 58f
Trade
    crocodilians, 93–94
    exotic species, 19, 123–124
Translocation programs, 49–50, 51
Treaties
    bird conservation conventions, 122t
    Convention on Biological Diversity, 16
    Convention on International Trade in Endangered Species of Wild Fauna and Flora, 15, 23
    Convention on the Conservation of Migratory Species of Wild Animals, 16–17
    International Convention for the Regulation of Whaling, 42
Trematodes, 86
Tuataras, 94
Tuna fishing, 39, 45
Turtle excluder devices, 90–91, 90f
Twain, Mark, 83

## U

Ultraviolet radiation, 85, 86f
UN Environment Programme (UNEP), 15
United States
    habitat destruction, 18
    land conservation, 9–10

National Forest Service management of species, 10*t*

numbers of endangered species, 5–6, 5*t*, 6*f*, 7*f*

Urbanization, 18

U.S. Army, 117–118

U.S. Bureau of Reclamation, 67–68

U.S. Fish and Wildlife Service (USFWS)

budget breakdown, 35*f*

funding, 34, 34*f*

litigation, 34

recovery potential priority ranking system, 33*t*

responsibilities, 3

U.S. Forest Service, 10

USFWS. *See* U.S. Fish and Wildlife Service

Utah prairie dogs, 102–103

Utah valvata snails, 74–75

## V

Valley elderberry longhorn beetles, 133–134

Verna pool fairy shrimp, 76–77

## W

Wading birds, 121–122, 121*f*, 122*f*

Water birds, 120–122

Water pollution, 57–58

WCPA (World Commission on Protected Areas), 17

Whales, 41–44, 41*f*, 43*t*, 44*f*, 45*t*

Whooping cranes, 121–122, 122*f*

Wilderness Act, 10

Wilderness Preservation System Areas, 10–11

Wildlife management, 4

Wilson, Edward O., 37

Wolves, 98–99, 99*f*

Wood storks, 121, 121*f*

Woodpeckers, 113–116, 116*f*

World Commission on Protected Areas (WCPA), 17

World Wildlife Fund (WWF), 23

## Y

Yellowstone National Park, 4, 9, 98

## Z

Zayante band-winged grasshoppers, 134

Zebra mussels, 74, 75*f*